SELECTED POETRY OF OGDEN NASH

SELECTED POETRY
OF
OGDEN NASH

650 Rhymes, Verses, Lyrics,
and Poems

INTRODUCTION BY ARCHIBALD MACLEISH

BLACK DOG & LEVENTHAL
NEW YORK

This edition published by arrangement with Little, Brown and Company, Inc.

Published by Black Dog & Leventhal Publishers, Inc.
151 West 19th Street
New York, NY 10011

Distributed by Workman Publishing Company
708 Broadway
New York, NY 10003

Manuafctured in the United States of America

j i h g f e d c

ISBN 1-884822-30-4

CONTENTS

1

2

3

4

MODERN LIFE— AND MIND YOUR MANNERS! 177

6

THE ODDEST ANIMAL OF ALL (GUESS WHO?) 313

7

8

9

10

11

TRAVELS & TRAVAILS 515

12

13

14

15

INTRODUCTION

ARCHIBALD MACLEISH

Ogden Nash's admirable obituary in the *New York Times* appeared under the heading "Master of Light Verse Dies." There are three things wrong with those five words. Nash's most important and most characteristic work is not in "verse." It is not "light." And his mastery, which was real enough, had nothing to do with a combination of the two. It consisted in the invention of a form, uniquely his own, which defied all the categories and, far more than that, altered the sensibility of his time: a form like the magic shoes in a Celtic tale which enable the wearer to enter an untraveled world —the untraveled world, in Nash's case, of the infinite banalities of the contemporary city.

Eliot had discovered that world with the aid of the ironic meters he borrowed so brilliantly from Laforgue, but only the sophisiticated knew of his famous journey. Nash settled there and then went back to fetch his readers. His colloquial couplets in rhymed prose, with their honest grins and innocent disguises, gave him entrance everywhere. And once his foot was in the door his readers had no choice but to listen. He was a humorist, wasn't he?—the author of delightful little jingles like "Candy /Is dandy/But liquor/Is quicker"? What risk was there in letting *him* in? He'd never tell you things you didn't want to know—show you your time as a Waste Land where Long Island used to be.

But of course he would and did, and to call the consequences "light verse" is hardly fair to anyone. For one thing the term is inaccurate. "Verse" is one of the vaguest words in the language except when it is used to make a distinction between verse and prose. When that happens it becomes a term of art, precise as are all such instruments. Verse, as distinguished from prose, is a form of composition founded on the *line*. Even what used to be called "free" verse—particularly what used to be called "free" verse—is composed of lines. In prose the basic element of structure is the sentence; in verse the sentence makes its peace with the line or the whole thing collapses. In prose the hearing ear pays no attention to the line's end at the margin of the page; in verse it is the line's end the ear is waiting for.

Apply all this to Nash's characteristic form. It has no *lines* in the verse sense; the line's end is a typographical accident with Nash and it is the sentence—the infinitely extensible sentence—which bears the burden. The hearing ear pays no more attention to the line's end in the print of his pieces than it would in a newspaper column. Nothing in the whole device suggests the structure of verse but the rhymes, and the rhymes are not used as verse would use them. They are not used, that is to say, to establish an enlarging counterpoint to the rhythm of the lines. They are used, instead, to force the sentences into couplets, or other combinations, which are often as funny as the assonances are outrageous. It is not the sound they play on but the sense. Or unsense. They are instruments of meaning. Often of zany meaning. But often, too, of new and impossible associations which can blow the mind.

That is one objection to the term: it is inaccurate. The other is the implication. "Light verse" carries a demeaning connotation. It implies that the art of poetry has its Macy's basement where a kind of second-rate excellence is the criterion. And this, of course, is an affront to poetry. There is only one kind of poetry: poetry. The art has no departments. It does not help that the newspaper meaning of "light verse" is verse with a sense of humor—as though poetry, which knows everything about mankind, knew nothing about human laughter. Who laughed at life the longest? Was it Shakespeare himself? Or Chaucer? Or Catullus? Or Li Po? Nash knew all this as well as anyone. And I suspect, although I do not know, that it had a good deal to do with his invention of a form which was *not* "light verse": a form which would enable him to examine the inanities of his time in a colloquial language most men understood because, like Molière's astonished character, they spoke it themselves.

In any case, and whatever the rationalization, Nash's first *New Yorker* publication shows how the form began. It was a piece written in 1930, when Mr. Herbert Hoover's Plateau of Permanent Prosperity had collapsed into the Great Depression carrying a generation with it—most painfully, a generation of the young. Nash was twenty-eight, a failed prep school teacher, a failed bond salesman, and a failed sonneteer, supporting himself, if that is the term, by composing advertising copy for a New York publisher. He was approaching the age at which a young man's commitment to art can no longer survive on hope. After thirty, failure begins to taste of finality and it becomes harder and harder to try again. But as one approaches thirty things have a way of happening. And they did for Ogden Nash in his grubby office on that 1930 afternoon. He found himself—or, if not precisely himself, then a form of language he could speak. It fell into half a dozen more or less rhymed couplets, which he might well have called (but didn't) "Portrait of the Artist as a Young Man," and it changed his life. It ended the failure, began a considerable literary success and, more astonishing than either, altered—or began to alter—the relation of his contemporaries to the time in which they lived:

I sit in an office at 244 Madison Avenue
And say to myself You have a responsible job, havenue?
Why then do you fritter away your time on this doggerel?
If you have a sore throat you can cure it by using a good goggeral.. .

A portrait certainly, but a portrait in the Cinquecento manner with a glimpse of the city in the background. Or, if not a glimpse, then a whiff. If one doesn't see Murray Hill beyond the copywriter's head as he leans from his window the way one sees the Duomo beyond the Saint, one can at least smell it: that penetrating pharmaceutical scent of face powder and sex which pervades the metropolises of our cosmetic civilization. The gargle taints the afternoon and it is that breath of antiseptic which puts the figure in the foreground at the center of its time. Even the young man's hope is somehow sterile—even the defeated artist's pain. The drugstore on the corner can take care of everything and that longing for the long-unwritten poem is no worse—or better—than a brief sore throat.

Mean it? With those hilarious rhymes? Of course he didn't mean it. He was laughing—had to be. Anyway Mr. Ross of the *New Yorker* published it, and the *New Yorker*, in its early years, was a humorous magazine. Also Ogden Nash soon joined the staff of the *New Yorker*. But still the question hung there. Did he? Didn't he? In any case he continued to work the same vein with the same sharp tool and the tool grew more and more effective as he went along until now, with the whole range of his work before us, we begin to see. Americans of the last quarter of the century—particularly young Americans—know better than their predecessors what was happening in those fusty years. They know what Nixon thought the country was, and what he tried to do to it—almost did. They understand what their fathers and their elder brothers didn't understand: that the rot of the Seventies came *out* of the society, not *down* on it from a crew of subversives at the top. And understanding that, they can see what a man who probed the intimacies of such a time with outrageous rhymes and comical couplets might have been up to. They may even conclude that Ogden Nash, though not a satirist in the Swiftian sense, had a satirist's concern for the humanity of human creatures. And they may come to read this book not for the laughs but for the tears—and for the love.

These remarks, I think, should end with a second portrait: not a portrait of the artist as a young man but as an artist; not a portrait of a satirist but of a man. I never met Ogden Nash in the ordinary sense: that is to say, I never exchanged a word with him. But I saw him once and I have never forgotten the man I saw. It was along in the Thirties, at St. George's outside of Newport, Rhode Island, where Nash had gone to school. The elder son of my friends Gerald and Sara Murphy had died there at the age of sixteen and I had been asked to write something to read at the planting of a tree which was to grow in the boy's memory. When the time came I found I had no voice to read what I had written and I stood there dumb and helpless. I don't know how long I would have waited, lost in that agony of shame, if I had not seen a young man crossing the lawn toward the little awkward group around the seedling tree. He said nothing, came close to me, looked me in the face, and I began to read. It was Ogden Nash.

1

LOVE AND MATRI-MOANING

*"Affection is a noble quality
It leads to generosity and jollity."*

THE STRANGE CASE OF THE LOVELORN
LETTER WRITER

Dear Miss Dix, I am a young lady of Scandinavian origin, and I
    am in a quandary.
I am not exactly broody, but I am kind of pondery.
I got a twenty-five waist and a thirty-five bust,
And I am going with a chap whose folks are very uppercrust.
He is the intellectual type, which I wouldn't want to disparage,
Because I understand they often ripen into love after marriage,
But here I am all set
For dalliance,
And what do I get?
Shilly-shalliance.
Just when I think he's going to disrobe me with his eyes,
He gets up off of the davenport and sighs.
Every time I let down my hair,
He starts talking to himself or the little man who isn't there.
Every time he ought to be worrying about me,
Why, he's worrying about his mother, that's my mother-in-law to be,
And I say let's burn that bridge when we come to it, and he says
    don't I have any sin sense,
His uncle and her live in incense.
Well, with me that's fine,
Let them go to their church and I'll go to mine.
But no, that's not good enough for Mr. Conscience and his mental
    indigestion,
He's got to find two answers for every question.
If a man is a man, a girl to him is a girl, if I correctly rememma,
But to him I am just a high pathetical dilemma.

What I love him in spite of
Is, a girl wants a fellow to go straight ahead like a locomotive and he
   is more like a loco-might-of.
Dear Miss Dix, I surely need your advice and solace.
It's like I was in love with Henry Wallace.
Well, while I eagerly await your reply I'm going down to the river to
   pick flowers. I'll get some rosemary if I can't find a camellia.
Yours truly, Ophelia.

THE JOYOUS MALINGERER

Who is the happy husband? Why, indeed,
'Tis he who's useless in the time of need;
Who, asked to unclasp a bracelet or a necklace,
Contrives to be utterly futile, fumbling, feckless,
Or when a zipper nips his loved one's back
Cannot restore the zipper to its track.
Another time, not wishing to be flayed,
She will not use him as a lady's maid.

Stove-wise he's the perpetual backward learner
Who can't turn on or off the proper burner.
If faced with washing up he never gripes,
But simply drops more dishes than he wipes.
She finds his absence preferable to his aid,
And thus all mealtime chores doth he evade.

He can, attempting to replace a fuse,
Black out the coast from Boston to Newport News,
Or, hanging pictures, be the rookie wizard
Who fills the parlor with a plaster blizzard.
He'll not again be called to competition
With decorator or with electrician.

At last it dawns upon his patient spouse
He's better at his desk than round the house.

THE STILLY NIGHT: A SOPORIFIC REFLECTION

There is one source of marital discord so delicate that I approach it
    on tiptoe,
And it reveals itself when the partners whose melancholy boast is
    that they are insomniacs are really somniacs, only not overt
    but crypto-.
He unwinds himself from the bedclothes each morn and piteously
    proclaims that he didn't sleep a wink, and she gives him a
    glance savage and murderous
And replies that it was she who didn't close an eye until cockcrow
    because of his swinish slumber as evidenced by his snores
    continuous and stertorous,
And his indignation is unconcealed,
He says she must have dreamed that one up during her night-long
    sweet repose, which he was fully conscious of because for
    eight solid hours he had listened to her breathing not quite so
    gentle as a zephyr on a flowery field.
Such is the genesis of many a myth,
Because her statement is a falsehood that is akin to truth, and his a
    truth that is to falsehood akith.
The fact is that she did awaken twice for brief intervals and he was
    indeed asleep and snoring, and he did awaken similarly and
    she was indeed unconscious and breathing miscellaneously,
But they were never both awake simultaneously.
Oh, sleep it is a blessed thing, but not to those wakeful ones who
    watch their mates luxuriating in it when they feel that their
    own is sorely in arrears.
I am certain that the first words of the Sleeping Beauty to her prince
    were, "You *would* have to kiss me just when I had dropped
    off after tossing and turning for a hundred years."

CONFESSION TO BE TRACED ON A
BIRTHDAY CAKE

Lots of people are richer than me,
Yet pay a slenderer tax;
Their annual levy seems to wane
While their income seems to wax.
Lots of people have stocks and bonds
To further their romances;
I've cashed my ultimate Savings Stamp—
But nobody else has Frances.

Lots of people are stronger than me,
And greater athletic menaces;
They poise like gods on diving boards
And win their golfs and tennises.
Lots of people have lots more grace
And cut fine figures at dances,
While I was born with galoshes on—
But nobody else has Frances.

Lots of people are wiser than me,
And carry within their cranium
The implications of Stein and Joyce
And the properties of uranium.
They know the mileage to every star
In the heaven's vast expanses;
I'm inclined to believe that the world is flat—
But nobody else has Frances.

Speaking of wisdom and wealth and grace—
As recently I have dared to—
There are lots of people compared to whom
I'd rather not be compared to.
There are people I ought to wish I was;

But under the circumstances,
I prefer to continue my life as me—
For nobody else has Frances.

THE STRANGE CASE OF MR. ORMANTUDE'S BRIDE

Once there was a bridegroom named Mr. Ormantude whose
      intentions were hard to disparage,
Because be intended to make his a happy marriage,
And he succeeded for going on fifty years,
During which he was in marital bliss up to his ears.
His wife's days and nights were enjoyable
Because he catered to every foible;
He went around humming her favorite hymns
And anticipating her whims.
Many a fine bit of repartee died on his lips
Lest it throw her anecdotes into eclipse;
He was always silent when his cause was meritorious,
And he never engaged in argument unless sure he was so
      obviously wrong that she couldn't help emerging victorious,
And always when in her vicinity
He was careful to make allowances for her femininity;
Were she snappish, he was sweetish,
And of understanding her he made a fetish.
Everybody said his chances of celebrating his golden wedding
      looked good,
But on his golden wedding eve he was competently poisoned by
      his wife who could no longer stand being perpetually
      understood.

THE ENTRAPMENT OF JOHN ALDEN
OR
WE PAINT THE LILY, WE BEARD MR. LONGFELLOW

Once there was a Pilgrim Father named Miles Standish,
Because despite many misconceptions few Pilgrim Fathers were
     named Praise-God Barebones or something equally outlandish.
Miles Standish was ordinarily a direct man, but in affairs of the
     heart he was inclined to crawfish,
Indeed, he might have been termed Standish-offish.
He had moved from Plymouth to Duxbury and he had a friend who
     was a born bachelor named John Alden
Who had also moved to Duxbury, though he might have done better
     to plump for Nahant or Saugus or Malden.
Well, Miles Standish fell in love with a Pilgrim maiden named
     Priscilla Mullens,
But whenever he approached her she fell into a fit of the sulks or
     sullens,
And he was afraid that if he offered her marriage in person she
     would grow even acider,
So the upshot was that be persuaded John Alden to be his ambassador,
And the offshoot of the upshot was that Priscilla welcomed John
     Alden as Penelope might have welcomed Odysseus
And she baked him a pumpkin pie that was simply delysseus,
And she evinced a frightening tendency to mingle,
And when he transmitted Miles Standish's proposal to her she asked
     him why he didn't speak for himself, but he really had nothing
     to say for himself except that he enjoyed being single.
Had he been a Method actor preparing for a play set in Greenpoint
     he could have told himself, "I can ad lib dis,"
But now with the image of Miles Standish looking over one shoulder
     and an amorous maiden snuggling against the other he stood
     silent between Priscilla and Charybdis.
This silence resulted in a union which eventually produced eleven
     children, several of them born in August,
And a recently discovered diary of John Alden's reveals that he
     often wished that instead of joining Miles Standish in
     Duxbury he had Nahanted or even Saugused.

HOW CAN ECHO ANSWER
WHAT ECHO CANNOT HEAR?

Why shouldn't I laud my love?
My love is highly laudable;
Indeed, she would be perfection
Were she only always audible.

Why shouldn't I laud her voice,
The welcomest sound I know,
Her voice, which is ever soft?
It is likewise gentle and low—

An excellent thing in woman
And the Wilson's thrush, or veery—
But there are maddening moments
When I wish I had wed a Valkyrie.

Whenever her talk is restricted
To topics inconsequential
She utters it face to face,
With clarity reverential.

Then why, when there's something important to say,
Does she always say it going away?
She'll remark, as she mounts the stairs to bed,
"Oh, some FBI man called and said . . . "
Then her words, like birds too swift for banding,
Vanish with her upon the landing.
"Don't you think we ought . . ." Then she's gone, whereat
The conclusion fades out like the Cheshire Cat.
Yes, her words when weighty with joy or dread
Seem to emerge from the back of her head;
The dénouement supreme, the point of the joke,
Is forever drifting away like smoke.
Knowing her custom, knowing the wont of her,
I spend my life circling to get in front of her.

I'll bet that the poet Herrick,
With Corinna gone a-Maying,
Had to run like a rabbit
To catch what she was saying.

A WORD TO HUSBANDS

To keep your marriage brimming,
With love in the loving cup,
Whenever you're wrong, admit it;
Whenever you're right, shut up.

THE STRANGE CASE OF THE
ENTOMOLOGIST'S HEART

Consider the case of Mr. Suggs.

He was an eminent entomologist, which is to say he knew nothing
but bugs.

He could tell the Coleoptera from the Lepidoptera,

And the Aphidae and the Katydididae from the Grasshoptera.

He didn't know whether to starve a cold or feed a fever, he was so
untherapeutical,

But he knew that in 1737 J. Swannderdam's *Biblia Naturae* had
upset the theories of Aristotle and Harvey by demonstrating
the presence of pupal structures under the larval cuticle.

His taste buds were such that he was always asking dining-car
stewards for their recipe for French dressing and mayonnaise,

But he was familiar with Strauss-Durckheim's brilliant treatise (1828)
on the cockchafer and that earlier (1760) but equally brilliant
monograph on the goat-moth caterpillar of P. Lyonnet's.

He was so unliterary that he never understood the difference
between *Ibid.* and *Anonymous,*

But he spoke of 1842 as the year in which Von Kölliker first
described the formation of the blastoderm in the egg of the
midge *Chironomus.*

Mr. Sugg's specialty was fireflies, which he knew inside and out and
from stem to stern,

And he was on the track of why they blaze and don't burn,

And then one day he met a girl as fragrant as jessamine,

And he found her more fascinating than the rarest eleven-legged
specimen,

But being a diffident swain he wished to learn how the land lay
before burning his bridges,

So he bashfully asked her mother what she thought of his chances,
and she encouragingly said, At sight of you my daughter
lights up like a firefly, and Mr. Suggs stammered, Good
gracious, what a strange place for a girl to light up!, and
rapidly returned to his goat-moth caterpillars, blastoderms
and midges.

I NEVER EVEN SUGGESTED IT

I know lots of men who are in love and lots of men who are married
      and lots of men who are both,
And to fall out with their loved ones is what all of them are most
      loth.
They are conciliatory at every opportunity,
Because all they want is serenity and a certain amount of impunity.
Yes, many the swain who has finally admitted that the earth is flat
Simply to sidestep a spat,
Many the masculine Positively or Absolutely which has been diluted
      to an If
Simply to avert a tiff,
Many the two-fisted executive whose domestic conversation is
      limited to a tactfully interpolated Yes,
And then he is amazed to find that he is being raked backwards over
      a bed of coals nevertheless.
These misguided fellows are under the impression that it takes two
      to make a quarrel, that you can sidestep a crisis by
      nonaggression and nonresistance,
Instead of removing yourself to a discreet distance.
Passivity can be a provoking *modus operandi*;
Consider the Empire and Gandhi.
Silence is golden, but sometimes invisibility is golder.
Because loved ones may not be able to make bricks without straw,
      but often they don't need any straw to manufacture a bone to
      pick or a chip for their soft white shoulder.
It is my duty, gentlemen, to inform you that women are dictators all,
      and I recommend to you this moral:
In real life it takes only one to make a quarrel.

TO MY VALENTINE

More than a catbird hates a cat,
Or a criminal hates a clue,
Or the Axis hates the United States,
That's how much I love you.

I love you more than a duck can swim,
And more than a grapefruit squirts,
I love you more than gin rummy is a bore,
And more than a toothache hurts.

As a shipwrecked sailor hates the sea,
Or a juggler hates a shove,
As a hostess detests unexpected guests,
That's how much you I love.

I love you more than a wasp can sting,
And more than the subway jerks,
I love you as much as a beggar needs a crutch,
And more than a hangnail irks.

I swear to you by the stars above,
And below, if such there be,
As the High Court loathes perjurious oaths,
That's how you're loved by me.

DON'T BE CROSS, AMANDA

Don't be cross, Amanda,
Amanda, don't be cross,
For when you're cross, Amanda,
I feel an albatross
Around my neck, or dank gray moss,
And my eyes assume an impervious gloss.
Amanda,
Dear Amanda,
Don't be cross.

Do not frown, Amanda,
Amanda, do not frown,
For when you frown, Amanda,
I wamble like a clown,
My mouth is stuffed with eiderdown,
And I spatter coffee upon your gown.
Amanda,
Dear Amanda,
Do not frown.

Don't clam up, Amanda,
Amanda, do not clam,
For when you clam, Amanda,
I don't know where I am.
What is it that I did you damn?
Shall I make amends for a sheep, or a lamb?
Amanda,
Dear Amanda,
Do not clam.

Please be gay, Amanda,
Amanda, please be gay,
For when you're gay, Amanda,
The stars come out by day,
The police throw parking tags away,
And I want to kick up my heels and bray.
Amanda,
Dear Amanda,
Please be gay.

THE SOLITUDE OF MR. POWERS

Once there was a lonely man named Mr. Powers.

He was lonely because his wife fixed flowers.

Mr. Powers was a gallant husband, but whenever he wished to
     demonstrate his *gallantry*

His beloved was always out with six vases and a bunch of something
     or other in the pantry.

He got no conversation while they ate

Because she was always nipping dead blossoms off the centerpiece
     and piling them on her plate.

He could get no conversation after meals because if he happened to
     begin one

She would look at the mantel and wonder if she shouldn't switch the
     small fat vase with the tall thin one.

Yes, even when she wasn't actually fixing flowers there was no
     forgetting about them,

Because before fixing them she was busy cutting them, and after
     fixing them she was busy fretting about them.

Mr. Powers began to shave only once a week because no one cared
     whether his chin was scratchy;

He felt as lonely as *Cavalleria* without *Pagliacci*.

Finally he said Hey!

I might as well be alone with myself as alone with a lot of vases that
     have to have their water replenished every day,

And he walked off into the dawn,

And his wife just kept on refilling vases and never noticed that he
     was gone.

Beware of floral arrangements;

They lead to marital estrangements.

THE NYMPH AND THE SHEPHERD
or
SHE WENT THAT-A-WAY

Few things are less endearing than a personal comparison,
But I know a lady who is very like the elusive mother of Mr. Milne's
     James James Morrison Morrison.
She would be a perfect wife could she but be restrained by a leash
     or a fetter,
Because she has the roving tendencies of an Irish setter.
Her husband assists her from the cab and stops to pay the fare,
And when he turns around she isn't there,
She is a hundred yards off, blithe as a flock of linnets,
And in a fair way to do the mile under four minutes.
He assists her from the train and by the time he has caught a porter
     she is at the top of the moving stairway,
And again to do the mile under four minutes she is in a fair way.
She shoots ahead of him in London crowds and leaves him behind
     fumbling with lire in Pisa,
Despite the fact that he is in sole possession of all the travelers'
     checks and their joint passport and visa.
If in the Louvre she exclaims, "Oh, look at the Mona Lisa!" and he
     pauses to look at the Mona Lisa,
By the time he has looked she is three corners and forty
     masterpieces away, and himself alone with the same old
     money and passport and visa.
Sometimes he is touched and flattered by her faith in him, but
     mostly he feels like Queen Victoria's chair,
Which Queen Victoria never looked behind at before she sat down,
     because she just knew it would be there.

THE SELF-EFFACEMENT OF ELECTRA THORNE

Everybody knows who is the greatest actress ever born;
Why, if you rolled the Misses Hayes and Cornell into one and
      tripled them, you would only begin to approximate Electra
      Thorne.
Some call Electra Thorne ill-tempered because when her dear old
      mother let her go on with her slip showing she kicked her
      dear old mother in the breeks,
But gosh, everybody around the theater had been wanting to do that
      for weeks.
It seems unfair to call her prone to temperamental rage
Simply because she insisted on the firing of an elderly bit player
      because he reminded her of her father, whose financial
      failure forced her out of Sarah Lawrence onto the stage.
As for egocentricity, good heavens!
What's egocentric about wanting the marquee to read

ELECTRA THORNE
IN
OPHELIA AND HAMLET
WITH
MAURICE EVANS
?

Yet on their honeymoon there was some trepidation in the mind of
      Hoover Grimalkin, her groom;
He was wondering how to register for the room.
He was a writer who had won three Pulitzer Prizes, two Critics'
      Awards and an Oscar,
And he was at work an the libretto of a bebop version of *Tosca*.
His bride had assured him that she did not wish her career to
      intrude upon their private life,

He was the artist in the family, she said, and her only desire was to
        be a common, ordinary, everyday, just plain wife.
But Mr. Grimalkin had not been totally unobservant during his
        wooing;
He had a distinct feeling: no billing, no cooing.
So, thinking quickly, he asked Electra to register, he said his
        handwriting was a disgrace.
And she registered as "Mrs. Hoover Grimalkin and husband," and
        now he walks her poodle every day in Sutton Place.

THERE'LL ALWAYS BE A WAR
BETWEEN THE SEXES
or
A WOMAN CAN BE SOMETIMES PLEASED,
BUT NEVER SATISFIED

I used to know a breadwinner named Mr. Purefoy who was far from
    the top of the heap,
Indeed he could only be called a breadwinner because he had once
    won half a loaf of whole wheat in the Irish Sweep.
His ambition was feverish,
His industry was eager-beaverish,
His wife was a thrifty helpmeet who got full value for every
    disbursement,
Yet their financial status showed no betterment, just perpetual
    worsement.
The trouble with these two was that they dissipated their energies,
They didn't play the percenages.
If he got angry at a slovenly, insolent waiter when they were dining
    in town
She would either bury her face in the menu or try to calm him down.
If she got angry at the woman in front of her at the movies and
    loudly suggested that she push her hat a little lower,
He pretended he didn't know her.
He defended his unappreciative employer against her loyal wifely
    ire,
And when he got burned up about the bills from the friendly
    exorbitant little grocer around the corner she tried to put out
    the fire.
One day they had a thought sublime,
They thought, Let's both get mad at the same person or situation at
    the same time.
I don't know about Mars, but Earth has not a denizen,
Who can withstand the wrath of a husband and wife being wrathful
    in unison.

To be said, little remains;
Only that after they merged their irascibility, it required the full
time of three Certified Public Accountants and one Certified
Private Accountant to keep track of their capital gains.

TUNE FOR AN ILL-TEMPERED CLAVICHORD

Oh, once there lived in Kankakee
A handy dandy Yankakee,
A lone and lean and lankakee
Cantankakerous Yankakee.
He slept without a blankaket,
And whiskikey, how he drankaket,
This rough and ready Yankakee,
The bachelor of Kankakee.
He never used a hankakee,
He jeered at hanky-pankakee;
Indeed, to give a frank account,
He didn't have a bank account.
And yet at times he hankakered
In marriage to be anchachored.
When celibacy rankakles,
One dreams of pretty ankakles.
He took a trip to Waikiki
And wooed a girl named Psycheche,
And now this rugged Yankakee
'S a married man in Kankakee.
Good night, dear friends, and thankakee.

IT'S ABOUT TIME

How simple was the relationship between the sexes in the days
    of Francesca di Rimini;
Men were menacing, women were womeny.
When confronted with women, men weren't expected to understand
    them;
Their alternatives were, if rejected, to un-hand, and if accepted,
    to hand them.
I attribute much of our modern tension
To a misguided striving for intersexual comprehension.
It's about time to realize, brethren, as best we can,
That a woman is not just a female man.
How bootless, then, to chafe
When they are late because they have no watch with them, all
        eleven of their watches are on the dressing table or in the
        safe;
Give your tongue to the cat
When you ask what they want for their birthday and they say, Oh
        anything, and you get anything, and then discover it should
        have been anything but that.
Pocket the gold, fellows, ask not why it glisters;
As Margaret Fuller accepted the universe, so let us accept her
        sisters.
Women would I think be easier nationalized
Than rationalized,
And the battle of the sexes can be a most enjoyable scrimmage
If you'll only stop trying to create woman in your own image.

WHO UNDERSTANDS WHO ANYHOW?

There is one phase of life that I have never heard discussed in any
      seminar,
And that is that all women think men are funny and all men think
      that weminar.
Be the air the air of America or England or Japan,
It is full of husbands up in it saying, Isn't that just like a woman?
      And wives saying, Isn't that just like a man?
Well, it so happens that this is a unique fight,
Because both sides are right.
Each sex keeps on laughing at the other sex for not thinking the way
      they do,
Which is the cause of most domestic to-do and a-do,
Because breakfast is punctuated with spousely snorts,
Because husbands are jeering at their wives because they ignore the
      front page and read society and fashions, and wives are
      jeering at their husbands because they ignore the front page
      and read finance and sports,
And men think that women have an easy time because all they have
      to do is look after the household,
And what does that amount to but keeping an eye on the children
      and seeing that three meals a day are served and not allowing
      any litter to collect that would furnish a foothold for a
      mousehold?
And women think that men have an easy time because all they have
      to do is sit in an office all day long swapping stories and
      scratching up desks with their heels,
And going out to restaurants and ordering everything they like for
      their midday meals.
And oh yes, women like to resent the thought that they think men
      think they are toys,
And men like to bask in the thought that they think women think
      they are just big overgrown boys.
Well all these conflicting thoughts make for trouble at times but on
      the whole it is a sound idea for men and women to think
      different,

It is a topic upon which I am verbose and vociferant.
To it I dedicate my pen,
Because who would want to live in a world where the men all
      thought like women and the women all thought like men?
No, no, kind sirs, I will take all my hard-earned money,
And I will bet it on the nose of the tribe whose men and women
      continue to think each other are funny.

SEDATIVE REFLECTION

Let the love-lorn lover cure insomnia
By murmuring AMOR VINCIT OMNIA.

SONG FOR PIER SOMETHING OR OTHER

Steamer, steamer, outward bound,
Couldn't you, wouldn't you turn around?
Mightn't you double on your track?
Mightn't you possibly bring her back?
No, says the steamer, No, no, no!
We go, says the steamer, go, go, go!
Who, says the steamer, Who are you?
Boo! says the steamer.
Boo!

Steamer, steamer, are you sure
You can carry her secure?
Emerge from ice and storm and fog
With an uneventful log?
Chance, says the steamer, I am chance!
Chance, says the steamer, That's romance!
Who, says the steamer, Who are you?
Boo! says the steamer.
Boo!

Steamer, cogitate awhile,
Goddess unwittingly offended,
Are the males who prowl your decks
Attractive to the other sex?
Wait, says the steamer, Sit and wait.
Fate, says the steamer, I am Fate.
Who, says the steamer, Who are you?
Boo! says the steamer.
Boo!

Steamer, cogitate awhile,
Before you smile your final smile.
Seven days are yours to mock;
Steamer, wait until you dock.
Wait till she is safe ashore,
Steamer I do not adore!
Boo, says the steamer, and double boo!
Who, says the steamer,
Are you?

Steamer, steamer, I am he
Whose *raison d'etre* you bore to sea.
Steamer, lightly you weighed your anchor.
Try so lightly to weigh my rancor.
As soon as she is safely off you
I'll curse you from Sandy Hook to Corfu.

You who carried her off so boldly
Shall pay for it hotly, pay for it coldly,
With fog and howling hurricanes,
And icebergs in the shipping lanes,
And strikes of longshoremen and tugs,
And a passenger list of jitter bugs—
Pooh! says the steamer, Pooh for you!
Toodle-de-oodle-de-oo!

ABSENCE MAKES THE HEART GROW
HEART TROUBLE

I know a girl who is in Paris, France,
And I fear that every evening she goes out to dance,
And she ought to be pining for the undersigned,
But I fear that nothing is further from her mind,
And what is very suspicious, her letters say that she is being very
      quiet,
But my nerves deny it,
And I am unhappily sure that she is drinking champagne with
      aristocrats,
And exchanging cynicisms with sophistocrats.
She goes walking in the *Bois*
With elegant young men who are not *moi*.
She is receiving compliments from ambassadors,
And riding in *fiacres* with foreign agents who cry that for her they
      would betray the secrets of their lords and massadors.
Artists to have her pose for them are clamoring,
Tenors and symphony conductors tempt her with their entire
      repertoire from Pagliacci to Götterdämmerung;
Argentines and Brazilians
Seek to dazzle her with their dazzling millions;
Men of the world with etchings and monocles
Plead with her to become part of their personal chronicles;
Aides and equerries try to explain without too much bluntness and
      yet without too much shyness
The advantages a girl or a tailor enjoys when he or she is entitled to
      the subtitle of By Appointment to His Royal Highness.
Trips abroad are very nice for Davis Cup teams and Olympic teams,
      and that's about all you can say for them,
Because I think that when you are fond of somebody you would
      rather be with them than away from them,
So I wish that time would suddenly advance,
Because I want to be standing on the dock trying to find somebody
      on deck who will undoubtedly be wearing a terribly smart
      and perfectly terrible hat which she bought in Paris, France.

THE STRANGE CASE OF THE DEAD DIVORCEE

Once upon a time there was a beautiful woman named Mrs.
Geraldine McGregor Hamilton Garfinkle Boyce.

⌐

Her first husband, Mr. McGregor, divorced her for infidelity.

⌐

That wasn't his real reason, but he didn't want to blast her
reputation.

⌐

Her second husband, Mr. Hamilton, divorced her for infidelity, too.

⌐

He had better grounds, which he was too chivalrous to mention.

⌐

Her third husband, Mr. Garfinkle, was a cad.

⌐

He prepared a statement for the press setting forth his actual
motives for divorcing her.

⌐

Her white-haired old mother pled tearfully with him for seven hours,
pausing only to telephone her maid to bring over a dozen
clean handkerchiefs.

⌐

Mr. Garfinkle, if a cad, was a soft-hearted cad.

⌐

He destroyed his original damaging statement and informed the
press that he was divorcing his wife for infidelity.

⌐

It was in June that Mrs. Geraldin McGregor Hamilton Garfinkle
became Mrs. Geraldine McGregor Hamilton Garfinkle Boyce.

⌐

It was in July that Mr. Boyce slaughtered her with a priceless
heirloom, an ice-pick.

⌐

At the trial, Mr. Boyce pled guilty.

⌐

She was infidelitous, said Mr. Boyce, and I saw red.

⌐

Mr. Boyce's lawyer asked him if he didn't have a better excuse.

⸺

Maybe I have, said Mr. Boyce, but my lips are sealed.

⸺

De mortuis, you know, said Mr. Boyce.

⸺

I will only say that she was infidelitous.

⸺

Mr. Boyce was convicted and condemned to die.

⸺

Came Mr. Boyce's Execution Eve.

⸺

The reporters were already strapping their cameras to their ankles when a delegation waited upon the Governor.

⸺

The delegation consisted of Mr. McGregor, Mr. Hamilton and Mr. Garfinkle.

⸺

There are extenuating circumstances in the case of Mr. Boyce, said Mr. McGregor.

⸺

It is time the truth about Geraldine McGregor Hamilton Garfinkle Boyce were told, said Mr. Hamilton.

⸺

I would have told it long ago but for my soft heart, said Mr. Garfinkle.

⸺

Geraldine McGregor Hamilton Garfinkle Boyce was a juleper-in-the-manger, said Mr. McGregor, Mr. Hamilton, and Mr. Garfinkle.

⸺

She never drank but half a mint julep, they said.

⸺

But when she was offered a mint julep, did she quietly drink half of it and quietly give the other half to her husband when he had finished his?

⸺

Not Geraldine McGregor Hamilton Garfinkle Boyce! they said.

She said No thank you, I only want half of one, I'll drink half of my husband's, they said.

Other women's husbands get a julep and a half, they said.

Geraldine McGregor Hamilton Garfinkle Boyce's husbands get half a julep, they said.

The Governor pardoned Mr. Boyce forthwith.

Ten minutes later the Governor's butler discovered the body of the Governor's lady on the veranda.

The ice-pick that protruded from her heart was a priceless heirloom.

THE ANNIVERSARY

A marriage aged one
Is hardly begun;
A fling in the sun,
But it's hardly begun;
A green horse,
A stiff course,
And leagues to be run.

A marriage aged five
Is coming alive.
Watch it wither and thrive;
Though it's coming alive,
You must guess,
No or yes,
if it's going to survive.

A marriage aged ten
Is a hopeful Amen;
It's pray for it then,
And mutter Amen,
As the names
Of old flames
Sound again and again.

At twenty a marriage
Discovers its courage.
This year do not disparage,
It is comely in courage;
Past the teens,
And blue jeans,
It's a promising marriage.

Yet before twenty-one
It has hardly begun.
How tall in the sun,
Yet hardly begun!
But once come of age,
Pragmatically sage,
Oh, blithe to engage
Is sweet marri-age.

Tilt a twenty-first cup
To a marriage grown up,
Now sure and mature,
And securely grown up.
Raise twenty-one cheers
To the silly young years,
While I sit out the dance
With my dearest of dears.

I DIDN'T SAY A WORD
OR
WHO CALLED THAT PICCOLO PLAYER
A FATHER?

A man could be granted to live a dozen lives,
And he still wouldn't understand daughters and wives.
It may be because sometimes their ears are pierced for earrings,
But they have the most eccentric hearings.
Their hearings are in fact so sensitive
That you frequently feel reprchensitive.
At home, for instance, when near you,
Nobody can hear you.
After your most brilliant fireside or breakfast-table chats you can
          count on two fingers the responses you will have got:
Either, Don't mumble, dear, or, more simply, What?
I suppose if you're male and parental
You get used to being treated mental,
But you'd feel less psychically distant
If they weren't so inconsistent,
Because if you open your mouth in a hotel or a restaurant their
          eardrums quiver at every decibel,
And their embarrassment is almost, if not quite, inexprecibel.
Their eyes signal What's cooking? at you,
And their lips hiss, Shush, Daddy, everybody's looking at you!
Now, I realize that old age is a thing of beauty,
Because I have read Cicero's *De Senectute*,
But I prefer to approach senility in my own way, so I'll thank nobody
          to rush me,
By which I mean specifically that my voice in a tearoom is no louder
          than anybody else's, so why does everybody have to shush me?

TO A LADY PASSING TIME BETTER LEFT UNPASSED

O lady of the lucent hair,
Why do you play at solitaire?
What imp, what demon misanthrope,
Prompted this session of lonely hope?
What boredom drives you, and great Lord!
How can such as you be bored?
The gleaming world awaits your eye
While you essay futility.
That mouth is shaped for livelier sport
Than paging of a pasteboard court—
Why, even the Red Knave longing lingers,
While Black Queens wait, in those white fingers.—
See now the joy that lights your face
Squandered on some fortuitous ace,
Where formerly dark anger burned
When a five perverse would not be turned.
O, know you not, that darkling frown
Could topple Caesar's empire down;
That quick, bright joy, if flashed on men,
Could sudden build it up again?
Get up! Get up! Throw down the pack!
Rise in your gown of shining black!
Withdraw, my dear, while you are able
The slender feet from 'neath the table;
Remove from the regretful baize
The elbows curved in cunning ways.
Is there no game that pleasure brings
But fretting over painted things?
No gay, ecstatic end in view
But shuffle and begin anew?
Get up, I tell you, girl, get up!

Wine keeps not ever in the cup;
Even Love immortal, love undying,
Finds the loved one's Patience trying.
Let two-and-fifty rivals hiss me—
For God's sake, girl, come here and kiss me.

THE PRIVATE DINING ROOM

Miss Rafferty wore taffeta,
Miss Cavendish wore lavender.
We ate pickerel and mackerel
And other lavish provender.
Miss Cavendish was Lalage,
Miss Rafferty was Barbara.
We gobbled picked mackerel
And broke the candelabara,
Miss Cavendish in lavender,
In taffeta, Miss Rafferty,
The girls in taffeta lavender,
And we, of course, in mufti.

Miss Rafferty wore taffeta,
The taffeta was lavender,
Was lavend, lavender, lavenderest,
As the wine improved the provender.
Miss Cavendish wore lavender,
The lavender was taffeta.
We boggled mackled pickerel,
And bumpers did we quaffeta.
And Lalage wore lavender,
And lavender wore Barbara,
Rafferta taffeta Cavender lavender
Barbara abracadabra.

Miss Rafferty in taffeta
Grew definitely raffisher.
Miss Cavendish in lavender
Grew less and less stand-offisher.
With Lalage and Barbara

We grew a little pickereled,
We ordered Mumm and Roederer
Because the bubbles tickereled.
But lavender and taffeta
Were gone when we were soberer.
I haven't thought for thirty years
Of Lalage and Barbara.

THE PERFECT HUSBAND

He tells you when you've got on too much lipstick,
And helps you with your girdle when your hips stick.

THE UNSELFISH HUSBAND

Once upon a time there was a man named Orlando Tregennis and he
was in love with his wife,

And he thought he would express his love by serenading her but his
serenade wasn't very successful because his playing
interfered with his singing because all he could play was the
fife,

So then he said, I will climb the highest mountain in the world and
name it after my wife and then she will give me a look of
love, so he climbed the highest mountain in the world and his
wife was indeed whom he named it after,

But she didn't give him a look of love, she gave him a look of
laughter,

And not only a look of laughter but a look of menace,

Because he named it after his wife by naming it Mt. Mrs Orlando
Tregennis,

So then he said that he certainly was sorry that during the great war
he had absent-mindedly forgotten to join the army,

Because he said if he had been entitled to a bonus he would have
given her every penny even though she was already so
entrancing that no amount of mere money could make her a
jot or tittle more allury or charmy,

And she greeted this remark with ribald merriment,

And she said that possibly money wouldn't get her any further than
she was, but she'd like a chance to try the experiment,

So then Mr. Tregennis said, Well, I haven't any gold,

But I will give you my most precious possession, I will give you my
cold,

And he gave her his cold and first of all she tried to spurn it,

And then she tried to return it,

But he said No darling, now it's your very own cold,

It is yours to have and to hold,

Because if you reckon I don't give gifts for keeps you made a
mistake when you reckoned,

Because there hasn't been an Indian-giver in the Tregennis family
        since my great-great-grandfather, old Hiawatha Tregennis II.
But she wouldn't take no for an answer, but he wouldn't say yes, and
        Mr. Tregennis's precious cold went shuttling back and forth
        between them for the rest of their lives,
And I hope everybody will turn out to be such self-sacrificing
        husbands and wives.

REFLECTION ON CAUTION

Affection is a noble quality;
It leads to generosity and jollity.
But it also leads to breach of promise
If you go around lavishing it on red-hot momise.

I DO, I WILL, I HAVE

How wise I am to have instructed the butler to instruct the first
    footman to instruct the second footman to instruct the
    doorman to order my carriage;
I am about to volunteer a definition of marriage.
Just as I know that there are two Hagens, Walter and Copen,
I know that marriage is a legal and religious alliance entered into by
    a man who can't sleep with the window shut and a woman
    who can't sleep with the window open.
Moreover just as I am unsure of the difference between flora and
    fauna and flotsam and jetsam
I am quite sure that marriage is the alliance of two people one of
    whom never remembers birthdays and the other never
    forgetsam,
And he refuses to believe there is a leak in the water pipe or the gas
    pipe and she is convinced she is about to asphyxiate or
    drown,
And she says Quick get up and get my hairbrushes off the window
    sill, it's raining in, and he replies Oh they're all right, it's
    only raining straight down.
That is why marriage is so much more interesting than divorce,
Because it's the only known example of the happy meeting of the
    immovable object and the irresistible force.
So I hope husbands and wives will continue to debate and combat
    over everything debatable and combatable,
Because I believe a little incompatibility is the spice of life,
    particularly if he has income and she is pattable.

WHAT ALMOST EVERY WOMAN KNOWS
SOONER OR LATER

Husbands are things that wives have to get used to putting up with,
And with whom they breakfast with and sup with.
They interfere with the discipline of nurseries,
And forget anniversaries,
And when they have been particularly remiss
They think they can cure everything with a great big kiss,
And when you tell them about something awful they have done they
     just took unbearably patient and smile a superior smile,
And think, Oh she'll get over it after a while.
And they always drink cocktails faster than they can assimilate
     them,
And if you look in their direction they act as if they were martyrs
     and you were trying to sacrifice, or immolate them.
And when it's a question of walking five miles to play golf they are
     very energetic but if it's doing anything useful around the
     house they are very lethargic,
And then they tell you that women are unreasonable and don't know
     anything about logic,
And they never want to get up or go to bed at the same time as you
     do,
And when you perform some simple common or garden rite like
     putting cold cream on your face or applying a touch of
     lipstick they seem to think you are up to some kind of black
     magic like a priestess of Voodoo,
And they are brave and calm and cool and collected about the
     ailments of the person they have promised to honor and
     cherish,
But the minute they get a sniffle or a stomach-ache of their own, why
     you'd think they were about to perish,
And when you are alone with them they ignore all the minor
     courtesies and as for airs and graces, they utterly lack them,
But when there are a lot of people around they hand you so many
     chairs and ash trays and sandwiches and butter you with
     such bowings and scrapings that you want to smack them.

Husbands are indeed an irritating form of life,
And yet through some quirk of Providence most of them are really
very deeply ensconced in the affection of their wife.

BIOLOGICAL REFLECTION

A girl whose cheeks are covered with paint
Has an advantage with me over one whose ain't.

MACHINERY DOESN'T ANSWER, EITHER,
BUT YOU AREN'T MARRIED TO IT

Oh Daddy, look at that man, excuse my pointing, but just look at
      him!
He is in a frenzy or something, as if a red rag or something had been
      shook at him!
His eyes are rolling like a maniac's,
Oh isn't it shocking how insaniacs!
Oh Daddy, he is talking to thin air,
He is having a long conversation with somebody who isn't there!
He is talking to himself, he must be under the influence of either
      Luna or Bacchus;
Oh Daddy, Daddy, I think we had better go a long way away from
      him immediately because one in his condition might at any
      moment have an impulse to attacchus!

Nay, flush ye, hush ye, do not fret ye, my little white manchild,
Who if your parents hadn't been Caucasian would have been an
      ebony or copper or tan child,
Life will teach you many things, chief of which is that every man
      who talks to himself isn't necessarily out of his wits;
He may have a wife who knits.
Probably only he and his Maker
Know how many evenings he has spent trying to raise a conversation
      while his beloved created sweaters by the acre.

Ah, my inquiring offspring, you must learn that life can be very
      bitter,
But never quite so much so as when trying to pry a word out of a
      knitter.
Sometimes she knits and sits,
Sometimes she sits and knits,

And you tell her what you have been doing all day and you ask what
    she has been doing all day and nothing happens, and you tell
    her what you would like to do this evening and ask her what
    she would like to do this evening and nothing happens, and
    you think you will disintegrate if you don't get some
    response, and you speak tenderly of your courtship and your
    bridal,
And you might just as well try to get a response out of an Oriental
    idol,
And you notice a spasmodic movement of her lips,
And you think she is going to say something but she is only
    counting the number of stitches it takes to surround the hips;
And she furrows her beautiful brow, which is a sign that something
    is wrong somewhere and you keep on talking, and disregard
    the sign,
And she casts a lethal glance, as one who purls before swine,
And this goes on for weeks
At the end of which she lays her work down and speaks,
And you think now maybe you can have some home life but she
    speaks in a tone as far off as Mercury or Saturn,
And she says thank goodness that is finished, it is a sight and she
    will never be able to wear it, but it doesn't matter because
    she can hardly wait to start on an adorable new pattern,
And when this has been going on for a long time, why that's the time
    that strong men break down and go around talking to
    themselves in public, finally,
And it doesn't mean that they are weak mentally or spinally,
It doesn't mean, my boy, that they ought to be in an asylum, like
    Nijinsky the dancer,
It only means that they got into the habit of talking to themselves at
    home because they themselves were the only people they
    could talk to and get an answer.

VERY FUNNY, VERY FUNNY

In this foolish world there is nothing more numerous
Than different people's senses of humorous,
And the difference between different sense of humors
Is as wide as the gap between shorts and bloomers.
This is what humor boils down unto—
Are you him who doeth, or him who it's done to?
If a friend is dogged by some awful hoodoo,
Why, naturally, he doesn't laugh, but you do;
If the puppy is sick on your new Tuxedo,
Why, naturally, you don't laugh, but he do.
Humor depends on the point of view,
It's a question of what is happening to who;
It's a question facing which I surrender,
It's also a question of What's your gender?
Strong men have squandered the best of their life
In trying to coax a smile from their wife.
I know a wag named Septimus Best;
His wife won't laugh at his merriest jest.
Under her bed he hides a skeleton;
He fills her bathtub with glue and gelatin;
He draws whiskers on pictures of Cleopatra,
And he's disrespectful to Frank Sinatra;
And she just sits in her gown of taffeta
And refuses to smile, either during or afeter.
I guess a sense of humor is what
Husbands tell each other their wives haven't got.

A WARNING TO WIVES

"The outcome of the trial is another warning that if you must kill someone, you should spare the person possessing life insurance. . . . Figures are available to show that convictions are much more common in 'insurance murders' than in other types of homicides."

—BOSTON HERALD.

Speak gently to your husband, ma'am,
And encourage all his sneezes;
That nasty cough may carry him off,
If exposed to draughts and breezes.
And suppose the scoundrel lingers on,
And insists on being cured;
Well, it isn't a sin if a girl steps in—
Unless the brute's insured.

Oh, the selfishness of men, welladay, welladay!
Oh the sissies, oh the softies, oh the mice!
Egotistically they strive to keep themselves alive,
And insurance is their scurviest device.
Insurance!
It's insurance
That tries a lady's temper past endurance.
Yet it's safer, on the whole,
To practice self-control
If there's apt to be a question of insurance.

Arsenic soup is a dainty soup,
But not if he's paid his premium.
Or a .32 in a pinch will do,
If you're bored with the epithalemium.
But to make acquittal doubly sure—
No maybes, no perhapses—
You'll do well to wait to expunge your mate
Until his policy lapses.

The hypocrisy of men, welladay, welladay!
Whited sepulchers are much to be preferred.
They claim it's for their wives they evaluate their lives,
But it's fatal if you take them at their word.
Insurance!
Oh, insurance!
What holds potential widows fast in durance?
Not the Adlers and the Freuds,
But the Mutuals and Lloyds,
And the jury's evil mind about insurance.

NOTHING BUT NATURE

Ha ha ha! the sun is shining!
Yo ho ho! the sky is blue!
See the earth in peace reclining!
See the ocean reclining, too!
Tra la la! the birds are chirruping!
Fields are green and flowers are gay!
Maples swell with sap a-syruping!
Nature is spreading herself today!

Well, let's go out and trample on a violet,
Let's steal candy from a curly-headed tot,
Take a wrong number and deliberately dial it,
Let's plant thistles under squatters when they squat,
Let's throw pepper on the robins on their nests,
Let's tell Altman's we prefer to buy at Best's,
Let's cry Boo! at golfers as they putt,
Let's open windows that people want shut,
Let's step on somebody's nice white shoes,
Let's join a club and not pay dues,
Let's send bills and let's raise rents,
Let's put mosquitoes in campers' tents,
Let's teach Nature not to spread so free
On a day when my love is off of me.

Yah yah yah! the rain is raining!
Zut alors! the wild waves boil!
Hear the homeless wind complaining!
Watch the shrubbery bite the soil!
Nya nya nya! come sleet, come icicles!
The world is a welter of freezing spray!
Pity the acrobats on high-wheeled bicycles!
Nature is having a tantrum today!

Well, lets buy lace from a visiting Armenian,
Let's give a beggar a nickel for a bath,
Let's praise Homer to a Homer-sick Athenian,
Let's spread sunbeams all along the path,
Let's go listen to the neighborhood bores,
Let's help mothers through revolving doors,
Let's go to church and fill the plate with money,
Let's tell the minister the sermon was a honey,
Let's teach whales to avoid harpooners,
Let's be kind to congressmen and crooners,
Let's make hunters make friends with moose,
Let's buy songbirds and turn them loose,
And that will teach Nature to tantrum when
My love is speaking to me again.

DON'T WAIT, HIT ME NOW!

If there are any wives present who wish to irritate the husbands or
       husbands who wish to irritate their wives,
Why I know an irritation more irritating than hives,
So if you think such an irritation expedient,
Here is the formula, in which the presence of a third person is the
       only essential extra ingredient;
Indeed is it beautifully simple,
But it is guaranteed to make a molehill out of a dimple
And what it consists of is that when you are annoyed with your
       husband or wife and want to do the opposite of woo them,
Why, you just talk at them instead of to them.
Suppose you think your Gregory danced too often with Mrs.
       Limbworthy at the club, you don't say to him directly,
       "Gregory I'll smack you down if you don't lay off that
       platinum-plated hussy,"
No, you wait till a friend drops in and then with a glance at Gregory
       say to her, "Isn't it funny what fools middle-aged men can
       make of themselves over anything blonde and slithery, do you
       understand how anybody sober and in their right mind could
       look twice at that Limbworthy job, but then of course darling,
       Gregory wasn't altogether in his right mind last night, was
       he?"
This is indeed more excruciating to Gregory than Shakespearean
       excursions and alarums,
Because there is no defense against caroms.
Or let us suppose you are irked by your Esmeralda's sudden passion
       for antiques.
Well you don't mention it for weeks,
No, you wait till a friend drops in and then with a glance at
       Esmeralda you say, "How anybody can be sucked in by this
       antique racket is beyond me, but there are some otherwise
       sensible women who'll mortgage their beauty treatments for a
       genuine early American paper doily or a guaranteed
       secondhand Killarney banshee,

But of course Esmeralda can't ever resist an opportunity to pick up
      some fossil to amaze her friends with, can she?"
And Esmeralda must sit quiet and take it with apparent docility,
Because the hit direct doesn't compare with the richochet in deadly
      unanswerability.
By this easy method can every Gregory score off every Esmeralda
      and every Esmeralda annihilate every Gregory,
And its only drawback besides eventual divorce is that it reduces all
      their friends to emotional beggary.

HOW TO HARRY A HUSBAND
or
IS THAT ACCESSORY REALLY NECESSARY?

Husband stands at door of flat,
Coat in elbow, hand on hat,
In his pocket, from broker shady,
Two good seats for *My Fair Lady*.
Patiently he stands there humming,
Coming, darling? Darling, coming?

But she's a freak and she's a hag,
She's got the wrong, she murmurs, bag,
She's got, she adds in wild distress,
To change the bag or change the dress.
She'd as soon appear with stockings ragged.
As be seen incongruously debaggèd.

Husband rings the bell for lift,
Hears it chunk and upward drift,
Well knows taxis in the rain
Rarer than the whooping crane.
Impatiently he stands there snarling,
Darling, coming? Coming, darling?

Another bag at last she chooses
And everything in the first bag loses.
She fumbles with many a dainty curse
For lipstick, glasses, keys, and purse.*
He grunts, as dies preprandial liquor,
To change from the skin out would have been quicker.

They disrupt the middle of the show,
Their seats are middle of the row,
They crawl and climb like tandem tractors
Between the audience and the actors,
Whose delicious rapport might have lagged
Had she been incongrously bebagged.

    *Then—
She turns it inside out and scratches
For handkerchief, cigarettes, and matches,
Tweezers, compact, and aspirin,
And Band-Aids redolent of My Sin,
Driver's license and Charga-Plate,
A sweepstake ticket one year late,
A colored chart of a five-day diet,
A Penguin commended by Gilbert Highet,
A tearful appeal from a charitymonger,
And a catalogue from Lewis & Conger.
This is she whose eyes start from their sockets
At the contents of her small son's pockets.

FRAILTY, THY NAME IS A MISNOMER

Once there was a couple named Mr. and Mrs. Pepperloaf and they
    were simply devoted,
Because each other was upon what they doted,
Arid in Mrs. Pepperloaf's eyes Mr. Pepperloaf could never err,
And he admitted only one flaw in her,
But it was a flaw which took many virtues to assuage,
Consisting in always asking him the date while she was reading the
    paper with the date clearly printed on every page,
And whenever he called her attention to this least admirable of her
    traits
She would retort that he didn't trust the paper's weather forecasts so
    then why should she trust its dates.
For eleven years his patience held
But finally he rebelled.
It was on the evening of Friday the seventh that she looked up from
    her paper and asked him the date,
And he replied firmly that she would find it at the top of the page so
    she looked at the top of the page and that was that, and
    presently they sat down to supper and ate,
And they were miserable because they had never disagreed and this
    contretemps was a beginner for them,
And at nine his employer's wife called up to ask where were they,
    she and eleven guests were waiting dinner for them,
And Mr. Pepperloaf asked Mrs. Pepperloaf how she could have so
    misreckoned,
And she said she knew that they had been invited out on the
    seventh but, according to the newspaper he had instructed
    her to consult, tonight was only the second,
And he picked up the paper and it was last week's, not today's,
And she said certainly, she had just been reading over some recipes
    for different delicious souffles,
And now she found the first flaw in him because she bad obeyed his
    order to look for the date in the paper, hadn't she, so his
    irritation was uncalled for and unseasonable.
Women would rather be right than reasonable.

WATCHMAN, WHAT OF THE FIRST FIRST LADY?

Everybody can tell you the date of George Washington's birth,
But who knows the date on which Mrs. George Washington first
    appeared on earth?
Isn't there any justice
For the former Mrs. Custis?
It's a disgrace to every United State
That we don't know more about our first president's only mate.
We all know a lot of stories about the wife of King Arthur
But you never bear any about Martha.
And we have all read a lot of romantic tales about Catherine the
    Great,
But nobody even writes them about Washington's mate.
And we have all seen Katharine Cornell, or was it Helen Hayes or
    Ethel Barrymore,
Impersonate Cleopatra, who wasn't even anybody's real wife but
    nothing more or less than a promiscuous un-American
    parrymore,
But has anybody done anything about the mistress of the nation's
    whitest house?
No, and yet but for her the nation would be the child of a man
    without a spouse.

ASIDE TO HUSBANDS

What do you do when you've wedded a girl all legal and lawful,
And she goes around saying she looks awful?
When she makes deprecatory remarks about her format,
And claims that her hair looks like a doormat?
When she swears that the complexion of which you are so fond
Looks like the bottom of a dried-up pond?
When she for whom your affection is not the least like Plato's
Compares her waist to a badly tied sack of potatoes?
Oh, who wouldn't rather be on a flimsy bridge with a hungry lion at
        one end and a hungry tiger at the other end and hungry
        crocodiles underneath
Than confronted by their dearest making remarks about her own
        appearance through clenched teeth?
Why won't they believe that the reason they find themselves the
        mother of your children is because you think of all the looks
        in the world, their looks are the nicest?
Why must we continue to be thus constantly ordealed and crisised?
I think it high time these hoity-toity ladies were made to realize that
        when they impugn their face and their ankles and their waist
They are thereby insultingly impugning their tasteful husbands'
        impeccable taste.

DOWN THE MOUSEHOLE, AND WHAT SCIENCE MISSED THERE

This is a baffling and forbidding world of disreputable international
    shakedowns,
And reputable scientists spending their lives trying to give mice
    nervous breakdowns.
Let us treat these scientists to a constructive suggestion on the
    house:
Have they thought to try their experiments on a married, or at least
    an engaged, mouse?
This suggestion is not frivolous or yeasty;
I want to tell them about a mouse I know, his name is Roger, who
    loses his mind at a twist of the wrist from his fiancée, later
    his wife, who first caught his eye because she seemed to him
    naught but, as he puts it, a wee sleekit cow'rin' tim'rous
    beastie.
Now, it is Roger's contention that to err is mouse-like, and being
    only mouse, though indeed his paternal grandmother was a
    mountain, he is all too often conscious of having erred not
    only as a mouse,
But as a mouse's spouse,
As a result of which when he is justly chastised,
He is, as a reasonable mouse, neither upset nor surprised.
It's a perfectly natural sequence, Roger says resignedly, that began
    with Adam and Eve in the garden:
Crime, punishment, apology, theater tickets, and eventual pardon.
What gets him down, he tells me, is when he has erred and doesn't
    know that he has erred,
When his conscience is clear as to thought, deed, misdeed, diet and
    word.
It is then, says Roger, that be is ready to pay the psychiatrist a
    lengthy visit,

Because he can't apologize without knowing what to apologize for,
     whereupon the coolness which chills him for whatever he has
     done that he doesn't know he has done grows all the cooler
     for the very reason that he has no idea what is it.
Worst of all, he adds in despair, is that while racking his brains to
     alight on what it can be that he erred about,
Why, he often loops an extra loop about his neck by apologizing for
     an error that if he hadn't apologized for it she would never
     have heard about.
So there you are, reputable scientists, it is in trying to recollect and
     expiate sins that it never knew were sins,
That is why a mouse is when it spins.

THE TROUBLE WITH WOMEN IS MEN

A husband is a man who two minutes after his head touches the
      pillow is snoring like an overloaded omnibus,
Particularly on those occasions when between the humidity and the
      mosquitoes your own bed is no longer a bed, but an
      insomnibus,
And if you turn an the light for a little reading he is sensitive to the
      faintest gleam,
But if by any chance you are asleep and he wakeful, he is not slow
      to rouse you with the complaint that he can't close his eyes,
      what about slipping downstairs and freezing him a cooling
      dish of pistachio ice cream.
His touch with a bottle opener is sure,
But he cannot help you get a tight dress over your head without
      catching three hooks and a button in your coiffure.
Nor can he so much as wash his ears without leaving an inch of
      water on the bathroom linoleum,
But if you mention it you evoke not a promise to splash no more but
      a mood of deep melancholium.
Indeed, each time he transgresses your chance of correcting his
      faults grows lesser,
Because he produces either a maddeningly logical explanation or a
      look of martyrdom which leaves you instead of him feeling
      the remorse of the transgressor.
Such are husbandly foibles, but there are moments when a foible
      ceases to be a foible.
Next time you ask for a glass of water and when he brings it you
      have a needle almost threaded and instead of setting it down
      he stands there holding it out to you, just kick him fairly hard
      in the stomach, you will find it thoroughly enjoible.

TIN WEDDING WHISTLE

Though you know it anyhow
Listen to me, darling, now,

Proving what I need not prove
How I know I love you, love.

Near and far, near and far,
I am happy where you are;

Likewise I have never learnt
How to be it where you aren't.

Far and wide, far and wide,
I can walk with you beside;

Furthermore, I tell you what,
I sit and sulk where you are not.

Visitors remark my frown
When you're upstairs and I am down,

Yes, and I'm afraid I pout
When I'm indoors and you are out;

But how contentedly I view
Any room containing you.

In fact I care not where you be,
just as long as it's with me.

In all your absences I glimpse
Fire and flood and trolls and imps.

Is your train a minute slothful?
I goad the stationmaster wrothful.

When with friends to bridge you drive
I never know if you're alive,

And when you linger late in shops
I long to telephone the cops.

Yet how worth the waiting for,
To see you coming through the door.

Somehow, I can be complacent
Never but with you adjacent.

Near and far, near and far,
I am happy where you are;

Likewise, I have never learnt
How to be it where you aren't.

Then grudge me not my fond endeavor,
To hold you in my sight forever;

Let none, not even you, disparage
Such valid reason for a marriage.

LOVE UNDER THE REPUBLICANS
(OR DEMOCRATS)

Come live with me and be my love
And we will all the pleasures prove
Of a marriage conducted with economy
In the Twentieth Century Anno Donomy.
We'll live in a dear little walk-up flat
With practically room to swing a cat
And a potted cactus to give it hauteur
And a bathtub equipped with dark brown water.
We'll eat without undue discouragement
Foods low in cost but high in nouragement
And quaff with pleasure, while chatting wittily,
The peculiar wine of Little Italy.
We'll remind each other it's smart to be thrifty
And buy our clothes for something-fifty.
We'll stand in line on holidays
For seats at unpopular matinees,
And every Sunday we'll have a lark
And take a walk in Central Park.
And one of these days not too remote
I'll probably up and cut your throat.

THAT REMINDS ME

Just imagine yourself seated on a shadowy terrace,
And beside you is a girl who stirs you more strangely than an
    heiress.
It is a summer evening at its most superb,
And the moonlight reminds you that To Love is an active verb,
And your hand clasps hers, which rests there without shrinking,
And after a silence fraught with romance you ask her what she is
    thinking,
And she starts and returns from the moon-washed distances to the
    shadowy veranda,
And says, Oh I was wondering how many bamboo shoots a day it
    takes to feed a baby Giant Panda.
Or you stand with her on a hilltop and gaze on a winter sunset,
And everything is as starkly beautiful as a page from Sigrid Undset,
And your arm goes round her waist and you make an avowal which
    for masterfully marshaled emotional content might have been
    a page of Ouida's or Thackeray's,
And after a silence fraught with romance she says, I forgot to order
    the limes for the Daiquiris.
Or in a twilight drawing room you have just asked the most
    momentous of questions,
And after a silence fraught with romance she says, I think this little
    table would look better where that little table is, but then
    where would that little table go, have you any suggestions?
And that's the way they go around hitting below our belts;
It isn't that nothing is sacred to them, it's just that at the Sacred
    Moment they are always thinking of something else.

2

PARENTS—AND OH, THOSE CHILDREN!

*"Of all the things that I would rather,
It is to be my daughter's father."*

CHILDREN'S PARTY

May I join you in the doghouse, Rover?
I wish to retire till the party's over.
Since three o'clock I've done my best
To entertain each tiny guest;
My conscience now I've left behind me.
And if they want me, let them find me.
I blew their bubbles, I sailed their boats,
I kept them from each other's throats.
I told them tales of magic lands,
I took them out to wash their hands.
I sorted their rubbers and tied their laces,
I wiped their noses and dried their faces.
Of similarity there's lots
Twixt tiny tots and Hottentots.
I've earned repose to heal the ravages
Of these angelic-looking savages.
Oh, progeny playing by itself
Is a lonely fascinating elf,
But progeny in roistering batches
Would drive St. Francis from here to Natchez.
Shunned are the games a parent proposes;
They prefer to squirt each other with hoses,
Their playmates are their natural foemen
And they like to poke each other's abdomen.
Their joy needs another's woe to cushion it,
Say a puddle, and somebody littler to push in it.
They observe with glee the ballistic results
Of ice cream with spoons for catapults,
And inform the assembly with tears and glares
That everyone's presents are better than theirs.
Oh, little women and little men,
Someday I hope to love you again,
But not till after the party's over,
So give me the key to the doghouse, Rover.

THE FACTS OF LIFE

Daughter, dim those reverent eyes;
Daddy must apologize.
Daddy's not an engineer;
Never will be, now, I fear.
Daddy couldn't drive a train,
Not for all the sherry in Spain.

Daddy's not a fireman, too;
He couldn't do what firemen do.
Clanging bells and screaming sirens
Are not part of his environs.
In case of fire, no hero he;
Merely a humble rescuee.

Also, greatly to his grief,
Daddy's not an Indian chief.
Daddy cannot stealthy walk
Or wield a lethal tomahawk.
Hark to Daddy's secret grim:
Feathers only tickle him.

Better learn it now than later;
Daddy's not an aviator.
Daddy cannot soar and swoop,
Neither can he loop the loop.
Parachutes he never hung on to,
And what is worse, he doesn't want to.

As long as Daddy's being defiant,
Daddy, child, is not a giant.
You'll travel far if you would seek
A less remarkable physique.
That's why he feels a decade older
When you are riding on his shoulder.

Another thing that Daddy ain't,
I frankly tell you, is a saint.
Daddy, my faithful catechumen,
Is widely known as all too human.
Still, if you watch him, you will find
He does his best, when so inclined.

One final skeleton while I dare;
Daddy's not a millionaire.
Alas, his most amusing verse
Is not a Fortunatus purse.
What I should buy for you, my sweeting,
Did journals end in both ends meeting!

There, child, you have the dismal truth,
Now obvious as an absent tooth.
Your doom it is to be the daughter
Of one as flat as barley water.
Do you mind so much, since he was made so?
What's that, my own?—I was afraid so.

DID SOMEONE SAY "BABIES"?

Everyone who has a baby thinks everybody who hasn't a baby ought
to have a baby,
Which accounts for the success of such plays as the Irish Rose of
Abie,
The idea apparently being that just by being fruitful
You are doing something beautful,
Which if it is true
Means that the common housefly is several million times more
beautiful than me or you.
Who is responsible for this propaganda that fills all our houses from
their attics to their kitchens?
Is it the perambulator trust or the safety pin manufacturers or the
census takers or the obstetritchens?
Men and women everywhere would have a lot more chance of
acquiring recreation and fame and financial independence
If they didn't have to spend most of their time and money tending
and supporting two or three unattractive descendants.
We could soon upset this kettle of fish, forsooth,
If every adult would only come out and tell every other adult the
truth.
To arms, adults! Kindle the beacon fires!
Women, do you want to be nothing but dams? Men, do you want to
be nothing but sires?
To arms, Mr. President! Call out the army, the navy, the marines, the
militia, the cadets and the middies.
Down with the kiddies!

RAINY DAY

Linell is clad in a grown of green.
She walks in state like a fairy queen.
Her train is tucked in a winsome bunch
Directly behind her royal lunch.
With a dignified skip and a haughty hop
Her golden slippers go clippety-clop.
I think I am Ozma, says Linell.
I'm Ozma too, says Isabel.

Linell has discovered a filmy veil;
The very thing for a swishy tail.
The waves wash over the nursery floor
And break on the rug with a rumbling roar;
The swishy tail gives a swishy swish;
She's off and away like a frightened fish.
Now I'm a mermaid, says Linell.
I'm mermaid too, says Isabel.

Her trousers are blue, her hair is kinky,
Her jacket is red and her skin is inky.
She is hiding behind a green umbrella;
She couldn't be Alice, or Cinderella,
Or Puss in Boots, or the Fiddlers Three;
Gracious Gulliver, who can she be?
I'm Little Black Sambo, says Linell.
I'm Sambo, too, says Isabel.

Clack the shutters. The blinds are drawn.
Click the switch, and the lights are gone.
Linell is under the blankets deep,
Murmuring down the hill to sleep.
Oh, deep in the soft and gentle dark
She stirs and chirps like a drowsy lark.
I love you, Mummy, says Linell.
Love Mummy too, says Isabel.

ADVENTURES OF ISABEL

Isabel met an enormous bear,
Isabel, Isabel, didn't care;
The bear was hungry, the bear was ravenous,
The bear's big mouth was cruel and cavernous.
The bear said, Isabel, glad to meet you,
How do, Isabel, now I'll eat you!
Isabel, Isabel, didn't worry.
Isabel didn't scream or scurry.
She washed her hands and she straightened her hair up,
Then Isabel quietly ate the bear up.

Once in a night as black as pitch
Isabel met a wicked old witch.
The witch's face was cross and wrinkled,
The witch's gums with teeth were sprinkled.
Ho ho, Isabel! the old witch crowed,
I'll turn you into an ugly toad!
Isabel, Isabel, didn't worry,
Isabel didn't scream or scurry,
She showed no rage and she showed no rancor,
But she turned the witch into milk and drank her.

Isabel met a hideous giant,
Isabel continued self reliant.
The giant was hairy, the giant was horrid,
He had one eye in the middle of his forehead.
Good morning, Isabel, the giant said,
I'll grind your bones to make my bread.
Isabel, Isabel, didn't worry,
Isabel didn't scream or scurry.
She nibbled the zwieback that she always fed off,
And when it was gone, she cut the giant's head off.

Isabel met a troublesome doctor,
He punched and he poked till he really shocked her.
The doctor's talk was of coughs and chills
And the doctor's satchel bulged with pills.
The doctor said unto Isabel,
Swallow this, it will make you well.
Isabel, Isabel, didn't worry,
Isabel didn't scream or scurry.
She took those pills from the pill concocter,
And Isabel calmly cured the doctor.

THE GENTLEMAN LADY'S MAID

A treat which I consider mild
Is dressing an impatient child.
It proves impossible to insert
The child in socks or drawers or shirt.
The process baffles brain and brawn,
The socks will just go halfway on,
The drawers cut the child in two
And the shirt won't let the head get through.
It's presently clear that one can not
Force last month's clothes on this month's tot.

EPISTLE TO THE OLYMPIANS

Dear parents, I write you this letter
Because I thought I'd better;
Because I would like to know
Exactly which way to grow.

My milk I will leave undrunk
If you'd rather have me shrunk,
If your love it will further kindle,
I'll do my best to dwindle;

Or, on the other hand,
Do you wish me to expand?
I'll stuff like a greedy rajah
If you really want me larger.

All that I ask of you
Is to tell me which to do;
To whisper in accents mild
The proper size for a child.

I get so very confused
By the chidings commonly used.
Am I really such a dunce
As to err two ways at once?

When one mood you are in,
My bigness is a sin:
"Oh what a thing to do
For a great big girl like you!"

But then another time
Smallness is my crime;
"Stop doing whatever you're at;
You're far too little for that!"

Kind parents, be so kind
As to kindly make up your mind
And whisper in accents mild
The proper size for a child.

THE ROMANTIC AGE

This one is entering her teens,
Ripe for sentimental scenes,
Has picked a gangling unripe male,
Sees herself in bridal veil,
Presses lips and tosses head,
Declares she's not too young to wed,
Informs you pertly you forget
Romeo and Juliet.
Do not argue, do not shout;
Remind her how that one turned out.

GRANDPA IS ASHAMED

A child need not be very clever
To learn that "Later, dear" means "Never."

FIRST CHILD . . . SECOND CHILD

FIRST

Be it a girl, or one of the boys,
It is scarlet all over its avoirdupois,
It is red, it is boiled; could the obstetrician
Have possibly been a lobstertrician?
His degrees and credentials were hunky-dory,
But how's for an infantile inventory?
Here's the prodigy, here's the miracle!
Whether its head is oval or spherical,
You rejoice to find it has only one,
Having dreaded a two-headed daughter or son;
Here's the phenomenon all complete,
It's got two hands, it's got two feet,
Only natural, but pleasing, because
For months you have dreamed of flippers or claws.
Furthermore, it is fully equipped:
Fingers and toes with nails are tipped;
It's even got eyes, and a mouth clear cut;
When the mouth comes open the eyes go shut,
When the eyes go shut, the breath is loosed
And the presence of lungs can be deduced.
Let the rockets flash and the cannon thunder,
This child is a marvel, a matchless wonder.
A staggering child, a child astounding,
Dazzling, diaperless, dumfounding,
Stupendous, miraculous, unsurpassed,
A child to stagger and flabbergast,
Bright as a button, sharp as a thorn,
And the only perfect one ever born.

SECOND

Arrived this evening at half-past nine.
Everybody is doing fine.
Is it a boy, or quite the reverse?
You can call in the morning and ask the nurse.

WATER FOR THE GANDER

You take a man who has ever possessed an infant son or daughter,
And he feels pretty superior about drinks of water.
His voice is full of paternal lenience
As he describes how their thirst is always adjusted to his utmost
       inconvenience,
And you gather that there is no rest for the married,
If only because of the little ones who choose to be perpetually
       inopportunely arid.
I assume that these little ones have never seen their sire in session
At his business or profession,
So listen closely, infant son and infant daughter,
His business or profession is what he carries on between getting up
       to get a drink of water.
It requires a dozen visits to the nearest water cooler or fount
Before he can face drawing up a report or balancing an account.
You may be interested to note
That the driest point in America is not Death Valley, but a man with
       lots of important work on his desk's throat.
Therefore, children, when he next complains at midnight about your
       everlasting thirst,
Simply ask him how many hours he spent that day at his desk and
       how many at the water cooler, and he may answer you, but I
       bet he has to go and get himself a drink of water first.

TO A SMALL BOY STANDING ON MY SHOES
WHILE I AM WEARING THEM

Let's straighten this out, my little man,
And reach an agreement if we can.
I entered your door as an honored guest.
My shoes are shined and my trousers are pressed,
And I won't stretch out and read your funnies
And I won't pretend that we're Easter bunnies.
If you must get somebody down on the floor,
What in the hell are your parents for?
I do not like the things that you say
And I hate the games that you want to play.
No matter how frightfully hard you try,
We've little in common, you and I.
The interest I take in my neighbour's nursery
Would have to grow, to be even cursory,
And I would that performing sons and nephews
Were carted away with the daily refuse,
And I hold that frolicsome daughters and nieces
Are ample excuse for breaking leases.
You may take a sock at your daddy's tummy
Or climb all over your doting mummy,
But keep your attentions to me in check,
Or, sonny boy, I will wring your neck.
A happier man today I'd be
Had someone wrung it ahead of me.

DADDY'S HOME, SEE YOU TOMORROW

I always found my daughters' beaux
Invisible as the emperor's clothes,
And I could hear of them no more
Than the slamming of an auto door.
My chicks would then slip up to roost;
They were, I finally deduced,
Concealing tactfully, pro tem,
Not beaux from me but me from them.

THE ABSENTEES

The healthy human child will keep
Away from home, except to sleep.
Were it not for the common cold,
Our young we never would behold.

A BOY'S WILL IS THE WIND'S WILL?

Mr. Longfellow spoke only part of the truth,
Though a fatherly poet of pre-eminent rank;
A girl's will is the twister's will.
It can drive a parent through a two-inch plank.

FATHER, DEAR FATHER, GO JUMP IN THE LAKE
or
YOU'RE COSTLIER THAN YOU THINK

Once there was a man named Mr. Arents,
And he was the severest of parents.
Every time his seven children asked him when they could have a
      convertible he answered, bye and bye,
And he confiscated all their phonograph records that had songs with
      people singing, Aye yi aye yi.
He complained that they smoked too many cigarettes,
And he would neither feed nor bathe their pets.
He insulted all their friends at 4 A.M.
By standing at the head of the stairs in his pajamas and remarking,
      Ahem.
He insisted that they put on their shoes before they ate,
And objected when they scooped the middles out of the rolls and
      deposited the crust on their plate.
That was the erstwhile Mr. Arents,
The most unreasonable of parents.
You ought to see the new Mr. Arents,
He is a veritable model of forbearance.
He feels that whatever his seven children request,
It behooves him to behave at their behest.
Mr. Arents has had a warning,
Wherefore he brings them seven apples and seven convertibles each
      morning;
He is currying favor
Against the day his voice begins to quaver;
Any good will that his children may bear him, he wants to pad it,
He wants them to remember him as a right guy when he had it.
He knows that he is now an asset but he fears that all too soon
He will be an elderly liability in a chimney corner slurping porridge
      from a wooden spoon.

Mr. Arents has recently been told by an annuity salesman something
  that makes him feel so singluar that he has shrunk to Mr.
  Arent:
Namely, it is easier for one parent to support seven children than for
  seven children to support one parent.

MY DADDY

I have a funny daddy
Who goes in and out with me,
And everything that baby does
My daddy's sure to see,
And everything that baby says
My daddy's sure to tell.
You *must* have read my daddy's verse.
I hope he fries in hell.

THE CHILD IS FATHER TO THE MAN,
BUT WITH MORE AUTHORITY

Once there were some children and they were uninterested in
        chores,
And they never picked anything up or put anything back or brought
        anything in from out-of-doors,
They didn't want to take care of anything, just to play with it,
And their parents let them get away with it.
Little did they know that Nemesis
Was on the premises.
Their regrets were at first scant
When they were left alone on their island summer home because
        their parents were called away by the convalescence of a
        wealthy aunt.
They prepared to take advantage of nobody being around,
And this is what they found,
This is how they were hoist with their own petards,
There wasn't a deck with more than fifty-one cards,
And when they tried to play the handsome phonograph with which
        they were equipped,
The records were either lost, warped or chipped,
There were bows but no arrows, and bats and gloves but no ball,
And the untethered rowboat had drifted beyond recall,
And when they were wet the only towels were those strewn on the
        bathroom floor where moisture lingers,
And when they were cold they couldn't light a fire because all the
        matches had been used by people seeing how far down they
        would burn without burning their fingers.
Such experiences certainly taught them a lesson, and when their
        parents returned to their native heath,
Why, the first thing these children did was to leave the window open
        so it rained in on the piano, and go to bed without brushing
        their teeth.

LINES TO BE EMBROIDERED ON A BIB
or
THE CHILD IS FATHER OF THE MAN, BUT NOT FOR QUITE A WHILE

So Thomas Edison
Never drank his medicine;
So Blackstone and Hoyle
Refused cod-liver oil;
So Sir Thomas Malory
Never heard of a calory;
So the Earl of Lennox
Murdered Rizzio without the aid of vitamins or calisthenox;
So Socrates and Plato
Ate dessert without finishing their potato;
So spinach was too spinachy
For Leonardo da Vinaci:
Well, it's all immaterial,
So eat your nice cereal,
And if you want to name your own ration,
First go get a reputation.

PIANO TUNER, UNTUNE ME THAT TUNE

I regret that before people can be reformed they have to be sinners,
And that before you have pianists in the family you have to have
     beginners.
When it comes to beginners' music
I am not enthusic.
When listening to something called "An Evening in My Doll
     House," or "Buzz, Buzz, Said the Bee to the Clover,"
Why I'd like just once to hear it played all the way through, instead
     of that hard part near the end over and over.
Have you noticed about little fingers?
When they hit a sour note, they lingers.
And another thing about little fingers, they are always strawberry-
     jammed or cranberry-jellied-y,
And "Chopsticks" is their favorite melody,
And if there is one man who I hope his dentist was a sadist and all
     his teeth were brittle ones,
It is he who invented "Chopsticks" for the little ones.
My good wishes are less than frugal
For him who started the little ones going boggie-woogal,
But for him who started the little ones picking out "Chopsticks" on
     the ivories,
Well I wish him a thousand harems of a thousand wives apiece, and
     a thousand little ones by each wife, and each little one
     playing "Chopsticks" twenty-four hours a day in all the
     nurseries of all his harems, or wiveries.

SOLILOQUY IN CIRCLES

Being a father
Is quite a bother.

You are free as air
With time to spare,

You're a fiscal rocket
With change in your pocket,

And then one morn
A child is born.

Your life has been runcible,
Irresponsible,

Like an arrow or javelin
You've been constantly travelin',

But mostly, I daresay,
Without a *chaise percée*,

To which by comparison
Nothing's embarison.

But all children matures,
Maybe even yours.

You improve them mentally
And straighten them dentally,

They grow tall as a lancer
And ask questions you can't answer,

And supply you with data
About how everybody else wears lipstick sooner and stays up later,

And if they are popular,
The phone they monopular.

They scorn the dominion
Of their parent's opinion,

They're no longer corralable
Once they find that you're fallible

But after you've raised them and educated them and gowned them,
They just take their little fingers and wrap you around them.

Being a father
Is quite a bother,
But I like it, rather.

THE PARENT

Children aren't happy with nothing to ignore,
And that's what parents were created for.

TABLEAU AT TWILIGHT

I sit in the dusk. I am all alone.
Enter a child and an ice-cream cone.

A parent is easily beguiled
By sight of this coniferous child.

The friendly embers warmer gleam,
The cone begins to drip ice cream.

Cones are composed of many a vitamin.
My lap is not the place to bitamin.

Although my raiment is not chinchilla,
I flinch to see it become vanilla.

Coniferous child, when vanilla melts
I'd rather it melted somewhere else.

Exit child with remains of cone.
I sit in the dusk. I am all alone,

Muttering spells like an angry Druid,
Alone, in the dusk, with the cleaning fluid.

THERE'S NOTHING LIKE INSTINCT. FORTUNATELY.

I suppose that plumbers' children know more about plumbing than
  plumbers do, and welders' children more about welding than
  welders,
Because the only fact in an implausible world is that all young know
  better than their elders.
A young person is a person with nothing to learn,
One who already knows that ice does not chill and fire does not
  burn.
It knows that it can read indefinitely in the dark and do its eyes no
  harm,
It knows it can climb on the back of a thin chair to look for a
  sweater it left on the bus without falling and breaking an arm.
It knows it can spend six hours in the sun on the first day at the
  beach without ending up a skinless beet,
And It knows it can walk barefoot through the barn without running
  a nail in its feet.
It knows it doesn't need a raincoat if it's raining or galoshes if it's
  snowing,
And knows how to manage a boat without ever having done any
  sailing or rowing.
It knows after every sporting contest that it had really picked the
  winner,
And that its appetite is not affected by eating three chocolate bars
  covered with peanut butter and guava jelly, fifteen minutes
  before dinner.
Most of all it knows
That only other people catch colds through sitting around in drafts
  in wet clothes.
Meanwhile psychologists grow rich
Writing that the young are ones parents should not undermine the
  self-confidence of which.

TARKINGTON, THOU SHOULD'ST BE LIVING IN THIS HOUR

O Adolescence, O Adolescence,
I wince before thine incandescence.
Thy constitution young and hearty
Is too much for this aged party.
Thou standest with loafer-flattened feet
Where bras and funny papers meet.
When anxious elders swarm about
Crying "Where are you going?", thou answerest "Out,"
Leaving thy parents swamped in debts
For bubble gum and cigarettes.

Thou spurnest in no uncertain tone
The sirloin for the ice-cream cone;
Not milk, but cola, is thy potion;
Thou wearest earrings in the ocean,
Blue jeans at dinner, or maybe shorts,
And lipstick on the tennis courts.

Forever thou whisperest, two by two,
Of who is madly in love with who.
The car thou needest every day,
Let hub caps scatter where they may.
For it would start unfriendly talk
If friends should chance to see thee walk.

Friends! Heavens, how they come and go!
Best pal today, tomorrow foe,
Since to distinguish thou dost fail
Twixt confidante and tattletale,
And blanchest to find the beach at noon
With sacred midnight secrets strewn.

Strewn! All is lost and nothing found.
Lord, how thou leavest things around!
Sweaters and rackets in the stable,
And purse upon the drugstore table,
And cameras rusting in the rain,
And Daddy's patience down the drain.

Ah well, I must not carp and cavil,
I'll chew the spinach, spit out the gravel,
Remembering how my heart has leapt
At times when me thou didst accept.
Still, I'd like to be present, I must confess,
When thine own adolescents adolesce.

REFLECTION ON BABIES

A bit of talcum
Is always walcum.

A CHILD'S GUIDE TO PARENTS

Children, I crave you kind forbearance;
Our topic for today is Parents.

Parents are generally found in couples,
Except when divorce their number quadruples.

Mostly they're married to each other.
The female one is called the mother.

Paternal pride being hard to edit,
The male, or father, claims the credit,

But children, hark! Your mother would rather,
When you arrived, have been your father.

At last on common ground they meet:
Their child is sweetest of the sweet.

But burst not, babe, with boastful glee;
It is themselves they praise, not thee.

The reason Father flatters thee, is—
Thou must be wonderful, aren't thou his?

And Mother admires *her* offspring double,
Especially after all that trouble.

The wise child handles father and mother
By playing one against the other.

Don't! cries this parent to the tot;
The opposite parent asks, Why not?

Let baby listen, nothing loth,
And work impartially on both.

In clash of wills, do not give in;
Good parents are made by discipline;

Remember the words of the wise old senator:
Spare the tantrum, and spoil the progenitor,

But joy in heaping measure comes
To children whose parents are under their thumbs.

PEDIATRIC REFLECTION

Many an infant that screams like a calliope
Could be soothed by a little attention to its diope.

ASK DADDY, HE WON'T KNOW

Now that they've abolished chrome work
I'd like to call their attention to home work.
Here it is only three decades since my scholarship was famous,
And I'm an ignoramus.
I cannot think which goes sideways and which goes up and down, a
      parallel or a meridian,
Nor do I know the name of him who first translated the Bible into
      Indian, I see him only as an enterprising colonial Gideon.
I have difficulty with dates,
To say nothing of the annual rainfall of the Southern Central States.
Naturally the correct answers are just back of the tip of my tongue,
But try to explain that to your young.
I am overwhelmed by their erudite banter,
I am in no condition to differentiate between Tamerlane and Tam
      o' Shanter.
I reel, I sway, I am utterly exhausted;
Should you ask me when Chicago was founded I could only reply I
      didn't even know it was losted.

SONG TO BE SUNG BY THE FATHER OF
INFANT FEMALE CHILDREN

My heart leaps up when I behold
A rainbow in the sky;
Contrariwise, my blood runs cold
When little boys go by.
For little boys as little boys,
No special hate I carry,
But now and then they grow to men,
And when they do, they marry.
No matter how they tarry,
Eventually they marry.
And, swine among the pearls,
They marry little girls.

Oh, somewhere, somewhere, an infant plays,
With parents who feed and clothe him.
Their lips are sticky with pride and praise,
But I have begun to loathe him.
Yes, I loathe with a loathing shameless
This child who to me is nameless.
This bachelor child in his carriage
Gives never a thought to marriage,
But a person can hardly say knife
Before he will hunt him a wife.

I never see an infant (male),
A-sleeping in the sun,
Without I turn a trifle pale
And think Is *he* the one?
Oh, first he'll want to crop his curls,
And then he'll want a pony,
And then he'll think of pretty girls

And holy matrimony.
He'll put away his pony,
And sigh for matrimony.
A cat without a mouse
Is he without a spouse.

Oh, somewhere he bubbles bubbles of milk,
And quietly sucks his thumbs.
His cheeks are roses painted on silk,
And his teeth are tucked in his gums.
But alas, the teeth will begin to grow,
And the bubbles will cease to bubble;
Given a score of years or so,
The roses will turn to stubble.
He'll sell a bond, or he'll write a book,
And his eyes will get that acquisitive look,
And raging and ravenous for the kill,
He'll boldly ask for the hand of Jill.
This infant whose middle
Is diapered still
Will want to marry
My daughter Jill.

Oh sweet be his slumber and moist his middle!
My dreams, I fear, are infanticiddle.
A fig for embryo Lohengrins!
I'll open all of his safety pins,
I'll pepper his powder, and salt his bottle,
And give him readings from Aristotle.
Sand for his spinach I'll gladly bring,
And Tabasco sauce for his teething ring.
Then perhaps he'll struggle through fire and water
To marry somebody else's daughter.

SOME OF MY BEST FRIENDS ARE CHILDREN

Ichneumons are fond of little ichneumons,
And lions of little lions,
But I am not fond of little humans;
I do not believe in scions.

Of course there's always our child,
But our child is different,
Our child appeals
To the cultivated mind.
Ours is a lady;
Boys are odoriferant;
Ladies are the sweetness;
Boys are the rind.

Whenever whimsey colides with whimsy
As parents compare their cherubs,
At the slightest excuse, however flimsy,
I fold my tent like the Arabs.

Of course there's always our child,
But our child is charminger,
Our child's eyes
Are a special kind of blue;
Our child's smile
Is quite a lot disarminger;
Our child's tooth
Is very nearly through.

Mankind, I consider, attained its zenith
The day it achieved the adult;
When the conversation to infants leaneth,
My horse is bridled and saddult.

Of course there's always our child,
But our child is wittier;
Our child's noises
Are the nicest kind of noise;
She has no beard
Like Tennyson or Whittier;
But Tennyson and Whittier
Began as little boys.

The Politician, the Parent, the Preacher,
Were each of them once a kiddie.
The child is indeed a talented creature.
Did I want one? Oh, heaven forbidde!

But now there's always our child,
And our child's adorable.
Our child's an angel
Fairer than the flowers;
Our child fascinates
One who's rather borable;
And incidentally,
Our child is ours.

AFTER THE CHRISTENING

Come along, everybody, see the pretty baby,
Such a pretty baby ought to be adored.
Come along, everybody, come and bore the baby,
See the pretty baby, begging to be bored.

Hurry, hurry, Aunt Louise,
Silly names are sure to please.
Bother what the baby thinks!
Call her Kitchy-kitch and Binks,
Call her Wackywoo and Snookums,
Just ignore her dirty lookums,
Who than she is fairer game
For every kind of silly name?
Baby cannot answer back,
Or perhaps an aunt she'd lack.

Come along, everybody, isn't she a darling?
Such a little darling ought to be enjoyed.
Come along, everybody, let's annoy the baby,
Such a darling darling begs to be annoyed.

Goodness Gracious, Uncle George!
Home at last from Valley Forge?
Won't you try on her the whoops
That cheered the Continental troops?
Stand a little closer, please;
That will put her at her ease;
And babies find it hard to hear,
So place your mouth against her ear—
I gues she heard it, Uncle George;
I'm sure they did at Valley Forge.

Come along, everybody, see the little lady,
Isn't she adorable and kissable and pleasing?
Come along, everybody, come and tease the baby,
Here's a lady baby available for teasing!

Cousin Charles was always chummy;
He's about to poke her tummy.
Grandpa almost chokes on chuckles,
Tickling with his beard her knuckles;
All of Granny's muscles ache
From half an hour of patty-cake;
God-mamma with glee begins
A noisy count of baby's chins;
God-papa with humor glows
Playing piggie with her toes.
See the happy prideful parents,
Do they think of interference?
Certainly not, while baby gives
Such wholesome fun to relatives.

Up and at her, everybody, at the pretty baby,
Tell her she's a dumpling, tell her she's a dear.
Everybody knows the way to woo a baby—
Tickle her and pinch her and yodel in her ear.

LITTLE FEET

Oh, who would live in a silent house,
As still as a waltz left unwritten by Strauss,
As undisturbed as a virgin dewdrop,
And quiet enough to hear a shoe drop?
Who would dwell
In a vacuum cell,
In a home as mute as a clapperless bell?
Oh, a home as mute as a bell that's clapperless
Is forlorn as an Indian in Indianapolis.

Then ho! for the patter of little feet,
And the childish chatter of voices sweet,
For the ringing laughter and prancing capers
That soothe your ear as you read the papers,
For the trumpets that blow and the balls that bounce
As you struggle to balance your old accounts,
For the chubby arms that encircle your neck,
And the chubby behinds that your lap bedeck,
And sirens who save their wiliest wooing
For the critical spot in whatever you're doing.

Shakespeare's, I'm sure, was a silent house,
And that of Good King Wenceslaus,
And Napoleon's dwelling, and Alexander's,
And whoever's that wrote *The Dog of Flanders.*
Yes, Shelley and Keats
And other élites,
They missed the patter of little feets,
For he who sits and listens to pattering
Will never accomplish more than a smattering.

Then ho! for the patter of little feet!
Some find these footfalls doubly sweet,
Subjecting them to the twofold use
Of paternal pride and a good excuse.
You say, for instance, my modest chanteys
Are not so fine as Pope's or Dante's?
My deeds do not compare with those
Of Nelson, or Michelangelo's?
Well, my life is perpetual Children's Hour,
Or boy! would immortal genius flower!

THUNDER OVER THE NURSERY

Listen to me, angel tot,
Whom I love an awful lot,
It will save a barrel of bother
If we understand each other.

Every time that I'm your herder
You think you get away with murder.
All right, infant, so you do,
But only because I want you to.

Baby's muscles are prodigious,
Baby's beautiful, not higious,
She can talk and walk and run
Like a daughter of a gun.

Well, you may be a genius, child,
And I a parent dull and mild;
In spite of which, and nevertheless,
I could lick you yet, I guess.

Forgive me, pet, if I am frank,
But truth is money in the bank;
I wish you to admire and love yourself,
But not to get too far above yourself.

When we race, you always win;
Baby, think before you grin.
It may occur to you, perhaps,
That Daddy's running under wraps.

When you hide behind the chair
And Daddy seeks you everywhere,
Behind the door, beneath the bed—
That's Daddy's heart, not Baby's head.

When I praise your speech in glee
And claim you talk as well as me,
That's the spirit, not the letter.
I know more words, and say them better.

In future, then, when I'm your herder,
Continue getting away with murder;
But know from him who murder endures,
It's his idea much more than yours.

A GOOD PARENT'S GARDEN OF VISION

In my bachelor days, no parent I,
My spirits fell as the weeks ran by,
And, tossing on my pallet, I dolefully thought
Of Time, the tri-motored Juggernaut,
Or paused at whiles amid my gardening
To listen for the sound of my arteries hardening.
But now I eargerly listen for
Senility knocking at the door.
Come dotage, envelop me in your arms,
Old age, I ween, has its special charms.
I'll camp awhile by Jordan's water
And enjoy being a nuisance to my daughter.
The loving offspring of Mr. N.
Won't trouble her head with raw young men,
Young men who cry she is lissome and flowery,
Young men who inquire about her dowery.
She'll make young men all keep their distances.
She'll listen to her father's reministances,
She'll fondly lay out his favorite slippers,
And when he wears arctics, she'll zip his zippers,
She'll nogg his eggs and she'll toast his kippers,
And disparage the quips of the current quippers
She'll light his pipe and she'll mix his drinks
And tell her father every thought she thinks.
And he in his way and she in hern
Will be merrry as a melody by Mr. Kern.

And he in his way and she in hern
Will be merry as ashes in a funeral urn.
She'll discourage his pipe and she'll hide his drinks,
And conceal from her father every thought she thinks.

She'll make audible comments on his taste in togs,
She'll put his eggs in custards and not in noggs,
She'll object to the odor of kippering kippers,
She will laugh Ha Ha! at the current quippers,
She will leave the room when he dons his slippers,
When his buttons unbutton she will advocate zippers.
She'll see that parents keep their proper distances,
And she'll give young men a lot of reministances,
She'll look at her father like a beetle from the Bowery,
And ask why she hasn't a decent dowery,
And the only moments she'll be really merry
Will be pricing plots at the cemetery.

PART III: THE AWAKENING

O pleasing daughter of Mr. N.,
His forebodings are happily beyond your ken,
And I gravely doubt that his querulous words
Retard the digestion of your whey and curds,
For children all choose their own sweet way—
Say Disobey, and they Datobey.
It's not that they're all in the train of Belial,
It's only their way of being filial.
Some grow up hideous, others beautiful,
Some ungrateful and others dutiful;
Why try to prognosticate which yours will be?
There's nothing to do but wait and see.
Only nasty parents lose their nerve
At the prospect of getting what they deserve.
With a conscience as clear as mountain water
I await the best from my loving daughter.

JUDGMENT DAY

This is the day, this is the day!
I knew as soon as the sun's first ray
Crept through the slats of the cot,
And opened the eyes of a tot,
And the tot would rather have slept.
And, therefore, wept.
This is the day that is wrong,
The day when the only song
Is a skirling lamentation
Of continuous indignation,
When the visage is ireful,
The voice, direful,
And the early, pearly teeth
Snick like a sword in the sheath.
When the fists are clenched,
And the cheeks are drenched
In full-fed freshets and tumbling, tumultuous torrents
Of virtuous abhorrence,
When loud as the challenging trumpets of John at Lepanto
Rings the clarion, "I don't want to."
This is the day, the season,
Of wrongs without reason,
The day when the prunes and the cereal
Taste like building material.
When the spinach tastes only like spinach, and honey and sugar
Raise howls like the yowls of a quarrelsome puma or cougar,
When the wail is not to be hushed
Nor the hair to be brushed.
When life is frustration, and either
A person must be all alone or have somebody with her, and tolerates
      neither,

When outdoors is worse than in, and indoors than out, and both too
      dull to be borne,
And dolls are flung under the bed and books are torn,
When people humiliate a person
With their clumsily tactful attempts to conciliate a person,
When music no charm possesses,
Nor hats, nor mittens, nor dresses,
When the frowning fortress is woe
And the watchword is No.
You owners of children who pass this day with forbearance,
You indeed are parents!

IT MUST BE THE MILK

There is a thought that I have tried not to but cannot help but think,
Which is, My goodness how much infants resemble people who have
    had too much to drink.
Tots and sots, so different and yet so identical!
What a humiliating coincidence for pride parentical!
Yet when you see your little dumpling set sail across the nursery
    floor,
Can you conscientiously deny the resemblance to somebody who is
    leaving a tavern after having tried to leave it a dozen times
    and each time turned back for just one more?
Each step achieved
Is simply too good to be believed;
Foot somehow follows foot
And somehow manages to stay put;
Arms wildly sempahore,
Wild eyes seem to ask, Whatever did we get in such a dilemma for?
And their gait is more that of a duckling than a Greek goddessling
    or godling,
And in inebriates it's called staggering but in infants it's called
    toddling.
Another kiship with topers is also by infants exhibited,
You discover yourself too tired to sleep.
O torpor and sloth, torpor and sloth,
These are the cooks that unseason the broth.
Tropor is harrowing, sloth it is irksome—
Everyone ready? Let's go out and worksome.

OUR CHILD DOESN'T KNOW ANYTHING
or
THANK GOD!

I am now about to make a remark that I suppose most parents will
      think me hateful for,
Though as a matter fo fact I am only commenting on a condition that
      they should be more than grateful for.
What I want to say is, that of luckiness it seems to me to be the
      height
That babies aren't very bright.
Now listen to me for a minute, all you proud progenitors who boast
      that your bedridden infant offspring of two months or so are
      already bright enough to get into Harvard or Stanford or
      Notre Dame or Fordham;
Don't you realize that the only thing that makes life at all bearable
      to those selfsame offspring is being rather backward, and that
      if they had any sense at all they would lose no time in
      perishing of boredom?
Good heavens, I can think of no catastrophe more immense
Than a baby with sense,
Because one thing at least, willy-nilly, you must believe,
And that is, that a baby has twenty-four hours a day to get through
      with just the same as we've.
Some people choose to wonder about virtue and others about crime,
But I choose to wonder how babies manage to pass the time.
They can't pass it in tennis or badminton or golf,
Or in going around resucing people from Indians and then marrying
      somebody else the way Pocahontas did with the Messrs.
      Smith and Rolfe;
They can't pass it in bridge or parchesi or backgammon,
Or in taking the subway to Wall Street and worshipping Mammon;
How then do they manage to enthuse themselves,
And amuse themselves?
Well, partly they sleep,

And mostly they weep,
And the rest of the time they relax
On their backs,
And eat, by régime specifically, but by nature omnivorously,
And vocalize vocivorously.
That, to make it short,
Is about all they can do in the way of sport;
So whatever may come,
I am glad that babies are dumb.
I shudder to think what for entertainment they would do
Were they as bright as me or you.

BIRDIES, DON'T MAKE ME LAUGH

Once there was a poem, and it was serious and not in jest,
And it said children ought to agree like little birdies in their nest.
Oh forsooth forsooth!
That poem was certainly more poetry than truth,
Because do you believe that little birdies in their nest agree?
It doesn't sound very probable to me.
Ah no, but I can tell you what does sound probable,
And that is that life in a nest is just one long quarrel and
     squabbable.
Look at that young mother robin over in that elm, or is it a beech,
She has two little robins and she thinks she has solved her problem
     because she has learned not to bring home just one worm but
     a worm for each.
She is very pleased with her understanding of fledgling psychology,
     but in just about two minutes she is going to lose a year's
     growth,
Because she's going to find that one little robin gets no worms and
     the other little robin gets both,
And if one little robin gets out of the nest on the wrong side and
     nothing can please it,
Why the other little robin will choose that moment to tease it,
And if one little robin starts a game the other little robin will stop it,
And if one little robin builds a castle the other little robin will
     knock it down and if one little robin blows a bubble the other
     little robin will pop it.
Yes, I bet that if you walked up to any nest and got a good revealing
     glimpse,
Why, you would find that our little feathered friendlets disagree just
     like human imps,
And I also bet that their distracted feathered parents quote
     feathered poetry to them by whoever the most popular
     feathered poet may be,

All about why don't they like little children in their nurseries agree.
Well, to put the truth about youth in a very few words,
Why the truth is that little birds do agree like children and children
 do agree like little birds,
Because you take offsprings, and I don't care whether a house or a
 tree is their abode,
They may love each other but they aren't going to agree with each
 other anywhere except in an ode.
It doesn't seem to have occurred to the poet,
That nobody agrees with anybody else anyhow, but adults conceal it
 and infants show it.

"MY CHILD IS PHLEGMATIC . . . "
—ANXIOUS PARENT

Anxious Parent, I guess you have just never been around;
I guess you just don't know who are the happiest people anywhere to
    be found;
So you are worried, are you, because your child is turning out to be
    phlegmatic?
Forgive me if I seem a trifle unsympathetic.
Why do you want your child to be a flashing, coruscating gem?
Don't you know the only peace the world can give lies not in flame
    but in phlegm?
Don't you know that the people with souls of putty
Are the only people who are sitting prutty?
They never get all worked up at the drop of a pin or a feather or a
    hat,
They never go around saying bitterly to themselves: "Oh God, did I
    really do, did I really say that?"
They never boil over when they read about stool pigeons getting girls
    into reformatories by making treacherous advances;
They never get perfectly futily harrowed about Sacco and Vanzetti,
    or Alice Adamses who don't have good times at dances;
They never blink an eyelash about colleges that are going to the
    dogs because of football overemphasis;
They never almost die with indignation over a lynching near Natchez
    or Memphis.
No, when they eat they digest their food, a go to bed they get right to
    sleep,
And four phlegmatic angels a stolid watch over them keep.
Oh to be phlegmatic, Oh to be stolid, Oh to be torpid, Oh to be
    calm!
For it is only thus, Anxious Parent, that we can get through life
    without a qualm.

3

VICES, VICES EVERYWHERE

*"Purity
Is Obscurity."*

THE VISIT

She welcomes him with pretty impatience
And a cry of Greetings and salutations!
To which remark, no laggard, he
Ripostes with a Long time no see.
Recovering her poise full soon,
She bids him Anyhoo, sit ye doon,
And settling by the fireside,
He chuckles, Thank you, kind sir, she cried.
Snug as a bug, the cup he waits
That cheers but not inebriates.
She offers him a truly ducal tea,
Whipped up, she says, with no diffewclty.
A miracle, if I didn't know you,
He says—It only shows to go you.
Eying her o'er the fragrant brew,
He tells her her smile is picturescue,
And now he whispers, a bit pajamaly,
That he's fed to the teeth with his whole fam damily,
Perhaps she'll forgive an old man's crotchet
And visit Bermuda on his yachat.
She says she might, despite Dame Rumor,
Because he is a who than whom none is whomer.
He sidles close, but no cigar—
Until the yachat, au reservoir.

NATURE KNOWS BEST

I don't know exactly how long ago Hector was a pup,
But it was quite long ago, and even then people used to have to start
their day by getting up.
Yes, people have been getting up for centuries,
They have been getting up in palaces and Pullmans and
penitentiaries.
The caveman had to get up before he could go out and track the
brontosaurus,
Verdi had to get up before he could sit down and compose the Anvil
Chorus,
Alexander had to get up before he could go around being dominant,
Even Rip Van Winkle had to get up from one sleep before he could
climb the mountain and encounter the sleep which has made
him prominent.
Well, birds are descended from birds and flowers are descended
from flowers,
And human beings are descended from generation after generation
of ancestors who got up at least once every twenty-four hours,
And because birds are descended from birds they don't have to be
forced to sing like birds, instead of squeaking like rats,
And because flowers are descended from flowers they don't have to
be forced to smell like flowers, instead of like burning rubber
or the Jersey flats,
But you take human beings, why their countless generations of
ancestors who were always arising might just as well have
spent all their lives on their mattresses or pallets,
Because their descendants haven't inherited any talent for getting
up at all, no, every morning they have to be forced to get up
either by their own conscience or somebody else's, or alarm
clocks or valets.
Well, there is one obvious conclusion that I have always held to,
Which is that if Nature had really intended human beings to get up,
why they would get up naturally and wouldn't have to be
compelled to.

CAT NAPS ARE TOO GOOD FOR CATS

Oh, early every afternoon
I like a temporary swoon.
I do not overeat at luncheon,
I do not broach the bowl or puncheon;
Yet the hour from two to three
Is always sleepy-time to me.

Bolt upright at my desk I sit,
My elbows digging into it,
My chin into my hands doth fit,
My careful fingers screen my eyes,
And all my work before me lies,
Which leads inquisitive passer-bys
Who glance my way and see me nod,
To think me wide awake, if odd.

I would not sell my daily swoon
For all the rubies in Rangoon.
What! sell my swoon? My lovely swoon?
Oh, many and many's the afternoon
I've scoured the woods with Daniel Boone,
And sipped a julep with Lorna Doone
And former Governor Ruby Laffoon.
I'll sell my soul before my swoon,
It's not for sale, my swoon's immune.

From two to three each afternoon
Mine are the Mountains of the moon.
Mine a congenital silver spoon.
And I can lead a lost platoon
Or dive for pearls in a haunted lagoon,
Or guide a stratosphere balloon.
Oh, where the schooner schoons, I schoon,
I can talk lion, or baboon.

Or make a crooner cease to croon.
I like to swoon, for when I swoon
The universe is my macaroon.
Then blessings on thee, my afternoon torpor,
Thou makest a prince of a mental porpor.

THE CLUB CAR

Come, child, while rambling through the nation
Let's practice our pronunciation.
The liquid confluence here we see
Of r-i-b and a-l-d.
When first potato chips he nibbled,
That gentleman was merely ribald,
But now that he is four-rye-highballed,
We may properly pronounce him ribald.

THIS WAS TOLD ME IN CONFIDENCE

Oh, I do like a little bit of gossip
In the course of a cozy little chat,
And I often wonder why
My neighbors all imply
I'm a pussy, I'm a tabby, I'm a cat.
Mrs. Dooley murmured meow at me this morning;
Mrs. Cohen would have cut me if she could;
But my feelings aren't so filmy,
That names are going to kill me,
And a little bit of gossip does me good.

Oh, I do like a little bit of gossip;
I am pleased with Mr. Moffet's double life.
It's provocative to watch
Mr. Taylor guzzle Scotch;
I wonder if he knows about his wife?
The sheriff wants a word with Mrs. Walker;
She doesn't pay her bills the way she should;
Yet I hear from several sources
That she gambles on the horses—
Oh, a little bit of gossip does me good.

Oh, I do like a little bit of gossip;
It seems to lend a savor to my tea;
The deplorable mistakes
That everybody makes
Are calories and vitamins to me.
If I tell you Mrs. Drew is off to Reno,
You are not to breathe a word, that's understood;
For I said to Mrs. Drew
That I heard it all from you—
Oh, a little bit of gossip does me good.

Oh, I do like a little bit of gossip,
But for scandal or for spite there's no excuse;
To think of Mrs. Page
Telling lies about my age!
Well, her tongue is like her orals, rather loose.
Mrs. Murgatroyd eats opium for breakfast,
And claims I'm running after Mr. Wood;
That sort of vicious slander
Arouses all my dander—
But a little bit of gossip does me good.

IT FIGURES

A lady from near Rising Sun,
She flattened her boy friend in fun,
Saying, Don't worry kid,
That's for nothing you did,
It's for something I dreamt that you done.

THE STRANGE CASE OF MR. DONNYBROOK'S BOREDOM

Once upon a time there was a man named Mr. Donnybrook.

He was married to a woman named Mrs. Donnybrook.

Mr. and Mrs. Donnybrook dearly loved to be bored.

Sometimes they were bored at the ballet, other times at the cinema.

They were bored riding elephants in India and elevators in the Empire State Building.

They were bored in speakeasies during Prohibition and in cocktail lounges after Repeal.

They were bored by Grand Dukes and garbagemen, debutantes and demimondaines, opera singers and operations.

They scoured the Five Continents and the Seven Seas in their mad pursuit of boredom.

This went on for years and years.

One day Mr. Donnybrook turned to Mrs. Donnybrook.

My dear, he said, we have reached the end of our rope.

We have exhausted every yawn.

The world holds nothing more to jade our titillated palates.

Well, said Mr.Donnybrook, we might try insomnia.

So they tried insomnia.

About two o'clock the next morning Mr. Donnybrook said, My, insomnia is certainly quite boring, isn't it?

Mrs. Donnybrook said it certainly was, wasn't it?

Mr. Doonybrook said it certainly was.

Pretty soon he began to count sheep.

Mrs. Donnybrook begain to count sheep, too.

After awhile Mr. Donnybrook said, Hey, you're counting my sheep!

Stop counting my sheep, said Mr. Donnybrook.

Why, the very idea, said Mrs. Donnybrook.

I guess I know my own sheep, don't I?

How? said Mr. Donnybrook.

They're cattle, said Mrs. Donnybrook.

They're cattle, and longhorns at that.

Furthermore, said Mrs. Donnybrook, us cattle ranchers is shore tired o' you sheepmen plumb ruinin' our water.

I give yuh fair warnin', said Mrs. Donnybrook, yuh better git them woolly Gila monsters o' yourn back across the Rio Grande afore mornin' or I'm a goin' to string yuh up on the nearest cottonwood.

Carramba! sneered Mr. Donnybrook. Thees ees free range, no?

No, said Mrs. Donnybrook, not for sheepmen.

She strung him up on the nearest cottonwood.

Mr. Donnybrook had never been so bored in his life.

SONG BEFORE BREAKFAST

Hopeful each morning I arise
And splash the cobwebs from my eyes.
I brush my teeth and scrape my chin
And bravely at the mirror grin.
Sternly I force myself to say,
Huzza! Huzza! another day!
Oh happy me! oh lucky I!
Another chance with life to vie!
Another golden opportunity
To rise and shine in this community!
Another target for my aim!
Another whack at wealth and fame!
Almost I feel within me stir
A budding force of character.
Who knows, indeed, but what I might
Perhaps have altered overnight?
Today may be the day, who knows,
That sees me triumph o'er my foes:
Gluttony, simony, and sloth,
And drawing on the table cloth;
Perjury, arson, envy, pride,
And renting tales of homicide;
Barratry, avarice and wrath
And blowing bubbles in the bath.
The differences this day may bring!
Perhaps I'll work like anything;
I'll travel to my tasks on foot,
And in the bank the carfare put,
And buy a haircut when I need it,
And if I get a letter, read it,
And every eve improve myself
By inching through the Five Foot Shelf.
The things I want to do, I won't,

And only do the things I don't.
What lordly aspirations dawn
The while I draw my trousers on!
Oh beamish morning, big with hope
And noble tasks with which to cope,
If I should fail you, do not sorrow;
I'll be a better man tomorrow.

CARLOTTA

There was an old man in a trunk
Who inquired of his wife, "Am I drunk?"
She replied with regret,
"I'm afraid so, my pet,"
And he answered, "It's just as I thunk."

PRAYER AT THE END OF A ROPE

Dear Lord, observe this bended knee,
This visage meek and humble,
And heed this confidential plea,
Voiced in a reverent mumble.

I ask no miracles nor stunts,
No heavenly radiogram;
I only beg for once, just once,
To not be in a jam.

One little moment thy servant craves
Of being his own master;
One placid vale between the waves
Of duty and disaster.

Oh, when the postman's whistle shrills,
Just once, Lord, let me grin:
Let me have settled last month's bills
Before this month's come in.

Let me not bite more off the cob
Than I have teeth to chew;
Please let me finish just one job
Before the next is due.

Consider, too, my social life,
Sporadic though it be;
Why is it only mental strife
That pleasure brings to me?

For months, when people entertain,
Me they do not invite;
Then suddenly invitations rain,
All for the self-same night.

R.S.V.P.'s I pray thee send
Alone and not in bunches,
Or teach me I cannot attend
Two dinners or two lunches.

Let me my hostess not insult
Not call her diamonds topaz;
Else harden me to the result
Of my fantastic faux pas.

One little lull, Lord, that's my plea,
Then loose the storm again;
Just once, this once, I beg to be
Not in a jam. Amen.

I HAVE IT ON GOOD AUTHORITY

There are two kinds of people who blow through life like a breeze,
And one kind is gossipers, and the other kind is gossipees,
And they certainly annoy each other,
And they certainly enjoy each other,
Yes, they pretend to flout each other,
But they couldn't do without each other,
Because gossipers are lost without a thrill and a shock,
Because they like to sit in rocking chairs and gossip and rock and
      rock and gossip and gossip and rock,
And if the gossipees weren't there to give them a thrill and a shock
      their life would be all rocking and no gossip,
Which would be as flat as music without people named Sacha and
      Yehudi and Ossip,
While on the other hand everybody errs
If they think the gossipees could be happy without the gossipers,
Because you don't have to study under Freud or Adler or Coué
To know that it isn't any fun being a roué if nobody notices that you
      are a roué,
And indeed connoisseurs agree
That even gossipers don't know anything about gossip until they
      have heard one gossipee gossiping about another gossipee.
Another good thing about gossip is that it is within everybody's
      reach,
And it is much more interesting than any other form of speech,
Because suppose you eschew gossip and just say Mr. Smith is in
      love with his wife,
Why that disposes of the Smiths as a topic of conversation for the
      rest of their life,
But suppose you say with a smile, that poor little Mrs. Smith thinks
      her husband is in love with her, he must be very clever,

Why then you can enjoyably talk about the Smiths forever.
So a lot of people go around determined not to hear and not to see
     and not to speak any evil,
And I say Pooh for them, are you a man or a mouse, are you a
     woman or a weevil?
And I also say Pooh for sweetness and light,
And if you want to get the most out of life why the thing to do is to
     be a gossiper by day and gossipee by night.

POLITICAL REFLECTION

Discretion is the better part of virtue;
Commitments the voters don't know about can't hurt you.

HEARTS OF GOLD
or
A GOOD EXCUSE IS WORSE THAN NONE

There are some people who are very resourceful
At being remorseful,
And who apparently feel that the best way to make friends
Is to do something terrible and then make amends.
They come to your party and make a great hit with your Victorian
        aunt and with her freely mingle,
And suddenly after another drink they start a lot of *double entendre*
        the *entendre* of which is unfortunately not *double* but single,
And if you say anything to them they take umbrage,
And later when you are emptying the ash trays before going to bed
        you find them under the sofa where they have crept for a good
        night's slumbrage.
Then next day they are around intoning apologies
With all the grace and conviction of a high-paid choir intoning
        doxologies.
There are people in every group
Who will jog your elbow at table just when you are lifting a spoonful
        of very hot soup,
Or at a musicale or something while you're listening to a ravishing
        obbligato
Will forget their cigarettes and burn a hole in your clothes the size
        of a medium-sized tomato.
And then you are presented with a lot of form-fitting apologies
Quite good enough, I am sure, for inclusion in one of the higher-
        class anthologies.
Everybody says these people have hearts of gold,
But nevertheless they are always talking when you're putting, or
        splashing mud on you from their car, or giving you a cold,
And they are always sure that today you don't mind their inflicting
        on you any sorrow,

Because they'll give you so much pleasure when they smilingly
     apologize tomorrow,
But I myself would rather have a rude word from someone who has
     done me no harm
Than a graceful letter from the King of England saying he's sorry he
     broke my arm.

WHICH THE CHICKEN, WHICH THE EGG?

He drinks because she scolds, he thinks;
She thinks she scolds because he drinks;
And neither will admit what's true,
That he's a sot and she's a shrew.

OH SHUCKS, MA'AM, I MEAN EXCUSE ME

The greatest error ever erred
Is a nice girl with a naughty word.
For naughty words I hold no brief,
They fill my modest heart with grief,
But since it's plainer every day,
That naughty words are here to stay,
At least let's send them back again
To where they come from: namely, men.
For men, although to language prone,
Know when to leave the stuff alone;
The stevedore, before each damn,
Stops to consider where he am;
The lumberjack is careful, too,
Of what he says in front of who;
And if surrounded by the young,
The taxi driver curbs his tongue.
The reason men speak softly thus is
That circumstances alter cusses,
And naughty words scream out like sirens
When uttered in the wrong environs.
But maidens who restrict their hips
Place no such limits on their lips;
Once they have learned a startling Verb,
No tactful qualms their heads disturb;
They scatter Adjectives hither and thence
Regardless of their audience,
And cannot hold a Noun in trust
But have to out with it, or bust,
And that's why men creep into crannies
When girls play cribbage with their grannies,
And nervous husbands develop hives

When ministers call upon their wives,
And fathers tie themselves in knots
When damsels stoop to caress their tots,
For who knows what may not be heard
From a nice girl with a naughty word?
One truth all womankind nonplusses:
That circumstances alter cusses.

REFLECTION ON A WICKED WORLD

Purity
Is obscurity.

PAPPY WANTS A POPPY

When I a winsome babe did creep,
I'm told that I was fond of sleep,
And later, as a handsome stripling,
Gave up my life to sleep and Kipling.
At thirty, proud and in my prime,
They found me sleeping half the time,
And now that I am forty-four,
Why, sleep I doubly do adore.
As headlines range from odd to oddest
My own requirements grow more modest;
I ask no cloud of daffodils,
But just a cask of sleeping pills.
Wrapped in a robe of rosy slumber
How happily my dreams I number:
Europe erupts in bumper crops;
Bubble Gum King swells up and pops;
Big hussy novel wilts on cob;
In Georgia, Negro lynches mob;
The Have-nots simply love the Haves,
And people understand the Slavs;
Good fairies pay my income taxes,
And Mrs. Macy shops at Saks's.
In an era opened by mistake
I'd rather sleep than be awake.
Indeed, at times I can't recall
Why ever I wake up at all.

HUSH, HERE THEY COME

Some people get savage and bitter when to backbiters they refer,
But I just purr.
Yes, some people consider backbiters to be rankest of the rank,
But frankly, I prefer them to people who go around being frank,
Because usually when you are backbitten behind your back you
      don't know about it and it doesn't leave a trace,
But frankness consists of having your back bitten right to your face,
And as if that weren't enough to scar you,
Why you are right there in person to scotch the defamation, and if
      you don't happen to be able to scotch it, why where are you?
Frank people are grim, but genuine backbiters are delightful to have
      around,
Because they are so anxious that if what they have been saying
      about you has reached your ears you shouldn't believe it, that
      they are the most amiable companions to be found;
They will entertain you from sunset to dawn,
And cater encouragingly to all your weaknesses so that they can
      broadcast them later on,
So what if they do gnaw on your spine after enjoying your beer and
      skittles?
I don't blame them the least of jots or tittles,
Because certainly no pastime such diversion lends
As talking friends over analytically with friends,
So what if as they leave your house or you leave theirs backbiters
      strip your flesh and your clothes off,
At least it is your back that they bite, and not your nose off.
I believe in a place for everything and everything in its place,
And I don't care how unkind the things people say about me so long
      as they don't say them to my face.

POSSESSIONS ARE NINE POINTS OF CONVERSATION

Some people, and it doesn't matter whether they are paupers or
    millionaires,
Think that anything they have is the best in the world just because it
    is theirs.
If they happen to own a 1921 jalopy,
They look at their neighbor's new de luxe convertible like the wearer
    of a 57th Street gown at a 14th Street copy.
If their seventeen-year-old child is still in the third grade they sneer
    at the graduation of the seventeen-year-old children of their
    friends,
Claiming that prodigies always come to bad ends,
And if their roof leaks,
It's because the shingles are antiques.
Other people, and it doesn't matter if they are Scandinavians or Celts,
Think that anything is better than theirs just because it belongs to
    somebody else.
If you congratulate them when their blue-blooded Doberman
    pinscher wins the obedience championship, they look at you
    like a martyr,
And say that the garbage man's little Rover is really infinitely
    smarter;
And if they smoke fifteen-cent cigars they are sure somebody else
    gets better cigars for a dime.
And if they take a trip to Paris they are sure their friends who went
    to Old Orchard had a better time.
Yes, they look on their neighbor's ox and ass with covetousness and
    their own ox and ass with abhorrence,
And if they are wives they want their husband to be like Florence's
    Freddie, and if they are husbands they want their wives to be
    like Freddie's Florence.
I think that comparisons are truly odious, I do not approve of this
    constant proud or envious to-do;
And furthermore, dear friends, I think that you and yours are
    delightful and I also think that me and mine are delightful
    too.

LINES INDITED WITH ALL THE DEPRAVITY OF POVERTY

One way to be very happy is to be very rich
For then you can buy orchids by the quire and bacon by the flitch.
And yet at the same time
People don't mind if you only tip them a dime.
Because it's very funny
But somehow if you're rich enough you can get away with spending
      water like money
While if you're not rich you can spend in one evening your salary
      for the year
And everybody will just stand around and jeer.
If you are rich you don't have to think twice about buying a judge or
      a horse,
Or a lower instead of an upper, or a new suit, or a divorce,
And you never have to say When,
And you can sleep every morning until nine or ten,
All of which
Explains why I should like very, very much to be very, very rich.

HOW LONG HAS THIS BEEN GOING ON?
OH, QUITE LONG

Some people think that they can beat three two's with a pair of aces,
And other people think they can wind up ahead of the races,
And lest we forget,
The people who think they can wind up ahead of the races are
     everybody who has ever won a bet.
Yes, when you first get back five-sixty for two, oh what a rosy-toed
     future before you looms,
But actually your doom is sealed by whoever it is that goes around
     sealing people's dooms;
And you are lost forever
Because you think you won not because you were lucky but because
     you were clever.
You think the race ended as it did, not because you hoped it,
But because you doped it,
And from then on you withdraw your savings from the bank in ever-
     waxing wads
Because you are convinced that having figured out one winner you
     can figure out many other winners at even more impressive
     odds,
And pretty soon overdrawing your account or not betting at all is the
     dilemma which you are betwixt
And certainly you're not going to not bet at all because you are sure
     you will eventually wind up ahead because the only reason
     the races haven't run true to form, by which you mean your
     form, is because they have been fixed,
So all you need to be a heavy gainer
Is to bet on one honest race or make friends with one dishonest
     trainer.
And I don't know for which this situation is worse,
Your character or your purse.
I don't say that race tracks are centers of sin,
I only say that they are only safe to go to as long as you fail to begin
     to win.

A DRINK WITH SOMETHING IN IT

There is something about a Martini,
A tingle remarkably pleasant;
A yellow, a mellow Martini;
I wish that I had one at present.
There is something about a Martini,
Ere the dining and dancing begin,
And to tell you the truth,
It is not the vermouth—
I think that perhaps it's the gin.

There is something about an old-fashioned
That kindles a cardiac glow;
It is soothing and soft and impassioned
As a lyric by Swinburne or Poe.
There is something about an old-fashioned
When dusk has enveloped the sky,
And it may be the ice,
Or the pineapple slice,
But I strongly suspect it's the rye.

There is something about a mint julep.
It is nectar imbibed in a dream,
As fresh as the bud of the tulip,
As cool as the bed of the stream.
There is something about a mint julep,
A fragrance beloved by the lucky.
And perhaps it's the tint
Of the frost and the mint,
But I think it was born in Kentucky.

There is something they put in a highball
That awakens the torpidest brain,
That kindles a spark in the eyeball,
Gliding singing through vein after vein.

There is something they put in a highball
Which you'll notice one day, if you watch;
And it may be the soda,
But judged by the odor,
I rather believe it's the Scotch.

Then here's to the heartening wassail,
Wherever good fellows are found;
Be its master instead of its vassal,
And order the glasses around.
For there's something they put in the wassail
That prevents it from tasting like wicker;
Since it's not tapioca,
Or mustard, or mocha,
I'm forced to conclude it's the liquor.

REMINISCENT REFLECTION

When I consider how my life is spent,
I hardly ever repent.

DON'T EVEN TELL YOUR WIFE, PARTICULARLY

All good men believe that women would rather get rid of a piece of
        gossip than a bulge,
And all good women believe that gossip is a feminine weakness in
        which men never indulge.
Rather than give ear to scandalous rumors,
Why, men would rather play golf in bloomers,
And rather than talk behind each other's backs,
They would go shopping in a mink coat and slacks.
It is one of each scx's uniquenesses
That men's talk is all of humanity's aspirations, and women's all of
        their friends' weaknesses.
Yes, this is a universal credo that no amount of evidence can alter,
Including that of Petronius, Suetonius, Pepys, Boswell, the locker
        room of the country club, and Mrs. Winchell's little boy,
        Walter.
Allow me to ask and answer one question before departing for
        Mount Everest or Lake Ossipee:
Who says men aren't gossipy?—Men say men aren't gossipy.

SO DOES EVERYBODY ELSE, ONLY NOT SO MUCH

O all ye exorcizers come and exorcize now, and ye clergymen draw
        nigh and clerge,
For I wish to be purged of an urge.
It is an irksome urge, compounded of nettles and glue,
And it is turning all my friends back into acquaintances, and all my
        acquaintances into people who look the other way when I
        heave into view.
It is an indication that my mental buttery is butterless and my
        mental larder lardless,
And it consists not of "Stop me if you've heard this one," but of "I
        know you've heard this one because I told it to you myself,
        but I'm going to tell it to you again regardless,"
Yes I fear I am living beyond my mental means
When I realize that it is not only anecdotes that I reiterate but what
        is far worse, summaries of radio programs and descriptions of
        cartoons in newspapers and magazines.
I want to resist but I cannot resist recounting the bright sayings of
        celebrities that everybody already is familiar with every
        word of;
I want to refrain but cannot refrain from telling the same audience
        on two successive evenings the same little snatches of
        domestic gossip about people I used to know that they have
        never heard of.
When I remember some titillating episode of my childhood I figure
        that if it's worth narrating once it's worth narrating twice, in
        spite of lackluster eyes and drooping jaws,
And indeed I have now worked my way backward from titillating
        episodes in my own childhood to titillating episodes in the
        childhood of my parents or even my parents-in-laws,
And what really turns my corpuscles to ice,
I carry around clippings and read them to people twice.

And I know what I am doing while I am doing it and I don't want to
do it but I can't help doing it and I am just another Ancient
Mariner,
And the prospects for my future social life couldn't possibly be
barrener.
Did I tell you that the prospects for my future social life couldn't
possibly be barrener?

REFLECTIONS OF THE FALLIBILITY OF NEMESIS

He who is ridden by a conscience
Worries about a lot of nonscience;
He without benefit of scruples
His fun and income soon quadruples.

BIRTH COMES TO THE ARCHBISHOP

Ministers
Don't like bar sinisters.
They consider that sort of irregularity
As the height of vulgarity
And go around making remarks
About the need for patrolling the beaches and parks.
They hate to see any deadlock
Between sin and wedlock
And get very nervous
When people omit the marriage service.
They regard as villains
Owners of unauthorized chillains,
A point of view
Which of course doesn't embarrass me or you
But makes things very inconvenient
For many really quite nice girls who may have been just a bit
    lenient.

So although none of us is in danger
Of the arrival of an inexplicable little stranger
Still I think we ought to join with a lot of others
And wish the best of luck to the nation's unmarried mothers.

INTER-OFFICE MEMORANDUM

The only people who should really sin
Are the people who can sin with a grin,
Because if sinning upsets you,
Why, nothing at all is what it gets you.
Everybody certainly ought to eschew all offences however venial
As long as they are conscience's menial.
Some people suffer weeks of remorse after having committed the
      slightest peccadillo,
And other people feel perfectly all right after feeding their husbands
      arsenic or smothering their grandmother with a pillow.
Some people are perfectly self-possessed about spending their lives
      on the verge of delirium tremens,
And other people feel like hanging themselves on a coathook just
      because they took that extra cocktail and amused their fellow
      guests with recitations from the poems of Mrs. Hemans.
Some people calmly live a barnyard life because they find
      monogamy dull and arid,
And other people have sinking spells if they dance twice in an
      evening with a lady to whom they aren't married.
Some people feel forever lost if they are riding on a bus and the
      conductor doesn't collect their fare,
And other people ruin a lot of widows and orphans and all they
      think is, Why there's something in this business of ruining
      widows and orphans, and they go out and ruin some more and
      get to be a millionaire.
Now it is not the purpose of this memorandum, or song,
To attempt to define the difference between right and wrong;
All I am trying to say is that if you are one of the unfortunates who
      recognize that such a difference exists,
Well, you had better oppose even the teeniest temptation with
      clenched fists,

Because if you desire peace of mind it is all right to do wrong if it
        never occurs to you that it is wrong to do it,
Because you can sleep perfectly well and look the world in the eye
        after doing anything at all so long as you don't rue it,
While on the other hand nothing at all is any fun
So long as you yourself know it is something you shouldn't have
        done.
There is only one way to achieve happiness on this terrestrial ball,
And that is to have either a clear conscience, or none at all.

TURNS IN A WORM'S LANE

I've never bet on a so-called horse
That the horse didn't lose a leg.
I've never putted on a golfing course
But the ball behaved like an egg.
I've never possessed three royal kings
But somebody held three aces;
In short, I'm a lad whose presence brings
The joy to bankers' faces.

And everybody says, "What a splendid loser!"
Everybody says, "What a thoroughgoing sport!"
And I smile my smile like an amiable Duse,
I leer like a lawyer in the presence of a tort.
And I crack my lips,
And I grin my grin,
While someone else
Rakes my money in.
Yes, I smile a smile like the Mona Lisa,
Though my spirits droop like the Tower of Pisa.
Yes, I chortle like a military march by Sousa
And everybody says, "What a splendid loser!"

I'll buy a tome, an expensive tome,
On the art of double dealing,
And I'll wrap it up and I'll take it home,
While the bells of Hell are pealing.
I'll stealthily study the ebony arts
Of men like the great Houdini,
Till both in foreign and local parts
I'm known as a darned old meany.

And everyone will say, "What a nasty winner!"
And everyone will say, "What a dreadful sport!"
And they'll all stop inviting me to come to dinner,
For I used to be a dimple and I want to be a wart.
But I won't care,
And I'll win with a scowl,
Foul means or fair,
But preferably foul.

I'll jeer my victims everytime I vanquish,
And if I lose I shall scream with anguish.
And people will say, "What a dreadful sport!"
And I'll say, "Phooie!" or something of the sort.

THE TERRIBLE PEOPLE

People who have what they want are very fond of telling people who
> haven't what they want that they really don't want it,
And I wish I could afford to gather all such people into a gloomy
> castle on the Danube and hire half a dozen capable Draculas
> to haunt it.
I don't mind their having a lot of money, and I don't care how they
> employ it,
But I do think that they damn well ought to admit they enjoy it.
But no, they insist on being stealthy
About the pleasures of being wealthy,
And the possession of a handsome annuity
Makes them think that to say how hard it is to make both ends meet
> is their bounden duty.
You cannot conceive of an occasion
Which will find them without some suitable evasion.
Yes indeed, with arguments they are very fecund;
Their first point is that money isn't everything, and that they have no
> money anyhow is their second.
Some people's money is merited,
And other people's is inherited,
But wherever it comes from,
They talk about it as if it were something you got pink gums from.
Perhaps indeed the possession of wealth is constantly distressing,

But I should be quite willing to assume every curse of wealth if I
could at the same time assume every blessing.
The only incurable troubles of the rich are the troubles that money
can't cure,
Which is a kind of trouble that is even more troublesome if you are
poor.
Certainly there are lots of things in life that money won't buy, but it's
very funny—
Have you ever tried to buy them without money?

A PLEA FOR A LEAGUE OF SLEEP

Some people lead a feverish life,
For they with restlessness are rife.
They revel in labors energetic,
Their fare is healthful and ascetic,
Their minds are keen, their hands are earthy,
Each day they work on something worthy.
Something accomplished, something done,
Comprises their idea of fun.

My life with joy is sometimes fraught,
But mostly when I'm doing naught.
Yea, I could spend my whole career
A pillow underneath my ear.
How wise was he who wittily said
That there is nothing like a bed.
A mattress is what I like to creep on;
The right side is the one I sleep on.

Heroes who moil and toil and fight
Exist on eight hours' sleep a night.
I call this but a miserly budget,
Yet I assure you that they grudge it.
I've heard them groan, times without number,
At wasting a third of their lives in slumber.
All right, you Spartans who build and delve,
You waste eight hours, and I'll waste twelve.

No honester man is to be found
Than he who sleeps the clock around.
Of malice and ambition free,
The more he sleeps, the sleepier he.
No plots and schemes infest his head,
But dreams of getting back to bed.
His spirit bears no worldly taint;
Scratch a sluggard, and find a saint.

Stalin and Hitler while they sleep
Are harmless as a baby sheep;
Tyrants who cause the earth to quake
Are only dangerous when awake.
This world would be a happier place,
And happier the human race,
And all our pilots be less Pontius,
If people spent more time unconscious.

INVOCATION
("Smoot Plans Tariff Ban on Improper Books"—NEWS ITEM)

Senator Smoot (Republican, Ut.)
Is planning a ban on smut.
Oh root-ti-toot for Smoot of Ut.
And his reverent occiput.
Smite, Smoot, smite for Ut.,
Grit your molars and do your dut.,
Gird up your l—ns,
Smite h—p and th—gh,
We'll all be Utah
By and by.

Smite, Smoot, for the Watch and Ward,
For Hiram Johnson and Henry Ford,
For Bishop Cannon and John D., Junior,
For Governor Pinchot of Pennsylvania,
For John S. Sumner and Elder Hays
And possibly Edward D. Bernays,
For Orville Poland and Ella Boole,
For Mother Machree and the Shelton pool.
When smut's to be smitten
Smoot will smite
For G—d, for country,
And Fahrenheit.

Senator Smoot is an institute
Not to be bribed with pelf;
He guards our homes from erotic tomes
By reading them all himself.
Smite, Smoot, smite for Ut.,
They're smuggling smut from Balt. to Butte!
Strongest and sternest
Of your s—x
Scatter the scoundrels
From Can. to Mex.!

Smite, Smoot, for Smedley Butler,
For any good man by the name of Cutler,
Smite for the W.C.T.U.,
For Rockne's team and for Beader's crew,
For Florence Coolidge and Admiral Byrd,
For Billy Sunday and John D., Third,
For Grantland Rice and for Albie Booth,
For the Woman's Auxiliary of Duluth,
Smite, Smoot,
Be rugged and rough,
Smut if smitten
Is front-page stuff.

PORTRAIT OF THE ARTIST AS A
PREMATURELY OLD MAN

It is common knowledge to every schoolboy and even every Bachelor
    of Arts,
That all sin is divided into two parts.
One kind of sin is called a sin of commission, and that is very
    important,
And it is what you are doing when you are doing something you
    ortant,
And the other kind of sin is just the opposite and is called a sin of
    omission and is equally bad in the eyes of all right-thinking
    people, from Billy Sunday to Buddha,
And it consists of not having done something you shuddha.
I might as well give you my opinion of these two kinds of sin as long
    as, in a way, against each other we are pitting them,
And that is, don't bother your head about sins of commission
    because however sinful, they must at least be fun or else you
    wouldn't be committing them.
It is the sin of omission, the second kind of sin,
That lays eggs under your skin.
The way you get really painfully bitten
Is by the insurance you haven't taken out and the checks you
    haven't added up the stubs of and the appointments you
    haven't kept and the bills you haven't paid and the letters
    you haven't written.
Also, about sins of omission there is one particularly painful lack of
    beauty,
Namely, it isn't as though it had been a riotous red-letter day or
    night every time you neglected to do your duty;
You didn't get a wicked forbidden thrill
Every time you let a policy lapse or forget to pay a bill;
You didn't slap the lads in the tavern on the back and loudly cry

Whee,

Let's all fail to write just one more letter before we go home, and this
round of unwritten letters is on me.

No, you never get any fun

Out of the things you haven't done,

But they are the things that I do not like to be amid,

Because the suitable things you didn't do give you a lot more trouble
than the unsuitable things you did.

The moral is that it is probably better not to sin at all, but if some
kind of sin you must be pursuing,

Well, remember to do it by doing rather than by not doing.

OH, STOP BEING THANKFUL ALL OVER THE PLACE

In the glittering collection of paste diamonds one in particular ranks
     very high,
And that is the often-quoted remark of the prominent and
     respectable dignitary who on seeing a condemned man on his
     way to the scaffold crashed into a thousand anthologies by
     remarking, There but for the grace of God go I.
Here is a deplorable illustration
Of sloppy ratiocination;
Here is a notable feat
Of one-way thinking on a two-way street.
It must certainly have been the speaker's lucky day,
Or otherwise he would have been run over by his speech turning
     around and coming back the other way,
Because did he stop to work out his premise to its logical
     conclusion? Ah no,
He just got it off and let it go,
And now whenever people are with people they want to impress with
     their combined greateartedness and book-learning they cry
Oh look at that condemned man on his way to the scaffold, there but
     for the grace of God go I.
Which is so far so good, but they neglect to continue with the
     heretofore unspoken balance of the theme, which is equally
     true,
That there but for the grace of God goes Jimmie Durante or the
     Prince of Wales or Aimee Semple McPherson or Dr.
     Wellington Koo,
Or Moses or Napoleon or Cleopatra or P. T. Barnum,
Or even William or Dustin Farnum.

So away with you, all you parrot-like repeaters of high-sounding
　　phrases that you never stop to consider what they actually
　　mean,
I wouldn't allow you to stay in any college of which I was the Dean.
I can never listen to you without thinking Oh my,
There but for the grace of God speak I.

HA! ORIGINAL SIN!

Vanity, vanity, all is vanity
That's any fun at all for humanity.
Food is vanity, so is drink,
And undergarments of gossamer pink,
P. G. Wodehouse and long vacations,
Going abroad, and rich relations,
The kind of engagements you want to keep,
A hundred honors, and twelve hours' sleep.
Vanities all—Oh Worra, worra!
Rooted in Sodom and Gomorrah.

Vanity, vanity, all is vanity
That's any fun at all for humanity.
That is the gist of the prophet's case,
From Bishop Cannon to Canon Chase.
The prophet's chant and the prophet's chatter,
But somehow it never seems to matter,
For the world hangs on to its ancient sanity
And orders another round of vanity.
Then Hey! for Gomorrah! and Nonny! for Sodom!
Marie! the Chanel model for Modom!

NEVERTHELESS

I am not fond of Oliver Montrose.
Oliver is a person I despise;
The purple veins that bulbify his nose,
The crimson veins that irrigate his eyes.
His wheezy breath his vinous weakness shows;
He is the slave of whisky, beer and gin.
I am not fond of Oliver Montrose;
I hate the sinner. But what a warming sin!

Bibesco Poolidge is a man of jowl;
I've never seen a dewlap, but on him;
He shines with the grease of many a basted fowl;
Ten thousand sauces round his innards swim.
The ghosts of hosts of kine about him prowl,
Lamb, pig, and game blood trickles from his chin;
I cannot look on him without a scowl;
I hate the sinner. But what a luscious sin!

I do not dote on Murgatroyd Van Rust,
So tasty to the tenderest of genders.
Practically everything that has a bust
Surveys his suave ensemble and surrenders.
The way he parts his hair I do not trust;
Let the phone ring, I loathe his knowing grin.
You cannot see his diary for the dust,
I hate the sinner. Still, if one had to sin . . .

O Mammonites and spendthrifts, draw ye nigh,
Fingernail-biters and sluggards, come on in,
Consider now how tolerant am I
Who hate the sinner, yet who love the sin.

MR. JUDD AND HIS SNAIL, A SORRY TALE
or
NEVER UNDERESTIMATE THE WISDOM OF A
SAGE OF THE AGES

I offer one small bit of advice that Billy Graham could write a whole
    column on:
Never ignore any bit of advice offered by King Solomon.
I call your attention to the case of Philander Judd.
His veins were distended with optimism and sporting blood.
His interest in racing was enormous,
But he was by nature nonconformous.
He was not one of those who set their horses or greyhounds whirling
    around the track to their heart's content, or a gogo,
He said he knew that something fast could go fast, he was interested
    in how fast could something slow go.
He considered conventional races pallid and stale,
So his entire stable consisted of one thoroughbred gastropod, or
    snail.
The snail, of course, is a mollusk akin to the whelk and the slug,
    and, as is known to every gastropodist,
It moves complacently on one ventral muscular foot, to the
    bewilderment of every biped chiropodist.
Mr. Judd entered his snail in every kind of race but one, for which
    he refused to name it,
And that one was a claiming race, because he was afraid that
    somebody, perhaps a Gallic gourmet, might claim it.
His snail was beaten in December by a tortoise, so he dropped it
    down a couple of classes,
And in January it lost by eight lengths to a jug of molasses.
By now Mr. Judd was deeply indebted to his bookie,
But being an honorable man, he couldn't get out of town or stoop to
    any other form of welsher's hookey.
At last he thought he saw a way to settle with his creditors;
He found the perfect spot for his snail, a race in which an amoeba
    and a glacier were the other two competitors.

The amoeba posed a real threat, but from the glacier he did not
      flinch;
He had clocked it for a full month, during which it had moved only
      three-quarters of an inch.
Therefore, although he could not be certain to win the race,
He knew he had a sure thing to place.
Yes, that was what he happily reckoned,
And he bet his remaining roll on the snail for second.
Well, the amoeba outdistanced the snail and the snail outdistanced
      the glacier, and then just at the finish line something out of
      the ordinary occurred;
The amoeba split apart and finished one two, and the snail ran third.
Mr. Judd had forgotten what Solomon once told the Queen of Sheba:
Never trust an Egyptian or an amoeba.

WHILE HOMER NODDED: A FOOTNOTE TO THE ILIAD

In the days when the hollow ships of the well-greaved Achaeans
      were beached off Priam's city there was a two-faced Achaean
      named Antiscrupulos,
And he was so two-faced that his duplicity was doubled, it was
      quadrupulous.
He was the owner of a mighty fleet which was not under Achaean
      registry, it flew the flag of the Hesperides,
And his ships were never hollow, they were always full of costly
      cargoes such as maidens available for sacrifice, and lotus, the
      predecessor of L.S.D., and cantharides.
He was far too busy to spend any time hurling insults at Hector on
      the ringing plains of windy Troy,
He was always furrowing the wine-dark sea in search of costlier
      cargoes, and nearly always accompanied by a fascinating
      hetaera, which was the contemporary term for a daughter of joy.
But once he didn't take her with him and he got home a day early
      and what did he behold?

There was his hetaera in a compromising situation with a shower of
      gold,
And he said, How do you excuse such misconduct? and she said, I
      don't need any excuse,
This isn't really a shower of gold, it's aegis-bearing Zeus.
Well, Antiscrupulos was very moral about other people's morals,
      anent which he was a veritable bluenose,
And he was also jealous as a dozen Heras or Junos,
So after precautiously sacrificing a surplus maiden to aegis-bearing
      Zeus he accused aegis-bearing Zeus of being a compulsive
      seducer and a menace to Achaean womanhood both mortal
      and immortal,
And Zeus did not incinerate him with a thunderbolt, he just gave a
      thunderous self-satisfied lecherous chortle.
Antiscrupulos grew even more indignant and ventured on further prods,
He said, How can you chortle off your licentious behavior, you who
      should set an example of marital fidelity for us humans, you
      who bear the dread responsibility of being monarch of
      Olympus and king of all gods?
He said, Tell me, O king of all the gods, for your godless
      philandering can you offer the shadow of an excuse, the ghost
      of an excuse, the wraith of an excuse, even the wraithiest?
And Zeus said, Yes, I'm an athiest.

LITTLE PRETTY PENNY, LET'S SQUANDER THEE

Why do so many billionaires go in for penuriousness
Instead of luxuriousness?
Why are so many prosperous potential sybarites
Afraid of being termed flibbertigibberites?
Too many tycoons who would relish a display of extravagance
Explore the edges of ostentation in a sort of timid circumnavigance.
If I were Mr. Onassis do you know what I would do? I would buy
      Neiman-Marcus
And give it for Easter to Mr. Niarchos.
If I were Mr. Niarchos I might buy the Parthenon
And present it to the Huntington Hartford Museum after changing
      its name to the General MacArthurnon.
Were I the favorite customer of Harry Winston
I might well acquire the Green Bay Packers and give them to
      Rutgers for use in the game with Princeton.
Or were I a Nizam counting my rubies and emeralds and wives in
      my Oriental palace
I'd find it a change of pace to present Dallas to Madame Callas, or
      even Madame Callas to Dallas.
Were I an Aga or a Khan fond of a friend despite his gross addiction
      to food and drink who might therefore be described as
      crapulous,
I would give him a deed to Le Pavillon and Lüchow's and La Tour
      d'Argent and all the Indian pudding in Indianapulous.
I'd like to say to Gulbenkian or a Rockefeller, why don't you show in
      what league you are?
Why don't you transport the Taj Mahal and use it as a guesthouse in
      Antigua?
Had I the wells of an H. L. Hunt I would be openhanded like
      Cardinal Wolsey, not close-fisted like Cardinal Mazarin,
I would raise and refit the *Andrea Doria* just for a cruise around
      Manhattan Island and set before my guests a feast Lucullan,
      yea, even Belshazzaran.

Upon arising next noon I would taper on to prodigality again by
      making the kind of humble propitiatory offering that Midas
      might have made to Zeus or Hera,
I would spend a modest $1700 on an appropriate gift for President
      de Gaulle, an item advertised by a Park Avenue shop
      consisting of a limestone fossil fish plaque 60 million years
      old, a relic of the Eocene Era.
I would also, may my tribe increase,
Present every taxi-driver in New York with a lifetime supply of
      cigars costing not less than a dollar apiece.
Whether glory or infamy would be my lot I know not which,
But I would surely carve for myself a special niche among the rich.

ROULETTE US BE GAY

The trouble with games of chance is that they don't do much to
      stimulate your pulse
Unless you risk some money on the results,
And the trouble with playing for money is not that it is a sin,
But that you have got either to lose or win,
And the trouble with losing is not only that you need the money,
      which is an important point, very true,
But also that you never lose it except to somebody who is very much
      richer than you,
And the trouble with winning, if you can bring yourself to imagine
      any trouble with winning, is that except in the most
      glamorous fiction
You never win except from somebody to whom you know that the
      money that they pay over to you is all that stands between
      them and eviction.
Another thing about games of chance
Is a thing at which I look askance,
And that is that no matter how far at any time you may be ahead,
You are always well behind when it is time for bed,
While on the other hand if you start out by losing as steadily and
      heavily as if you were afflicted with Tutankhamen's curse
You finish up even worse,
So you can take it as understood

That your luck changes only if it's good.
And this, my friends, is a brief history of the major troubles with
    gambling but I feel that no improving lesson from it will be
    learned
As long as there is nothing so delightful in the world as money you
    haven't earned.

THE GOSSIP THAT NEVER SHOULD BE UNLOOSED IS GOSSIP THAT CAN'T COME HOME TO ROOST (1969)

There are two kinds of gossip, and they differ from each other quite
    a lot,
Because one kind of gossip is sportsmanlike and the other kind is
    definitely not.
This latter kind, shall I tell you what it is?
It is chatter about Ari and Jackie and Mia Farrow and the Aga Khan
    and Vanessa Redgrave and Richard and Liz,
About Prince Philip and his domestic financial snarls,
And about the eligibility of mates for the eligible Tricia Nixon and
    the eligible Princess Anne and even eligibler Prince Charles.
It is pregnant with spicy speculation and insinuation horrendous,
With innuendo innuendous,
None of which is subject to apology, retraction or even discreet
    voluntary revisal,
Because the gossipers run no risk of retaliation or reprisal,
Because after all, no matter how lurid your hints about Mia or Jackie
    or Prince Philip or even Tricia,
They don't hear you, so there's no chance they will answer back or
    sue for slander or call out the militia.
No, the only sportsmanlike gossip is that in which such cozy
    immunity ends,
It is when you join your best friend in frank confidential discussion
    of the failings of all your other best friends.
Although you know full well that as long as human nature endures
This best friend will shortly repeat to those best friends your
    summary of their failings and then join them in a frank
    confidential discussion of yours.

NO TROUBLE AT ALL, IT'S AS EASY AS FALLING OFF A PORTABLE BAR

I often appeal to the Lord of hosts, because a host I often find myself,
And to the frustrations of hostmanship I cannot blind myself.
I invariably fail the ultimate test:
Outguessing the guest.
Would that I could anticipate
How my guests will elect to dissipate.
Now ice and glasses glisten within easy reach,
The guests old friends, the liquors lined up on the bar in accordance
    with the well-known taste of each.
Comes Polyhymnia, the semi-teetotaller for whom you have brought
    her favorite brand of sherry;
Tonight she would like just straight bourbon on the rocks with
    perhaps a little sugar and bitters and, if it's not too much
    trouble, a slice of orange and a maraschino cherry.
And Alistair, his cheek by years of aged scotch all motley mottled—
Beefeater gin for him with just an ounce and a half of lime juice,
    preferably British-bottled.
Here's Otho, a martini man as sure as da Gama's name was Vasco;
He'll take a Bloody Mary, only with a tequila base and maybe an
    extra dash of Worcestershire sauce and lemon and just two
    drops of Tabasco.
And Ethel, for whose sole benefit a stock of Dubonnet you carry—
This time she requests Campari.
Wilfred is smugly off the stuff, so you have provided every current
    alternative or proxy;
He declines tomato juice, ginger ale, Coke, Sprite, Squirt, Fresca,
    and Bitter Lemon, and wistfully supposes you haven't
    anything in the way of Bevo or Moxie.
At long last Lily, surely fairest flower of the lot;
You ask her what she would like, and she replies, "Oh, anything at
    all, dear, what have you got?"
Well, I'll tell you what I've got and what she's going to get this time,
    by cracky:
My customary aperitif, pawpaw juice and *sake*.

HOW TO GET ALONG WITH YOURSELF
OR
I RECOMMEND SOFTENING OF THE OUGHTERIES

When I was young I always knew
The meretricious from the true.
I was alert to call a halt
On other people's every fault.
My creed left no more chance for doubt
Than station doors marked IN and OUT.
A prophet with righteousness elated,
Dogmatic and opinionated,
Once self-convinced, I would not budge;
I was indeed a hanging judge.
I admitted, in either joy or sorrow,
No yesterday and no tomorrow.
My summary of life was reckoned
By what went on that very second.
I scoffed when kindly uncles and aunts
Said age would teach me tolerance,
For tolerance implies a doubt
That IN is IN and OUT is OUT.
But now that I am forty-nine
I'm tolerant, and like it fine.
Since the faults of others I condone,
I can be tolerant of my own.
I realize the sky won't fall
If I don't pay my bills at all.
The King of Sweden it will not irk
To hear that I neglect my work,
And tombfuls of historic dead
Care not how late I lie abed.
Oh, tolerance is the state of grace
Where everything falls into place,
So now I tolerantly think
I could tolerate a little drink.

SIC SEMPER MR. SHERMAN'S TEMPER
or
KINDLY PLACE YOUR ORDER IN ENGLISH

I have a friend named Mr. Sherman who is far from dodderin',
But he lives old-fashioned instead of moderun.
He believes that the terminology of drinking has long been complete,
And it needs new wrinkles like Manhattan needs a hole in the street.
He thinks the phrase whisky on ice
Is both descriptive and precise,
So of rocks he keeps a store
Which he gathered on the stern New England shore,
And when guests ask for bourbon on the rocks they get bourbon on
  the rocks and they squint at their bourbon on the rocks jitterily
Because he fulfills their request literally,
And when they clamor for that new favorite, bouillon on the rocks,
  his eyes are so moist that he melts them with them,
And then he dips the rocks in bouillon and pelts them with them.
As for the folksy he-men who slap him on the back and bellow for
  bourton and branch water, they don't do it a second time or a
  third,
He takes them at their word;
He has imported a dozen Mason jars of genuine branch water from
  the Ozarks, and every serving contains three tadpoles and a
  crawfish,
After receiving which even a governor of Tennessee would switch to
  Scotch and soda and behave a little more standoffish.

NEVER MIND THE OVERCOAT,
BUTTON UP THAT LIP

Persons who have something to say like to talk about the arts and
  politics and economics,
And even the cultural aspects of the comics.

Among persons who have nothing to say the conversational content
     worsens;
They talk about other persons,
Sometimes they talk about persons they know personally, and
     rearrange their lives for them,
And sometimes they talk about persons they know through the
     tabloids, and rearrange their husbands and wives for them.
I have better things to talk about than fortune hunters who harry debs;
The causerie in my coterie is of how come Sir Arthur rewrote "The
     Red-headed League" under the title of "The Adventure of the
     Three Garridebs."
Gossip never darkens my doors
And I wouldn't trade one Gaboriau for a hatful of Gabors.
Do not praise me because to curious ears I will not pander,
I myself am not responsible for my absention from libel and slander.
For this laudable trait there is a coony little old lady whom I am
     under obligation to;
She taught me that if you hear a juicy tidbit and don't repeat it
     within twenty-four hours, why, after that it is juiceless and
     there is no temptation to.
If you heed this precept you will never find yourself in a gossiper's
     role;
I know, because in 1915 when I discovered that Marie Jeanne Bécu
     Du Barry wasn't married to Louis XV I sat on the item for
     twenty-four hours and from that day till this I haven't
     breathed it to a living soul.

A STITCH TOO LATE IS MY FATE

There are some people of whom I would certainly like to be one,
Who are the people who get things done.
They balance their checkbooks every month and their figures always
     agree with the bank's,
And they are prompt in writing letters of condolence or thanks.

They never leave anything to chance,

But always make reservations in advance.

When they get out of bed they never neglect to don slippers so they
never pick up athlete's foot or a cold or a splinter,

And they hang their clothes on hangers every night and put their
winter clothes away every summer and their summer clothes
away every winter.

Before spending any money they insist on getting an estimate or a
sample,

And if they lose anything from a shoelace to a diamond ring it is
covered by insurance more than ample.

They have budgets and what is more they live inside of them,

Even though it means eating things made by recipes clipped from
the Sunday paper that you'd think they would have died of
them.

They serve on committees

And improve their cities.

They are modern knight errants

Who remember their godchildren's birthdays and the anniversaries
of their godchildren's parents,

And in cold weather they remember the birds and supply them with
sunflower seed and suet,

And whatever they decide to do, whether it's to save twenty-five per
cent of their salary or learn Italian or write a musical comedy
or touch their toes a hundred times every morning before
breakfast, why they go ahead and do it.

People who get things done lead contented lives, or at least I guess
so,

And I certainly wish that either I were more like them or they were
less so.

THE STRANGE CASE OF THE IRKSOME PRUDE

Once upon a time there was a young man named Harold Scrutiny.

Harold had many virtues and practically no vices.

He smoked, to be sure.

Also he drank and swore.

Moreover, he was a pickpocket.

But, for all that, Harold was no prude.

I am no prude, Harold often said.

But Detective Guilfoyle of the Pickpocket Squad is a prude, the old prude, said Harold.

One day Harold went into the subway to pick some pockets.

There was a man on the platform penciling a beard on the lady on the toothpaste placard.

Hey, said Harold.

Hey who, said the man.

Hey you, that's hey who, said Harold.

Aren't you going to give her a moustache?

Sure I'm going to give her a moustache, said the man.

What do you think I am?

I think you're somebody that puts the beard on ladies on toothpaste placards before they put on the moustache, said Harold.

Don't you know enough to put the moustache on first?

＊

You put the moustache on first, why then you can turn it up or turn it down, whichever you want, said Harold.

＊

You try to turn a moustache down after the beard's on, it runs into the beard, said Harold.

＊

It don't look like a moustache, only like a beard grows up and down both.

＊

Go on, said the man, go on and pick some pockets.

＊

Harold turned to his work, but his mind was elsewhere.

＊

Suddenly the lady on the toothpaste placard got off the toothpaste placard and arrested him.

＊

It was Detective Guilfoyle of the Pickpocket Squad all the time.

＊

You got a beard grows up and down both, said Harold.

＊

Detective Guilfoyle searched Harold.

＊

He certainly was surprised at what he found.

＊

So was Harold.

＊

Harold hadn't picked any pockets at all because his mind was elsewhere.

＊

He had picked a peck of pickled peppers.

＊

Detective Guilfoyle wanted to call Harold a name, but he couldn't because he was a prude.

＊

Harold picked his pocket and later became the smokingest swearingest, drinkingest Assistant District Attorney the county ever had.

＊

Don't be a prude.

WHERE THERE'S A WILL, THERE'S VELLEITY

Seated one day at the dictionary I was pretty weary and also pretty
      ill at ease,
Because a word I had always liked turned out not to be a word at all,
      and suddenly I found myself among the v's,
And suddenly among the v's I came across a new word which was a
      word called *velleity*,
So the new word I found was beter than the old word I lost, for
      which I thank my tutelary deity,
Because velleity is a word which gives me great satisfaction,
Because do you know what it means, it means *low degree of volition
      not prompting to action*,
And I always knew I had something holding me back but I didn't
      know what,
And it's quite a relief to know it isn't a conspiracy, it's only velleity
      that I've got,
Because to be wonderful at everything has always been my
      ambition,
Yes indeed, I am simply teeming with volition,
So why I never was wonderful at anything was something I couldn't
      see
While all the time, of course, my volition was merely volition of a
      low degree,
Which is the kind of volition that you are better off without it,
Because it puts an idea in your head but doesn't prompt you to do
      anything about it.
So you think it would be nice to be a great pianist but why bother
      with practicing for hours at the keyboard,
Or you would like to be the romantic captain of a romantic ship but
      can't find time to study navigation or charts of the ocean or
      the seaboard;
You want a lot of money but you are not prepared to work for it,
Or a book to read in bed but you do not care to go into the nocturnal
      cold and murk for it;
And now if you have any such symptoms you can identify your
      malady with accurate spontaneity;

It's velleity,
So don't forget to remember that you're velleitous, and if anybody
     says you're just lazy,
Why, they're crazy.

SEEING EYE TO EYE IS BELIEVING

When speaking of people and their beliefs I wear my belief on my
     sleeve;
I believe that people believe what they believe they believe.
When people reject a truth or an untruth it is not because it is a
     truth or an untruth that they reject it,
No, if it isn't in accord with their beliefs in the first place they
     simply say, "Nothing doing," and refuse to inspect it.
Likewise when they embrace a truth or an untruth it is not for either
     its truth or its mendacity,
But simply because they have believed it all along and therefore
     regard the embrace as a tribute to their own fair-mindedness
     and sagacity.
These are enlightened days in which you can get hot water and cold
     water out of the same spigot,
And everybody has something about which they are proud to be
     broad-minded but they also have other things about which
     you would be wasting your breath if you tried to convince
     them that they were a bigot,
And I have no desire to get ugly,
But I cannot help mentioning that the door of a bigoted mind opens
     outwards so that the only result of the pressure of facts upon
     it is to close it more snugly.
Naturally I am not pointing a finger at me,
But I must admit that I find any speaker far more convincing when I
     agree with him than when I disagree.

HOME, 99 44/100% SWEET HOME

Most of the time, oh most of the time,
I like to sit at home,
With a good fire, and a good chair,
And a good detective tome.
What can a man, can a family man
Ask in the way of cheer
More than a pipe, and a reading lamp,
And a modest mug of beer?
Most of the time, the wealth of the Indies
Wouldn't tempt me to blowouts or shindies.

But once in a while,
Oh, once in a while,
It's pleasant to paint the town,
To frolic and revel,
A regular devil,
And do the evening brown.
To buy an orchid, or maybe two,
And woo the way that you used to woo,
To press the loot from the babies' banks
On waiters who fail to murmur thanks,
To dine and wine and dance and sup,
And ride in a cab till the sun comes up,
And to feel thereafter, in sundry ways,
Simply awful for days and days.
Home is heaven and orgies are vile,
But I *like* an orgy, once in a while.

Home is the place, oh home is the place
That no place else is like,
So who would freeze in the South, like Byrd,
Or discover peaks, like Pike?
Who so animal, who so low
As to pant for the Great White Way?
Who would give up a night at home

For one in a cabaret?
Most of the time I'd swim to Australia
As soon as engage in a Saturnalia.

But once in a while,
Oh, once in a while,
It's pleasant to loop the loop,
To daringly seize
The flying trapeze
With a cry of Allez-oop!
To jump the rails, kick over the traces,
To go on the town and visit places,
Sit ten at a table meant for two,
And choke on smoke as you used to do,
To tread the floor with the dancing bears,
They on your feet, and you on theirs,
To have flings at things that philosophers true shun,
And undermine your constitue-shun.
Home is heaven and orgies are vile,
But you *need* an orgy, once in a while.

FABLES BULFINCH FORGOT

CHLOË AND THE ROUÉ

When Lord Byron wrote so glowingly of the isles of Greece
It was not more coincidence or caprice.
Nobody than Lord Byron could have been sorrier
About the death of a heroic Grecian warrior,
But nobody after so short a period
Could find consolation in the company of a nymph or a Nereid,
So all praise to the nymphs of the isles of Greece.
May their tribe increase.
But their tribe won't increase if they all behave like a nymph named
      Chloë,
Who lived on the southernmost isle of Greece where it is swampy,
      not snowy.
Chloë caught the attention of Zeus,
And he slipped away from the banquet hall mumbling some
      ridiculous excuse,
And when Hera called after him to come back, she knew what it
      meant when he got all skittish and scampery,
He said he'd be back for breakfast, he just had to see a mortal about
      a lamprey,
And he didn't want to tell a lie so he disguised himself as a lamprey-
      fisherman but he couldn't find his lamprey-fishing clothes,
So aside from his lamprey-spear he was as naked as a narcissus or a
      rose,
And he tracked Chloë through the swamp and offered her his heart
      and a golden chariot, a dandy four-wheeler,
But she refused because she was a Southern nymph, a Hellenic
      Dixiecrat, and she had been taught never to trust a nude
      eeler.

THE THIRTEENTH LABOR OF HERCULES

Some people think the nose of the Sphinx was flattened by
      Napoleon's cannoneers,

But it wasn't, not by several thousand years.
Credit should go to a person who dressed like Adam and talked like
        Pericles,
This person being known to us as Hercules and to the illiterate
        Greeks as Heracles,
And Hercules performed twelve fabulous labors,
Which caused all the inhabitants of Ultima Thule to exclaim
        Begorra and Bejabers,
And just when he thought he was through with labors he was told by
        the gods, several of whom were his cousin,
That he must make it a baker's dozen.
They said that all brawn and no brain makes a dull demigod, so on
        immortality it was no dice
Unless he stumped the Sphinx thrice,
And Hercules said, Well I'll be a duck-billed platypus,
Here is a chance to avenge my friend Oedipus,
And he assumed an expression deceptively pleasant,
And he asked the Sphinx, Who is the heavyweight champion? and
        she said, Ezzard Charles, and he said, No it ezzant,
And he said, I'll give you another bone to pick at,
Why did Orpheus give up conducting and throw away his baton?
        and she said, I bet you don't know, either, and he said,
        Because there were more Bacchantes than he could shake a
        stick at,
And the Sphinx said, You can't stump me three times in a row, and
        he said, A house full, a hole full, you cannot catch a bowlful,
        can you riddle me that without straining?
And she said, Smoke? and Hercules said, No thank you, I'm in
        training.
From that point
The Sphinx's nose has been out of joint.

Once there was a Greek divinity of the sea named Ceto and she
    married a man named Phorcus,
And the marriage must have been pretty raucous;
Their remarks about which child took after which parent must have
    been full of asperities,
Because they were the parents of the Gorgons, and the Graeae, and
    Scylla, and the dragon that guarded the apples of the
    Hesperides.
Bad blood somewhere.
Today the Gorgons are our topic, and as all schoolboys including
    you and me know,
They were three horrid sisters named Medusa and Euryale and
    Stheno,
But what most schoolboys don't know because they never get beyond
    their Silas Marners and their Hiawathas,
The Gorgons were not only monsters, they were also highly talented
    authors.
Medusa began it;
She wrote *Forever Granite*.
But soon Stheno and Euryale were writing, too, and they addressed
    her in daily choruses,
Saying we are three literary sisters just like the Brontës so instead of
    Gorgons why can't we be brontësauruses?
Well, Medusa may have been mythical but she wasn't mystical,
She was selfish and egotistical.
She saw wider vistas
Than simply being the sister of her sisters.
She replied, tossing away a petrified Argonaut on whom she had
    chipped a molar,
You two can be what you like, but since I am the big *fromage* in this
    family, I prefer to think of myself as the Gorgon Zola.

The Greeks called the king of the gods Zeus and the Romans called
    him Jupiter.
Not that the Romans were stupider,
Jupiter being Roman for Zeus Pater, or Zeus the Father,
Which was appropriate, rather.
Zeus Pater is not to be confused with Walter Pater,
Who flourished later.
I don't even know if Walter Pater had a wife,
But I bet he never poured into a lady's room disguised as a shower
    of gold in his life.
Zeus Pater, on the other hand, was so eager to escape the restraint of
    his jealous queen that once he nearly killed a guard,
And in order to forward his unsavory amours he impersonated just
    about everybody except Hildegarde.
One day he tiptoed out through heaven's portal
And picked up the handkerchief of a succulent mortal,
But when he wished to continue the acquaintance, he had run out of
    impersonations, he had nothing new to go as.
Juno always recognized him and followed him like Ruth after Boaz.
But this mortal happened to be Leda
And she was a great reader,
And when they were the equivalent of introduced,
Instead of Zeus, she thought the name was Proust,
And hey, hey!
The perplexing problem of what to impersonate was solved when she
    told him how much she admired *Swann's Way*.

4

MODERN LIFE—AND MIND YOUR MANNERS!

*"I find it very difficult to enthuse
Over the current news."*

THE SPOON RAN AWAY WITH THE DISH?

The ideal TV commercial pins the attention of the viewer,
And I am suffering from one that has pinned my wandering thoughts
　　like shish kebab on a skewer.
Did I ever prick up my ears
When the other night a smiling announcer presented what he called
　　the most revolutionary dishwashing discovery in twelve years!
I readily agree that the new discovery is great;
What pinned my attention was trying to remember what
　　revolutionized dishwashing in 1948.
I was in the most frustrating of the countless predicaments I have
　　been among,
Because the answer wasn't even on the tip of my tongue.
I could remember that in 1948 the Cleveland Indians took the World
　　Series, four games to two, from the Boston Braves, and
　　Citation won the Derby;
Also that 1948 marked the publication of *The Golden Hawk*, by
　　Frank Yerby.
Frank Yerby did not win the Nobel award for literature that year, but
　　T. S. Eliot did—may he long on life have lease—
And there was no Nobel award for peace.
I recalled clearly that the Pulitzer Prize went to *Tales of the South
　　Pacific*, by James Michener,
But that was literary stuff—I was groping for something pantrier,
　　something kitchener.
For that twelve-year-old dishwashing discovery my mind continues
　　sleeplessly to grope.
Could it have been the discovery of dish towels? Of paper plates? Of
　　hot water? Of soap?
Of course, there was my wife's welcome discovery that without my
　　assistance it took her only half the time to get the dishes
　　spotless and arid,
But that was in 1931, shortly after we were married.
Anyhow, that's the way my brain has been eroded,
Worrying about a once-revolutionary method of dishwashing that has
　　now been outmoded.

UNFORTUNATELY, IT'S THE ONLY GAME IN TOWN

Often I think that this shoddy world would be more nifty
If all the ostensible fifty-fifty propositions in it were truly fifty-fifty.
How unfortunate that the odds
Are rigged by the gods.
I do not wish to be impious,
But I have observed that all human hazards that mathematics would
  declare to be fifty-fifty are actually at least fifty-one-forty-nine
  in favor of Mount Olympius.
In solitaire, you face the choice of which of two black queens to put
  on a red king; the chance of choosing right is an even one,
  not a long one,
Yet three times out of four you choose the wrong one.
You emerge from a side street onto an avenue, with the choice of
  turning either right or left to reach a given address
Do you walk the wrong way? Yes.
My outraged sense of fair play it would salve
If just once I could pull the right curtain cord the first time, or guess
  which end of the radiator lid conceals the valve.
Why when choosing between two lanes leading to a highway
  tollhouse do I take the one containing a lady who first hands
  the collector a twenty-dollar bill and next drops her change
  on the ground?
Why when quitting a taxi do I invariably down the door handle when
  it should be upped and up it when it should be downed?
By the cosmic shell game I am spellbound.
There is no escape; I am like an oyster, shellbound.
Yes, surely the gods operate according to the fiercest exhortation
  W. C. Fields ever spake:
Never give a sucker an even break.

THE INVITATION SAYS FROM FIVE TO SEVEN

There's nothing like an endless party,
A collection of clammy little groups,
Where a couple of the guests are arty
And the rest of the guests are goops.
There's the confidential girlish chatter—
It soothes you like a drug—
And the gentle pitter-patter
As the anchovies hit the rug.
There's the drip, drip, drip of the mayonnaise
As the customers slither through the canapés,
There are feuds that are born,
There are friendships that pine away,
And the big cigar that smolders on the Steinaway.
The major trouble with a party
Is you need a guest to give it for,
And the best part of any guest
Is the last part out the door.

There's nothing like an endless party,
And there hasn't been since ancient Rome.
Here's Silenus making passes at Astarte
While Mrs. Silenus begs him to go home.
There is bigamy about the boudoirs,
There is bundling at the bar,
And the sideboard where the food was
Has the aspect of an abattoir.
You wonder why they pursue each other's wives,
Who by now resemble the cream cheese and the chives.
There's a corpse on the floor
From New Rochelle or Scarborough,
And its mate is swinging from the candelabara.
The best location for a party
Is in a room without a floor,
And the best way to give a party
Is leave town the night before.

WHAT, NO SHEEP?

WHAT, NO SHEEP? These are a few of the 600 products sold in the "sleep shop" of a New York department store.

—From an advertisement of the
Consolidated Edison Company in the TIMES

I don't need no sleepin' medicine—
I seen a ad by ole Con Edison.
Now when I lay me on my mattress
You kin hear me snore from hell to Hatteras,
With muh Sleep Record,
Muh Vaporizer,
Muh Electric Slippers,
Muh Yawn Plaque,
Muh Slumber Buzzer,
Muh miniature Electric Organ,
An' muh wonderful Electric Blanket.

My old woman couldn't eat her hominy—
Too wore out from the durned insominy.
She give insominy quite a larrupin'
Sleeps like a hibernatin' tarrapin,
With her Eye Shade,
Her Clock-Radio,
Her Sinus Mask,
Her Massagin' Pillow,
Her Snore Ball,
Her miniature Electric Organ,
An' her wonderful Electric Blanket.

Evenin's when the sunlight westers
I pity muh pioneer an-cestors.
They rode the wilderness wide and high,
But how did they ever go sleepy-bye

Without their Eye Shade,
Their Clock-Radio,
Their Sleep Record,
Their Vaporizer,
Their Sinus Mask,
Their Electric Slippers,
Their Yawn Plaque,
Their Slumber Buzzer,
Their Massagin' Pillow,
Their Snore Ball,
Their miniature Electric Organ,
An' their wonderful Electric Blanket?

POLITICAL REFLECTION

Like an art-lover looking at the Mona Lisa in the Louvre
Is the *New York Herald Tribune* looking at Mr. Herbert Houvre.

RING OUT THE OLD, RING IN THE NEW, BUT DON'T GET CAUGHT IN BETWEEN

1. FIRST CHIME

If there is anything of which American industry has a superfluity
It is green lights, know-how, initiative and ingenuity.
If there is one maxim to American industry unknown
It is, Let well enough alone.
Some people award American industry an encomium
Because it not only paints the lily, it turns it into a two-toned job
          with a forward look and backward fins and a calyx trimmed
          with chromium.
I don't propose to engage in a series of Lincoln-Douglas debates,
But take the matter of paper plates.
The future of many a marriage would have been in doubt
But for paper plates, which have imparted tolerability to picnics and
          the maid's day out,
But the last paper plates I handled had been improved into plastic
          and they are so artistic that I couldn't throw them away,
And I ended up by washing them against another day.
Look at the automotive industry, how it never relaxes;
It has improved the low-priced three so much that instead of a
          thousand dollars they now cost twenty-nine seventy-five, not
          including federal and local taxes.
Do you know what I think?
Ordinary mousetraps will soon be so improved that they will be too
          good for the mice, who will be elbowed out by mink.

2. SECOND CHIME

That low keening you hear is me bemoaning my fate;
I am out of joint, I was born either too early or too late.
As the boll said to the weevil,
Get yourself born before the beginning or after the end, but never in
          the middle of a technological upheaval.

I am adrift, but know not whether I am drifting seaward or
      shoreward,
My neck is stiff from my head trying to turn simultaneously
      backward and forward.
One way I know I am adrift,
My left foot keeps reaching for the clutch when the car has an
      automatic shift.
Another way that I am adrift I know,
I'm in a car that I've forgotten has a clutch and I stall it when the
      light says STOP and again when the light says GO.
I find that when dressing I behave as one being stung by
      gallinippers
Because half my trousers are old style and half new and I am forever
      zipping buttons and buttoning zippers.
I can no longer enjoy butter on my bread;
Radio and TV have taught me to think of butter as "You know what"
      or "The more expensive spread."
I am on the thin ice of the old order while it melts;
I guess that perhaps in this changing world money changes less than
      anything else.
That is one reason money is to me so dear;
I know I can't take it with me, I just want the use of some while I am
      here.

THE SECOND MONTH IT'S NOT ITEMIZED

I go to my desk to write a letter,
A simple letter without any frills;
I can't find space to write my letter,
My desk is treetop high in bills.

I go to my desk to write a poem
About a child of whom I'm afraid;
I can't get near it to write my poem
For the barrel of bills, and all unpaid.

I go to my desk for an aspirin tablet,
For a handy bottle of syrup of squills,
I reach in the drawer for the trusty bicarbonate;
My fingers fasten on nothing but bills.

I go to my desk to get my checkbook
That checks may blossom like daffodils,
Hundreds of checks to maintain my credit;
I can't get through the bills to pay my bills.

I've got more bills than there are people,
I've got bigger bills than Lincoln in bronze,
I've got older bills than a Bangor & Aroostook day coach,
I've got bills more quintuplicate than Dionnes.

There's a man named Slemp in Lima, Ohio,
Since 1930 he has been constantly ill,
And of all the inhabitants of this glorious nation
He is the only one who has never sent me a bill.

The trouble with bills, it costs money to pay them,
But as long as you don't, your bank is full.
I shall now save some money by opening a charge account
With a fuller, a draper, and a carder of wool.

OAFISHNESS SELLS GOOD, LIKE AN
ADVERTISEMENT SHOULD

I guess it is farewell to grammatical compunction,
I guess a preposition is the same as a conjunction,
I guess an adjective is the same as an adverb,
And "to parse" is a bad verb.
Blow, blow, thou winter wind,
Thou are not that unkind
Like man's ingratitude to his ancestors who left him the English
       language for an inheritance;
This is a chromium world in which even the Copley Plazas and the
       Blackstones and the Book Cadillacs are simplified into
       Sheratons.
I guess our ancient speech has gone so flat that we have to spike it;
Like the hart panteth for the water brooks I pant for a revival of
       Shakespeare's *Like You Like It*.
I can see the tense draftees relax and purr
When the sergeant barks, "Like you were."
—And don't try to tell me that our well has been defiled by
       immigration;
Like goes Madison Avenue, like so goes the nation.

AND HOW KEEN WAS THE VISION OF SIR LAUNFAL?

Man's earliest pastime, I suppose,
Was to play with his fingers and his toes.
Then later, wearying of himself,
He devised the monster and the elf,
Enlivening his existence drab
With Blunderbore and Puck and Mab.
A modern man, in modern Maryland,
I boast my private gate to fairyland,
My kaleidoscope, my cornucopia,
My own philosopher's stone, myopia.
Except when rationalized by lenses,
My world is not what other men's is;
Unless I have my glasses on,
The postman is a leprechaun,
I can wish on either of two new moons,
Billboards are graven with mystic runes,
Shirts hung to dry are ragtag gypsies,
Mud puddles loom like Mississipsies,
And billiard balls resemble plums,
And street lamps are chrysanthemums.
If my vision were twenty-twenty,
I should miss miracles aplenty.

I SPY
or
THE DEPRAVITY OF PRIVACY

My voice is a minor one, but I must raise it;
I come not only to bury privacy, but to praise it.
Yes, this is my long farewell to privacy;
Democracy seems to have turned into a sort of Lady Godivacy.
We are living in an era by publicity bewitched,
Where the Peeping Toms are not blinded, but enriched.
Keyhole-itis is contagious, and I fear that by our invasion of the
        privacy of the people who clamor for their privacy to be
        invaded,
Well, we are ourselves degraded;
And now that we can't leave the privacy of public personalities
        alone
We end up by invading our own.
What puts a neighbor's teeth on edge?
Your growing a hedge.
He is irked because he can't see what you're doing on your own
        lawn, raising tulips,
Or swigging juleps,
And curiosity is what he is in his knees up to,
And also exhibitionism, because he not only wants to know what *you*
        are doing, he wants you to know what *he's* up to,
So he has a picture window to look out through that he never lowers
        the blinds on, so you can't help looking in through it,
And you are forced to observe the nocturnal habits of him and his
        kin through it.
Things have reached a pretty pass; even my two goldfish, Jael and
        Sisera,
Complain that they have no more privacy than a candidate's viscera.
Well, privacy is a wall,
And something there is that does not love it: namely, the Pry family,
        Pauline and Paul.

FEE FI HO HUM,
NO WONDER BABY SUCKS HER THUMB

I don't know whether you know what's new in juvenile literature or
    not,
But I'll tell you what's new in juvenile literature, there's a new plot.
I grew up on the old plot, which I considered highly satisfactory,
And the hope of having stories containing it read to me restrained
    me occasionally from being mendacious or refractory.
There were always two older sons and a youngest son, or two older
    daughters and a youngest daughter,
And the older pair were always arrogant, selfish rascals, and the
    youngest was always a numskull of the first water,
And the older ones would never share their bread and cheese with
    little old men and women, and wouldn't help them home with
    their loads,
And ended up with their fingers caught in cleft logs, or their
    conversation issuing in the form of toads,
And the youngest numskulls never cared what happened to their
    siblings, because they had no family loyalty,
They just turned over all their bread and cheese to elderly
    eccentrics and ended up married to royalty, which I suppose
    explains what eventually happened to royalty.
That was admittedly not a plot to strain the childish understanding,
But it was veritably Proustian compared to the new plot that the
    third generation is demanding.
When these haggard looks?
I am trapped between one lovable grandchild and her two detestable
    favorite books.
The first is about a little boy who lost his cap and looked everywhere
    for it, behind the armchair and inside the refrigerator and
    under the bed,
And where do you think he found it? On his head!

The second is about a little girl who lost one shoe on the train, and
   until she found it she would give the porter and the other
   passengers no peace,
And finally where do you think she found it? In her valise!
A forthcoming book utilizing this new plot will tell the story of a
   child who lost her grandfather while he was reading to her,
   and you'll never guess where she discovered *him*.
Spang in the middle of Hans Christian Andersen and the Brothers
   Grimm.

SONG OF THE OPEN ROAD

I think that I shall never see
A billboard lovely as a tree.
Indeed, unless the billboards fall
I'll never see a tree at all.

HO, VARLET! MY TWO CENTS' WORTH
OF PENNY POSTCARD!

One thing about the past,
It is likely to last.
Some of it is horrid and some sublime,
And there is more of it all the time.
I happen to be one who dotes
On ruins and moats;
I like to think on the days when knights were bold and ladies
  demure,
And I regret that my strength is only as the strength of nine because
  my heart is not one hundred per cent pure.
However, I also like to think on periods other than the Arthurian,
I like to think on the period when most types of invertebrate marine
  life flourished and coral-reef building began—namely, the
  Silurian.
I believe that Cro-Magnon caves and huts on stilts in lakes would
  make nifty abodes,
And I am given to backward glances o'er traveled roads.
Because I am one in whom Waverley romanticism prevails,
I guess that is why I am fascinated by the United States mails.
The attitude of the Post Office Department is much to my taste;
It holds that posthaste makes post waste.
In these drab days when trains and airplanes fill the grade crossings
  and skies by the million,
The mails are still carried by dusty couriers on fat palfreys, riding
  pillion.
So as a dreamy-eyed antiquarian I hereby, dear Post Office
  Department, express my appreciation to you:
Thanks to whom we can diurnally eat archaic and have it, too.

I'LL EAT MY SPLIT-LEVEL TURKEY IN THE BREEZEWAY

A lady I know disapproves of the vulgarization of Christmas; she
    believes that Christmas should be governed purely by
    spiritual and romantic laws;
She says all she wants for Christmas is no more suggestive songs
    about Santa Claus.
Myself, I am more greedy if less cuddle-y.
And being of '02 vintage I am perforce greedy fuddy duddily,
So my own Christmas could be made glad
Less by the donation of anything new than just by the return of a few
    things I once had.
Some people strive for gracious living;
I have recurrent dreams of spacious living.
Not that I believe retrogression to be the be-all and the end-all,
Not that I wish to spend the holidays sitting in a Turkish corner
    smoking Sweet Caps and reading *Le Rouge et le Noir* by
    Stendhal,
Nor do I long for a castle with machicolations,
But I would like a house with a porte-cochere so the guests wouldn't
    get wet if it rained the evening of my party for my rich
    relations.
Also, instead of an alcove I'd like a dining room that there wasn't
    any doubt of,
And a bathtub that you didn't have to send $7.98 to Wisconsin for a
    device that enables you to hoist yourself out of,

And if there is one thought at which every cockle of my heart perks
　　up and warms,
It is that of an attic in which to pile old toys and magazines and
　　fancy dress costumes and suitcases with the handle off and
　　dressmaker's forms.
I'd like a house full of closets full of shelves,
And above all, a house with lots of rooms all with doors that shut so
　　that every member of the family could get off alone by
　　themselves.
Please find me such a relic, dear Santa Claus, and when you've done
　　it,
Please find me an old-fashioned cook and four old-fashioned maids
　　at $8.00 a week and a genial wizard of a handyman to run it.

FAMILY COURT

One would be in less danger
From the wiles of the stranger
If one's own kin and kith
Were more fun to be with.

DO YOU PLAN TO SPEAK BANTU?
or
ABBREVIATION IS THE THIEF OF SANITY

The merchant, as crafty a man is he
As Haughton or Stagg or Zuppke;
He sells his wares by the broad turnpike,
Or, as some would have it, tpke.

The merchant offers us merchandise
Frozen or tinned or sudsy,
And the way that he spells his merchandise,
I have to pronounce it mdse.

'Twixt the wholesale price and the retail price
The merchant doth daily hustle,
His mdse he sells at the retail price,
But he buys his mdse whsle.

Let us purchase some whsle mdse, love,
And a shop will we set up
And the turnpike runs through the township, love,
Where the tpke runs through the twp.

And you shall be as precious, love,
As a mermaidsk from Murmansk,
And I will tend the customers, love,
In a suit with two pr. pantsk.

CAESAR KNIFED AGAIN
or
CULTURE BIZ GETS HEP, BOFFS PROFS

To win the battle of life you have to plan strategical as well as
      tactical,
So I am glad that our colleges are finally getting practical.
If they're going to teach know-how
It's up to them to show how,
And one way to show it
Is to get rid of dead languages taught by professors who are also
      dead but don't know enough to know it.
It's high time to rescue our kids from poetry and prunes and prisms;
Once they start in on ideas and ideals they'll end up spouting
      ideologies and isms.
Get them interested in hotel management and phys. ed. and
      business administration instead of the so-called finer arts
And you'll cut off the flow of eggheads and do-gooders and bleeding
      hearts.
Every campus gets what it deserves and deserves what it gets,
So what do you want on yours—a lot of pinko longhairs, or
      red-blooded athaletes and drum majorettes?
Another thing, now every autumn it's like the coach had to open up
      a *new* factory,
But get rid of the classics and he can play his stars year after year
      until they're ready for the glue factory,
Because they can never graduate, but no crowd of self-appointed
      reformers can raise a nasty aroma,
Because the reason they can never graduate is there won't be
      anybody left who can write the Latin for their diploma.
So now let's all go the Victory Prom
And join in singing Alma Mom.

ANYBODY ELSE HATE NICKYNAMES?

These are the times when all our feminine notables are beautified
And, unfortunately, the times when all our masculine notables are
     cutified.
This is the day of public diminutives,
Of Virginny instead of Virginiatives.
You don't remember Addison Sims of Seattle, you remember Addie,
Who today drives a Caddie.
Today we are much togetherer than we were,
And Jerry is hurt unless you call him Jer.
Honest Jack disappears, and Jackies turn up like bad pennies,
And Lennies and Kennies.
O tempora! O mores! Or rather, O tempy, O mory!
O Binnorie, O Binnorie!
O idols with mouths of babes and feet of straw!
O shades of Jackie L. Sullivan and Jackie J. McGraw!
This infantilism has almost knocked me flat,
But I'm still fighting like a one-eyed Kilkenneth cat.

THIS IS MY OWN, MY NATIVE TONGUE

Often I leave my television set to listen to my wireless,
So, often I hear the same song sung by the same singer many times a
day, because at repeating itself the wireless is tireless.
There is one such song from which at sleepy time I can hardly bear
to part,
A song in which this particular singer, who apparently has offended
a nameless character in an undescribed way, states that he
apawlogizes from the bawttom of his heart.
I am familiar with various accents—I know that in Indiana you
stress the "r" in Carmen,
And that in Georgia if a ladybug's house is on far she sends for the
farmen.
And I have paaked my caah in Cambridge, and elsewhere spoken
with those who raise hawgs and worship strange gawds—but
here I am, late in life's autumn,
Suddenly confronted with somebody's apawlogies and bawttom.
I tell you whawt,
Things were different when I was a tawddling tawt.
I may have been an indifferent schawlar,
Lawling around in my blue serge suit and doodling on my Eton
cawllar;
In fact, I didn't even pick up much knawledge
In a year at cawllege;
I guess that of normal intelligence I had only about two thirds,
But, by gum, I was taught, or, by gum, was I tot, to pronounce my
words.
And now they've gawt me wondering:
Was it the dawn or the don that from China cross the bay came up
thundering?
As a tot, was I tawddling or was I toddling?
When I doodled, was I dawdling or was I dodling?
I have forgawtten oll I ever knew of English, I find my position as an
articulate mammal bewildering and awesome.
Would God that I were a tender apple blawssom.

DO SPHINXES THINK?

There is one thing I do not understand,
Which is how anybody successfully cuts the fingernails on their
right hand,
Because it is easy to cut your left-hand fingernails, but with your
right-hand fingernails, why you either have to let them grow
ad infinitum,
Or else bitum.
Then there is another problem that keeps my brain working in two
twelve-hour shifts,
Which is Why doesn't the fact that everything that goes up must
come down, apply to elevators, or as the British say, lifts?
You have been standing on the tenth floor waiting to descend to the
ground floor since Bob Son of Battle was a pup,
And all you see is elevators going up, up, up,
And first your impatience, and eventually your curiosity, grows keen,
When you see the same elevator going up a dozen times without
having been down in between.
Is there a fourth dimension known only to elevator attendants,
Or do they, when they get to the top, glide across the roof to the next
building and there make their descendance?
Whatever the secret is, to know it I should adore,
For I am tired of being marooned without my ten favorite movie
actresses on the tenth floor.
An answer to the third baffler, however, would make the greatest
difference in this dear old life o' mine,
Which is, ought I to hope to feel terrible, or to feel fine?
Because how can I tell which hope to nurse,
Because when I feel terrible I know that after a while I'll feel better,
and when I feel fine I know that after a while I'll feel worse.

Is it better to feel terrible and know that pretty soon you'll feel fine
      or to feel fine and know that pretty soon you'll feel terrible,
      that is the question,
And I am open to suggestion,
And when you consider further that probably nobody can every feel
      either fine or terrible anyhow, because how can you feel fine
      when you know that you're going to feel terrible or how can
      you feel terrible *et cetera* it all grows very confusing,
So let's leave everything in the hands of Dorothy Dix and Ted
      Husing.

HI-HO THE AMBULANCE-O

People on wheels hate people on feet,
It takes two to make a one-way street.
Traffic commission plan and study,
And nearly every is a body.

THE PARTY NEXT DOOR

I trust I am not a spoil sport, but there is one thing I deplore,
And that is a party next door,
I am by nature very fond of everybody, even my neighbors,
And I think it only right that they should enjoy some kind of
      diversion after their labors,
But why don't they get their diversion by going to the movies or the
      Little Theater or the Comédie Française or the Commedia
      dell'arte?
Why do they always have to be giving a party?
You may think you have heard a noise because you heard an
      artillery barrage or an avalanche or the subway's horrendous
      roar,
But you have never really heard anything until you have heard a
      party next door.
At a party next door the guests stampede like elephants in wooden
      shoes and gallop like desperate polo players,
And all the women are coloratura sopranos and all the men are train
      announcers and hogcallers and saxophone solo players.
They all have screamingly funny stories to tell to each other,
And half of them get at one end of the house and half of them get at
      the other end of the yard and then they yell to each other,
And even if the patrolman looks in from his beat they do not
      moderate or stop,
No, they just seduce the cop.
And at last you manage to doze off by the dawn's early light,
And they wake you up all over again shouting good night,
And whether it consists of two quiet old ladies dropping in for a
      game of bridge or a lot of revelers getting really sort of out-of-
      bounds-like,
That's what a party next door always sounds like,
So when you see somebody with a hoarse voice and a pallid face and
      eyes bleary and red-rimmed and sore,
It doesn't mean they've been on a party themselves, no, it probably
      means that they have experienced a party next door.

THE EVENING OUT

You have your hat and coat on and she says she will be right down,
And you hope so because it is getting late and you are dining on the
other side of town,
And you are pretty sure she can't take long,
Because when you left her she already looked as neat and snappy as
a Cole Porter song,
And so goes ten minutes, and then fifteen minutes, and then half an
hour,
And you listen for the sound of water running because you suspect
she may have gone back for a bath or a shower,
Or maybe she is taking a nap,
Or possibly getting up a subscription for the benefit of the children
of the mouse that she said mean things about last night but
she is now sorry got caught in a trap,
Or maybe she decided her hair was a mess and is now shampooing
it,
But whatever she is up to, she is a long time doing it,
And finally she comes down and says she is sorry she couldn't find
the right lipstick, that's why she was so slow,
And you look at her and she looks marvelous but not a bit more
marvelous than she did when you left her forty-five minutes
ago,
And you tell her she looks ravishing and she says No, she is a sight,
And you reflect that you are now an hour late, but at any rate she is
now groomed for the rest of the night,
So you get to your destination and there's the ladies' dressing room
and before you know it she's in it,
But she says she'll be back in a minute,
And so she is, but not to tarry,
No, only to ask you for her bag, which she has forgotten she had
asked you to carry
So you linger in the lobby

And wish you had a nice portable hobby,

And you try to pass the time seeing how much you can remember of
the poetry you learned in school, both good verse and bad
verse,

And eventually she re-appears just about as you have decided she
was in the middle of Anthony Adverse,

And she doesn't apologize, but glances at you as if you were
Bluebeard or Scrooge,

And says why didn't you tell her she had on too much rouge?

And you look to see what new tint she has acquired,

And she looks just the same as she did before she retired,

So you dine, and reach the theater in time for the third act, and then
go somewhere to dance and sup,

And she says she looks like a scarecrow, she has to go straighten up,

So then you don't see her for quite a long time,

But at last you see her for a moment when she comes out to ask if
you will lend her a dime,

The moral of all which is that you will have just as much of her
company and still save considerable on cover charges and
beverages and grub

If instead of taking her out on the town, you settle her in a nice
comfortable dressing room and then go off and spend the
evening at the Club.

HOW NOW, SIRRAH? OH ANYHOW

Oh, sometimes I sit around and think, what would you do if you
        were up a dark alley and there was Caesar Borgia,
And he was coming torgia,
And brandished a poisoned poniard,
And looked at you like an angry fox looking at the plumpest rooster
        in a boniard?
What that certainly would be an adventure,
It would be much more exciting than writing a poem or selling a
        debenture,
But would you be fascinated,
Or just afraid of being assassinated?
Or suppose yoiu went out dancing some place where you generally
        dance a lot,
And you jostled somebody accidentally and it turned out to be Sir
        Lancelot,
And he drew his sword,
Would you say *Have at you!* or would you say *Oh Lord!?*
Or what if you were held up by a bandit,
And he told you to hand over your money, would you try to disarm
        him and turn him over to the police, or would you over just
        meekly hand it?
What would you do if you were in a luxurious cosmopolitan hotel
        surrounded by Europeans and Frenchmen,
And a beautiful woman came up to you and asked you to rescue her
        from some mysterious master mind and his sinister
        henchmen?
Would you chivalrously make her rescue your personal objective,
Or would you refer her to the house detective?
Yes, and what if you were on trial for murdering somebody whom for
        the sake of argument we might call Kelly or O'Connor,
And you were innocent but were bound to be convicted unless you
        told the truth and the truth would tarnish a lady's honor,

Would you elect to die like a gentleman or like like a poltroon,
Or put the whole thing in the hands of an arbitration commitee
    headed by Heywood Broun?
Yes, often as through life I wander
This is the kind of question I ponder,
And what puzzles me most is why I even bother to ponder when I
    already know the answer,
Because anybody who won't cross the street till the lights are green
    would never get far as a Musketeer or a Bengal Lancer.

BENJAMIN

There was a brave girl of Connecticut
Who flagged the express with her pecticut,
Which her elders defined
As presence of mind,
But deplorable absence of ecticut.

UP FROM THE WHEELBARROW

Some people understand all about machinery,
And to them it is just like beautiful poetry or beautiful scenery,
Because they know how to control and handle it,
Because they understandle it,
Yes, when they are confronted with a complicated piece of
      machinery,
Why, they are as cool and collected as a dean sitting in his deanery,
And I certainly wish I were among them because if there is one
      thing that makes me terrified and panical,
It is anything mechanical and nowadays everything is mechanical.
O thrice unhappy home
Whose master doesn't know the difference between a watt and an
      ohm!
O radio glum and silent as a glum and silent burial
When no one knows what to do about the grounding or the aerial!
O four-door sedan cantankerous and stubborn and Mad Hattery,
With none to give a thought to occasionally changing the oil or once
      in a while checking on the battery!
O telephone and vacuum cleaners and cameras and electric toasters
      and streamlined locomotives and artificial refrigeration,
O thermostats and elevators and cigarette-lighters and air-
      conditioning units and all ye other gadgets that make ours a
      mighty nation,
I think you are every one a miracle,
And you do wonderful things and it's probably only because I don't
      see how you do what you do that when I think of you I
      become hystirical,
And of course that is silly of me because what does it matter how
      you function so long as all I have to do to get you to function
      is push a button or throw a switch,
Always assuming that I can remember which is which,
So keep on functioning, please,
Because if you don't I shall starve or freeze.

BOOP-BOOP-ADIEUP, LITTLE GROUP!

There are several generally recognized grounds for divorce,
And there are moments when stealing is a starving man's only
      recourse;
There are gatherings when it is perfectly proper to tell a dubious
      story if there is sufficient wit in it,
And there are provocations under which it is allowable to pull away
      an old lady's chair as she is about to sit in it,
But there is one unpardonable sin and in extenuation of it let us
      quote no Ballads of Reading Gaol and in praise of it let us
      chant no merry madrigals,
And that is amateur theadrigals.
Now, the urge to dress up and pretend to be somebody else is a
      universal human weakness,
Like never going to church except on Easter and then crowding out
      all the people who have been there the other fifty-one
      Sundays of the year, or never going to the races except for the
      Belmont or the Preakness.
So if some alternate All-Eastern left tackle who has been told he
      looks like Noel Coward wants to toss badinage back and forth
      like a medicine ball with a Junior Leaguer who has been told
      that with her glasses off she looks like Gertrude Lawrence,
Why that's their business, like drinking sidecars in bed or putting
      maple walnut ice cream on their oysters, and if they kept it to
      themselves it could be viewed with tolerance as well as
      abhorrence,
But the trouble is that they refuse to indulge their depraved
      appetites in the privacy of deserts or cloisters,
The kick is missing unless a lot of people are on hand to watch them
      drink sidecars in bed or put maple walnut ice cream on their
      oysters,
So they inveigle all their friends and relatives and all the relatives of
      their friends and all the friends of their relatives, in the name
      of various worthy charities,

Into paying for the privilege of sitting for three hours on piano stools
and watching them project their personalities across the
footlights with the gusto and élan of Oriental beggars
exhibiting their physical peculiarities.
Tonight I am being taken to see the Troubadour Players do the
Merchant of Venice.
I shall go with the same eagerness with which, if I weren't me, I
should pay three-thirty to watch me play tennis.

EVERYBODY TELLS ME EVERYTHING

I find it very difficult to enthuse
Over the current news.
Just when you think that at least the outlook is so black that it can
grow no blacker, it worsens,
And that is why I do not like the news, because there has never
been an era when so many things were going so right for so
many of the wrong persons.

LET'S NOT PLAY LOTTO, LET'S JUST TALK

If anybody says conversation in our day is as good as it was in
      Dr. Johnson's,
Why, that's a lot of nonsense.
The art of conversation has been lost, or at least mislaid,
And no modern phrase-coiner can think of a fresher word for spade
      than spade.
Take the causerie of the most effervescent coterie,
It sounds like something sworn to before a notary.
Where are yesterday's epigrams, banter and badinage?
All you hear is who behaved scandalously at the club dance and
      how hard it is to get a new car into an old garage.
The maxim, the apothegm, yea, even the aphorism, die like echoes
      in the distance,
Overwhelmed by such provocative topics as clothes, beauticians,
      taxes and the scarcity of competent domestic assistants.
Come, sprinkle ashes and coffee substitutes upon my head,
I weep for the art of conversation, it is dead.
But wait a minute, the art of conversation is not dead, see it arise,
      vigorous, stimulating and untroubled,
Just as you start to play six spades, vulnerable, doubled and
      redoubled.

UNDER THE FLOOR

Everybody knows how the waters come down at Lodore,
But what about voices coming up through the floor?
Oh yes, every time that into a task you set your teeth
Something starts talking in the room underneath,
And no matter how many authorities you quiz,
You can never find out who or what it is;
You know one thing about it and nothing more,
That it is just something that goes around making noises that come
      up through the floor.
Sometimes it sings the Indian Love Call and sometimes it sings
      Lead, Kindly Light, by Cardinal Newman,
But even then it doesn't sound human,
And sometimes it gobbles,
And the sound wibbles and wobbles,
And sometimes it snarls like a ghoul interrupted at its unholy feast,
And sometimes it just mutters like blood going down the drain of a
      tub after a murderer has finished dismembering the
      deceased;
It cackles, it crackles, it drones, it buzzes, it chortles,
It utters words but in no tongue spoken by mortals,
Yes, its language is a mystery for evermore,
The language of whatever it is that makes the noise that comes up
      through the floor,
And you shiver and quiver and wonder,
What's under?
Is it banshees or goblins or leprechauns, or trolls or something?
Or pixies or vampires of lost souls or something?
What is it below?
Better not, better no know.
Don't let it upset you,
But also don't overlook the possibility that someday whatever it is
      that makes the noises that come up through the floor may
      come up through the floor and get you.

NO WONDER OUR FATHERS DIED

Does anybody mind if I don't live in a house that is quaint?

Because, for one thing, quaint houses are generally houses where plumbing ain't,

And while I don't hold with fanatical steel-and-glass modernistic bigots,

Still, I do think that it simplifies life if you live it surrounded by efficient pipes and faucets and spigots.

I admit that wells and pumps and old oaken buckets are very nice in a poem or ode,

But I feel that in literature is where they should have their permanent abode,

Because suppose you want a bath,

It is pleasanter to be able to take it without leaving a comfortable stuffy room and going out into the bracing fresh air and bringing back some water from the end of a path.

Another thing about which I am very earnest,

Is that I do like a house to be properly furnaced,

Because if I am out in the bracing fresh air I expect to be frozen,

But to be frigid in a stuffy room isn't what I would have chosen.

And when you go to bed in a quaint house the whole house grumbles and mutters,

And you are sure the walls will be shattered by clattering shutters.

At least you hope it's the shutters but you fear it's a gang of quaint ghosts warming up for twelve o'clock,

And you would lock yourself snugly in but the quaint old key won't turn in the quaint old lock,

So you would pull the bedclothes snugly up over your head and lie there till a year from next autumn,

Were it not a peculiarity of bedclothes in quaint houses that if you pull them up on top, why your feet stick out at the bautum,

But anyhow you find a valley among the hilltops of your mattress and after a while slumber comes softly stealing,

And that is when you feel a kiss on your cheek and you think maybe
      it is a goodnight kiss from your guardian angel, but is isn't,
      it's a leak in the ceiling.
Oh, I yield to none in my admiration of the hardy colonists and their
      hardy spouses,
But I still feel that their decadent descendants build more
      comfortable houses.

THE PEOPLE UPSTAIRS

The people upstairs all practice ballet.
Their living room is a bowling alley.
Their bedroom is full of conducted tours
Their radio is louder than yours.
They celebrate week ends all the week.
When they take a shower, your ceilings leak.
They try to get their parties to mix
By supplying their guests with Pogo sticks,
And when their orgy at last abates,
They go to the bathroom on roller skates.
I might love the people upstairs wondrous
If instead of above us, they just lived under us.

There are several things in life that keep me guessing,
And one of them is what are the French words for French leave and
French fried potatoes and French dressing,
And I am also a trifle vague
About how you ask people to a Dutch treat or talk to them like a
Dutch uncle in The Hague.
And why do restaurants put signs in their windows advertising
REAL HOME COOKING and expect the customers to come
rushing in all panting and overjoyed
When the reason that half the people who eat in restaurants are
eating in restaurants is because with home cooking they have
become cloyed?
And when is a violin a fiddle?
And when the tide goes out here does it go in somewhere else or
does it just pile up and make the ocean deeper in the
middle?
And who is the brownie whose duty it is to see that the theater
curtain never goes up on time except the one evening that
you are late?
And who is the railroad dispatcher who arranges his dispatching so
that every time you are about to see something interesting out
of your train window your view is cut off by a hundred-car
freight?
These are the kind of riddles and conundrums with which life
Is far too rife,
But fortunately for the human race thinking people eventually
discover that there is only one satisfactory way of dealing
with a riddle or conundrum.
And that is to stop worrying about the answers and just get clean out
from undrum.

THE QUEEN IS IN THE PARLOR

Let's all go over to Lily's,
And we'll all play games;
We'll act like regular sillies,
We'll assume ridiculous names,
We'll embarrass the butler,
And shock the maids,
With some of our subtler
Sly charades.
Come along, come along to Lily's,
Effervescent incessantly Lily's,
Come along, come along to Lily's,
And we'll all play games.

Lily is loaded with strictures
And many a palpable hit
For people who won't draw pictures,
For people who won't be IT.
There are sharpened pencils
And virgin papers,
All the utensils
For mental capers.
Here's a new one! You're going to love it!
Just enter into the spirit of it!
The name of the game is, Who Is Whom?
Harold, you have to leave the room;
I hope a few minutes alone won't bore you;
We'll whistle when we are ready for you.
Amanda, sit on the chandelier;
You represent Eternity, dear;
Now let me think—oh yes, Louise,
Stand on the sofa—on one leg, please;
You're Nelson—oh, it was Nelson's arm!

Well, a change of limbs lends whimsical charm.
George and Edward are Scrooge and Marley;
Pincus, you be Bonnie Prince Charlie.
Now, do I dare be Cleopatra?
No, really I don't! Why George, you flattra!
Everyone ready? This is fun!
Harold must guess us, every one,
And portray us all in a cartoon trim
While we each write a sonnet on him.
Hoo hoo, Harold! Hoo hoo! Hoo hoo!
Come in now, Harold, we're ready for you!
Hoo hoo, Harold—Oh no! Not that!
Harold is missing, and so's his hat.

Let's go over to Lily's
We'll all play games;
We'll bloom like daffy-down-dillies
And romp like Colonial Dames.
Anne, think of a number!
George, pick a card!
But I shall slumber
And slumber hard.
Come along, come along to Lily's,
Energetic aesthetically Lily's
Come along, come along to Lily's,
The Queen of the Parlor Games!

EXPERIENCE TO LET

Experience is a futile teacher,
Experience is a prosy preacher,
Experience is a fruit tree fruitless,
Experience is a shoe-tree bootless.
For sterile wearience and drearience,
Depend, my boy, upon experience.
The burnt child, urged by rankling ire,
Can hardly wait to get back at the fire,
And, mulcted in the gambling den,
Men stand in line to gamble again.
Who says that he can drink or not?
The sober man? Nay nay, the sot.
He who has never tasted jail
Lives well within the legal pale,
While he who's served a heavy sentence,
Renews the racket, not repentance.
The nation bankrupt by a war
Thinks to recoup with just one more;
The wretched golfer, divot-bound,
Persists in dreams of the perfect round.
Life's little suckers chirp like crickets
While spending their all on losing tickets.
People whose instinct instructs them naught
But must by experience be taught,
Will never learn by suffering once,
But ever and ever play the dunce.
Experience! Wise men do not need it!
Experience! Idiots do not heed it!
I'd trade my lake of experience
For just one drop of common sense.

THE FRIENDLY TOUCH

You go into a store and select half-a-dozen shirts and charge them,
And finally you get them paid for along about the time you either
      have to give them away or enlarge them,
And you don't go back to the store because although it has nice
      shirts, still, for your modest budget it's rather expensive,
And the possibilities of a charge account are too extensive,
You need some more shirts,
But your conscience hurts;
Your bureau drawer is emptied
But you refuse to be temptied;
You say, No, they have nice shirts but they look on any purchase
      under two hundred dollars with boredom,
And I simply can't afforedom.
Well, everything is simply splendid,
And suddenly you get a letter from them saying they have been
      looking over their accounts and note that they have not
      served you since April 15th, 1931, and in what way have
      they offended?
This is followed by other letters even more imploring,
Indeed the tone become positively adoring;
They beg you to purchase something from them,
They egg you to purchase something from them;
They hint that if their plea you ignore,
Why, they will simply close up their store,
And you succumb to their appealings,
And buy half-a-dozen shirts just so as not to hurt their feelings.
Well, their feelings seem to recover all right from the wreck,
Because around the middle of the following month you get a letter
      from them saying they have been looking over their accounts
      and how about favoring them with a check?
This is followed by other letters even more suggestive of lovers'
      meetings ending in journeys,

And in about two weeks they turn over their share of the
       correspondence to their attorneys,
So you send the check and the affair is ended,
And you swear off and in about a year you get a letter from them
       saying they have been looking over their accounts and note
       that they have not served you since October 2nd, 1936, and
       in what way have they offended?
Some people chase their own coattails in revolving doors,
And other people write letters for stores.

THE CITY

Here men walk alone
For most of their lives,
What with hydrants for dogs,
And windows for wives.

SPLASH!

Some people are do-it-some-other-timers and other people are do-it-
      nowers,
And that is why manufacturers keep on manufacturing both bathtubs
      and showers,
Because some bathers prefer to recline
On the cornerstone of their spine,
While others, who about their comfort are less particular,
Bathe perpendicular.
Thus from the way people lave themselves
You can tell how under other circumstances they will behave
      themselves.
Tubbers indulge in self-indulgence,
And they loll soaking until they are a moist mass of warm rosy
      effulgence,
And finally they regretfully hoist themselves up and shiver and say
      Brrrr! even though the atmosphere is like an orchid-house
      and the mirror is coated with steam,
And they pat at their moistness with a towel as soft as whipped
      cream,
So it is obvious that the tubber is a sybaritic softie,
And will never accomplish anything lofty.
How different is the showerer, whose chest is often festooned with
      hair such as bedecked our ancestors arboreal!
He has no time to waste on luxuriousness, but skims through the
      spray with the speed of a Democratic politician skimming
      through a Republican editorial,
After which he grates himself on something which he calls a towel,
But which anybody covered with human skin instead of cowhide
      would call a file or a spur or a rowel,
And thus at the same time he avoids procrastination
And improves his circulation,
So we see that the showerer is a Spartan,

And sternly guides his ambitious life along the lines laid down by
      baccalaureate preachers and Bruce Barton,
And this is the reason that in the game of life although occasional
      points are won by the tubber,
The showerer always gets game and rubber.
Sometimes tubbers and showerers get into arguments about tubs and
      showers and become very warlike and martial,
But I myself have always been strictly impartial,
Yes, I am neutrally anchored halfway between Calais and Dover,
And all I will impartially and neutrally say is that there are three
      things you can't do in a shower, and one is read, and the
      other is smoke, and the other is get wet all over.

ROADBLOCK

Justice has been rerouted
From present to future tense;
The law is so in love with the law
It's forgotten common sense.

WOMAN PULLS THE WIRES

I have been idly leafing through the Book of Proverbs and the Book
of Deuteronomy,
But I have failed to find what I was seeking, which was a few pithy
words on the subject of lovely woman and her weakness for
peculiar economy,
And at first I couldn't understand the omission and then I thought,
Why of course!
The Book of Proverbs and the Book of Deuteronomy were written
before the days of Marconi and Morse,
And to appreciate lovely woman really entangled in the coils of
economy you are unable
Until you have seen her in the coils of composing a telegram or a
radiogram or a cable.
The occasion may be one of life and death, but she does not wire at
once, she frugally decides to wait,
Because she is determined to save the pennies that are saved by
getting the night or week-end rate,
So suppose you are out of town and your wife wants to tell you that
the children have turned into wart hogs and somebody will
give you a million dollar contract if you call them up right
away and she has shot the minister's wife and eloped with the
minister,
She will not squander money on a rush message, no, she sends it
creeping overnight, thus saving a sum so tidy that you can't
see it even in these days when the financial outlook is pretty
sinister.
Or suppose that she instead of you is out of town and she decides
that she should have brought along a certain dress,
Why then she sends you a costly rush wire but she is still
economical and the instructions are so terse that you have
nothing to act on but a wrong guess,
So it takes about twenty dollars worth of electricity to get
straightened out and you are quite broke and burst,

All of which could have been avoided if she had spent an extra
   thirty cents at first.
Oh I often think that most of the misery in the world is caused by
   the telegraph companies who make you pay extra for all
   words over ten,
And I realize they have a right to a profit, but I wish they would
   abolish all their present special rates and start all over again
   with just one for lovely economical women, and one for men.

WHAT DO YOU WANT, A MEANINGFUL DIALOGUE, OR A SATISFACTORY TALK?

Bad money drives out good.
That's Gresham's law, which I have not until recently understood.
No economist I, to economics I have an incurable allergy,
But now I understand Gresham's law through obvious analogy.
Just as bad money drives the good beyond our reach,
So has the jargon of the hippie, the huckster and the bureaucrat
   debased the sterling of our once lucid speech.
What's worse, it has induced the amnesia by which I am faced;
I can't recall the original phraseology which the jargon has replaced.
Would that I had the memory of a computer or an elephant!
What used I to say instead of uptight, clout and thrust and relevant?
Linguistics becomes an ever eerier area, like I feel like I'm in Oz,
Just trying to tell it like it was.

BANKERS ARE JUST LIKE ANYBODY ELSE, EXCEPT RICHER

This is a song to celebrate banks,
Because they are full of money and you go into them and all you
　　　hear is clinks and clanks,
Or maybe a sound like the wind in the trees on the hills,
Which is the rustling of the thousand dollar bills.
Most bankers dwell in marble halls,
Which they get to dwell in because they encourage deposits and
　　　discourage withdralls,
And particularly because they all observe one rule which woe
　　　betides the banker who fails to heed it,
Whis is you must never lend any money to anybody unless they
　　　don't need it.
I know you, you cautious conservative banks!
If people are worried about their rent it is your duty to deny them
　　　the loan of a single penny, even though it be worth only 3 $\frac{7}{10}$
　　　francs.
Yes, if they request fifty dollars to pay for a baby you must look at
　　　them like the English looking at Joan of Arc,
And tell them what do they think a bank is, anyhow, they had better
　　　go get the money from their friendly neighborhood shark.
But suppose people come in and they have a million and they want
　　　another million to pile on top of it,
Why, you brim with the milk of human kindness and you urge them
　　　to accept every drop of it,
And you lend them the million so then they have two million and
　　　this gives them the idea that they would be better off with
　　　four,
So they already have two million as security so you have no
　　　hesitation in lending them two more,
And all the vice-presidents nod their heads in rhythm,
And the only question asked is do the borrowers want the money
　　　sent or they want to take it withm.

But please do not think that I am not fond of banks,
Because I think they deserve our appreciation and thanks,
Because they perform a valuable public service in eliminating the
      jackasses who go around saying that health and happiness
      are everything and money isn't essential,
Because as soon as they have to borrow some unimportant money to
      maintain their health and happiness they starve to death so
      they can't go around any more sneering at good old money,
      which is nothing short of providential.

I HAD NO IDEA IT WAS SO LATE

Consider the man without a watch.
He is like a soda without Scotch.
Of the male character I can quickly give you the gist;
It is the reach for the pocket or the glance at the wrist.
From the moment they are fledglings
Males discipline themselves with timings and schedulings.
Be they lovers, golfers, or railroad engineers,
Time is the essential ingredient in their careers,
And there is nothing more surly
Than a watchless man who doesn't know whether he is late or early,
And clocks are no good to him because he can't take them along,
And anyhow a clock is only something that you compare with your
        watch and find the clock is several minutes wrong.
If there is one thing that every man thinks how sublime it is,
It is to know what time it is.
Women don't like watches, they only tolerate them when they are
        embedded in brooches or bracelets or belts,
Or in some way disguised to look like something else.
Yes, it's obvious that women don't like them or need them,
Because with women's watches you need a microscope and a map to
        read them.
Time is something they resent, and they fight it with peculiarly
        feminine resistence;
They refuse to acknowledge its existence.
In this sexual conflict in attitude toward time who am I to tip the
        scales?
I only know that more males wait for females than females wait for
        males.

FIRST PAYMENT DEFERRED

Let us look into the matter of debt
Which is something that the longer you live, why the deeper into it
    you get,
Because in the first place every creditor is his debtor's keeper,
And won't let you get into debt in the first place unless you are
    capable of getting in deeper,
Which is an unfortunate coincidence
Because every debtor who is capable of getting deeper into debt is
    attracted only to creditors who will encourage him to get
    deeper into debt, which is a most fabulous and unfair You-
    were-a-creditor-in-Babylon-and-I-was-a-Christian-debtor
    Elinor Glyncidence.
Some debtors start out with debts which are little ones,
Such as board and lodging and victual ones;
Other debtors start out by never demanding that their bills be
    itemized,
Which means that they are bitten by little creditors upon the backs
    of bigger creditors and are so on ad infinitumized.
Veteran debtors dabble in stocks,
Or their families get adenoids or appendicitis or pox,
Any of which means that debt is what they get beneather and
    beneather,
Either to them who told them about the stocks or to them who
    administer the chloroform and ether.
Some debts are fun while you are acquiring them,
But none are fun when you set about retiring them,
So you think you will reform, you think instead of sinking into debt
    you will ascend into credit,
So you live on a budget and save twenty-five per cent of your salary
    and cut corners and generally audit and edit,
And that is the soundest idea yet,
Because pretty soon your credit is so good that you can charge
    anything you want and settle down for eternity into peaceful
    and utterly irremediable debt.

THE STRANGE CASE OF MR. O'BANION'S COME-UPPANCE

Once there was a man named Mr. O'Banion,
And he was a depressing companion.
He was so cynical
That it was practically clinical.
He was also a skeptic,
And would never eat a hamburger without first immersing it in
     antiseptic.
He believed that actresses exist on amours and marijuana,
And that St. George's dragon was really a large iguana.
He stated that every man has his price,
And he was sure that bartenders use the same olive twice.
He was especially derisive of the names of summer cottages,
He said they stuck in his craws, of which he had developed two, and
     in his epiglottages.
He said there was nothing more fraudulent than a summer cottage's
     cognomen,
And one day he pointed out to his Scout troup that there were three
     large opaque billboards between Seaview Villa and the
     ocean, and that everybody was restless at Dunroamin.
He hinted that at Lilac Lodge you couldn't even raise dandelions,
     and scoffed that Mon Repos and Beau Sejour would be the
     last place to find a French menu in,
And just as he remarked that Stuffed Sea Gull would be an apter
     name for Eagle's Eyrie, he was carried off by an eagle, and it
     was genuine.

WHY THE POSTMAN HAS TO RING TWICE
or
YELLOW ENVELOPE, WHERE HAVE YOU GONE?

Captain Ahab's desire was the White Whale.
My desire is to receive a telegram by telegraph messenger and not
      by telephone or mail.
If I should be asked, What hath God wrought? by Samuel F. B.
      Morse's ghost,
I should reply, He hath wrought the Telephone Company and the
      United States Post,
And I am still trying to read the riddle
Of how the Telegraph Company got that cozy seat in the middle.
Oh Company uncertain, coy, and hard to please,
In the unprogressive olden times they relied on reliable elderly boys
      with bicycles and puttees,
But now a telegram seems to something that if they can't mail it or
      phone it,
They disown it.
You stand convicted of impudence and effrontry
If you wish a telegram delivered, not mailed, to a person without a
      telephone in either the city or, what they never heard of, the
      country.
Do not try to appease me, I am unappeasable,
For every time I send an important telegram to be personally
      delivered I am inevitably notified just too late the next day
      that delivery was impractical and unfeasible.
Telegraph Company, you are the darling of my heart, I adore you,
In token of which I present you with a new slogan: Don't write,
      telegraph; we will mail it for you.

TWO GOES INTO TWO ONCE, IF YOU CAN GET IT THERE

All my life I have been a witness of things,
Among which I keep witnessing the eternal unfitness of things.
Daily it is my wont
To notice how things that were designed to fit each other, don't.
Getting a cigarette into a cigarette-holder is like the round hole and
      the square peg,
And getting the cork back into the vermouth bottle is like
      reinserting the cuckoo in the egg.
Why is the card-case always just a smidgin smaller than the deck?
Why does it take a 15¾ collar to encircle a 15½ neck?
Experience is indeed a teacher, and I have learned this fact from it,
That no suitcase is large enough to recontain the clothes you just
      unpacked from it.
No wonder the grapes set on edge the teeth of the little foxes;
The minute you buy a dozen silver or brocade or leather match-box
      holders the match-box makers change the size of the boxes.
I am baffled, I weave between Scylla and Charbydis, between a writ
      of replevin and a tort;
I shall console myself with the reflection that even in this world,
      ever perverse and ever shifting, two pints still make one
      cavort.

CONSIDER THE LAPEL, SIR

Have you bought a suit at Spand and Spitz?
They won't let you wear it unless it fits.
That's what they warn you in all their ads,
And Spand and Spitz are scrupulous lads.
Spand and Spitz are intensely scrupulous,
You can't wear their suit if the seat is droopulous.
Do you want it for slumming, or tea at the Ritz?
They won't let you wear it unless it fits.
The pants they carry are envy arousers,
In fact, they are not pants, they are trousers.
You select a suit and you call it quits,
As far as you are concerned, it fits.
You put your money and keys and comb in it,
You prepare to pay, and walk on home in it,
When her comes Spitz and here comes Spand,
They look at you like a swollen gland,
Spitz swears to Spand, who swears to Spitz,
They won't let you wear it unless it fits.
You adore the suit, you appeal to Spand,
He jerks it apart with loving hand;
You wish to wear it, you cry to Spitz,
He rips it off, while Spand on you sits.
It may be the suit that you're who it's made for,
The suit you have fought for and bought and paid for;
But if Spand and Spitz don't admit it fits you,
To wear it away, you must learn jujitsu.
The hell with this esthetic palaver
When you just want to cover your threadbare cadaver.

HAVE YOU TRIED STAYING AWAKE?
or
THEY'LL FIND A WAY TO STOP THAT, TOO

Most people's downy couches have a footboard and a headboard,
And some people's downy couches also have a bed-board.
I must tell you before I forgets
That a bed-board is different from a bed *and* board, which is what
      when your wife leaves it you are no longer responsible for her
      debts,
But if you can't get to sleep because your couch is so downy that
      you wallow and roll like a tug-boat off Cape Hatteras,
Why, you make it un-downy by slipping a bed-board under your
      matteras,
Thereby earning, whether you wear pajamas or a gown,
The unusual privilege of getting to sleep by walking the plank lying
      down.
O Civilization, O Progress, O Human Ingenuity!
O Fatuity in Perpetuity!
One genius chooses downy couches to set his mind uon,
And he spends a lifetime tinkering with Angeldust and Fogfoam and
      Bubblemist until he has invented the downiest couch ever
      reclined upon,
Whereupon another genius immediately invents a slab or wood that
      you can put under it to harden it,
And up-and-coming dealers may now feature the most irresistible of
      downy couches and the most immovable of bed-boards
      simultaneously, like the poison bottle with the antidote on the
      label, so if I giggle in my hammock I hope you will pardon it.

I'LL TAKE THE HIGH ROAD COMMISSION

In between the route marks
And the shaving rhymes,
Black and yellow markers
Comment on the times.

All along the highway
Hear the signs discourse:

MEN
SLOW
WORKING
;
SADDLE
CROSSING
HORSE
.

Cryptic crossroad preachers
Proffer good advice,

Helping wary drivers
Keep out of Paradise.

Transcontinental sermons,
Transcendental talk:

SOFT
CAUTION
SHOULDERS
;
CROSS
CHILDREN
WALK
.

Wisest of their proverbs,
Truest of their talk,
Have I found that dictum:

CROSS
CHILDREN
WALK

.

When Adam took the highway
he left his sons a guide:

CROSS
CHILDREN
WALK
;
CHEERFUL
CHILDREN
RIDE

.

MRS. PURVIS DREADS ROOM SERVICE
or
MR. PURVIS DREADS IT, TOO

Some say the fastest living creature is the cheetah,
Others nominate a duenna getting between a señor and a señorita,
Which goes to show that their knowledge of natural history is clear
      as a bell,
But they've never had their clothes off in a hotel.
Some hold out for the speed with which a Wagnerian quits an opera
      by Puccini,
Others for the speed with which an empty stomach is hit by a dry
      Martini.
These are speeds on whose superior speediness they persistently
      dwell,
Which simply proves that they've never had their clothes off in a
      hotel.
If you want to spite your face you can cut your nose off,
And if you want to spite people who think that cheetahs and
      duennas and dry Martinis are speedy, you can go to a hotel
      and take your clothes off,
Because some people can run the hundred in ten seconds and others
      would need only nine to circle the earth at the equator,
And they are the ones who knock on your triple-locked door just as
      your're ready for the bath and before you can say Wait a
      minute! they stalk in and if you're a man they're the maid
      and if you're a woman they're the waiter.
So I say Hats off to our hotel managers,
I hope they all get mistaken for Japanese beetles by scarlet
      tanagers,
Because there are two dubious thrills they guarantee every guest,
And one is a fleet-footed staff that laughs at locksmiths, because the
      other is a triple lock that will open only from the outside and
      only if the inmate is completely undressed.

THE OUTCOME OF MR. BUCK'S SUPERSTITION

Let me tell you of Aloysius Buck
Who had a pathetic belief in luck.
While the soup was waiting for him to sup
He would see a pin and pick it up.
When eating fish he toyed with the fishbones,
Making believe that they were wishbones,
And his bedside table was leaning over
Under bushel baskets of four-leafed clover.
His wife was a model of patience and tact
But at last her pleasant nature cracked.
For a birthday present he gave her a horseshoe.
She said, My dear, I'm going to divorce you.
He promised that if she'd remain Mrs. Buck
He'd never again believe in luck.
I was a fool, said Aloysius,
I'll never again be superstitious.
He brought home the blackest cats he could catch
And lit three cigarettes upon one match,
He walked his wife underneath a ladder
And often trampled on his own shadder,
And to make his un-superstition clearer
He put his foot through his wife's best mirror.
His wife was a model of patience and tact.
But at last her pleasant nature cracked
Though she liked his face and admired his carriage
She went to court and dissolved their marriage
When he said, Let's have eleven children as fast as we're able,
Then we can always sit down thirteen at table.

POLTERGUEST, MY POLTERGUEST

I've put Miss Hopper upon the train,
And I hope to do so never again,
For must I do so, I shouldn't wonder
If, instead of upon it, I put her under.

Never has host encountered a visitor
Less desirabler, less exquisiter,
Or experienced such a tangy zest
In beholding the back of a parting guest.

Hoitiful-toitiful Hecate Hopper
Haunted our house and haunted it proper,
Hecate Hopper left the property
Irredeemably Hecate Hopperty.

The morning paper was her monopoly
She read it first, and Hecate Hopperly,
Handing on to the old subscriber
A wad of Dorothy Dix and fiber.

Shall we coin a phrase for "to unco-operate"?
How about trying "to Hecate Hopperate"?
On the maid's days off she found it fun
To breakfast in bed at quarter to one.

Not only was Hecate on a diet,
She insisted that all the family try it,
And all one week end we gobbled like pigs
On rutabagas and salted figs.

She clogged the pipes and she blew the fuses,
She broke the rocker that Grandma uses,
And she ran amok in the medicine chest,
Hecate Hopper, the Polterguest.

Hecate Hopper the Polterguest
Left stuff to be posted or expressed,
And absconded, her suavity undiminished,
With a mystery story I hadn't finished.

If I pushed Miss Hopper under the train
I'd probably have to do it again,
For the time that I pushed her off the boat
I regretfully found Miss Hopper could float.

PERIOD PERIOD

PERIOD I

Our fathers claimed, by obvious madness moved,
Man's innocent until his guilt is proved.
They would have known, had they not been confused,
He's innocent until he is accused.

PERIOD II

The catch phrase "Nothing human to me is alien"
Was coined by some South European rapscallion.
This dangerous fallacy I shall now illumine:
To committees, nothing alien is human.

SUPPOSE I DARKEN YOUR DOOR

It seems to me that if you must be sociable it is better to go and see
      people than to have people come and see you,
Because then you can leave when you are through.
Yes, the moment you begin to nod
You can look at your watch and exclaim Goodness gracious, it is ten
      o'clock already, I had no idea it was so late, how very odd!
And you politely explain that you have to get up early in the
      morning to keep an important engagement with a man from
      Alaska or Siam,
And you politely thank your host and hostess for the lovely time and
      politely say good night and politely scram,
But when you yourself are the home team and the gathering is under
      your own roof,
You haven't got a Manchurian's chance of being aloof.
If you glance at your watch it is grievous breach of hospitality and a
      disgrace,
And if you are caught in the midst of a yawn you have to pretend
      you were making a face and say Come on everybody, let's see
      who can make the funniest face.
Then as the evening wears on you feel more and more like an
      unsuccessful gladiator,
Because all the comfortable places to sit in are being sat in by
      guests and you have to repose on the window sill or the
      chandelier or the radiator,
And somebody has always brought along a girl who looks like a loaf
      of raisin bread and doesn't know anybody else in the room,
And you have to go over to the corner where she is moping and try
      to disperse her gloom,
And finally at last somebody gets up and says they have to get back
      to the country or back to town again,

And you feebly say Oh it's early, don't go yet, so what do they do but
sit down again,

And people that haven't said a word all evening begin to get lively
and people that have been lively all evening get their second
wind and somebody says Let's all go out in the kitchen and
scramble some eggs,

And you have to look at him or her twice before you can convince
yourself that anybody who would make a suggestion like that
hasn't two heads or three legs,

And by this time the birds are twittering in the trees or looking in
the window and saying Boo,

But nobody does anything about it and as far as I know they're all
still here, and that's the reason I say that it is better to go and
see people than to have people come and see you.

WE WOULD REFER YOU TO OUR SERVICE
DEPARTMENT, IF WE HAD ONE

It fills me with elation
To live in such a mechanical-minded nation,
Surrounded not only by the finest scenery
But also the most machinery,
Where every prospect is attractive
And people are radioactive,
Reading books with show-how
Written by scientists with know-how.
Breathes there with soul so dead a fossil
Who never to himself hath said, Production is colossal?
Obviously civilization is far from a crisis
When the land teems with skilled craftsmen skillfully manufacturing
   gadgets and mechanical devices.
Millions of washing machines and electric refrigerators
Are shipped from the shipping rooms of their originators,
Streamlined dreamlined automobiles roll off the assembly lines in
   battalions and droves,
Millions of radios pour from the factories for housewives to listen to
   in the time they save through not having to slice their pre-
   sliced loaves,
So when everybody has a houseful and a garageful of mechanical
   perfection no one has any worries, but if you want a worry, I
   will share one,
Which is, Why is it that when seemingly anybody can make an
   automobile or a washing machine, nobody can repair one?
If you want a refrigerator or an automatic can opener or a razor that
   plays "Begin the Beguine" you can choose between an old
   rose or lavender or blue one,
But after you've got it, why if anything goes wrong don't think you'll
   find anybody to fix it, just throw it away and buy a new one.
Oh well, anyhow here I am nearly forty-five,
And still alive.

MALICE DOMESTIC

A Mrs. Shepherd of Danbudy, Conn.,
She tried to steal our cook,
She may have thought to stay anon.,
But now she's in a book!
Oh—Mrs.—Shepherd,
OH! Mrs. SHEPHERD!
I'll hunt you hither, I'll hunt you yon.
Did you really hope to remain anon.?
Didn't you know the chance you took
Making a pass at a poet's cook?

Oh, Mrs. S. of the Nutmeg State,
No human shame she knew,
Her carnal appetites to sate,
Our home she walked into.
Oh—Mrs.—Shepherd!
OH! Mrs. SHEPHERD!
By hook and by crook and by telephone
You attempted to rape us of our own.
You ruptured the laws of God and man
And made a pass at Matilda Ann.

Then here's a health to Matilda Ann
Whose soups are soundly peppered,
Whose commonest meats are godlike feats,
Who resisted Mrs. Shepherd.
But—Oh—Mrs.—Shepherd!
OH! Mrs. SHEPHERD!
You ruptured the laws of man and God
When in our kitchen you softly trod.
You tiptoed hither, you tiptoed yon,
You fondly hoped to remain anon.,
But householders all, the nation over,

Shall hear the name of the lawless rover
Who by telephone and by hook and crook
Attempted to alienate our cook.
Go back to your home in Danbury, Conn.,
And carry this curse to ponder on:
I hope that your soup is washy-wishy,
Your salad sandy, your butter fishy,
Your oatmeal scorched and your sirloins boiled,
Your soufflé soggy, your sherbet oiled,
Till all your neighbors in Danbury, Conn.,
As they watch the Shepherds grow feeble and wan,
Say: "She should have thought of the chance she took,
Making a pass at a poet's cook."

WHO DID WHICH?
or
WHO INDEED?

Oft in the stilly night,
When the mind is fumbling fuzzily,
I brood about how little I know,
And know that little so muzzily.
Ere slumber's chains have bound me,
I think it would suit me nicely,
If I knew one tenth of the little I know,
But knew that tenth precisely.

O Delius, Sibelius,
And What's-his-name Aurelius,
O Manet, O Monet,
Mrs. Siddons and the Cid!
I know each name
Has an oriflamme of fame,
I'm sure they all did something,
But I can't think what they did.

Oft in the sleepless dawn
I feel my brain is hominy
When I try to identify famous men,
Their countries and anno Domini.
Potemkin, Pushkin, Ruskin,
Velásquez, Pulaski, Laski;
They are locked together in one gray cell,
And I seem to have lost the passkey.

O Tasso, Picasso,
O Talleyrand and Sally Rand,
Elijah, Elisha,
Eugene Aram, Eugène Sue,
Don Quixote, Donn Byrne,
Rosencrantz and Guildenstern,
Humperdinck and Rumpelstiltskin,
They taunt me, two by two.

At last, in the stilly night,
When the mind is bubbling vaguely,
I grasp my history by the horns
And face it Haig and Haigly.
O, Snow-Bound *was written by Robert Frost,*
And Scott Fitzgerald wrote Paradise Lost,
Croesus was turned to gold by Minos,
And Thomas à Kempis was Thomas Aquinas.
Two Irish Saints were Patti and Micah,

The Light Brigade rode at Balalaika,
If you seek a roué to irk your aunt,
Kubla-Khan but Immanuel Kant,
And no one has ever been transmogrified
Until by me has been biogrified.

Gently my eyelids close;
I'd rather be good than clever;
And I'd rather have my facts all wrong
Then have no facts whatever.

ANY MILLENNIUMS TODAY, LADY?

As I was wandering down the street
With nothing in my head,
A sign in a window spoke to me
And this is what it said:

"Are your pillows a pain in the neck?
Are they lumpy, hard, or torn?
Are they full of old influenza germs?
Are the feathers thin and forlorn?
Bring 'em to us,
We do the trick;

Re-puff,
Replenish,
Re-curl,
Re-tick,
We return your pillows, spanned-and-spicked,
Re-puffed, replenished, re-curled, re-ticked."

As I was wandering down the street
With too much in my head,
The sign became a burning bush,
And this is what it said:

"Is the world a pain in the neck?
Is it lumpy, hard, or torn?
Is it full of evil ancestral germs
That were old before you were born?
Bring it to us,
We do the trick,
Re-puff,
Replenish,
Re-curl,
Re-tick,

In twenty-four hours we return the world
Re-puffed, replenished, re-ticked, re-curled."

As I was wandering down the street
I heard the trumpets clearly,
But when I faced the sign again
It spoke of pillows merely.
The world remains a derelict,
Unpuffed, unplenished, uncurled, unticked.

OH, PLEASE DON'T GET UP!

There is one form of life to which I unconditionally surrender,
Which is the feminine gender.
I think there must be some great difference in the way men and
women are built,
Because women walk around all day wearing shoes that a man
would break his neck the first step he took in them because
where a man's shoe has a heel a woman's shoe has a stilt.
Certainly a man shod like a woman would just have to sit down all
day, and yet my land!
Women not only don't have to sit, but prefer to stand,
Because their pleasure in standing up is exquisite,
As everybody knows who has ever watched a woman pay a call or a
visit,
Because the proportions of feminine social chitchat are constant,
always;
One part of sitting down in the sitting room to four parts standing up
saying good-by in foyers and hallways,
Which is why I think that when it comes to physical prowess,
Why woman is a wow, or should I say a wowess.

I'LL WRITE THEIR NUMBER DOWN WHEN
WE GET HOME

Words, idle words, are what people's social life contains a goodly
store of,
And the idlest words are contained in the wishful phrase beginning,
Why don't we see more of?
By the time your age is medium,
Well, your most exotic evenings are placid to the point of tedium,
Because whenever you step out you find yourself steping out amid
faces and ideas that are, to say the least, familiar,
Which is a situation which moves only from the willy-nilly to the
willy-nillier,
But once in every eleven blue moons you encounter a newcomer in
your little coterie,
And it doesn't matter whether he is a veteran or a veterinary or a
vestryman or a vegetarian or a notable or a Notogæan or a
notary,
Because his fresh point of view is as beneficial to anemic
conversation as a transfusion or a tonic,
And his wife is equally attractive and stimulating, and the future
would be cute as a button if it weren't so inevitably ironic,
Because on the way home you say "My I like those people, why
don't we see more of them?" and it is agreed that Yes we
certainly must, and from then on they might as well be living
in the ancient Anglian kingdom of Mercia,
Because you never see them again because you never do anything
about it except to murmur "Why don't we see more of them?"
and that is why the best definition I can think of for at least
one man's social life is simply inertia.

THE VERY UNCLUBBABLE MAN

I observe, as I hold my lonely course,
That nothing exists without a source.
Thus, oaks from acorns, lions from cubs,
And health and wealth from the proper clubs.
There are yacht clubs, golf clubs, clubs for luncheon,
Clubs for flowing bowl and puncheon,
Clubs for dancing, clubs for gambling,
Clubs for sociable Sunday ambling,
Clubs for imbibing literature,
And clubs for keeping the cinema pure,
Clubs for friendship, clubs for snobbery,
Clubs for smooth political jobbery.
As civilization onward reels,
It's clubs that grease the speeding wheels.

Alas!

Oh, everybody belongs to something,
But I don't belong to anything;
No, I don't belong to anything, any more than the miller of Dee,
And everything seems to belong
To people who belong to something,
But I don't belong to anything,
So nothing belongs to me.

Racquet, Knickerbocker, Union League,
Shriners parading without fatigue,
Oddfellows, Red Men, Woodmen of the World,
Solvent Moose and Elks dew-pearled,
Tammany tigers, Temperance doves,
Groups of various hates and loves,
Success is the thing that all have an air of,
Theirs are the summonses taken care of,
Theirs are the incomes but not the taxes,

Theirs are the sharpest, best-ground axes;
Millions of members of millions of bands,
Greeting fellow members with helping hands;
Good fellows all in incorporated hordes,
Prosperity is what they are moving towards.

Alas!

Oh, everybody belongs to something,
But I don't belong to anything;
Yes, I belong to nothing at all, from Kiwanis to the R.F.C.,
And everything definitely belongs
To people who belong to lots of things,
But I don't belong to anything,
So nothing belongs to me.

PLEASE KEEP ON FORWARDING

Some people are born simply to pay postage due,
Which is like being born simply to tread on the gum that other
people chew.
Anybody sensible
Knows that the demand for extra postage heralds the arrival of
tidings unconditionally dispensable;
There is no instance thus far
Of a postage-due envelope having contained either a check or a
confession of murder or an invitation to dine with Winston
Churchill and Hedy Lamarr;
It is postage-due mail that requests your presence at a benefit and
encloses two tickets that will be charged to you unless you
write a letter returning them to the requester;
It is postage-due mail that electrifies you with a full report of the
graduation exercises at the kindergarten that you attended,
while going on five, for one semester.
Yet such is the fascination of getting nothing for something that
whenever the postman whistles,
People hasten to proffer good money for misdirected and
understamped epistles.
I know a man whose moral sense is checkered,
And next to looking through keyholes he likes reading other people's
mail, but not their postage-due mail, he says he'd rather
browse in the *Congressional Record.*

ELECTION DAY IS A HOLIDAY

People on whom I do not bother to dote
Are people who do not bother to vote.
Heaven forbid that they should ever be exempt
From contumely, obloquy and various kinds of contempt.
Some of them like Toscanini and some like Rudy Vallée,
But all of them take about as much interest in their right to ballot as
    their right to ballet.
They haven't voted since the heyday of Miss Russell (Lillian)
And excuse themselves by saying What's the difference of one vote
    in fifty million?
They have such refined and delicate palates
That they can discover no one worthy of their ballots,
And then when someone terrible gets elected
They say, There, that's just what I expected!
And they go around for four years spouting discontented criticisms
And contented witticisms,
And then when somebody to oppose the man they oppose gets
    nominated
They say Oh golly golly he's the kind of man I've always
    abominated,
And they have discovered that if you don't take time out to go to the
    polls
You can manage very nicely to get through thirty-six holes.
Oh let us cover these clever people very conspicuously with
    loathing,
For they are un-citizens in citizens' clothing.
They attempt to justify their negligence
On the grounds that no candidate appeals to people of their
    integligence,
But I am quite sure that if Abraham Lincoln (Rep.) ran against
    Thomas Jefferson (Dem.)
Neither man would be appealing enough to squeeze a vote out of
    them.

ONE NIGHT IN OZ

O She whom I cannot abide,
Our hostess sat us side by side,
But must the heavy silence scream
Our heartfelt mutual disesteem?
Can we not mitigate our plight
If you turn left and I turn right?
This tasty fare will tastier taste
If by each other we are not faced;
Why shouldn't our acquaintance end,
Friend of a friend of a friend of a friend?
You do not love my way of life,
Myself, my children or my wife,
And too self-satisfied for tact,
Don't bother to conceal the fact,
While I my feelings may not hint
Till I can see them forth in print.
Our juxtaposition as we dine
Results from no intrigue of mine.
You'd wished yon titled refugee
Whose dollars jetted here with he,
While I, whose hopes are mild and mere,
Had but desired to not be here.
Discovering who sits next to who,
Your face fell one inch, mine fell two.
Yet o'er our hostess's well-meant food
Did I refrain from being rude,
A minor courtesy which I grieve
To note that you could not achieve.
Well, Madam, if you wish it so,
Hitch up your girdle, here we go.
O living sneer, poor painted peril,
Yours is the snobbery of the sterile.
Of hounds and huntin' you discourse
Who never sat upon a horse.

You, who have never penned a line
That would not shame a Bantu of nine,
Serve up the great as chummy nicknames
And little intimate make-you-sick names.
How glibly in your talk you glue
Bohemia to Park Avenue,
Unwitting that your gossipy speech
Stamps you a hanger-on in each.
Ah, let us our acquaintance end,
Friend of Hemingway's friend's friend's friend;
I'm just as glad as glad can be
To feel towards you as you towards me.

THERE'S ALWAYS AN UBBLEBUB

There are some fiestas that the moment you arrive at them you
      realize this is not your night to howl,
Because your hostess is still patting sofa cushions in the parlor and
      your host is upstairs applying the styptic pencil to his jowl,
And you apologize for being premature,
And when your hostess snarls "Oh that's all right," she is lying in
      her teeth, you may be sure,
And you wish she would keep on patting cushions and let you go out
      and walk around the block,
But she just sits there asking how you like their city and looking at
      the clock,
And at last in comes another guest whose name sounds like Miss
      Ubblebub, which seems highly improbable,
And she is wearing a dress that she wore first as a bridesmaid
      during the Harding administration and hair that hesitates
      between the waveable and the bobbable,
And you may not have suspected your hostess of craft,
But suddenly she is superintending appetizers and you and Miss
      Ubblebub are off in a corner as snug as two barnacles on a
      raft,
And an hour later when the last guest has been cocktailed and
      canapéed you have certainly run, as far as Miss Ubblebub is
      concerned, your conversational gamut,
And when at dinner you find yourself seated next to Miss Ubblebub,
      I think you may be excused an ardent shucks, or even a quiet
      damut.

SUPPOSE HE THREW IT IN YOUR FACE

Please don't anybody ask me to decide anything, I do not know a nut
      from a meg,
Or which came first, the lady or the tiger, of which came next, the
      chicken or the egg.
I am, alas, to be reckoned
With the shortstop who can't decide whether to throw to first or
      second,
Nor can I decide whether to put, except after c,
E before i, or i before e.
But where this twilight mind really goes into eclipse
Is in the matter of tips.
I stand stricken before the triple doom,
Whether, and How Much, and Whom.
Tell me, which is more unpleasant,
The look from him who is superior to a tip and gets it, or from him
      who isn't and doesn't?
I had rather be discovered playing with my toes in the Aquarium
Than decide wrongly about an honorarium.
Oh, to dwell forever amid Utopian scenery
Where hotels and restaurants and service stations are operated by
      untippable unoffendable machinery.

I'M SURE SHE SAID SIX-THIRTY

One of the hardest explanations to be found
Is an explanation for just standing around.
Anyone just standing around looks pretty sinister,
Even a minister;
Consider then the plight of the criminal,
Who lacks even the protective coloration of a hyminal,
And as just standing around is any good criminal's practically daily
      stint,
I wish to proffer a hint.
Are you, sir, a masher who blushes as he loiters,
Do you stammer to passers-by that you are merely expecting a street
      car, or a dispatch from Reuter's?
Or perhaps you are a safeblower engaged in casing a joint;
Can you look the patrolman in the eye or do you forget all the *savior-
faire* you ever loint?
Suppose you are a shoplifter awaiting an opportunity to lift a shop,
Or simply a novice with a length of lead pipe killing time in a dark
      alley pending the arrival of a wealthy fop,
Well, should any official ask you why you are just standing around,
Do you wish you could simply sink into the ground?
My dear sir, do not be embarrassed, do not reach for your gun or
      your knife,
Remember the password, which, uttered in a tone of quiet despair,
      is the explanation of anyone's standing around anywhere at
      any hour for any length of time: "I'm waiting for my wife."

NOW TELL ME ABOUT YOURSELF

Everybody speaks of being patronized,
Yet nobody speaks of the truly irksome shambles which is, or are,
      being matronized,
By which I mean that there is nothing more impolitely and
      noticeably aloof
Than a woman of a certain sort sounding out a man of whose certain
      sort she hasn't yet got definite affidavits or proof.
She displays the great names of her acquaintance for his benefit like
      a *nouveau riche* displaying his riches.
And fixes him with the stare of a psychiatrist to see if there is one at
      which he twitches.
George Washington and George Sand and Lloyd George to her are
      Georgie,
And she would have addressed the Borgias behind their backs as
      Borgie.
She always wants to know, first, where do you come from, and
      second, do you of course know Babs and Bonzo Beaver there,
      which you never do, often for your own very good reasons, but
      you try to make your reply a polite one.
So you murmur, "Well, I don't really know them, but I know *of*
      them," and she at once assigns you to your proper side of the
      tracks, and it is not the right one.
When she discusses national affairs she doesn't talk exactly
      treasonably.
But she refers to that part of the nation which lies outside of New
      York in the bright tone of one referring to a little tailor she
      has just discovered who does alterations very reasonably.
Please do not get the impression that a matronizing woman causes
      me to froth at the mouth or slaver;
I only wish to notify you that whenever you want her you can have
      her.

DO, DO, DO WHAT YOU DONE, DONE, DONE
BEFORE, BEFORE, BEFORE

There is a man whose name must be, I think, Mr. Oglethrip, and if
you will bring me his head on a silver charger I will award
you the hand of my daughter and a lien on my future salary,

And nobody has ever seen him but when you go to an amateur
performance of any kind he is always sitting in the upper left-
hand corner of the gallery,

And he has the hands of a blacksmith and a heart full of
enthusiasm,

And compared to the rest of the audience, well Mr. Oglethrip is not
as chusiasm,

Because seasoned amateur performance attenders generally weigh
their applause carefully so as not to be either a spendthrift or
a hoarder,

Because unless the performers of any performance are your
grandmother or your favorite cousin or something your aim is
to applaud just enough to not hurt their feelings and not
enough to induce them to duplicate the order,

And some girl who once handed you a cup of cocoa at a church
supper appears and renders an imitation of Helen Hayes as
Portia,

And your applause preserves the delicate balance between ecstasy
and nausea,

And she is just about to resign the stage to the next performer and
everything is as right as a couple of trivets,

When hark! What is that thunder in the upper left-hand corner of
the gallery, can Mr. Oglethrip be driving rivets?

No, but he is clapping his horny hands and before you can catch
your breath,

Why, the cocoa girl is back with an imitation of Judith Anderson's
Lady Macbeth.

Mr. Oglethrip's cup has no brim,

Mr. Oglethrip is he to whom what is too much for anybody else is
never enough for him,

If Mr. Oglethrip heard Conrad Hilton sing "Trees,"
He would want a reprise.
Do you know a picture program that Mr. Oglethrip would find simply
      peachy?
A double bill in which each picture contained a dual role for Don
      Ameche.
I think it would be nice
If when you cut off Mr. Oglethrip's head to bring to me on a silver
      charger you would cut it off twice.

YOU AND ME AND P. B. SHELLEY

What is life? Life is stepping down a step or sitting in a chair,
And it isn't there.
Life is not having been told that the man has just waxed the floor,
It is pulling doors marked PUSH and pushing doors marked PULL and
      not noticing notices which say PLEASE USE OTHER DOOR.
It is when you diagnose a sore throat as an unprepared geography
      lesson and send your child weeping to school only to be
      returned an hour later covered with spots that are indubitably
      genuine,
It is a concert with a trombone soloist filling in for Yehudi Menuhin.
Were it not for frustration and humiliation
I suppose the human race would get ideas above its station.
Somebody once described Shelley as a beautiful and ineffective
      angel beating his luminous wings against the void in vain,
Which is certainly describing with might and main,
But probably means that we are all brothers under our pelts,
And Shelley went around pulling doors marked PUSH and pushing
      doors marked PULL just like everybody else.

COMPLAINT TO FOUR ANGELS

Every night at sleepy-time
Into bed I gladly climb.
Every night anew I hope
That with the covers I can cope.

Adjust the blanket fore and aft,
Swallow next a soothing draught;
Then a page of Scott or Cooper
May induce a healthful stupor.

O the soft luxurious darkness,
Fit for Morgan, or for Harkness!
Traffic dies along the street.
The light is out. So are your feet.

Adjust the blanket aft and fore,
Sigh, and settle down once more.
Behold, a breeze! The curtains puff.
One blanket isn't quite enough.

Yawn and rise and seek your slippers,
Which, by now, are cold as kippers.
Yawn, and stretch, and prod yourself,
And fetch a blanket from the shelf.

And so to bed again, again,
Cozy under blankets twain.
Welcome warmth and sweet nirvana
Till eight o'clock or so mañana.

You sleep as deep as Keats or Bacon;
Then you dream and toss and waken.
Where is the breeze? There isn't any.
Two blankets, boy, are one too many.

O stilly night, why are you not
Consistent in your cold and hot?
O slumber's chains, unlocked so oft
With blankets being donned or doffed!

The angels who should guard my bed
I fear are slumbering instead.
O angels, please resume your hovering;
I'll sleep, and you adjust the covering.

THE DARKEST HALF-HOUR
or
TOO EARLY IS THE TIME FOR ALL GOOD GUESTS TO COME TO THE AID OF THE PARTY

They are ready for their party.

He feels as elegant as the Sun King and she as divine as the Moon Goddess, Astarte.

They have asked the guests for 7:30 on this, they hope, effulgent eve.

And by 7:05 they are in the living room, poised braced, anticipatory, and on the *qui vive*.

Eagerly they await the doorbell, or, in certain climes,

The ripple of those melodious Wistful Vista chimes.

He starts to light a cigarette, but she halts him with gestures frenzied—

The ashtrays have just been cleansèd.

She starts to sit on the sofa, and he, the most impartial umpire who never umped,

Evens the count by reminding her that the sofa has just been plumped.

Then she divides the olives by the number of guests and hopes she has not been too frugal,

And wishes that the caviar were not the sticky reddish kind but genuinely Belugal.

He nervously whistles a snatch from the *Peer Gynt Suite* by Grieg,

And wonders if his vodka—domestic, not Polish—is fit for compounding a White Russian, an Orange Julius, a Bog Fog, or a Palm Bay Intrigue.

By 7:25 she is pacing the floor and nibbling at her fingernails, destroying the opalescent symmetry acquired at the afternoon manicure,

And he inquires, "Are you sure it was *this* Saturday and not next that you asked them for?"—a question not recommended as the ideal panic cure.

At 7:30 they are tense as mummers awaiting the rise of the curtain,
      and at 7:31 they have abandoned their mumming—
They are convinced that nobody is coming.
So he says how about a quick one, and just as he has one hand in
      the ice bucket and the other on the gin,
Why, the first couple walks in.
You will be glad to learn that the party turned out to be absolutely
      fabulous;
Indeed, some say the best since the one at which a horse was named
      consul by the late Emperor Heliogabulus.

ALLOW ME, MADAM, BUT IT WON'T HELP

Adorable is an adjective and womankind is a noun,
And I often wonder why, although adorable womankind elects to talk
      standing up, it elects to put on its coat sitting down.
What is the outstanding characteristic of matinees, tea rooms and
      table d'hôtes?
Women, sitting firmly and uncomfortably on their coats;
Woman at whose talents a contortionist would hesitate to scoff,
Because they also sat down on their coats to take them off.
What is *savoir-faire*?
It is the ability to pick up eighty-five cents in nickels and a lipstick
      with the right hand while the left hand is groping wildly over
      the back of a chair.
Yes, and if you desire *savoir-faire* that you could balance a cup on,
Consider the calmness of a woman trying to get her arm into the
      sleeve of a coat that she has sat down on too far up on.
Women are indeed the salt of the earth,
But I fail to see why they daily submit themselves voluntarily to an
      operation that a man only undergoes when he is trying to put
      on his trousers in an upper berth.

I WONDER WHAT THEY BROUGHT
FROM GHENT TO AIX

My newspaper in winter helps light the fire but it doesn't help warm
the depths of my heart, colloquially known as cockles.
The front page is a showcase of dire disasters, doomful doings and
dismal debacles.
The entertainment section is of my dejected mood no alleviator or
temperer;
Such are the current movies that even the printed pitch for them
would add a blush to the painted check of a degenerate
Roman emperor.
On the society page the Croesus-cum-Arts group has taken over
noblesse oblige with no ifs or buts;
The popping of corks mingles with the cries of Burn, baby, burn! till
you can't tell the chic from the guts.
The sports page is as thrilling as a lecture on bimetallism by
Winnie-the-Pooh;
Nothing there but basketball, a game which won't be fit for people
until they set the basket umbilicus-high and return the
giraffes to the zoo.
The columnists five times a week on what the administration might
do or should do pontificate and speculate,
And each believes that of the truth his own conception is alone
immaculate.
And don't forget that blight on the ballot, the poll weevil.
I often wish that the film could be reversed and my newspaper could
turn back first to pulp and then to murmuring pines and
hemlocks and I could carve Everybody go home on their
trunks in the forest primeval.

BUT I COULD NOT LOVE THEE, ANN, SO MUCH, LOVED I NOT HONORÉ MORE

Some find the world in a grain of sand, I in the correspondence of
    Ann Landers.
I eavesdrop unabashed as she spoons out her acerb sauce with even
    hand on lachrymose geese and truculent ganders.
Her desk is positively formicating, which means swarming with
    moving beings, although I might well employ the other word
    that sounds like unto it,
Because her mail consists mostly of letters from those embittered
    ones who have discovered about illicit sex that often there are
    more headaches than fun to it.
A present-day Emma Lazarus, she cries Give me your huddled
    problems, the wretched refuse of your wrongs, unwrap for me
    your festering sores and stigmas;
Your poison is my meat, be it alcoholism, infidelity, frigidity,
    satyriasis, premarital pregnancy or borborygmus.
Yes, if anyone's Gordian love-knot requires a blade more cutting
    than Alexander's,
Let them call on Ann Landers.
No pussy-footer she, no purveyor of admonitions soothing or polite;
It's Tell the bum to jump in the lake, tell the old bag to go fly a kite.
If Anne of Cleves could have written to Ann Landers
I bet Henry would have thought twice before calling her the mare of
    Flanders.
From a human comedy as varied as Balzac's I choose for you one
    excerpt, the ultimate in wails of poignant woe,
The plaint of a teen-ager who doubted the affection of her boy friend
    because the only compliment he ever paid her was You sweat
    less than any fat girl I know.

NEVER WAS I BORN TO SET THEM RIGHT

Since the non-book and the anti-hero are now accepted elements of
modern negative living
I feel justified in mentioning a few examples of the march of
progress for which I suggest a heartfelt non-thanksgiving.
I not only like Turkish towels or a reasonable facsimile on emerging
from the tub,
I also like towels after washing my hands, even paper ones that you
rip untimely from a reluctant device that warns you, Blot, do
not rub.
I do not like the contraptions that have replaced towels in every
washroom from the humblest Howard Johnson to the
haughtiest Statler or Hilton,
Those abominations which you stand cringingly in front of waiting
for them to scorch you with a blast of air from a hell hotter
than any imagined by Dante or Milton.
I like the common incandescent lamp whose light is produced in
a filament rendered luminous by the passage of current
through it,
I do not like the fluorescent lamp in which light is produced by
passage of electricity through a metallic vapor or gas
enclosed in a tube or bulb, I resent it, I rue it, I eschew it.
You stumble into a dark room and press a switch and then stand in
continuing darkness for half a minute wondering if you have
blown a fuse sky-high,
And then the fluorescent fixture flickers and hesitates and finally
lights up and you see your face in the mirror and it is yellow
and green and purple like a recently blackened eye.
I do not like bottle openers shaped like a mermaid or a fish or even
an axolotl,
They may be all right for driving thumbtacks with but they're no
good for opening a bottle.
I do not like the substitution at toll-booths of the electronic coin-
basket for the human collector,

I accept it as grudgingly as Hecuba might have accepted the
      substitution of Polyphemus for Hector.
The collector would even lean into your car to accept the coin from
      your right hand, but you have to toss it at the basket with
      your left,
And I happen to be the least ambidextrous northpaw who ever
      chunked a pebble at a newt or an eft.
I do not like the thrifty European airmail stationery combining
      envelope with letter, I have never faced one but I trembled;
You need a well-honed paper knife to open it, and even then end up
      with eight or sixteen fragments which must be painstakingly
      reassembled.
Speaking of envelopes, I particularly dislike in our non-civilization
      the return envelope with postage prepaid which the Internal
      Revenue Department does not enclose with its annual
      demands; of needlessly irritating the taxpayer this is the most
      picayune of their many ways;
When I drain my bank account to write them a check I think they
      might at least blow me to a nickel's worth of postage,
      especially as it wouldn't cost them anything anyways.

MAY I DRIVE YOU HOME, MRS. MURGATROYD?

Here's a statement that anybody who feels so inclined is welcome to
   make a hearty mental meal of:
People who possess operator's licenses ought never to ride in a car that
   anybody else is at the wheel of.
It seems to be their point of view
That you are some kind of fanatic bent on murdering or mutilating them
   even in the face of the certainty that in so doing you must
   murder or mutilate yourself too.
They are always jumping and wincing and jamming their feet down on
   an imaginary brake,
Or making noises as if they had just discovered that their bed was
   inhabited by a snake,
Or else they start a casual conversation that begins with remarks about
   the weather and other banalities,
And leads up to a pointed comment on the horrifying number of annual
   automobile fatalities.
They tell you not only about cars that actually are coming but also cars
   that might be coming, and they do it so kindly and gently
That it's obvious they consider you deaf and blind as well as rather
   deficient mently.
And when at last you somehow manage to get to where you've been
   going to they say thank you in a voice full of plaster of Paris and
   bitter aloes,
And get down out of the car as if they were getting down off the gallows,
And they walk away with the Is-it-really-over expression of a lot of
   rescued survivors
And you go off and make a lot of remarks to yourself about back-seat
   drivers,
And you vow that come what may you yourself will never join their
   ranks, no indeed,
And then the next day somebody gives you a lift and you find yourself
   bathed with cold moisture the moment they shift the gears into
   third speed.
The truth of the matter, mesdames and sirs,
Is that we are all born chauffeurs;
Or, to put it another way before retiring to curl up with a bad book on
   the sofa,
Everybody in the car can drive better than the chauffeur.

ONE FROM ONE LEAVES TWO

Higgledy piggledy, my black hen,
She lays eggs for gentlemen.
Gentlemen come every day
To count what my black hen doth lay.
If perchance she lays too many,
They fine my hen a pretty penny;
If perchance she fails to lay,
The gentlemen a bonus pay.

Mumbledy pumbledy, my red cow,
She's cooperating now.
At first she didn't understand
That milk production must be planned;
She didn't understand at first
She either had to plan or burst,
But now the government reports
She's giving pints instead of quarts.

Fiddle de dee, my next-door neighbors,
They are giggling at their labors.
First they plant the tiny seed,
Then they water, then they weed,
Then they hoe and prune and lop,
They they raise a record crop,
Then they laugh their sides asunder,
And plow the whole caboodle under.

Abracadabra, thus we learn
The more you create, the less you earn.
The less you earn, the more you're given,
The less you lead, the more you're driven,
The more destroyed, the more they feed,
The more you pay, the more they need,
The more you earn, the less you keep,
And now I lay me down to sleep.

I pray the Lord my soul to take
If the tax-collector hasn't got it before I wake.

5

THE ANIMAL KINGDOM

"He who attempts to tease the cobra
Is soon a sadder he, and sobra."

THE PYTHON

The python has, and I fib no fibs,
318 pairs of ribs.
In stating this I place reliance
On a seance with one who died for science.
This figure is sworn to and attested;
He counted them while being digested.

THE COELACANTH

Consider now the Coelacanth,
Our only living fossil,
Persistent as the amaranth,
And status quo apostle.
It jeers at fish unfossilized
As intellectual snobs elite;
Old Coelacanth, so unrevised
It doesn't know it's obsolete.

THE ELK

Moose makes me think of caribou,
And caribou, of moose,
With, even from their point of view,
Legitimate excuse.
Why then, when I behold an elk,
Can I but think of Lawrence Welk?

THE DOG PARADE

No, Mrs. Chutney, no, I am not going to Madison Square Garden,
I am not going to the dog show, and what do you think of that, and if,
    you think what you probably think, I beg your pardon.
Some people like not listening to Bing Crosby and other people like
    not listening to Lawrence Tibbett,
But I like not attending the annual canine exhibit.
The prizes are very nice, I am sure, and so are the donors,
And I guess the dogs are all right, but I'm afraid I can't stand the
    owners,
Because some of them breed dogs for love and some for riches,
But my experience has been that most of them do it just so they can
    startle their friends at the dinner table and the drawing room
    by babbling with self-conscious and unconsciousness about
    bitches,
So back, Mrs. Chutney, back to your breeding and beagling.
I find you are very fatigueling;
You are one of the reasons why when somebody says dogs are
    people's best friends,
My esteem for them ends,
Because whenever I hear of somebody whose best friend has four feet,
Well, that is the person that I would stay away from in droves rather
    than meet.
I think dogs are wonderful in their place,
But I refuse to admit that they are a superior or equal race;
I will not attribute to every precocious poodle or spaniel
The wisdom of a Daniel.
I know that some of them can count up to ten and carry the
    newspaper home in their mouth and stand upon their hind
    legs and waltz,
But so could I if I wanted to, so I am not thereby blinded to their
    faults.
When they are wet they do not smell like a rose.
And when they are dry they shed all over your furniture and clothes.
Another thing dogs do, and indeed have been doing from the days of
    Ulysses,

Is to turn all the authors who write about them into great big sissies.
Whoever you read, be it Homer or Albert Payson Terhune or
     Browning,
Their dogs do nothing but go around and be faithful to people and
     mourn on people's graves and rescue them from fire and
     drowning,
And I admit that this gives their pages a lovely lovable flavor,
And maybe that actually is how dogs spend their time, but all I can
     say is no dog has yet ever done me a favor.
To make a long story short, in the words of Omar Khayyam,
I don't mean that I don't like dogs. I just want to say that I don't
     think they are any better than I am.

THE GIRAFFE

I beg you, children, do not laugh
When you survey the tall giraffe.
It's hardly sporting to attack
A beast that cannot answer back.
Now you and I have shorter necks,
But we can chant of gin and sex;
He has a trumpet for a throat,
And cannot blow a single note.
It isn't that his voice he hoards;
He hasn't any vocal cords.
I wish for him, and for his wife,
A voluble girafter life.

CAPERCAILLIE, AVE ATQUE VAILLIE

One letter from a long correspondence on the capercaillie in the English magazine *Country Life* is headed "How to Outwit the Capercaillie" and reads, in part: ". . . the cock capercaillie is blind and deaf during the last part of each 'verse' of his love song, the part described by Mr. Richmond as sounding 'like a polar bear splashing into a swimming pool.' . . . Between verses and during the first two parts of them (the 'kek kek kek' and 'whoosh'), however, the cock is most alert . . ."

Spring, the sweet Spring, is the year's pleasant king;
Then blooms each thing, then maids dance in a ring,
Cold doth not sting, capercaillie then doth sing—
Kek kek kek, whoosh, kek kek kek, whoosh!

Sings he no cuckoo, jug-jug, pu-we, to-witta-woo,
Trills doth he oochew, lark song and tereu,
Hen doth he woo with wild Highland cockadoo—
Kek kek kek, whoosh, kek kek kek, whoosh!

The truant from school doth think to hear a ghoul,
Bee-stung bear in pool, or scold on ducking stool.
Nay, nay, young fool! Here cries a ravished soul—
Kek kek kek, whoosh, kek kek kek, whoosh!

To bird of caution rid, with rival now outbid,
Comes, as to Duncan did, stop't ear and closèd lid,
And archer, slyly hid, transfixes him amid
Kek, kek, kek, whoosh, and kek kek kek, whoosh.

Farewell, poor cock, which died a laughingstock—
Yet thy pibroch doth lately run amok,
While chicks of strange flock chant, as they roll and rock,
Kek kek kek, whoosh, kek kek kek, whoosh!

THE DOG

The truth I do not stretch or shove
When I state the dog is full of love.
I've also proved, by actual test,
A wet dog is the lovingest.

PASTORAL

Two cows
In a marsh,
Mildly munching
Foddler harsh.
Cow's mother,
Cow's daughter,
Mildly edging
Brackish water.
Mildly munching,
While heron,
Brackish-minded,
Waits like Charon.
Two cows,
Mildly mooing;
No bull;
Nothing doing.

THE SHREW

Strange as it seems, the smallest mammal
Is the shrew, and not the camel.
And that is all I ever knew,
Or wish to know, about the shrew.

THE PANDA

I love the Baby Giant Panda;
I'd welcome one to my veranda.
I never worry, wondering maybe
Whether it isn't Giant Baby;
I leave such matters to the scientists:
The Giant Baby—and Baby Giantists.
I simply wish a julep and a
Giant Baby Giant Panda.

THE WOMBAT

The wombat lives across the seas,
Among the far Antipodes.
He may exist on nuts and berries,
Or then again, on missionaries;
His distant habitat precludes
Conclusive knowledge of his moods.
But I would not engage the wombat
In any form of mortal combat.

THE SQUID

What happy appellations these
Of birds and beasts in companies!
A shrewdness of apes, a sloth of bears,
A sculk of foxes, a huske of hares.
An exaltation 'tis of larks,
And possibly a grin of sharks,
But I declare a squirt of squid
I should not like to be amid,
Though bachelors claim that a cloud of sepia
Makes a splendid hiding place in Leap Year.

THE OSTRICH

The ostrich roams the great Sahara.
Its mouth is wide, its neck is narra.
It has such long and lofty legs,
I'm glad it sits to lay its eggs.

THE PRAYING MANTIS

From whence arrived the praying mantis?
From outer space, or lost Atlantis?
I glimpse the grim, green metal mug
That masks this pseudo-saintly bug,
Orthopterous, also carnivorous,
And faintly whisper, Lord deliver us.

THE ABOMINABLE SNOWMAN

I've never seen an abominable snowman,
I'm hoping not to see one,
I'm also hoping, if I do,
That it will be a wee one.

THE MANATEE

The manatee is harmless
And conspicuously charmless.
Luckily the manatee
Is quite devoid of vanity.

THE SQUAB

Toward a better world I contribute my modest smidgin;
I eat the squab, lest it become a pigeon.

EXIT, PURSUED BY A BEAR

Chipmunk chewing the Chippendale,
Mice on the Meissen shelf,
Pigeon stains on the Aubusson,
Spider lace on the Delf.

Squirrel climbing the Sheraton,
Skunk on the Duncan Phyfe,
Silverfish in the Gobelins
And the calfbound volumes of *Life*.

Pocks on the pink Picasso,
Dust on the four Cézannes,
Kit on the keys of the Steinway,
Cat on the Louis Quinze.

Rings on the Adam mantel
From a thousand bygone thirsts,
Mold on the Henry Millers
And the Ronald Firbank firsts.

The lion and the lizard
No heavenly harmonies hear
From the high-fidelity speaker
Concealed behind the Vermeer.

Jamshid squats in a cavern
Screened by a waterfall,
Catered by Heinz and Campbell,
And awaits the fireball.

THE CENTIPEDE

I objurgate the centipede,
A bug we do not really need.
At sleepy-time he beats a path
Straight to the bedroom or the bath.
You always wallop where he's not,
Or, if he is, he makes a spot.

THE SHRIMP

A shrimp who sought his lady shrimp
Could catch no glimpse,
Not even a glimp.
At times, translucence
Is rather a nuisance.

LOCUST-LOVERS, ATTENTION!

My attention has been recently focused
Upon the seventeen-year locust.
This is the year
When the seventeen-year locusts are here,
Which is the chief reason my attention has been focussed
Upon the seventeen-year locust.
Overhead, underfoot, they abound,
And they have been seventeen years in the ground,
For seventeen years they were immune to politics and class war and
      capital taunts and labor taunts,
And now they have come out like billions of insect debutantes,
Because they think that after such a long wait,
Why they are entitled to a rich and handsome mate,
But like many another hopeful debutante they have been hoaxed
      and hocus-pocussed,
Because all they get is another seventeen-year locust.
Girl locusts don't make any noise,
But you ought to hear the boys.
Boy locusts don't eat, but it is very probable that they take a drink
      now and again, and not out of a spring or fountain,
Because they certainly do put their heads together in the treetops
      and render Sweet Adeline and She'll Be Comin' Round the
      Mountain.
I for one get bewildered and go all hot and cold
Everytime I look at a locust and realize that it is seventeen years
      old;
It is as fantastic as something out of H. G. Wells or Jules Verne or
      G. A. Henty
To watch a creature that has been underground ever since it hatched
      shortly previous to 1920,
Because locusts also get bewildered and go hot and cold because
      they naturally expected to find Jess Willard still the champ,
And Nita Naldi the vamp,
And Woodrow Wilson on his way to Paris to promote the perpetually
      not-yet-but-soon League,

And Washington under the thumb of Wayne B. Wheeler and the
      Anti-Saloon League.
Indeed I saw one locust which reminded me of a godmotherless
      Cinderella,
Because when it emerged from the ground it was whistling
      Dardanella.
Dear locusts, my sympathy for you is intense,
Because by the time you get adjusted you will be defunct, leaving
      nothing behind you but a lot of descendants who in turn will
      be defunct just as they get adjusted seventeen years hence.

THE HIPPOPOTAMUS

Behold the hippopotamus!
We laugh at how he looks to us,
And yet in moments dank and grim
I wonder how we look to him.
Peace, peace, thou hippopotamus!
We really look all right to us,
As you no doubt delight the eye
Of other hippopotami.

THE ANT

The ant has made himself illustrious
Through constant industry industrious.
So what?
Would you be calm and placid
If you were full of formic acid?

THE EMMET

The emmet is an ant (archaic),
The ant is just a pest (prosaic).
The modern ant, when trod upon,
Exclaims "I'll be a son-of-a-gun!"
Not so its ancestor, the emmet,
Which perished crying "Zounds!" or "Demmit!"

A DOG'S BEST FRIEND IS HIS ILLITERACY

It has been well said that quietness is what a Grecian urn is the still
      unravished bride of,
And that a door is what a dog is perpetually on the wrong side of.
I may add that a sachet is what many a housewife's linen is
      fragrantly entrusted to,
But that a cliché is what a dog owner must eventually get adjusted
      to.
What does the visitor say when your dog greets him with Southern
      hospitality and salutes him all kissin'-cousiny?
He says, He smells my dog on me, doesn't he?
And he asks, How old is he, and you say Twelve, and he appraises
      Spot with the eye of an antiquarian,
And says, Seven twelves are eighty something, why Spot in human
      terms you're an octogenarian,
But these two bromides are just the rattle before the strike,
Because then he says it's funny but he's noticed how often dogs and
      their masters look alike.
Such are the comments faced by dog owners from Peoria to
      Peshawar,
And frequently from a man who in canine terms is 322 years old,
      and he is the spit and image of his own Chihuahua.
The only escape is to have something instead of dogs but whatever I
      substituted I should probably err,
And if I ended up with raccoons every guest would turn out to be a
      raccoonteur.

THE SWAN

Scholars call the masculine swan a cob;
I call him a narcissistic snob.
He looks in the mirror over and over,
And claims to have never heard of Pavlova.

THE BAT

Myself, I rather like the bat,
It's not a mouse, it's not a rat.
It has not feathers, yet has wings,
It's quite inaudible when it sings.
It zigzags through the evening air
And never lands on ladies' hair,
A fact of which men spend their lives
Attempting to convince their wives.

THE CHIPMUNK

My friends all know that I am shy,
But the chipmunk is twice as shy as I.
He moves with flickering indecision
Likes stripes across the television.
He's like the shadow of a cloud,
Or Emily Dickinson read aloud.

THE MULES

In the world of mules
There are no rules.

FOR A GOOD DOG

My little dog ten years ago
Was arrogant and spry,
Her backbone was a bended bow
For arrows in her eye.
Her step was proud, her bark was loud,
Her nose was in the sky,
But she was ten years younger then,
And so, by God, was I.

Small birds on stilts along the beach
Rose up with piping cry,
And as they flashed beyond her reach
I thought to see her fly.
If natural law refused her wings,
That law she would defy,
For she could do unheard-of things,
And so, at times, could I.

Ten years ago she split the air
To seize what she could spy;
Tonight she bumps against a chair,
Betrayed by milky eye.
She seems to pant, Time up, time up!
My little dog must die,
And lie in dust with Hector's pup;
So, presently, must I.

THE CUCKOO

Cuckoos lead Bohemian lives,
They fail as husbands and as wives,
Therefore they cynically disparage
Everybody else's marriage.

THE BIRDS

Puccini was Latin, and Wagner Teutonic,
And birds are incurably philharmonic.
The skylark sings a roundelay,
The crow sings "The Road to Mandalay,"
The nightingale sings a lullaby
And the sea gull sings a gullaby.
That's what shepherds listened to in Arcadia
Before some one invented TV's and radia.

THE TORTOISE

Come crown my brows with leaves of myrtle;
I know the tortoise is a turtle.
Come carve my name in stone immortal;
I know the turtoise is a tortle;
I know to my profound despair;
I bet on one to beat a hare.
I also know I'm now a pauper
Because of its tortley turtley torpor.

THE WILD JACKASS

Have ever you harked to the jackass wild,
Which scientists call the onager?
It sounds like the laugh of a backward child,
Or a hepcat on a harmonica.
But do not sneer at the jackass wild,
There is method in his hee-haw,
For with maidenly blush and accent mild
The jenny-ass answers, shee-haw.

THE HAMSTER

There is not much about the hamster
To stimulate the epigramster.
The essence of his simple story,
He populates the laboratory,
Then leaves his offspring in the lurch,
Martyrs to medical research.
Was he as bright as people am,
New York would be New Hamsterdam.

THE PLATYPUS

I like the duck-billed platypus
Because it is anomalous.
I like the way it raises its family,
Partly birdly, partly mammaly.
I like its independent attitude.
Let no one call it a duck-billed platitude.

THE CATERPILLAR

I find among the poems of Schiller
No mention of the caterpillar,
Nor can I find one anywhere
In Petrarch or in Baudelaire,
So here I sit in extra session
To give my personal impression.
The caterpillar, as it's called,
Is often hairy, seldom bald;
It looks as if it never shaves;
When as it walks, it walks in waves;
And from the cradle to the chrysalis
It's utterly speechless, songless, whistleless.

THE TOUCAN

The toucan's profile is prognathous,
Its person is a thing of bathos.
If even I can tell a toucan
I'm reasonably sure that you can.

THE ASP

Whenever I behold an asp
I can't suppress a startled gasp.
I do not charge the asp with matricide,
But what about his Cleopatricide?

LISTEN TO THE LINOTYPE

In these days when we are living on the rim of a crater
I like the *New York Herald Tribune*, a paper that gets around to
      printing everything sooner or later.
Where else could I on October 2nd, 1947, have read or head
That in 1929 the mockingbird was chosen by the Mississippi
      Federation of Women's Clubs to be Mississippi State bird?
Since this fact had seemingly lain dormant for seventeen years
      before receiving mention
I naturally wondered if it had ever been brought to the
      mockingbird's attention.
I was relieved to learn from a venerable Maryland mockingbird of
      my acquaintance that in 1930 a notification ceremony was
      held in Jackson,
Attended by hordes of citizens, running the gamut from white to
      Protestant and Anglo-Saxon.
The mockingbirds stated that the signal honor was far signaler than
      any they had anticipated,
They had never dreamed of being Missississipated,
And then they scattered around a little suet and feed.
And voted the Mississippi Federation of Women's Clubs as the
      Federation of Women's Clubs most likely to succeed.
In gratitude for this information I showed my feathered friend an
      item from the same paper stating that the Tiber River, in
      Italy, is 253 miles long,
And he agreed with me when I said I wouldn't sell my subscription
      for a song.

DRAGONS ARE TOO SELDOM

To actually see an actual marine monster
Is one of the things that do before I die I wonster.
Should you ask me if I desire to meet the bashful inhabitant of Loch
      Ness,
I could only say yes.
Often my eye with moisture dims
When I think that it has never been my good fortune to gaze on one
      of Nature's whims.
Far from ever having seen a Gorgon
I haven't even seen the midget that sat in the lap of Mr. Morgan.
Indeed it is my further ill fortune or mishap
That far from having seen the midget that sat in it I have never even
      seen Mr. Morgan's lap.
Indeed I never much thought about Mr. Morgan's having a lap
      because just the way you go into churches and notice the
      stained glass more than the apses
When you think about multi-millionaires you don't think about their
      laps as much as their lapses;
But it seems that they do have laps which is one human touch that
      brings them a little closer to me and you,
And maybe they even go so far as to sometimes have hiccups too.
But regular monsters like sea serpents don't have laps or hiccups or
      any other characteristic that is human,
And I would rather see a second-rate monster such as a mermaid
      than a first-rate genius such as John Bunyan or Schiaparelli
      or Schubert or Schumann;
Yes, I would rather see one of the sirens
Than two Lord Byrons,
And if I knew that when I got there I could see Cyclops or Scylla
      and Charybdis or Pegasus
I would willingly walk on my hands from here to Dallas, Texas,
Because I don't mean to be satirical,

But where there's a monster there's a miracle,
And after a thorough study of current affairs, I have concluded with
      regret
That the world can profitably use all the miracles it can get,
And I think life would be a lot less demoralizing,
If instead of sitting around in front of the radio listening to torture
      singers sing torture songs we sat around listening to the
      Lorelei loreleising.

THE WASP

The wasp and all his numerous family
I look upon as a major calamily.
He throws open his nest with prodigality,
But I distrust his waspitality.

THE EEL

I don't mind eels
Except as meals.

THE LION

Oh, weep for Mr. and Mrs. Bryan!
He was eaten by a lion;
Following which, the lion's lioness
Up and swallowed Bryan's Bryaness.

THE SQUIRREL

A squirrel to some is a squirrel,
To others, a squirrel's a squirl.
Since freedom of speech is the birthright of each,
I can only this fable unfurl:
A virile young squirrel named Cyril,
In an argument over a girl,
Was lambasted from here to the Tyrol
By a churl of a squirl named Earl.

THE GUPPY

Whales have calves,
Cats have kittens,
Bears have cubs,
Bats have bittens.
Swans have cygnets,
Seals have puppies,
But guppies just have little guppies.

CREEPS AND CRAWLS

The insect world appealed to Fabre.
I find the insect world macabre.
In every hill of ants I see
A governed glimpse of what shall be,
And sense in every web contriver
Man's predecessor and survivor.
Someday, perhaps, my citronella
Will rank with Chamberlain's umbrella.

THE PORPOISE

I kind of like the playful porpoise,
A healthy mind in a healthy corpus.
He and his cousin, the playful dolphin,
Why they like swimmin like I like golphin.

THE JELLYFISH

Who wants my jellyfish?
I'm not sellyfish!

WHO CALLED THAT ROBIN
A PICCOLO PLAYER?

ROBINS GETTING LAZY.—Robins, now usually half tame and preferring
suburban to forest life, have become stupid and lazy in many cases.
—NEW YORK DAILY MIRROR

Hark hark the lark, no it is not a lark, it is a robin singing like a
      lark,
He is in disguise because he is now the target of a newspaper
      crusade like dirty books and vivisection and the man-eating
      shark.
He has been termed lethargic and fat,
It is said of him that he would rather live in Greenwich or Great
      Neck than in Medicine Hat,
It is rumored that at the Garden Club his wife once met an author,
And that he himself prefers a California Colonial bungalow to the
      tepee of Hiawatha,
And wears nylon instead of buckskin hosen,
And buys his worms at a super-market, cellophane-wrapped, and
      frozen.
In fact, the implication couldn't be clearer
That he is the spit and image of a reader of the *Mirror*.
Well for heaven's sake, how far can this scurrilous name-calling
      degenerate?
They are now attempting to besmirch a bird that I venerate.
His breast may be red, that is true,
But his heart is red, white and blue;
And as for being lazy, I know one robin that held down two jobs at
      once just so his younger brother (their parents had passed
      away uninsured) could get to be a transport pilot,
But if you mentioned it he was modest as a buttercup or vilot,
And the only reason he himself wasn't making those selfsame
      flights,
He had a bad head for heights.

If these editorial scandalmongers have to mong scandal about birds,
    let them leave the robin alone and turn their attention to the
    pelican;
It has an Oriental background and a triangular horny excrescence
    developed on the male's bill in the breeding season which
    later falls off without leaving trace of its existence, which for
    my money is suspicious and un-Amelican.

THE PURIST

I give you now Professor Twist,
A conscientious scientist.
Trustees exlaimed, "He never bungles!"
And sent him off to distant jungles.
Camped on a tropic riverside,
One day he missed his loving bride.
She had, the guide informed him later,
Been eaten by an alligator.
Professor Twist could not but smile.
"You mean," he said, "a crocodile."

THE PORCUPINE

Any hound a porcupine nudges
Can't be blamed for harboring grudges.
I know one hound that laughed all winter
At a porcupine that sat on a splinter.

THE PHOENIX

Deep in the study
Of eugenics
We find that fabled
Fowl, the Phoenix.
The wisest bird
As ever was,
Rejecting other
Mas and Pas,
It lays one egg,
Not ten or twelve,
And when it's hatched it,
Out pops itself.

THE DUCK

Behold the duck.
It does not cluck.
A cluck it lacks.
It quacks.
It is specially fond
Of a puddle or pond.
When it dines or sups,
It bottoms ups.

THE WAPITI

There goes the Wapiti,
Hippety-hoppity!

TWO DOGS HAVE I

For years we've had a little dog,
Last year we acquired a big dog;
He wasn't big when we got him,
He was littler than the dog we had.
We thought our little dog would love him,
Would help him to become a trig dog,
But the new little dog got bigger,
And the old little dog got mad.

Now the big dog loves the little dog,
But the little dog hates the big dog.
The little dog is eleven years old,
And the big dog only one;
The little dog calls him *Schweinhund*,
The little dog calls him Pig-dog,
She grumbles broken curses
As she dreams in the August sun.

The big dog's teeth are terrible,
But he wouldn't bite the little dog;
The little dog wants to grind his bones,
But the little dog has no teeth;
The big dog is acrobatic,
The little dog is a brittle dog;
She leaps to grip his jugular,
And passes underneath.

The big dog clings to the little dog
Like glue and cement and mortar;
The little dog is his own true love;
But the big dog is to her
Like a scarlet rag to a Longhorn,
Or a suitcase to a porter;
The day he sat on the hornet
I distinctly heard her purr.

Well, how can you blame the little dog,
Who was once the household darling?
He romps like a young Adonis,
She droops like an old mustache;
No wonder she steals his corner,
No wonder she comes out snarling,
No wonder she calls him *Cochon*
And even *Espèce de vache*.

Yet once I wanted a sandwich,
Either caviar or cucumber,
When the sun had not yet risen
And the moon had not yet sank;
As I tiptoed through the hallway
The big dog lay in slumber,
And the little dog slept by the big dog,
And her head was on his flank.

THE TURKEY

There is nothing more perky
Than a masculine turkey.
When he struts he struts
With no ifs or buts.
When his face is apoplectic
His harem grows hectic,
And when he gobbles
Their universe wobbles.

THE SHARK

How many Scientists have written
The shark is gentle as a kitten!
Yet this I know about the shark:
His bite is worser than his bark.

THE OCTOPUS

Tell me, O Octopus, I begs,
Is those things arms, or is they legs?
I marvel at thee, Octopus;
If I were thou, I'd call me Us.

THE KANGAROO

O Kangaroo, O Kangaroo,
Be grateful that you're in the zoo,
And not transmuted by a boomerang
To zestful tangy Kangaroo meringue.

TWO AND ONE ARE A PROBLEM

Dear Miss Dix, I am a young man of half-past thirty-seven.

My friends say I am not unattractive, though to be kind and true is
    what I have always striven.

I am open-minded about beverages so long as they are grape, brandy
    or malt,

And I am generous to practically any fault.

Well Miss Dix not to beat around the bush, there is a certain
    someone who thinks I am pretty nice,

And I turn to you for advice.

You see, it started when I was away on the road

And returned to find a pair of lovebirds had taken up their residence
    in my abode.

Well I am not crazy about lovebirds, but I must say they looked very
    sweet in their gilded cage,

And their friendship had reached an advanced stage,

And I had just forgiven her who of the feathered fiancés was the
    donor of

When the children caught a lost lovebird in the yard that we
    couldn't locate the owner of.

So then we had three, and it was no time for flippancy,

Because everybody knows that a lovebird without its own lovebird to
    love will pine way and die of the discrepancy,

So we bought a fourth lovebird for the third lovebird and they sat
    around very cozily beak to beak

And then the third lovebird that we had provided the fourth lovebird
    for to keep it from dying died at the end of the week,

So we were left with an odd lovebird and it was no time for
    flippancy,

Because a lovebird without its own lovebird to love will pine away
    and die of the discrepancy,

So we had to buy a fifth lovebird to console the fourth lovebird that
    we had bought to keep the third lovebird contented,

And now the fourth lovebird has lost its appetite, and Miss Dix, I am
       going demented.
I don't want to break any hearts, but I got to know where I'm at;
Must I keep on buying lovebirds, Miss Dix, or do you think it would
       be all right to buy a cat?

THE OYSTER

The oyster's a confusing suitor;
It's masc., and fem., and even neuter.
At times it wonders, may what come,
Am I husband, wife, or chum.

THE TERMITE

Some primal termite knocked on wood
And tasted it, and found it good,
And that is why your Cousin May
Fell through the parlor floor today.

THE PANTHER

The panther is like a leopard,
Except it hasn't been peppered.
Should you behold a panther crouch,
Prepare to say Ouch.
Better yet, if called by a panther,
Don't anther.

THE RHINOCEROS

The rhino is a homely beast,
For human eyes he's not a feast.
Farewell, farewell, you old rhinoceros,
I'll stare at something less prepoceros.

THE KITTEN

The trouble with a kitten is
THAT
Eventually it becomes a
CAT.

THE CALF

Pray, butcher, spare yon tender calf!
Accept my plea on his behalf;
He's but a babe, too young by far
To perish in the abattoir.
Oh, cruel butcher, let him feed
And gambol on the verdant mead;
Let clover tops and grassy banks
Fill out those childish ribs and flanks.
Then may we, at some future meal,
Pitch into beef, instead of veal.

THE FIREFLY

The firefly's flame
Is something for which science has no name.
I can think of nothing eerier
Than flying around with an unidentified glow on a person's
        posteerier.

THE GRACKLE

The grackle's voice is less than mellow,
His heart is black, his eye is yellow,
He bullies more attractive birds
With hoodlum deeds and vulgar words,
And should a human interfere,
Attacks that human in the rear.
I cannot help but deem the grackle
An ornithological debacle.

THE TURTLE

The turtle lives 'twixt plated decks
Which practically conceal its sex.
I think it clever of the turtle
In such a fix to be so fertile.

THE COW

The cow is of the bovine ilk;
One end is moo, the other, milk.

THE FISH

The fish, when he's exposed to air,
Displays no trace of *savoir-faire*,
But in the sea regains his balance
And exploits all his manly talents.
The chastest of the vertebrates,
He never even sees his mates,
But when they're finished, he appears
And O.K.'s all their bright ideas.

BUGS

Some insects feed on rosebuds,
And others feed on carrion.
Between them they devour the earth.
Bugs are totalitarian.

THE FLY

God in His wisdom made the fly
And then forgot to tell us why.

MR. BURGESS, MEET MR. BARMECIDE

Sometimes I play a game that is of interest only to me:
I try to think of the character in fiction who I would rather not be.
Sometimes, while my ideas I seek to adjust,
I would rather not be Lear, or Tess, or the hero of *A Handful of Dust*,
But eventually one incontrovertible conclusion emerges,
I would most of all rather not be Yowler the Bobcat in the Nature
stories of Thornton W. Burgess.
What with one generation and another, I have long been immersed
in Nature stories up to my ears,
And as far as I know, unless someone pilfered an installment to
wipe out an ashtray with, Yowler hasn't had a bite to eat in
twenty years.
Just as he has Johnny Chuck set up neat as you please,
Why, Johnny Chuck is tipped off by a Merry Little Breeze.
Just as he has a clean shot at Jumper the Hare, who would do his
system more good than a bucket of viosterol,
The same Merry Little Breeze tickles Jumper's sensitive nostril.
Currently, Yowler has his eye on the mouth-watering twins of Mrs.
Lightfoot, an addlepated deer,
But he might just as well dehydrate his mouth and go home; that
Merry Little Breeze is frolicking near.
Now the author pauses to draw a character sketch of this frustrated
carnivorous rover;
And writes, "Fortunately for him he had long ago learned to be
patient," which to my mind is stating the case under rather
than over.
Patient, indeed!
I cry with Cassius, "Upon what meat doth this our Yowler feed?"

THE GANDER

Be careful not to cross the gander,
A bird composed of beak and dander.
His heart is filled with prideful hate
Of all the world except his mate,
And if the neighbors do not err
He's overfond of beating her.
Is she happy? What's the use
Of trying to psychoanalyze a goose?

THE SEA-GULL

Hark to the whimper of the sea-gull;
He weeps because he's not an ea-gull.
Suppose you were, you silly sea-gull,
Could you explain it to your she-gull?

THE ROOSTER

The rooster has a soul more bellicose
Than all your Ludendorffs and Jellicoes.
His step is prouder than Davy Crockett's,
As he swaggers by with his hands in his pockets.

I HAPPEN TO KNOW

Hark to the locusts in their shrill armadas.
Locusts aren't locusts. Locusts are cicadas.

To seals in circuses I travel on bee lines.
Seals aren't seals. Seals are sea lions.

I'm a buffalo hunter. Want to see my license?
Buffaloes aren't buffaloes. Buffaloes are bisons.

I'm too old to be pedantically hocus-pocused.
I'll stand on the buffalo, the seal and the locust.

THE CAMEL

The camel has a single hump;
The dromedary, two;
Or else the other way around.
I'm never sure. Are you?

THE CANARY

The song of canaries
Never varies,
And when they're moulting
They're pretty revolting.

BARMAIDS ARE DIVINER THAN MERMAIDS

Fish are very good at swimming,
And the ocean with them is brimming.
They stay under water all year round,
And they never get drowned,
And they have a gift more precious than gold,
Which is that they never get cold.
No, they may not be as tasty as venison or mooseflesh,
But they never get gooseflesh.
They have been in the ocean since they were roe,
So they don't have to creep into it toe by toe,
And also they stay in it permanently, which must be a source of
      great satisfaction,
Because they don't have to run dripping and shivering up and down
      the beach waiting vainly for a healthy reaction
Indeed when I think how uncomplicated the ocean is for fish my
      thoughts grow jealous and scathing,
Because when fish bump into another fish it doesn't wring from them
      a cry of Faugh! and ruin their day's bathing.
No, if it's a bigger fish than they are, they turn around and beat it,
And if it's littler, they eat it.
Some fish are striped and some are speckled,
But none of them ever heard of ultra-violet rays and felt it necessary
      to lie around getting sand in their eyes and freckled.
Oh, would it not be wondrous to be a fish? No, it would not be
      wondrous,
Because we unmarine humans are at the top of the animal kingdom
      and it would be very undignified to change places with
      anything under us.

THE SMELT

Oh, why does man pursue the smelt?
It has no valuable pelt,
It boasts of no escutcheon royal,
It yields no ivory or oil,
Its life is dull, its death is tame,
A fish as humble as its name.
Yet—take this salmon somewhere else,
And bring me half a dozen smelts.

THE LAMA

The one-l lama,
He's a priest.
The two-l llama,
He's a beast.
And I will bet
A silk pajama
There isn't any
Three-l lllama.*

*The author's attention has been called to a type of conflagration known as the three-alarmer. Pooh.

THE SKINK

Let us do justice to the skink
Who isn't what so many think.
On consultation with a wizard
I find the skink a kind of lizard.
Since he is not a printer's whim,
Don't sniff and back away from him,
Or you may be adjudged too drunk
To tell a lizard from a skunk.

GLOSSINA MORSITANS, OR, THE TSETSE

A *glossina morsitans* bit rich Aunt Betsy.
Tsk tsk, tsetse.

THE RABBITS

Here's a verse about rabbits
That doesn't mention their habits.

THE PIG

The pig, if I am not mistaken,
Supplies us sausage, ham, and bacon.
Let others say his heart is big—
I call it stupid of the pig.

THE COBRA

This creature fills its mouth with venum
And walks upon its duodenum.
He who attempts to tease the cobra
Is soon a sadder he, and sobra.

6

THE ODDEST ANIMAL OF ALL
(GUESS WHO?)

"My fellow man I do not care for
I often ask me, what's he there for?"

WILL YOU HAVE YOUR TEDIUM
RARE OR MEDIUM?

Two things I have never understood: first, the difference between a
 Czar and a Tsar,
And second, why some people who should be bores aren't, and
 others, who shouldn't be, are.
I know a man who isn't sure whether bridge is played with a puck or
 a ball,
And he hasn't read a book since he bogged down on a polysyllable
 in the second chapter of *The Rover Boys at Putnam Hall.*
His most thrilling exploit was when he recovered a souvenir of the
 World's Fair that had been sent out with the trash,
And the only opinion he has ever formed by himself is that he looks
 better without a mustache.
Intellectually speaking, he has neither ears to hear with nor eyes to
 see with,
Yet he is pleasing to be with.
I know another man who is an expert on everything from witchcraft
 and demonology to the Elizabethan drama,
And he has spent a week end with the Dalai Lama,
And substituted for a mongoose in a fight with a cobra, and
 performed a successful underwater appendectomy,
And I cannot tell you how tediously his reminiscences affect me.
I myself am fortunate in that I have many interesting thoughts which
 I express in terms that make them come alive,
And I certainly would entertain my friends if they always didn't
 have to leave just when I arrive.

IF A BODER MEET A BODER, NEED A BODER CRY? YES.

I haven't much faith in bodings; I think that all bodings are daft
    bodings.
Forebodings are bad enough, but deliver me from aftbodings.
Aftbodings are what too many of us suffer from subsequent to
    making decisions even of the most inconsequential and
    niggling.
Aftbodings prevent people in restaurants from enjoying their
    haunch of venison, because they keep wondering if they
    shouldn't have ordered the roast crackling suckling pigling.
Aftbodings are what women are constantly up to their midriffs amid,
Because they are always afraid that the hats or dresses they didn't
    buy are more becoming than the ones they did.
Aftbodings trouble the young executive who has opted for a martini
    instead of a bloody mary, and plague the rascally artist who
    too late feels that he should have forged that Gainsborough
    instead of this Romney.
Aftbodings are the major cause of insomny.
Consider the lines "Of all sad words . . . the saddest are these: 'It
    might have been!'" whittled by J. G. Whittier;
As an example of aftboding, what could be prettier?
Indeed, I deem this an example of aftboding *in excelsis*,
Because J. G. Whittier wasn't even boding after his own decision
    but somebody else's.
I myself am more and more inclined to agree with Omar and with
    Satchel Paige as I grow older:
Don't try to rewrite what the moving finger has writ, and don't ever
    look over your shoulder.

AND SO MANHATTAN BECAME AN ISLE OF JOY

I do not know the name of the last chief of the Manhattan Indians, to
     me he is anonymous,
I suppose he had a name somewhere between the Powhatanish and
     the Sitting Bullish or the Geronimous.
I am sure, however, that his life followed the familiar pattern,
And that after three consecutive summers in which he had not been
     able to get out of town he was thoroughly sick of Manhattan.
He said that he was not just suffering from the nostalgia that
     senescence often brings,
But that people didn't use to go around digging up the trails to
     locate lost or hidden springs;
People, he said, to whom digging was undoubtedly some form of
     drug,
Because as soon as they filled in a hole they apologized and started
     digging again just where they had previously dug.
He said that the spreading tepees had crowded out the beavers and
     mooses,
And that he didn't feel safe on the trails after dark because of the
     delinquent papooses.
Manhattan, he said, was going to the bowwows,
The average brave and squaw simply couldn't afford the ridiculous
     number of scalps demanded for admission to any of the ten
     top powwows.
He said that although by the medicine man air pollution was strictly
     forbidden,
Yet the continuous fall of ashes from illegal smoke signals left his
     lungs feeling like the tribal refuse dump, or midden.
To his untutored mind, he said, life in Manhattan was so unpleasant
     that he didn't care to continue it,
So he sold the place for twenty-four dollars to Peter Minuit.
Do you know what he said when he found he had been
     hornswoggled? I will tell you what he said:
Boy, is my face red!

HOW TO TELL A QUAIL FROM A PARTRIDGE

You all know the story of the insomniac who got into such a state
Because the man upstairs dropped one shoe on the floor at eleven
        o'clock and the unhappy insomniac sat up until breakfast
        time waiting for him to drop the mate.
Well, here I lie in the interval between the beginning of day and the
        end of night,
Waiting for a Bob White to finish saying Bob White,
And much as I should like to be one who prayeth best because he
        loveth best all things both great and small,
I am afraid my feeling about Bob Whites will cause my ranking to be
        reduced considerably below that of St. Francis and St. Paul,
Which seems a shame, because my affection would remain
        undiminished
If he'd only say Bob White right out and get it finished.
But this particular Bob White just says Bob.
And then goes off on some other job,
And there are you in your resentful plight,
Waiting around for him to come back and say White.
Now nobody wants to be a slavedriver or a Cossack or a Hessian,
But you would think it possible to get through a simple sentence
        like Bob White in one session.
If he had to cope with some complicated speech like Cuckoo,
        pu-wee, to-witta-woo, jug-jug,
Why there'd be some excuse for remembering in the middle of it
        that he had to go see a man about a bug.
You could possibly sympathize with him, you think,
For hesitating over something silly like Spink spank spink;
And yes, you say to yourself as you toss on your sleepless pillow,
No self-respecting bird could be expected not to break down halfway
        through such a humiliating speech as willow tit-willow
        tit-willow,
But this isn't at all the same.
What are you going to do with a bird that can't even remember its
        own name?

If you were the King of Italy and you asked a man his name and he
    said Benito and then came back half an hour later and added
    Mussolini,
Would you ask him please to go ahead and form a Fascist State or
    would you tell him to tell it to Sweeney?
Well, I hope these bitter words of mine will have some effect in
    inducing Bob Whites to memorize their parts with all their
    might,
Or at least that from now on they'll go out only in couples, one to
    remember to say Bob and the other to remember to say
    White.

HIGH, LOW THE COMEDY: A WINTER'S TALE

Ice from the leaking hill glints on the terrace below.
My sunflower seed speckles the crusty snow.
High-perched on the white-topped wall, cardinal aflame,
Like one of Braddock's redcoats, easy game,
Come-kill-me target for all his absurd disguise,
Sun-fielder's sooty smudge around defensive eyes.
Vulnerable is cautious; timid, severe;
He orders mate to alight, prove the coast clear.
Hungry he watches, first pecks no lurking peril reveal.
Down he flutters, drives her off, approaches his meal.
Behind frozen azalea cat crouches, twitches,
Pupil and teacher of a hundred witches,
Here's insolence and ancient arrogance; he's sleek
With confidence, fierce whiskers boasting from each cheek.
Low-bellied he tenses muscles, springs in beauty hateful.
Balefire he fears not, knows not ice to footing fateful.
Cardinal flies away, saved by skidding cat-fall.
I shudder, as watching Lucifer do a pratfall.

THREE LITTLE MAIDS FROM SCHOOL

Here is the curious history of three adventurous ladies, each of
      whom was named Françoise.
They all had mastered the art of mistress-ship under the tutelage of
      their ambitious mammas.
They showed themselves eager students,
And at an early age could distinguish prudishness from prudence.
Like heliotropes their faces turned towards the Sun King, Louis
      Quatorze,
Who they thought was entitled to a little relaxation between wars.
First to feel the glow was Françoise Louise de la Baume Le Blanc,
      Duchesse de la Vallière.
She relaxed Louis to the extent of four children, none of whom got to
      be his heir,
And after the appearance at court of Françoise Athénaïs Rochechouart,
      Marquise de Montespan, Louis did not give her a fifth look,
So she retired to a convent and wrote a religious book.
Then Françoise de Montespan relaxed Louis to the extent of several
      more children, but unwisely entrusted their education to
      Françoise d'Aubigné, Marquise de Maintenon, formerly the
      impoverished widow Scarron,
For whom unwittingly she thus drew from the fire the jackpot
      marrons,
Because Françoise de Maintenon became queen and Françoise de
      Montespan retired to a convent which she herself had
      foresightedly founded,
And she didn't write a book but she started a rumor which proved
      that she could still fight even though permanently grounded.
There may have been some truth in it, but I myself think she went a
      bit too far;
She whispered that Mme. de Maintenon owed her success to the fact
      that her real name was Mme. de Pas-Maintenant-Louis-Mais-
      Plus-Tard.

THE SLIPSHOD SCHOLAR GETS AROUND TO GREECE

I sing of the ancient Greeks.

They had magnificent physiques.

They were also intellectual Titans,

And wore chlamyses and chitons.

Their minds were serene unless too much success induced hubris,

In which case the gods rendered them lugubrous.

They were preeminent in art and science,

And in their pottery they anticipated faïence.

Indeed they were our precursors in many ways; just think how their
man Homer did Milton and Tennyson precurse:

Because he could not think of a rhyme for orange he invented blank
verse.

Even the Stock Exchange reflects their far-off light;

Had the Greeks not bequeathed us their language, brokers would be
trading not in AT&T but in American Distantsound &
Distantwrite.

If the Greeks had never existed who would have been the most annoyed?

Freud.

Without their drama where would he have uncovered all those
complexes,

His pop-plexes and mom-plexes?

The path of Oedipus into the annals of analysis was straight,
Electra's rather more tortuous.

I shall try to map it for you though I may evoke offended cries of
De mortuis.

Electra persuaded her brother, Orestes, to murder their mother,
Clytemnestra, who had persuaded her lover, Aegisthus, to
murder Agamemnon, their father, whom Electra loved like
billy-o,

And Orestes did in fact murder Clytemnestra and her lover with
classic punctilio.

Thus was Agamemnon avenged and his adulterous slayers eradicated.

The Greek words for Electra were Accessory Before the Fact, but
Dr. Freud and I think of her simply as a daughter who was
over-daddycated.

LET ME BUY THIS ONE

Solomon said, Stay me with apples for I am sick with l'amour,
But I say, Comfort me with flagons, for I am sick with rich people
   talking and acting poor.
I have never yet met even a minor Croesus
Whose pocketbook didn't have paresis;
I have never yet been out with a tycoon for an evening in
   Manhattan's glamorous canyons
When the evening's bills weren't paid by the tycoon's impoverished
   but proud companions.
There is one fact of life that no unwealthy child can learn too soon,
Which is that no tycoon ever spends money except on another tycoon.
Rich people are people that you owe something to and take out to
   dinner and the theater and dancing and all the other
   expensive things there are because you know they are
   accustomed to the best and as a result you spend the
   following month on your uppers,
And it is a big evening to you but just another evening to them and
   they return the hospitality by saying that someday you must
   drop in to one of their cold Sunday suppers.
Rich people are also people who spend most of their time
   complaining about the income tax as one of life's greatest and
   most intolerable crosses,
And eventually you find that they haven't even paid any income tax
   since 1929 because their income has shrunk to fifty thousand
   dollars a year and everything has been charged off to losses,
And your own income isn't income at all, it is salary, and stops
   coming in as soon as you stop laboring mentally and manually,
But you have been writing out checks for the Government annually,
So the tax situation is just the same as the entertainment situation
   because the poor take their little pittance
And pay for the rich's admittance
Because it is a great truth that as soon as people have enough coupons
   in the safe-deposit vault or in the cookie jar on the shelf,
Why they don't have to pay anything themself,
No, they can and do just take all their coins and store them,

And other people beg to pay for everything for them,

And they certainly are allowed to,

Because to accept favors is the main thing that the poor are and the
      rich aren't too proud to,

So let us counterattack with sangfroid and phlegm,

And I propose a Twenty-second Amendment to the Constitution
      providing that the rich must spend as much money on us poor
      as we do on them.

THE COLLECTOR

I met a traveler from an antique show,
His pockets empty, but his eyes aglow.
Upon his back, and now his very own,
He bore two vast and trunkless legs of stone.
Amid the torrent of collector's jargon
I gathered he had found himself a bargain,
A permanent conversation piece post-prandial,
Certified genuine early Ozymandial,
And when I asked him how he could be sure,
He showed me P. B. Shelley's signature.

HE DIDN'T DARE LOOK
OR
THE PUZZLING UNIQUENESS
OF MR. SALTBODY'S MEEKNESS

I speak of Standish Saltbody, Harvard '24, a loyal Cantabridgin,
A timid man, a bashful man, whose makeup contained of arrogance
       not a modicum or a smidgin.
You would travel far to discover a character more retiring, more
       innately diffident,
His overdeveloped sense of self-unimportance was pathetically evident.
Yet in him a kindred soul is what Gailileo's persecutors might well
       have found
Because his very timidity led him to fear that Standish Saltbody was
       what the universe revolved around.
Small wonder that he was continually discomfited by a runaway pulse;
He was convinced that his most trivial act could generate the most
       appalling results.
He had not once attended the Yale game since undergoing
       graduation and valedictory
Because he was sure that his presence alone, although unsuspected
       by his team, was sufficient to guarantee an Eli victory.
Although Willie Mays was his hero, his very ideal, he would never
       watch him on TV
Because he was sure that although Willie couldn't know that Standish
       Saltbody was watching him from a distance of 2500 miles,
       that one fact would hoodoo him into looking at strike three.
His sense of responsibility and guilt reached a point at which from
       any positive move he was likely to refrain;
He was certain that any candidate he voted for would be defeated,
       just as his washing the car would bring on a torrential rain.
Thus we see that this meekest and most self-depreciative of God's
       creatures paradoxically felt himself to be omnipotent,
Since of any contretemps in his immediate world his words or deeds
       were obviously the precipitant;
And indeed, if of the cosmos he was not the hub,
How is it that he could make the telephone ring merely by settling
       down in the tub?

JUST HOLMES AND ME, AND
MNEMOSYNE MAKES THREE

I am told that my character has as many layers as an onyx,
But one layer is missing, which is an aptitude for mnemonics.
Mnemosyne (daughter of Uranus and Gaea, date of birth destroyed
    in fire at Alexandria) was the goddess of memory,
So she never said "Hail, Amory!" to a minor deity whose name was
    Emory.
She became a mother by Zeus—as what nubile Grecian female
    didn't?—and the children turned out to be the Muses, who
    later on helped Homer with their reminiscences of Achilles
    and Hector,
And she needed her innate talent, because she had nine names to
    remember when she summoned them to their ambrosia and
    nectar.
Me, I can never be elected to any office, because I am nearsighted
    and frequently forget the face of an acquaintance, and, worse,
    I invariably forget the name,
So I am solaced by the discovery that my lifelong hero Mr. Sherlock
    Holmes was once the same.
In "The Adventure of the Speckled Band" (*The Complete Sherlock
    Holmes*, Doubleday, 1953), the proposed victim of a fiendish
    plot introduces herself on page 294 as Miss Helen Stoner,
    stepdaughter of Dr. Grimesby Roylott, of Stoke Moran,
An unpleasant man,
Yet on page 299 Holmes says to her, "Miss Roylott . . . you are
    screening your stepfather," a slip that Miss Stoner left
    uncorrected, either through tact or because her mind was
    upon her approaching wedding,
For she had recently become betrothed to Mr. Percy Armitage,
    second son of Mr. Armitage, of Crane Water, near Reading.
Well, whatever caused Holmes's error and Miss Stoner's overlooking
    it, I have this reflection to cheer me as I step from the
    mounting block to the saddle of my high-wheeled bike:
Great minds forget alike.

THE MIND OF PROFESSOR PRIMROSE

My story begins in the town of Cambridge, Mass.,
Home of the Harvard Business and Dental Schools,
And more or less the home of Harvard College.
Now, Harvard is a cultural institution,
Squandering many a dollar upon professors,
As a glance at a Harvard football team makes obvious;
Professors wise and prowling in search of wisdom,
And every mother's son of them absent-minded.
But the absentest mind belonged to Professor Primrose.
He had won a Nobel award and a Pulitzer Prize,
A Guggenheim and a leg on the Davis Cup,
But he couldn't remember to shave both sides of his face.
He discharged the dog and took the cook for an airing;
He frequently lit his hair and combed his cigar;
He set a trap for the baby and dandled the mice;
He wound up his key and opened the door with his watch;
He tipped his students and flunked the traffic policeman;
He fed the mosquitoes crumbs and slapped at the robins;
He always said his prayers when he entered the theater,
And left the church for a smoke between the acts;
He mixed the exterminator man a cocktail
And told his guests to go way, he had no bugs;
He rode the streets on a bicycle built for two,
And he never discovered he wasn't teaching at Yale.
At last one summer he kissed his crimson flannels
And packed his wife in camphor, and she complained.
She had always hated camphor, and she complained.
"My dear," she ordered, "these *contretemps* must cease;
You must bring this absent mind a little bit nearer;
You must tidy up that disorderly cerebellum;
You must write today and enroll in the Pelman Institute."
He embraced his pen and he took his wife in hand,
He wrinkled a stamp and thoughtfully licked his brow,
He wrote the letter and mailed it, and what do you know?

In a couple of days he disappeared from Cambridge.
"For heaven's sake, my husband has disappeared,"
Said Mrs. Primrose. "Now isn't that just like him?"
And she cut the meat and grocery orders in half,
And moved the chairs in the living room around,
And settled down to a little solid comfort.
She had a marvelous time for seven years,
At the end of which she took a train to Chicago.
She liked to go to Chicago once in a while
Because of a sister-in-law who lived in Cambridge.
Her eye was caught at Schenectady by the porter;
She noticed that he was brushing off a dime,
And trying to put the passenger in his pocket.
"Porter," she said, "aren't you Professor Primrose?
Aren't you my husband, the missing Professor Primrose?
And what did you learn at the Pelman Institute?"
"Good Lawd, Maria," the porter said, "good Lawd!
Did you say *Pelman*? Ah wrote to de *Pullman* folks!"

WAITING FOR THE BIRDIE

Some hate broccoli, some hate bacon,
I hate having my picture taken.
How can your family claim to love you
And then demand a picture of you?
The electric chair is a queasy chair,
But I know an equally comfortless pair;
One is the dentist's, my good sirs,
And the other is the photographer's.
Oh, the fly in all domestic ointments
Is affectionate people who make appointments
To have your teeth filled left and right,
Or your face reproduced in black and white.
You open the door and you enter the studio,
And you feel less cheerio than nudio.
The hard light shines like seventy suns,
And you know that your features are foolish ones.
The photographer says, Natural, please,
And you cross your knees and uncross your knees.
Like a duke in a high society chronicle
The camera glares at you through its monocle
And you feel ashamed of your best attire,
Your nose itches, your palms perspire,
Your muscles stiffen, and all the while
You smile and smile and smile and smile.
It's over; you weakly grope for the door;
It's not; the photographer wants one more.
And if this experience you survive,
Wait, just wait till the proofs arrive.
You look like a drawing by Thurber or Bab,
Or a gangster stretched on a marble stab.
And all your dear ones, including your wife,
Say There he is, that's him to the life!
Some hate broccoli, some hate bacon,
But I hate having my picture taken.

WHAT'S IN A NAME? HERE'S WHAT'S
IN A NAME
or
I WONDER WHAT BECAME OF JOHN AND MARY

In movies I prefer something unpretentious, like "Marty,"
But who wants an unpretentious party?
I always say a nice, pretentious party will do more for your ego than
    doctors or medicine;
I wish you could have been at the one I tossed recently to celebrate
    the payment of my bill from Con Edison.
There was Cary Middlecoff, Carey Latimer, Cary Grant, Gary
    Cooper, Gary Crosby, and, I think but I'm not quite sure,
Garry Moore.
Also Rocky Marciano, Rocky Graziano, Rocky Castellani, Rock
    Hudson, and, showing great endurance,
A man from Prudential Insurance.
I don't want to talk your ear off,
But I mustn't forget Kim Stanley, Kim Hunter, Kim Novak, and
    Akim Tamiroff;
An added entry
Was Speed Lamkin and Race Gentry;
And guess who crowded together hotly discussing Schopenhauer and
    Nietzsche—
Donna Atwood, Donna Reed, and Don Ameche!
And who up for the conga should line
But Julie Andrews, Julie Wilson, Julie Harris, Julie Haydon, Julie
    Adams, and Jule Styne!
It was such a pretentious party that all my vapors did disappear.
I also had Katie and Audrey just to prove that it can Hepburn here.

A NECESSARY DIRGE

Sometimes it's difficult, isn't it, not to grow grim and rancorous
Because man's fate is so counter-clockwise and cantankerous.
Look at all the noble projects that die a-borning,
Look how hard it is to get to sleep at night and then how hard it is to
     wake up in the morning!
How easy to be unselfish in the big things that never come up and
     how hard in the little things that come up daily and hourly,
     oh yes,
Such as what heroic pleasure to give up the last seat in a lifeboat to
     a mother and babe, and what an irritation to give some
     housewife your seat on the Lexington Avenue Express!
How easy for those who do not bulge
To not overindulge!
O universe perverse, why and whence your perverseness?
Why do you not teem with betterness instead of worseness?
Do you get your only enjoyment
Out of humanity's annoyment?
Because a point I would like to discuss
Is, why wouldn't it be just as easy for you to make things easy for
     us?
But no, you will not listen, expostulation is useless,
Home is the fisherman empty-handed, home is the hunter
     caribouless and mooseless.
Humanity must continue to follow the sun around
And accept the eternal run-around.
Well, and if that be the case, why come on humanity!
So long as it is our fate to be irked all our life let us just keep our
     heads up and take our irking with insouciant urbanity.

THE SOLITARY HUNTSMAN

The solitary huntsman
No coat of pink doth wear,
But midnight black from cap to spur
Upon his midnight mare.
He drones a tuneless jingle
In lieu of tally-ho,
"I'll catch a fox
And put him in a box
And never let him go."

The solitary huntsman,
He follows silent hounds,
No horn proclaims his joyless sport,
And never a hoofbeat sounds.
His hundred hounds, his thousands,
Their master's will they know;
To catch a fox
And put him in a box
And never let him go.

For all the fox's doubling
They track him to his den.
The chase may fill a morning,
Or threescore years and ten.
The huntsman never sated
Screaks to his saddlebow,
"I'll catch another fox
And put him in a box
And never let him go."

MS. FOUND UNDER A SERVIETTE
IN A LOVELY HOME

... Our outlook is totally different from that of our American cousins, who have never had an aristocracy. Americans relate all effort, all work, and all of life itself to the dollar. Their talk is of nothing but dollars. The English seldom sit happily chatting for hours on end about pounds.

—NANCY MITFORD in *Noblesse Oblige*

Dear Cousin Nancy:

You probably never heard of me or Cousin Beauregard or Cousin
    Yancey,

But since you're claiming kin all the way across the ocean, we figure
    you must be at least partwise Southern,

So we consider you not only our kith and kin but also our kithin'
    couthern.

I want to tell you, when Cousin Emmy Lou showed us your piece it
    stopped the conversation flat,

Because I had twenty dollars I wanted to talk about, and Cousin
    Beauregard had ten dollars he wanted to talk about, and
    Cousin Yancey didn't have any dollars at all, and he wanted
    to talk about that.

But Cousin Emmy Lou looked over her spectacles, which the
    common people call glasses,

And she offered us a dollar to stop talking about dollars and start
    talking about the English upper classes

Cousin Beauregard wanted to know why the English aristocracy was
    called English when most of their names were French to
    begin with,

And now anybody with an English name like Hobbs or Stobbs has to
    accumulate several million of those pounds they seldom chat
    about, to buy his way in with.

Cousin Yancey said he could understand that—the St. Aubyns beat
    the hell out of the Hobbses in 1066—but there was a more
    important point that he could not determine,

Which is why the really aristocratic English aristocrats have names
    that are translated from the German.

Cousin Emmy Lou is pretty aristocratic herself; in spite of her
      weakness for hog jowl and potlikker, she is noted for her
      highborn pale and wan flesh,
And where most people get gooseflesh she gets swan flesh,
And she said she thought you ought to know that she had been over
      the royal roster
And she had spotted at least one impostor.
She noticed that the Wicked Queen said 'Mirror, mirror on the wall"
      instead of "Looking glass, looking glass on the wall," which
      is perfectly true,
So the Wicked Queen exposed herself as not only wicked but
      definitely non-U.
After that, we all loosened our collars
And resumed our conversation about dollars.

ARTHUR

There was an old man of Calcutta,
Who coated his tonsils with butta,
Thus converting his snore
From a thunderous roar
To a soft, oleaginous mutta.

THE STRANGE CASE OF MR. WOOD'S
FRUSTRATION
or
A TEAM THAT WON'T BE BEATEN
BETTER STAY OFF THE FIELD

Once there was a man named Mr. Culpepper Wood
And for him the best was none too good.
Unfortunately, he never got to get the best;
While somebody else was walking off with it, he was still looking for
　　　it with the rest.
When he got his name on the cup,
It was always as runner-up.
Nobody than he was kithier and kinnier,
But he came from one of the second families of Virginia.
His character was without a smirch,
But it never got him further than the Second Presbyterian Church.
He was of high financial rank,
But his account landed in the Second National Bank.
He finally realized he hadn't made the grade
When he was knocked down by a repossessed scooter and the Boy
　　　Scouts administered Second Aid.
It was then that he allowed that he reckoned
That he was tired of being second.
He took an advanced course in baby talk at a progressive university,
After which he spent three days in the desert without even a mirage
　　　to sip, and cried triumphantly, "Now me firsty."

LINES FRAUGHT WITH NAUGHT BUT THOUGHT

If you thirst to know who said, "I think, therefore I am," your thirst I
 will quench;
It was René Descartes, only what he actually said was, "*Je pense,
 donc je suis*," because he was French.
He also said it in Latin, "*Cogito, ergo sum*,"
Just to show that he was a man of culture and not a tennis tramp or
 a cracker barrel philosophy bum.
Descartes was one of the few who think, therefore they are,
Because those who don't think, but are anyhow, outnumber them by
 far.
If of chaos we are on the brink
It is because so many people only think that they think.
In truth, of anything other than thinking they are fonder,
Because thought requires the time and effort to reflect, cogitate,
 contemplate, meditate, ruminate and ponder.
Their minds are exposed to events and ideas but they have never
 pondered or reflected on them
Any more than motion picture screens meditate on the images that
 are projected on them.
Hence, our universal confusion,
The result of the unreasoned, or jumped at, conclusion.
People who just think that they think, they secretly think that
 thinking is grim,
And they excuse themselves with signs reading THIMK, or, as
 Descartes would have said, PEMSEZ, and THINK OR THWIM.
Instead of thoughts, they act on hunches and inklings,
Which are not thoughts at all, only thinklings.
Can it be because we leave to the Russians such dull pursuits as
 thinking that the red star continues to twinkle so?
I thinkle so.

JACK DO-GOOD-FOR-NOTHING: A CURSORY
NURSERY TALE FOR TOT-BAITERS

Once there was a kindhearted lad named Jack Do-Good-for-Nothing,
     the only son of a poor widow whom creditors did importune,
So he set out in the world to make his fortune.
His mother's blessing and a crust of bread was his only stake,
And pretty soon he saw a frog that was about to be devoured by a
     snake.
And he rescued the frog and drove the snake away,
And the frog vowed gratitude to its dying day,
And a little later on in his walk,
Why, he saw a little red hen about to be carried off by a hawk,
And he rescued the little red hen and drove the hawk away,
And the little red hen vowed that whenever he was in trouble his
     kindness she would repay,
And he walked a few more country blocks,
And he saw a bunny rabbit about to be gobbled up by a fox,
And he rescued the bunny rabbit before the fox could fall on it,
And the bunny rabbit thanked Jack and told him any time he
     needed help, just to call on it,
And after all this rescuing, Jack was huffing and puffing,
And a little farther on the snake and the hawk and the fox jumped
     him, and out of him they beat the stuffing;
They even stole his crust of bread and each ate a third of it,
And the frog and the little red hen and the bunny rabbit said they
     were very sorry when they heard of it.
You see, Jack against a cardinal rule of conduct had been a
     transgressor:
Never befriend the oppressed unless you are prepared to take on the
     oppressor.

MR. BARCALOW'S BREAKDOWN

Once there was a man, and he was named Mr. Barcalow, to be exact,
And he prided himself on his tact,
And he said, One thing about an apple, it may have a worm in it,
    and one thing about a chimney, it may have soot in it,
But one thing about my mouth, I never put my foot in it.
Whenever he entered a community
He inquired of his host and hostess what topics he could discuss
    with impunity,
So no matter beside whom he was deposited,
Why, he could talk to them without disturbing any skeletons that
    should have been kept closeted,
But one dire day he went to visit some friends,
And he started asking tactful questions about untactful
    conversational trends,
And his host said that here was one place that Mr. Barcalow
    wouldn't need his tact,
Because taboos and skeletons were what everybody there lacked,
And his hostess said, That's right, but you'd better not mention
    bathrooms to Emily, who you will sit by at lunch,
Because her grandmother was scalded to death in a shower shortly
    after complaining that there was no kick in the punch,
And his host said, Oh yes, and steer away from education when you
    talk to the Senator,
Because somebody said his seventeen-year-old nephew would have
    to burn down the schoolhouse to get out of the third grade
    and his nephew overheard them and did burn down the
    schoolhouse, including the music teacher and the janitor,
And his hostess said, Oh yes, and if you talk about love and
    marriage to Mrs. Musker don't be surprised if her eye sort of
    wanders,
Because her daughter is the one who had the divorce suit with
    thirty-seven co-responders,
And Mr. Barcalow said, Well, can I talk about sports,

And his hostess said, Well maybe you'd better not because Louise's
      sister, the queer one, was asked to resign from the club
      because she went out to play moonlight tennis in shorts, and
      Mr. Barcalow said That's not so terrible is it, everybody wears
      shorts, and his hostess said, Yes, but she forgot the shorts.
So Mr. Barcalow said, The hell with you all, and went upstairs and
      packed,
And that was the last that was ever heard of Mr. Barcalow and his
      tact.

MAYBE YOU CAN'T TAKE IT WITH YOU, BUT LOOK WHAT HAPPENS WHEN YOU LEAVE IT BEHIND

As American towns and cities I wander through,
One landmark is constant everywhere I roam;
The house that the Banker built in nineteen-two,
Dim neon tells me is now a funeral home.

THE STRANGE CASE OF THE CAUTIOUS MOTORIST

Have you read the biography of Mr. Schwellenbach? You can miss it
　　if you try.
Mr. Schwellenbach didn't have much to live for, but he didn't want
　　to die.
Statistics of automobile fatalities filled his brain,
And he never drove over 25 miles an hour, and always, I regret to
　　say, in the left-hand lane.
Whenever he stopped for a red light he cut off the ignition, put on
　　the hand brake, locked all the doors, checked his license and
　　registration cards, and looked in the glove compartment to
　　see if he had mice,
So when the light turned green everybody behind him had to wait
　　while he de-moused the car, reassured himself that he was
　　driving legally, unlocked the doors, released the hand brake,
　　reignited the ignition, pressed the wrong button and turned
　　on Bing Crosby instead of the motor, and the light turned
　　from green to red to green thrice.
Every autumn with the rains
Mr. Schwellenbach bought a new pair of chains.
He kept a record of every lethal blowout in the Western Hemisphere
　　since 1921 in his files,
And he turned in his tires for new ones every 750 miles.
Well, he was driving on his new tires at 25 miles an hour in the
　　left-hand lane of a dual highway last week, was
　　Mr. Schwellenbach,
And a car coming the other way owned by a loan shark who had
　　bought his old tires cheap had a blowout and jumped the
　　dividing line and knocked him to hellenbach.

MR. BETTS'S MIND A KINGDOM IS

Do you know my friend Mr. Betts?
He claims he forgets.
When urged by Mrs. Betts to tell you about their trip to California
  he says he has no memory,
He is in a dilemma, he looks dilemmary.
He looks like a high-school music teacher substituting at the last
  minute for Iturbi,
And then he gives you a precise blow by blow, palm tree by palm
  tree, movie star by movie star account, starting at the Grand
  Central and finishing with an appreciation of the waitresses'
  rear elevation at the Brown Derby.
My friend Mr. Betts
Claims he forgets.
When asked by Mrs. Betts to tell you about that radio program that
  made her laugh, she thought she'd smother,
He says everything goes in one ear and out the other,
After which he takes the floor like Winston Churchill,
And re-creates the entire half hour from the first joke about the
  ungainly spinster who can't get a man to the final
  commerchill.
Do you know my friend Mr. Betts?
I wish I could remember as accurately as he forgets.

JUST KEEP QUIET AND NOBODY WILL NOTICE

There is one thing that ought to be taught in all the colleges,
Which is that people ought to be taught not to go around always
    making apologies.
I don't mean the kind of apologies people make when they run over
    you or borrow five dollars or step on your feet,
Because I think that kind is sort of sweet;
No, I object to one kind of apology alone,
Which is when people spend their time and yours apologizing for
    everything they own.
You go to their house for a meal,
And they apologize because the anchovies aren't caviar or the
    partridge is veal;
They apologize privately for the crudeness of the other guests,
And they apologize publicly for their wife's housekeeping or their
    husband's jests;
If they give you a book by Dickens they apologize because it isn't by
    Scott,
And if they take you to the theater, they apologize for the acting and
    the dialogue and the plot;
They contain more milk of human kindness than the most capacious
    dairy can,
But if you are from out of town they apologize for everything local
    and if you are a foreigner they apologize for everything
    American.
I dread these apologizers even as I am depicting them,
I shudder as I think of the hours that must be spent in contradicting
    them,
Because you are very rude if you let them emerge from an argument
    victorious,
And when they say something of theirs is awful, it is your duty to
    convince them politely that it is magnificent and glorious,
And what particularly bores *me* with them,
Is that half the time you have to politely contradict them when you
    rudely agree with them,

So I think there is one rule every host and hostess ought to keep
      with the comb and nail file and bicarbonate and aromatic
      spirits on a handy shelf,
Which is don't spoil the denouement by telling the guests everything
      is terrible, but let them have the thrill of finding it out for
      themself.

YES AND NO

Oh would I were a politician,
Or else a person with a mission.
Heavens, how happy I could be
If only I were sure of me.

How would I strut, could I believe
That, out of all the sons of Eve,
God had granted this former youth
A binding option on His truth.

One side of the moon we've seen alone;
The other she has never shown.
What dreamless sleep, what sound digestion,
Were it the same with every question!

Sometimes with secret pride I sigh
To think how tolerant am I;
Then wonder which is really mine:
Tolerance, or a rubber spine?

IF FUN IS FUN, ISN'T THAT ENOUGH?

Child, the temptation please resist
To deify the humorist.
Simply because we're stuck with solons
Whose minds resemble lazy colons,
Do not assume our current jesters
Are therefore Solomons and Nestors.
Because the editorial column
Is ponderously trite and solemn
Don't think the wisdom of the ages
Awaits you in the comic pages.
There is no proof that Plato's brain
Weighed less than that of Swift or Twain.
If funny men are sometimes right
It's second guessing, not second sight;
They apply their caustic common sense
After, and not before, events.
Since human nature's a *fait accompli*
They puncture it regularly and promptly.
Some are sophisticates, some earthy,
And none are totally trustworthy;
They'll sell their birthright every time
To make a point or turn a rhyme.
This motto, child, is my bequest:
There's many a false word spoken in jest.

LOVE ME BUT LEAVE MY DOG ALONE

Once there was a handsome man named Mr. Beamington and he was
      to good causes the most generous of donors,
And he was so popular with dogs that he couldn't understand why
      he was so unpopular with their owners.
He was bold as an eagle, a cock eagle, yet gentle as a dove, a hen-
      dove,
And the dog didn't live that he couldn't make a friend of.
If you had a brace of ferocious spaniels
Mr. Beamington would soon be romping with them through your
      annuals and peranniels.
He fondled schnauzers
With no scathe to his trousers.
At his voice the pit bull eschewed the manners of the bull pit,
And assumed those of the pulpit.
He could discuss Confucianism with a Pekingese,
And address the Boston terrier on Beacon Hill in purest Beaconese.
Yes, Mr. Beamington had a way with dogs, dogs simply adored him,
Yet their owners abhorred him,
Because he reckoned without the third law of Paracelsus,
Which clearly states that every dog-owner considers his dog a one-
      man dog, and its affection his own and nobody elsus.
So the only people who liked him were the owners of a Cairn,
Which frequently bit him, thus reassuring them that its heart was
      not hisn but theirn.

IS THERE AN OCULIST IN THE HOUSE?

How often I would that I were one of those homely philosophical old
     codgers
Like, say, Mr. Dooley or Will Rogers,
Because I could then homelily call people's attention to the fact that
     we didn't see eye to eye with the Italians so we had a war
     with them, after which, to put it succinkly
We and the Italians became as close as Goodson and Todman or
     Huntley and Brinkley,
And we didn't see eye to eye with the Germans and we had to either
     fight or bootlick,
So we fought, and now everything between us and the Germans is
     gemütlich,
And the Japanese didn't see eye to eye with us, so they fought us the
     soonest,
And today we and the Japanese are of companions the boonest.
Now at the daily boasts of "My retaliation can lick your retaliation"
     I am with apprehension stricken,
As one who watches two adolescent hot-rodders careening headlong
     toward each other, each determined to die rather than
     chicken.
Once again there is someone we don't see eye to eye with, and
     maybe I couldn't be dafter,
But I keep wondering if this time we couldn't settle our differences
     before a war instead of after.

POOR MR. STRAWBRIDGE

Once there was a man who lived by the ocean named Mr.
      Strawbridge,
And all he wanted was a drawbridge,
But when people asked him what kind
He couldn't make up his mind.
His fingernails he would bite and his thumbs he would twiddle
Trying to decide whether he wanted one that revolved on a pivot or
      one that went up in the middle,
So finally everybody went to Mr. Strawbridge
And asked him why he wanted a drawbridge.
And Mr. Strawbridge smiled a smile seraphic
And said he wanted it because he wanted to interfere with traffic.
He said it gave him great satisfaction
To sit on his veranda and watch the Atlantic Ocean in action
But he said sometimes on Sundays and holidays he couldn't see the
      Atlantic for the motorists,
And he said he'd rather see the former than the latter even though
      they were handsome and respectable Kiwanians and Lions
      and Rotarists,
And he said maybe he was a silly old goose,
But it always gave him a pain to see a line of automobiles
      practically hooked up together like freight cars on a long
      freight train, particularly when the freight train was ten miles
      long and you never seemed to get to the caboose,
And he said that doubtless all the gipsying was most romantic,
But he still preferred looking at the Atlantic
And he said he didn't see why people went out in one automobile
      between a lot of other automobiles, because they didn't get
      any air or scenery,
No, they just got a view of the license plate in front and a lot of
      annoyance and dust and gasolinery,
And therefore, said Mr. Strawbridge,
Everybody else would see just as much and I would see much more
      if they were all held up somewhere by an open drawbridge,

So all his friends said he was a genius,
And they gave him a lot of orchids and gardenius,
But they never gave him a drawbridge
And that is why I call him poor Mr. Strawbridge.

A CAUTION TO EVERYBODY

Consider the auk;
Becoming extinct because he forgot how to fly, and could only walk.
Consider man, who may well become extinct
Because be forgot how to walk and learned how to fly before he
     thinked.

IT'S SNUG TO BE SMUG

Oh, sometimes I wish I had the wings of an angel because then I
      could fly through the air with the greatest of ease,
And if I wanted to be somewhere else I could get there without
      spending any money on taxis or railroad tickets or tips or
      fees,
Yes, I could fly to Paris and do as a Parisian, or fly to Rome and do
      as a Roman,
But on the other hand wings would necessitate my sleeping on my
      abdomen,
So I don't really wish I had the wings of an angel, but sometimes I
      wish I had the sweet voice of a thrush,
And then if I sang an Indian Love Lyric why thousands of beautiful
      beauties would harken and quiver and blush,
And it would be a treat to hear my rendition of Sweet Alice Ben
      Bolt,
But on the other hand who would go to harken to anybody who was
      known to eat insects and moult?
So I don't really wish I had the sweet voice of a thrush, but
      sometimes I wish I had the courage of a lion,
And then I could look life in the eye with a will of iron,
And to a goose, or a burglar, or even a butler, I wouldn't hesitate to
      say Boo!
But on the other hand I might encounter a goose or a burglar or a
      butler who had the courage of a lion too,
So I don't really wish I had the courage of a lion but sometimes I
      wish I had the innocence of a lamb,
And then I would never wake up crying Fie on me! and Damn!
But on the other hand innocence is a security on which it is hard to
      borrow,
Because all it means is that either you get eaten by a wolf today or
      else the shepherd saves you from the wolf so he can sell you
      to the butcher tomorrow,
So I do not really wish I had the innocence of a lamb,
I guess I'll stay just as I am.

DON'T GRIN, OR YOU'LL HAVE TO BEAR IT

It is better in the long run to possess an abscess or a tumor
Than to possess a sense of humor.
People who have senses of humor have a very good time,
But they never accomplish anything of note, either despicable or
      sublime,
Because how can anybody accomplish anything immortal
When they realize they look pretty funny doing it and have to stop to
      chortle?
Everybody admits that Michelangelo's little things in the Sistine
      Chapel are so immortal they have everybody reeling,
But I'll bet he could never have dashed them off if he had realized
      how undignified he looked lying up there with his stomach on
      the ceiling.
Yes, fatal handicaps in life are fortunately few,
But the most fatal of all is the faculty of seeing the other person's
      point of view,
And if your devoted mother suggests that you will some day be rich
      and famous, why perish the suggestion;
That is, perish it if you are afflicted with the suspicion that there are
      two sides to every question.
Good gracious, how could anybody corner wheat
If they were sissy enough to reflect that they were causing a lot of
      other people to be unable to afford to eat?
Look at mayors and congressmen and presidents, always excepting
      college presidents, such as Harvard's Conant;
Do you think they could get elected if they admitted even to
      themselves that there was anything to be said for their
      opponent?
No, no, genius won't get you as far as common everyday facility
Unless it is accompanied by a conviction of infallibility,
And people who have a sense of humor are extremely gullible,
But not enough so, alas, to believe that they are infullible.

PRIDE GOETH BEFORE A RAISE
or
AH, THERE, MRS. CADWALLADER-SMITH!

The Cadwallader-Smiths
Are People with Poise;
I consider them one of the minor joys,
Though frequently wishing
That I could share
Their imperturbable *savoir-faire*.

Madame is a modishly youthful matron,
Artfully dyed and I think enameled;
Monsieur is a generous opera patron,
A Man-about-Town, by trade untrammeled.
Oh the dapper dandies,
The haughty dames,
In the phalanx of hy-
Phenated names!
(Have you ever observed
That the name of Smith
Is the oftenest hy-
Phenated with?)
Now come the junior Cadwallader-Smiths,
Those perennial rotogravurian myths,
Maidens who scale the Alps and Rockies,
Debutantes with the world in tow,
Polo players and gentleman jockeys,
And athletes tailored in Savile Row.
Oh glamorous girls and golden boys,
They practically palpitate with poise!
Say me a word. It's a word they've got.
So what?

Well, though hardly copy for a great biographer,
They know how to twinkle for a news photographer.

They don't go to work, but they wallow in shekels,
And they sit on beaches and don't get freckles.
They exchange divorces without bearing malice,
And they all get presented at Buckingham Palace.
They receive reporters with a nonchalant air,
And they're dignified even in the barber chair,
They are dignified even in their testimonials
To beautifying lotions for the crude Colonials.
They take a paper and they read the headlines,
So they've heard of unemployment and they've heard of breadlines,
And they philanthropically cure them all
By getting up a costume charity ball.
They tipple nectar and they nibble lotus,
And they pay no attention to a jury notus,
And they don't get a summons when they run past stop-lights,
So they have the point of view of true cosmopolites.
They could all pay taxes, but they'd rather not.
So what?
Well, they're People with Poise,
The Cadwallader-Smiths,
With the sensitive senses of monoliths,
Which I freely admit
I could use myself,
Had I all I desire of profit and pelf.

PEEKABOO, I ALMOST SEE YOU

Middle-aged life is merry, and I love to lead it,
But there comes a day when your eyes are all right but your arm
      isn't long enough to hold the telephone book where you can
      read it,
And your friends get jocular, so you go to the oculist,
And of all your friends he is the joculist,
So over his facetiousness let us skim,
Only noting that he has been waiting for you ever since you said
      Good evening to his grandfather clock under the impression
      that it was him,
And you look at his chart and it says SHRDLU QWERTYOP, and
      you say Well, why SHRDNTLU QWERTYOP? and he says
      one set of glasses won't do.
You need two,
One for reading Erle Stanley Gardner's Perry Mason and Keats's
      "Endymion" with,
And the other for walking around without saying Hello to strange
      wymion with.
So you spend your time taking off your seeing glasses to put on your
      reading glasses, and then remembering that your reading
      glasses are upstairs or in the car,
And then you can't find your seeing glasses again because without
      them on you can't see where they are.
Enough of such mishaps, they would try the patience of an ox,
I prefer to forget both pairs of glasses and pass my declining years
      saluting strange women and grandfather clocks.

A CLEAN CONSCIENCE NEVER RELAXES

There is an emotion to which we are most of us adduced,
But it is one which I refuse to boost.
It is harrowing, browbeating, and brutal,
Besides which it is futile.
I am referring, of course,
To remorse.
Remorse is a violent dyspepsia of the mind,
But it is very difficult to treat because it cannot even be defined,
Because everything is not gold that glisters and everything is not a
    tear that glistens,
And one man's remorse is another man's reminiscence,
So the truth is that as far as improving the world is concerned,
    remorse is a duffer,
Because the wrong people suffer,
Because the very fact that they suffer from remorse proves they are
    innocuous,
Yes indeed, it is the man remorse passes over completely who is the
    virulent streptococcuous.
Do you think that when Nero threw a martyr to the lions remorse
    enveloped him like an affinity?
Why, the only remorse in the whole Colosseum was felt by the
    martyr who was reproaching himself for having dozed through
    the sermon on the second Sunday after Trinity.
So I think remorse ought to stop biting the consciences that feed it,
And I think the Communist Party ought to work out some plan for
    taking it away from those who have it and giving it to those
    who need it.

LITTLE MISS MUFFET SAT ON A PROPHET
AND QUITE RIGHT, TOO!

I am sure that if anybody into the condition of humanity cares to
      probe,
Why they will agree with the prophet Job,
Because the prophet Job said that man that is born of woman is of
      few days and full of trouble, that's what was said by the
      prophet Job,
And the truth of that statement can be confirmed by anybody who
      cares to probe.
So you would think that being born to trouble and woe, man would
      be satisfied,
And indeed that just by being born at all his passion for trouble
      would be gratisfied.
But is man content to leave bad enough alone?
Not so, he has to go out and create a lot more trouble and woe of his
      own.
Man knows very well that rheumatism and measles and ice and fog
      and pain and senility and sudden death are his for the
      asking, and, indeed, his whether he asks for them or not,
But when it comes to agony, man is a glutton and a sot,
His appetite for punishment is immense,
And any torture that Nature overlooked, he invents.
There is no law of Nature that compels a man to drink too much,
Or even to think too much,
And when Nature looked at her handiwork, for purposes of her own
      she certainly added gender to it,
But she didn't order everybody to dive overboard and surrender to it,
Yes, it may have been Nature who induced two people to love each
      other and end up by marrying each other,
But it is their own idea when they begin to lovingly torment and
      harry each other.
And it may have been Nature who developed the mosquito and the
      gnat and the midge,

But man developed golf and bridge,
And Nature may have thought up centipedes and ants,
But man all by himself thought up finance,
So this prophet will utter just one utterance instead of uttering them
      like the prophet Job in baker's twelves,
Which utterance is that people could survive their natural trouble
      all right if it weren't for the trouble they make for themselves.

OLD MEN

People expect old men to die,
They do not really mourn old men.
Old men are different. People look
At them with eyes that wonder when . . .
People watch with unshocked eyes;
But the old men know when an old man dies.

ONE MAN'S OPIATE

In the *Affendämmerung*, or twilight of the apes,
What is more fitting than that man should for reassurance turn to
     japes?
In chaos sublunary
What remains constant but buffoonery?
I know of a man named Daniel Deronda
And of buffoonery he is a veritable Golconda.
Once he was sipping a *fine* in a café in Montmartre,
When a man sat down at his table who wanted to discuss Sartre.
Daniel didn't wish to discuss Sartre, whose works filled him with
     ennui;
He told himself, "Dan, we can't put up with ennui, can we?"
So he said, "*Frappe, frappe*," and the man said, "*Qui va là?*" and he
     said, "*Alençon*," and the man said, "*Alençon qui?*"
And Daniel said, "*Alençonfants de la patrie.*"
The Sartre man, himself a lacemaker, was so taken aback that
     instead of exclaiming, "*Ma fwah!*" ("My faith!"), *il s'écria*,
     "*Mon fwah!*" which every goose knows means "My liver!"
And then threw himself into the Seine, a river.
I'm all for Daniel: In this age penumbral,
Let the timbrel resound in the tumbrel.

LOOK FOR THE SILVER LINING

I can't say that I feel particularly one way or the other towards
      bell-boys,
But I do admit that I haven't much use for the it's-just-as-well boys,
The cheery souls who drop around after every catastrophe and think
      they are taking the curse off
By telling you about somebody who is even worse off.
No matter how deep and dark your pit, how dank your shroud,
Their heads are heroically unbloody and unbowed.
If you have just lost the one love of your life, there is no possible
      doubt of it,
They tell you there are as good fish in the sea as ever came out of it.
If you are fined ten dollars for running past a light when you didn't
      but the cop says you did,
They say Cheer up think of the thousand times you ran past them
      and didn't get caught so you're really ten thousand bucks
      ahead, Hey old kid?
If you lose your job they tell you how lucky you are that you've
      saved up a little wealth
And then when the bank folds with the savings they tell you you
      sure are lucky to still have your health.
Life to them is just one long happy game,
At the conclusion of which the One Great Scorer writes not whether
      you won it or lost it, but how you played it, against your
      name.
Kismet, they say, it's Fate. What is to be, will be. Buck up! Take
      heart!
Kismet indeed! Nobody can make me grateful for Paris Green in the
      soup just by assuring me that it comes that way Allah carte.

THE SEVEN SPIRITUAL AGES OF
MRS. MARMADUKE MOORE

Mrs. Marmaduke Moore, at the age of ten
(Her name was Jemima Jevons then),
Was the quaintest of little country maids.
Her pigtails slapped on her shoulderblades;
She fed the chickens, and told the truth
And could spit like a boy through a broken tooth.
She could climb a tree to the topmost perch,
And she used to pray in the Methodist church.

At the age of twenty her heart was pure,
And she caught the fancy of Mr. Moore.
He broke his troth (to a girl named Alice),
And carried her off to his city palace,
Where she soon forgot her childhood piety
And joined in the orgies of high society.
Her voice grew English, or, say, Australian,
And she studied to be an Episcopalian

At thirty our lives are still before us,
But Mr. Moore had a friend in the chorus.
Connubial bliss was overthrown
And Mrs. Moore now slumbered alone.
Hers was a nature that craved affection;
She gave herself up to introspection;
Then, finding theosophy rather dry,
Found peace in the sweet Bahai and Bahai.

Forty! and still an abandoned wife.
She felt old urges stirring to life.
She dipped her locks in a bowl of henna
And booked a passage through to Vienna.
She paid a professor a huge emolument
To demonstrate what his ponderous volume meant.

Returning, she preached to the unemployed
The gospel according to St. Freud.

Fifty! she haunted museums and galleries,
And pleased young men by augmenting their salaries.
Oh, it shouldn't occur, but it does occur,
That poets are made by fools like her.
Her salon was full of frangipani,
Roumanian, Russian and Hindustani,
And she conquered par as well as bogey
By reading a book and going Yogi.

Sixty! and time was on her hands—
Maybe remorse and maybe glands.
She felt a need for a free confession,
To publish each youthful indiscretion,
And before she was gathered to her mothers,
To compare her sinlets with those of others,
Mrs. Moore gave a joyous whoop,
And immersed herself in the Oxford Group.

That is the story of Mrs. Moore,
As far as it goes. But of this I'm sure—
When seventy stares her in the face
She'll have found some other state of grace.
Mohammed may be her Lord and master,
Or Zeus, or Mithros or Zoroaster.
When a lady's erotic life is vexed
God knows what God is coming next.

WHAT I KNOW ABOUT LIFE

I have recently been pondering the life expectancy which the Bible
      allots to man,
And at this point I figure I have worked my way through nine
      fourteenths of my hypothetical span.
I have been around a bit and met many interesting people and made
      and lost some money and acquired in reverse order a family
      and a wife,
And by now I should have drawn some valuable conclusions about
      life.
Well I have learned that life is something about which you can't
      conclude anything except that it is full of vicissitudes,
And where you expect logic you only come across eccentricitudes.
Life has a tendency to obfuscate and bewilder,
Such as fating us to spend the first part of our lives being
      embarrassed by our parents and the last part being
      embarrassed by our childer.
Life is constantly presenting us with experiences which are
      unprecedented and depleting,
Such as the friend who starts drinking at three in the afternoon and
      explains it's only to develop a hearty appetite for dinner
      because it's unhealthy to drink without eating.
Life being what it is I don't see why everybody doesn't develop an
      ulcer,
Particularly Mrs. Martingale, the wife of a prominent pastry cook
      from Tulsa.
He had risen to fame and fortune after starting as a humble purveyor
      of noodles,
So he asked her what she wanted for her birthday and she said a
      new Studebaker and he thought she said a new strudel baker
      and she hated strudels.
So all I know about life is that it has been well said
That such things can't happen to a person when they are dead.

WHAT TO DO UNTIL THE DOCTOR GOES
or
IT'S TOMORROW THAN YOU THINK

Oh hand me down my old cigar with its Havana wrapper and its
    filling of cubeb,
Fill the little brown jug with bismuth and paregoric, and the pottle
    and cannikin with soda and rhubeb,
Lend me a ninety-nine piece orchestra tutored by Koussevitsky,
I don't want the ownership of it, I just want the usevitsky,
Bring me a firkin of Arkansas orators to sing me oratorios,
Remove these calf-clad Spenglers and Prousts and replace them
    with paper-covered Wodehouses and Gaboriaus,
Wrap up and return these secretarial prunes and prisms,
Let me have about me bosoms without isms.
Life and I are not convivial,
Life is real, life is earnest, while I only think I am real, and know I
    am trivial.
In this imponderable world I lose no opportunity
To ponder on picayunity.
I would spend either a round amount or a flat amount
To know whether a puma is only tantamount to a catamount or
    paramount to a catamount,
It is honey in my cup,
When I read of a sprinter sprinting the hundred in ten seconds flat,
    to think: Golly, suppose he stood up!
I guess I am not really reprehensible,
Just dispensable.

CURL UP AND DIET

Some ladies smoke too much and some ladies drink too much and
      some ladies pray too much,
But all ladies think that they weigh too much.
They may be as slender as a sylph or a dryad,
But just let them get on the scales and they embark on a doleful
      jeremiad;
No matter how low the figure the needle happens to touch,
They always claim it is at least five pounds too much;
No matter how underfed to you a lady's anatomy seemeth,
She describes herself as Leviathan or Behemoth;
To the world she may appear slinky and feline,
But she inspects herself in the mirror and cries, Oh, I look like a
      sea lion.
Once upon a time there was a girl more beautiful and witty and
      charming than tongue can tell,
And she is now a dangerous raving maniac in a padded cell,
And the first indication her friends and relatives had that she was
      mentally overwrought
Was one day when she said, I weigh a hundred and twenty-seven,
      which is exactly what I ought.
Oh, often I am haunted
By the thought that somebody might some day discover a diet that
      would let ladies reduce just as much as they wanted,
Because I wonder if there is a woman in the world strong-minded
      enough to shed ten pounds or twenty,
And say There now, that's plenty;
And I fear me one ten-pound loss would only arouse the craving for
      another,
So it wouldn't do any good for ladies to get their ambition and look
      like somebody's fourteen-year-old brother,
Because, having accomplished this with ease
They would next want to look like somebody's fourteen-year-old
      brother in the final stages of some obscure disease,
And the more success you have the more you want to get of it,

So then their goal would be to look like somebody's fourteen-year-
old brother's ghost, or rather not the ghost itself, which is
fairly solid, but a silhouette of it,
So I think it is very nice for ladies to be lithe and lissome,
But not so much so that you cut yourself if you happen to embrace
or kissome.

HOW DO YOU SAY HA-HA IN FRENCH?

There are several people who I can claim I am glad I am not,
without being accused of pride and effrontery,
And one of them is the bartender of a French restaurant in an
English-speaking country.
The conversation of the customers isn't calculated to keep a
bartender young,
Even when they converse in their mother tongue;
How much more dispiriting it must be when after the second Martini
They request a third because the first two are, not finished, but *finis*.
They select a *Maryland*, or cigarette,
And instead of Gotta light? it is *Avez-vous une allumette?*
When they cry *Garçon* after the school of Stratford atte Bowe or New
Rochelle or Nineveh,
It is moot whether they want the waiter or Mrs. Miniver.
Somehow, in a *bistro*, or French eatery,
Everybody suddenly discovers they can talk like Sasha Guitry,
But they really can't,
And if I were the bartender I should poke them in the *œil* with the
plume de ma tante.

COMPLIMENTS OF A FRIEND

How many gifted pens have penned
That Mother is a boy's best friend!
How many more with like afflatus
Award the dog that honored status!
I hope my tongue in prune juice smothers
If I belittle dogs or mothers,
But gracious, how can I agree?
I know my own best friend is Me.
We share our joys and our aversions,
We're thicker than the Medes and Persians,
We blend like voices in a chorus,
The same things please, the same things bore us.
If I am broke, then Me needs money;
I make a joke, Me finds it funny.
I know what I like, Me knows what art is;
We hate the people at cocktail parties,
When I can stand the crowd no more,
Why, Me is halfway to the door.
I am a dodo; Me, an auk;
We grieve that pictures learned to talk;
For every sin that I produce
Kind Me can find some soft excuse,
And when I blow a final gasket,
Who but Me will share my casket?
Beside us, Pythias and Damon
We're just two unacquainted laymen.
Sneer not, for if you answer true,
Don't you feel that way about You?

CORRECTION: *EVE* DELVED AND *ADAM* SPAN

The ladies of the garden club
Are in the other room,
And, fed on tea and sandwiches,
Their pretty fancies bloom,
I hear their gentle treble hubbub,
The ladies of the garden clubbub.

The ladies of the garden club,
Their words are firm and sure,
They know the lore of lime and mulch,
The poetry of manure.
Each spring they beautify our suburb,
The ladies of the garden cluburb.

Dear ladies of the garden club,
I love your natural zeal,
Your verdant thumbs, your canvas gloves,
The pads on which you kneel,
But I hear you making plans involving
Husbands in gardening instead of golfing.

Between the outer door and me
The flower ladies sit.
I'm frantic-footed, blind, and trapped,
Like mole in compost pit,
One timorous masculine minutia,
Caught between baby's-breath and fuchsia.

The air is sweet with talk of bulbs,
And phlox and mignonettes;
Arrangements drape the drawer that holds
My only cigarettes.
Would I had courage for an end run
Round herbaceous border and rhododendron!

Ranunculus can a prison make,
And hyacinth a cell;
I barely glimpse a patch of sky
Through wreath of immortelle.
And thus are fulfilled the baleful prophecies
Concerning men who are at home instead of their offices.

LUCY LAKE

Lawsamassy, for heaven's sake!
Have you never heard of Lucy Lake?
Lucy is fluffy and fair and cosy,
Lucy is like a budding posy.
Lucy speaks with a tiny lisp,
Lucy's mind is a will-o'-the-wisp.
Lucy is just as meek as a mouse,
Lucy lives in a darling house,
With a darling garden and darling fence,
And a darling faith in the future tense.
A load of hay, or a crescent moon,
And she knows that things will be better soon
Lucy resigns herself to sorrow
In building character for tomorrow.
Lucy tells us to carry on,
It's always darkest before the dawn.
A visit to Lucy's bucks you up,
Helps you swallow the bitterest cup.
Lucy Lake is meek as a mouse.
Let's go over to Lucy's house,
And let's lynch Lucy!

WHAT'S THE MATTER, HAVEN'T YOU GOT
ANY SENSE OF HUMOR?

There is at least one thing I would less rather have in the
        neighborhood than a gangster,
And that one thing is a practical prankster.
1 feel that we should differ more sharply than Montagues and
        Capulets or York and Lancaster,
Me and a practical prancaster.
If there is a concentration camp in limbo, that is the spot for which I
        nominate them,
Not because I don't like them, but simply because I abominate
        them.
The born practical prankster starts out in early youth by offering
        people a chair,
And when they sit down it isn't there,
And he is delighted and proceeds to more complicated wheezes,
Such as ten cent X-rays to see through people's clothes with and
        powders to give them itches and sneezes,
And his boutonnière is something that people get squirted in the eye
        out of,
And their beds are what he makes apple pie out of.
Then as he matures he widens his scope,
And he is no longer content to present people with exploding cigars
        and chocolate creams with centers of soap.
I have recently read with complete satisfaction of a practical
        prankster two of whose friends had just been married,
Which was of course in itself simply a challenge to be harried,
And it was a challenge he was eager to meet,
And he went to the roof of their hotel and tied a rope around his
        waist and a colleague lowered him to where he could clash a
        pair of cymbals outside the window of the nuptial suite,
And he weighed two hundred and eighty pounds and the rope broke,
And that to my mind is the perfect practical joke.

HAS ANYBODY SEEN MY NOUMENON*?

There is one point which I am more than human on,
And that's a noumenon.
On due reflection we are apt to find
That it is noumenons which lead us to believe that just this once two
      pair will beat three of a kind.
It is noumenons which whisper to our hearts that our futures will be
      brighter than our yores,
And noumenons which encourage us to laugh off the black clouds in
      the west and go ahead and move the supper table out of
      doors.
It is noumenons which, if you have no excuse for flouting natural
      laws, they supply it,
Such as kindling the hope that you can remain trim and lissome at
      forty without the nuisance of exercise or diet,
So now I shall go out and consume a hearty lunch,
But I know I shall remain trim and lissome in spite of it, because I
      have a strong noumenon, or overwhelming hunch.

Noumenon, n., an object known only by intuition, apart from any evidence of
ıe senses.

THE STRANGE CASE OF MR. PAUNCEFOOT'S
BROAD MIND

Once there was a man named Mr. Pauncefoot to whom Fate could
not have been meaner,

Because he was a born in-betweener.

Yes, he was one whom in an argument nothing but woe ever betides,

Because he always thought that there was much to be said on both
sides,

With the result that to his friends on the Left he was but a little
capitalistic bee busy distributing Tory pollen,

While on the Right he was rumored to be in the pay of Stalin.

Mr. Pauncefoot lived in a suburb, which was inevitable but rather a
pity,

Since the upshot was that he appeared as a city boy in the country
and a country boy in the city.

He was never invited to sing either solo or in a convivial quartet by
even the kindest Samaritan,

Because his voice was just a little too low for the tenor and just a
little too high for the baritan.

Mr. Pauncefoot was miserable until one day he read about the
donkey that starved to death between two haystacks because
it couldn't decide which haystack to begin on, and he said,
"That's an end of all my confusions,"

Only Mr. Pauncefoot didn't starve to death, quite the opposite, he
spent the rest of his days very happily eating his own words
between two conclusions.

THE SAGE OF DARIEN

Upon a peak in Darien
The Sage surveys his fellow men,
Exerting to its full capacity
His preternatural sagacity.
Sore eyes and empty stomach mutiny;
The Sage confines himself to scrutiny,
Occasionally sniffing through a tube
The vapor of a bouillon cube.
Thus, all his grosser instincts chastening,
He thinks to bring the vision hastening.
The truth about his fellow men,
He hopes, will bloom within his ken.
At last appears a tiny truth,
A sliver like a baby's tooth.
Now fast it grows, it swells, it waxes,
It multiplies itself like taxes.
The ultimate truth, for what it's worth,
Crowds minor truthlets off the earth.
The Sage cries Bother! through his beard;
Says he, Exactly what I feared.
I needn't have come to Darien
To scrutinize my fellow men;
It seems I've scaled this natural steeple
To learn what I've always known about people;
To confirm through sacrifice intense
The fact that people have no sense.
People are born in pain and woe,
In woe and pain through life they go,
Harpies attend their to-and-froing,
And yet the blockheads keep on going.
Republics rob them, monarchies milk them,
Revolutions unfailingly bilk them;
Tyrants imprison them and slaughter them;
Promoters take their stocks and water them;
Statements and bills pile high around them;

Sheriffs and credit departments hound them;
By ten-ton trucks they are forced from the roads;
Every October they change their abodes;
Frequent expensive diseases smite them;
Sunbeams burn them, mosquitoes bite them;
Employers jeer at their shiny diplomas;
Advertisers insult their aromas;
People are born in pain and woe,
In woe and pain through life they go;
They have no cause at all for thanksgiving.
And yet the idiots keep on living.
Upon a peak in Darien
The Sage renounced his fellow men.
His fellow men he did renounce,
And leapt, and lit, and didn't bounce.

DR. FELL? I THOUGHT SO

Some people relate anecdotes about Samuel Goldwyn and Gregory
  Ratoff;
I sing of Dr. Fell, who slips in the only vacant barber chair while
  you are taking your hat off.
Does a young man go to a picture with a girl he hopes to make a
  bride of?
The immovable Dr. Fell is what the only two empty seats are one on
  each side of.
You are marooned downtown on a night when the rain is a Niagara
  and the wind is a bayonet,
And after twenty minutes of futile whistling you catch a taxi driver's
  eye and as he slows down Dr. Fell emerges miraculously from
  a hydrant, steps into the cab and drives away in it.
Dr. Fell obviously works with the assistance of a brownie or a
  malevolent dwarf,
For it is he who by monopolizing the middle of the road reaches the
  ferry ahead of you and slides into the last space, thus leaving
  you to two hours' uninterrupted contemplation of the wharf.
Yes, I fear that Dr. Fell is a monopolist and an obstructionist,
But I would not grudge him the obstructive monopoly of that portion
  of a whirlpool where the suction is the suctionest.

JUST WRAP IT UP, AND I'LL THROW IT
AWAY LATER

Men think that men have more sense than women and women think
        that any woman has more sense than any man,
An issue which I eagerly evade, for who am I to pass judgment on
        the comparative reasoning processes of, say, Mr. Lunt and
        Miss Fontanne?
However, I ask you to visualize, please, a clear-thinking American
        male who needs a hat, or a left sock, or an ashtray in the form
        of the statue Civic Virtue by the sculptor MacMonnies,
And what does he do, he goes into the likeliest shop and buys it and
        returns to the regular evening race with the children for first
        go at the funnies.
Kindly contrast this with the procedure of his wife or sister or aunt
        who drops into a store for three ounces of flax for the
        spinning wheel or an extra minuet for the spinet,
And what happens, the doorstep is crawling for days with people
        delivering lampshades and bedspreads and dirndls and
        chairs that expand into bridge tables and bridge tables that
        expand into chaises longues, and husbands who can't bear it
        simply have to grin it.
Man's idea of shopping is to buy what he needs and get through with
        it.
Woman's idea is to have everything she has never needed sent home
        and then figure out what to do with it.
It is as true today as in the day of David and Goliath or Corbett and
        Fitzsimmons,
That men go into a shop to supply a want, and women principally to
        stimulate their imaginations, but men's imaginations need no
        extra stimulus as long as their world is filled with beautiful
        unanswerable womens.

SONG FOR DITHERERS

I journey not whence nor whither,
I languish alone in a dither;
I journey not to nor fro,
And my dither to me I owe.
I could find a pleasanter name for it
Had I somebody else to blame for it,
But alas that beneath the sun
Dithers are built for one.
This is the song of the dither,
For viol, bassoon or zither,
Till the greenest simpletons wither
This is the song of the dither;
When regular troubles are wrong with you,
Others are guilty along with you;
Dithers are private trouble
Where you privately stew and bubble.
Come hither, somebody, come hither,
Would you care for a share of my dither?
I want somebody else to be mad at;
"Have at you!" to cry, and be had at.
I am tired of being angry at me,
There is room in my dither for three,
There is room in my dither for two;
We could butt at each other and moo;
We could hiss like the serpent, and slither
Through the tropical depths of my dither;
Like bees we could fight along beelines,
Or spit at each other like felines;
I care not who gaineth the laurel,
All I want is a foe and a quarrel.
Alone in my dither I pine.

For the sake of the days of lang syne,
For your white-haired old feyther and mither,
Come along, come along to my dither.
With no foe in my dither but me,
I swoon, I lay doon, and I dee.

AND THREE HUNDRED AND SIXTY-SIX
IN LEAP YEAR

Some people shave before bathing,
And about people who bathe before shaving they are scathing,
While those who bathe before shaving,
Well, they imply that those who shave before bathing are
      misbehaving.
Suppose you shave before bathing, well the advantage is that you
      don't have to make a special job of washing the lather off
      afterwards, it just floats off with the rest of your
      accumulations in the tub,
But the disadvantage is that before bathing your skin is hard and
      dry and your beard confronts the razor like a grizzly bear
      defending its cub.
Well then, suppose you bathe before shaving, well the advantage is
      that after bathing your skin is soft and moist, and your beard
      positively begs for the blade,
But the disadvantage is that to get the lather off you have to wash
      your face all over again at the basin almost immediately after
      washing it in the tub, which is a duplication of effort that
      leaves me spotless but dismayed.
The referee reports, gentlemen, that Fate has loaded the dice,
Since your only choice is between walking around all day with a
      sore chin or washing your face twice.

THOUGHTS THOUGHT ON AN AVENUE

There would be far less masculine gaming and boozing
But for the feminine approach to feminine fashions, which is
      distinctly confusing.
Please correct me if, although I don't think I do, I err;
But it is a fact that a lady wants to be dressed exactly like
      everybody else but she gets pretty upset if she sees anybody
      else dressed exactly like her.
Nothing so infuriates her as a similar hat or dress,
Especially if bought for less,
Which brings up another point which I will attempt to discuss in my
      guttural masculine jargon;
Her ideal raiment is costlier than her or her dearest friend's purse
      can buy, and at the same time her own exclusive and amazing
      bargain.
Psychologists claim that men are the dreamers and women are the
      realists,
But to my mind women are the starriest-eyed of idealists,
Though I am willing to withdraw this charge and gladly eat it
      uncomplaineously
If anyone can explain to me how a person can wear a costume that is
      different from other people's and the same as other people's,
      and more expensive than other people's and cheaper than
      other people's, simultaneously

LINES TO A THREE-NAME LADY

Mrs. Hattie Boomer Spink,
You puzzle me a lot.
Do you, I wonder, ever think?
And, if you do, of what?

Oh, solons bow like slender reeds
Beneath your firm resolve.
Your words I know, I know your deeds—
But whence do they evolve?

Do you employ a cerebrum,
And eke a cerebellum?
Or do you simply let 'em come,
With Gabriel at the hellum?

Your native mental processes
Imply some secret canker;
Instead of thoughts, antipathies;
Instead of reason, rancor.

The ripple in your skull that spreads
From some primeval pebble,
How quickly washes o'er the heads
Of prophet and of rebel!

You three-name women, Mrs. Spink,
You puzzle me a lot.
Do you, I wonder, ever think?
And if you do, of what?

When gossip first began to link
Your name with that of Mr. Spink,
O Hattie Boomer, did you think?
—And what's become of Mr. Spink?

NO DOCTORS TODAY, THANK YOU

They tell me that euphoria is the feeling of feeling wonderful, well,
  today I feel euphorian,
Today I have the agility of a Greek god and the appetite of a
  Victorian.
Yes, today I may even go forth without my galoshes,
Today I am a swashbuckler, would anybody like me to buckle any
  swashes?
This is my euphorian day,
I will ring welkins and before anybody answers I will run away.
I will tame me a caribou
And bedeck it with marabou.
I will pen me my memoirs.
Ah youth, youth! What euphorian days them was!
I wasn't much of a hand for the boudoirs,
I was generally to be found where the food was.
Does anybody want any flotsam?
I've gotsam.
Does anybody want any jetsam?
I can getsam.
I can play chopsticks on the Wurlitzer,
I can speak Portuguese like a Berlitzer.
I can don or doff my shoes without tying or untying the laces
  because I am wearing moccasins,
And I practically know the difference between serums and
  antitoccasins.
Kind people, don't think me purse-proud, don't set me down as
  vainglorious,
I'm just a little euphorious.

A VISIT FROM DR. FELL

Dr. Fell is at the door and my *mens sana* is about to depart from my
    corpore sano,
For this is the hour of the chocolate fingerprints in the books and
    the coconut-marshmallow icing on the piano.
Dr. Fell is notable for the southern-central section of his silhouette,
And he lands in your frailest chair like somebody from the ninth
    floor of a burning hotel landing in a net.
Hitherto, the plumbing has functioned as sweetly as a hungry
    mosquito lapping up citronella,
But the plumbing is where Dr. Fell disposes of any unwanted object,
    from an old cigar to an old umbrella.
Dr. Fell's little finger projecting from his glass as he drinks couldn't
    possibly be genteeler or archer,
But whatever glasses you had a dozen of on his arrival you only have
    eleven of on his departure.
Every man but Dr. Fell has his own conception of enough;
Dr. Fell will not only nonchalantly knock a half-completed jigsaw
    puzzle onto the floor but nonchalantly carry off a key piece
    buried in his cuff.
Come on in Dr. Fell, you must take pot-luck with us, no, wait a
    minute, I forgot,
Today we can only offer you kettle-luck, last time you were here you
    ran the ice-pick through the pot.

SLOW DOWN, MR. GANDERDONK, YOU'RE LATE

Do you know Mr. Ganderdonk, he is no Einstein, he has no theories
      of Time and Space,
But he is the only man I know can be both the hare and the tortoise
      in the same race.
Mr. Ganderdonk's proclivity
Is divoty Relativity.
Put him behind you in a twosome or a foursome,
His speed is awesome.
His relationship to your rear
Is that of a catamount to a deer,
And while you are still reaching for your putter
He is standing on the edge of the green going mutter mutter,
But once through you in his foursome or twosome,
His torpor is gruesome.
He is a golfer that the thought of other golfers simply hasn't
      occurred to;
He has three swings for every shot, the one he hopes to use, the one
      he does use, and finally the one he would have preferred to.
His world from tee to cup
Consists of those behind him pressing him and those in front of him
      holding him up,
Wherefore the rest of the world is his foe
Because the rest of the world is either too fast or too slow.
For Mr. Ganderdonk there is only one correct pace and that is his,
Whatever it is.

Once there was a girl named Miriam,
And she spent part of her time in a delirium,
And she said, I wish the world were a little less mysterious,
Because I do like to know when I am delirious,
But I have discovered that whenever I regard the world and judge it
    logical and normal and headed for the millennium at a mile a
    minute,
Why that's the time I ought to be enclosed in a spacious park with
    an asylum in it,
But whenever everybody else seems to be running around in a
    delirium,
Why that's the time when somebody may be fuzzy-minded, but it
    isn't Miriam.
So finally she convened an enormous convention, national and
    international,
And she said, Please I wish everybody would help me to determine
    when I am delirious and when I am rational,
Because, she said, at present I am just a bit hazy,
Because when I am crazy you all seem perfectly sane, but when I
    am sane you all seem perfectly crazy,
So, she said, forgive me if I am too personal or informal,
But I hope from now on you will all behave so that I will think you
    are delirious if I am delirious, and normal if I am normal,
So they all said, What a good idea, hurrah for Miriam!
Who are we? Who are we? We are the boys and girls of the Eastern
    and Western hemispheres, and we are going to help her with
    her delirium!
So from then on manias were declared reprehensible,
And everybody tried to be sensible,
And there wasn't any more war,
And there were only as many people dancing at night clubs as could
    comfortably get on the floor,
And all the rich people cried Soak the rich, and all the poor people
    cried No that would retard recovery, soak the poor!

And the tailors made men's and women's coats with the buttons on
the same side, and that stopped a lot of argument between
husbands and wives as to the comparative intelligence of men
and women, you may be sure.

And what with one thing and another everybody was sensible and
lived happily ever after and they said they owed it all to
Miriam,

So they offered her the dictatorship of the world, but she never used
it, only in a delirium.

WE DON'T NEED TO LEAVE YET, DO WE?
OR, YES WE DO

One kind of person when catching a train always wants to allow an
    hour to cover the ten-block trip to the terminus,
And the other kind looks at them as if they were verminous,
And the second kind says that five minutes is plenty and will even
    leave one minute over for buying the tickets,
And the first kind looks at them as if they had cerebral rickets.
One kind when theater-bound sups lightly at six and hastens off to
    the play,
And indeed I know one such person who is so such that it frequently
    arrives in time for the last act of the matinee,
And the other kind sits down at eight to a meal that is positively
    sumptuous,
Observing cynically that an eight-thirty curtain never rises till eight-
    forty, an observation which is less cynical than bumptuous.
And what the first kind, sitting uncomfortably in the waiting room
    while the train is made up in the yards, can never
    understand,
Is the injustice of the second kind's reaching their seat just as the
    train moves out, just as they had planned,
And what the second kind cannot understand as they stumble over
    the first kind's feet just as the footlights flash on at last
Is that the first kind doesn't feel the least bit foolish at having
    entered the theater before the cast.
Oh, the first kind always wants to start now and the second kind
    always wants to tarry,
Which wouldn't make any difference, except that each other is what
    they always marry.

LISTEN . . .

There is a knocking in the skull,
An endless silent shout
Of something beating on a wall,
And crying, Let me out.

That solitary prisoner
Will never hear reply,
No comrade in eternity
Can hear the frantic cry.

No heart can share the terror
That haunts his monstrous dark;
The light that filters through the chinks
No other eye can mark.

When flesh is linked with eager flesh,
And words run warm and full,
I think that he is loneliest then,
The captive in the skull.

Caught in a mesh of living veins,
In cell of padded bone,
He loneliest is when he pretends
That he is not alone.

We'd free the incarcerate race of man
That such a doom endures
Could only you unlock my skull,
Or I creep into yours.

ELECTRA BECOMES MORBID

Abandon for a moment, friends,
Your frivolous means, your futile ends;
Life is not wholly beer and skittles,
A treasure hunt for love and victuals;
And so at times I think we ought
To pause and think a sobering thought.
Myself, I feel a dark despair
When I consider human hair.
I'm chicken-hearted, beetle-browed,
As I behold the heedless crowd,
Knowing each carefree individual
The slave of hair that runs on schedule.
On every human head or chin
It's falling out or growing in.
Your whistling adolescent scholar,
Released from Ye Olde Tonsorial Parlor,
Runs up his neck with fingers tense
Like sticks along a picket fence.
His scalp is all Bay Rum and bristles,
Therefore he's pleased and therefore whistles.
Yea, he rejoices, quite unknowing
That all the time his hair is growing.
O woe is you, unhappy scholar,
Next month you'll be back in the tonsorial parlor.

II

Myself I feel a dark despair,
When I consider human hair,
(Fine filaments sprouting from the skin),
Reflecting, as I stroke my chin,
That men and women everywhere
Unconsciously are growing hair,
Or, if the other hand you choose,
With every breath a hair they lose.
Unbid it cometh, likewise goeth,
And oftentimes it's doing boeth.
This habit is the chief determinant
Why permanent waves are less than permanent.
You rise, Madame, you face your mirror,
You utter cries of shame and terror.
What though to males you look all right?
For heaven's sake, your hair's a sight.
You hasten to the Gallic lair
Where lurks Maurice, or Jean or Pierre.
Between arrival and departure
You suffer hours of vicious torture,
At last emerging, white and weak,
But sure at least your mane is chic.
Thus you rejoice, my dear, unknowing
That all the time your hair is growing.
The waves so dearly purchased
Next month will have grown a foot or so away from your head.

I've said, I think, I think we ought
To think at times a sobering thought.
Man's lot it is to be a field
For crops that no nutrition yield,
That filter through his tender skin
And ripen on his head or chin.
I face mankind and shudder, knowing
That everybody's hair is growing;
That lovers, linked in darkened hallways,
Are capped with hair that groweth always;
That millions, shaven in the morning,
At eve find beards their jowls adorning;
That hair is creeping through the scalps
Of yodelers yodeling in the Alps,
And pushing through the epidermises
Of peasants frolicking at kermises;
And poking bravely through the pores
Of cannibals on tropic shores;
That freezing, scorching, raining, snowing,
People's hair is always growing.
I contemplate with dark despair
The awful force of growing hair,
Although admitting to be quite honest,
That it will be worth a million Niagaras to humanity if Science can
      ever get it harnessed.

PEOPLE

Some people are popular with other people because their wit is
    pointed
And they can sing tenor and are double-jointed
And have bad experiences in the Shetlands and the Hebrides
And have private anecdotes about public celebrities,
And are bright and amusing in the entr'acte
And always do the right thing in backgammon and contr'acte.

Other people are unpopular with other people because they discuss
    Bertrand Russell
And keep wanting you to feel their muscle
And point out that your furniture is oak, not mahogany,
And tell you all about their ancestors and progeny
And advise you to move to a suburb
And get away from all this tumult and huburb.

Both kinds of people, however, will eventually succumb to acidity;
Or perhaps they will be victims of the humidity
Or even approach metempsychosis
Through the various stages of cirrhosis.
But whatever the manner of their passing may be
It's all all right with me.

SO PENSEROSO

Come, megrims, mollygrubs and collywobbles!
Come, gloom that limps, and misery that hobbles!
Come also, most exquisite melancholiage,
As dank and decadent as November foliage!
I crave to shudder in your moist embrace,
To feel your oystery fingers on my face.
This is my hour of sadness and of soulfulness,
And cursed be he who dissipates my dolefulness.
I do not desire to be cheered,
I desire to retire, I am thinking of growing a beard,
A sorrowful beard, with a mournful, a dolorous hue in it,
With ashes and glue in it.
I want to be drunk with despair,
I want to caress my care,
I do not wish to be blithe,
I wish to recoil and writhe,
I will revel in cosmic woe,
And I want my woe to show.
This is the morbid moment,
This is the ebony hour.
Aroint thee, sweetness and light!
I want to be dark and sour!
Away with the bird that twittersl
All that glitters is jitters!
Roses, roses are gray,
Violets cry Boo! and frighten me.
Sugar is stimulating,
And people conspire to brighten me.
Go hence, people, go hence!
Go sit on a picket fence!
Go gargle with mineral oil,
Go out and develop a boil!

Melancholy is what I brag and boast of,
Melancholy I mean to make the most of,
You beaming optimists shall not destroy it.
But while I am it, I intend to enjoy it.
Go, people, feed on kewpies and soap,
And remember, please, that when I mope, I mope!

A BAS BEN ADHEM

My fellow man I do not care for.
I often ask me, What's he there for?
The only answer I can find
Is, Reproduction of his kind.
If I'm supposed to swallow that,
Winnetka is my habitat.
Isn't it time to carve Hic Jacet
Above that Reproduction racket?

To make the matter more succinct:
Suppose my fellow man extinct.
Why, who would not approve the plan
Save possibly my fellow man?
Yet with a politician's voice
He names himself as Nature's choice.

The finest of the human race
Are bad in figure, worse in face.
Yet just because they have two legs
And come from storks instead of eggs
They count the spacious firmament
As something to be charged and sent.

Though man created smocks and snoods
And one-way streets and breakfast foods,
And double features and mustard plasters,
And Huey Longs and Lady Astors,
He hails himself with drum and fife
And bullies lower forms of life.

Not that I think that much depends
On how we treat our feathered friends,
Or claim the wart hog in the zoo
Is nearer God than me or you;
Just that I wonder, as I scan,
The wherefore of my fellow man.

7

Senescence and Obsolescence

*"At another year
I would not boggle
Except that when I jog
I joggle."*

When I was ten I didn't want to be president,
Or a woman-wary cowboy like William S. Hart;
I didn't even want to be a fireman.
I wanted to drive a racer a mile a minute.
Where is the sound-effects man to give me the cobble-clop of the
        milkman's horse on Charlton Street,
The lighting expert to capture the glow in the grate,
The wavering kobold dance of shadows on the ceiling?
I sniff again the fringes of smoke from the shifting, sifting coals,
Soft and insidious, skunk-like sweet, furring the tongue and throat.
Savannah in 1912 hadn't heard of air pollution.
Gulp breakfast now and bundle
Into the bathtub tonneau of the splendid Royal Tourist,
It's almost time for the start of the fabulous Grand Prize.
The sun has unraveled the mist, but it's cold in the wooden stands,
Cold and hard on the bottom.
The mechanics below in the pits pause to blow on their fingers.
How vast the machines in the eyes of a little boy!
Strange as gorgons or minotaurs each with its magic name:
Mercedes, Apperson Jackrabbit, Blitzen Benz, Fiat and Lozier;
Fiat devil-red, Mercedes and Benz fog-gray,
Apperson blue, and Lozier insipid white,
And for every monster a master, Perseus in helmet and goggles.
Their names roar by in my mind:
Spenser Wishart, Ralph DePalma,
Bruce Brown and Caleb Bragg
And perhaps another half-dozen of mythopoeic heroes.
Only Barney Oldfield missing;
He never came to Savannah, and we reckoned we hadn't missed
        much.
The flag drops, they are off like panicking razorback hogs,
Under their wheels crushed oyster shell explodes.
Red, blue, gray and white they streak to the first of the turns in the
        highway

Wearily banked for this moment by black men in black and white
  stripes.
The driver crowds for position, the spare tire racked behind him,
At his side his trusty mechanic, pumping oil in a fury;
They vanish around the turn.
How long is the course? Five miles? Ten miles?
It stretches from there to now.

THE MIDDLE

When I remember bygone days
I think how evening follows morn;
So many I loved were not yet dead,
So many I love were not yet born.

THE WRONGS OF SPRING
OR
NO ALL FOOLS' DAY LIKE AN ALL OLD FOOLS' DAY

Just because I'm sixty-three,
Shall April folly forbidden be?
Though the locks above my scalp
Be thin as snow on August Alp,
Must I then leave April foibles
To sprouts of louts and hobbledehoibles?
I still remain the out-to-win type,
And I reply, 'Not on your tintype!'
I will find a zany zebra,
I will teach the beast algebra;
Buy a Peugeot or a Simca,
Present it to a worthy YMCA;
Seek me out a sporting bishop,
Fit him with slaloms from a ski shop;
Roam through Perth and other Amboys,
Gathering luscious fraises and framboise,
To feast on with meringues and Nesselrodes
The while I drink a toast to Cecil Rhodes.
I'll write to some forlorn Penelope,
"S(ealed) W(ith) A K(iss)" on the envelope;
I'll memorize the works of Euripides
And match the footwork of centipedes.
I'll turn my mind to projects grandiose—
Regal, imperial, Ozymandiose—
Be Orientally lethargical,
Sybaritic, Maharajical,
And write, while lolling in my tub,
A syllabus on syllabub.
So I'll pace out my seven ages
By various frolicsome ambages—
A word that means, in Webster's phrase,
By roundabout or winding ways.
Thus, when April hoots her girlish laughter
My senile cackle shall echo after.

THE SUNSET YEARS OF SAMUEL SHY

Master I may be,
But not of my fate.
Now come the kisses, too many too late.
Tell me, O Parcae,
For fain would I know,
Where were these kisses three decades ago?
Girls there were plenty,
Mint julep girls, beer girls,
Gay younger married and headstrong career girls,
The girls of my friends
And the wives of my friends,
Some smugly settled and some at loose ends,
Sad girls, serene girls,
Girls breathless and turbulent,
Debs cosmopolitan, matrons suburbulent,
All of them amiable,
All of them cordial,
Innocent rousers of instincts primordial,
But even though health and wealth
Hadn't yet missed me,
None of them,
Not even Jenny,
Once kissed me.

These very same girls
Who with me have grown older
Now freely relax with a head on my shoulder,
And now come the kisses,
A flood in full spate,
The meaningless kisses, too many too late.
They kiss me hello,
They kiss me goodbye,
Should I offer a light, there's a kiss for reply.
They kiss me at weddings,

They kiss me at wakes,
The drop of a hat is less than it takes.
They kiss me at cocktails,
They kiss me at bridge,

It's all automatic, like slapping a midge.
The sound of their kisses
Is loud in my ears
Like the locusts that swarm every seventeen years.

I'm arthritic, dyspeptic,
Potentially ulcery,
And weary of kisses by custom compulsory.
Should my dear ones commit me
As senile demential,
It's from kisses perfunctory, inconsequential.
Answer, O Parcae,
For fain would I know,
Where were these kisses three decades ago?

THE REWARD

In my mind's reception room
Which is what, and who is whom?
I notice when the candle's lighted
Half the guests are uninvited,
And oddest fancies, merriest jests,
Come from these unbidden guests.

IT IS INDEED SPINACH

People by whom I am riled
Are people who go around wishing O that Time would backward turn
      backward and again make them a child.
Either they have no sense, or else they go around repeating
      something they have heard, like a parakeet,
Or else they deliberately prevarikete,
Because into being a marathon dancer or a chiropodist or a tea-
      taster or a certified public accountant I could not be
      beguiled,
But I could sooner than I could into being again a child,
Because being a child is not much of a pastime,
And I don't want any next time because I remember the last time.
I do not wish to play with my toes,
Nor do I wish to have codliver oil spooned down my throat or
      albolene pushed up my nose.
I don't want to be plopped at sundown into a crib or a cradle
And if I don't go to sleep right away be greeted with either a lullaby
      or an upbraidal.
I can think of nothing worse
Than never being out of sight of a parent or nurse;
Yes, that is the part that I don't see how they survive it,
To have their private life so far from private.
Furthermore, I don't want to cry for the moon,
And I do want to hold my own spoon;
I have more ambitious ideas of a lark
Than to collect pebbles in my hat or be taken for a walk in the park;
I should hate to be held together with safety pins instead of buttons
      and suspenders and belts,
And I should particularly hate being told every time I was doing
      something I liked that it was time to do something else.
So it's pooh for the people who want Time to make them a child
      again because I think they must already be a child again or
      else they would stand up and own up
That it's much more fun to be a grown-up.

YOU CAN BE A REPUBLICAN, I'M A GENOCRAT

Oh, "rorty" was a mid-Victorian word
Which meant "fine, splendid, jolly"
And often to me it has reoccurred
In moments melancholy.
For instance, children, I think it rorty
To be with people over forty.

I can't say which, come eventide,
More tedious I find;
Competing with the juvenile stride,
Or meeting the juvenile mind.
So I think it rorty, yes, and nifty,
To be with people over fifty.

The pidgin talk the youthful use
Bypasses conversation.
I can't believe the code they choose
Is a means of communication.
Oh to be with people over sixty
Despite their tendency to prolixty!

The hours a working parent keeps
Mean less than Latin to them,
Wherefore they disappear in jeeps
Till three and four A.M.
Oh, to be with people you pour a cup for
Instead of people you have to wait up for!

I've tried to read young mumbling lips
Till I've developed a slant-eye,
And my hearing fails at the constant wails
Of, If I can't, why can't I?
Oh, to be beside a septuagenarian,
Silent upon a peak in Darien!

They don't know Hagen from Bobby Jones,
They never heard Al Smith,
Even Red Grange is beyond their range,
And Dempsey is a myth.
Oh golly, to gabble upon the shoulder
Of someone my own age, or even older!

I'm tired of defining hadn't oughts
To opposition mulish,
The thoughts of youth are long long thoughts,
And Jingo! Aren't they foolish!
All which is why, in case you've wondered
I'd like a companion aged one hundred.

LAMENTS FOR A DYING LANGUAGE—III

In the nice-minded Department of Prunes and Prisms,
It's I for you
And euphemisms.
Hence the phrase I would eagerly jettison:
"Senior citizen."
Shall we retranslate
Joel 2:28?
To the sociologist squeamish
The words "Your old men shall dream dreams" are less than
        beamish,
So "Your senior citizens shall dream dreams" it shall henceforth be,
Along with Hemingway's "The Senior Citizen and the Sea."
I, though no Joel, prophesy that someday while the senior citizens
        are projecting the image of an age-adjusted social group,
The old men will rise up and knock them for a loop.

COME, COME, KEROUAC! MY GENERATION
IS BEATER THAN YOURS

My dictionary defines progress as an advance toward perfection.
There has been lots of progress during my lifetime, but I'm afraid it's
 been heading in the wrong direction.
What is the progress that I see?
The headwaiter has progressed to being a maître-d';
The airways have advanced backward like so many squids,
And the radio jokes about Bing's horses have become the TV jokes
 about Bing's kids.
We have progressed from a baseball czar to a football czar, and I
 suppose we'll eventually have a huntin' and a shootin' and a
 swimmin' czar,
And now the designers of automobile seats tell us that men's hip
 spreads have progressed to being broader than women's are.
Oriental menaces have not let progress pass them by,
And we have advanced from Fu-Manchu to Chou En-lai.
Once, you just put "The Two Black Crows" on the talking machine
 and wound the handle and it played, but now science has
 stacked the deck,
And if you want to hear one Little Golden Record you must be a
 graduate of Cal. Tech or M.I.T. (which is sometimes known as
 No-Cal. Tech).
Progress may have been all right once, but it went on too long;
I think progress began to retrogress when Wilbur and Orville started
 tinkering around in Dayton and at Kitty Hawk, because I
 believe that two Wrights made a wrong.

COME ON IN, THE SENILITY IS FINE

People live forever in Jacksonville and St. Petersburg and Tampa,
But you don't have to live forever to become a grampa.
The entrance requirements for grampahood are comparatively mild,
You only have to live until your child has a child.
From that point on you start looking both ways over your shoulder,
Because sometimes you feel thirty years younger and sometimes
       thirty years older.
Now you begin to realize who it was that reached the height of
       imbecility,
It was whoever said that grandparents have all the fun and none of
       the responsibility.
This is the most enticing spiderweb of a tarradiddle ever spun,
Because everybody would love to have a baby around who was no
       responsibility and lots of fun,
But I can think of no one but a mooncalf or a gaby
Who would trust their own child to raise a baby.
So you have to personally superintend your grandchild from diapers
       to pants and from bottle to spoon
Because you know that your own child hasn't sense enough to come
       in out of a typhoon.
You don't have to live forever to become a grampa, but if you do
       want to live forever,
Don't try to be clever;
If you wish to reach the end of the trail with an uncut throat,
Don't go around saying Quote I don't mind being a grampa but I
       hate being married to a gramma Unquote.

PREFACE TO THE PAST

Time all of a sudden tightens the tether,
And the outspread years are drawn together.
How confusing the beams from memory's lamp are;
One day a bachelor, the next a grampa.
What is the secret of the trick?
How did I get so old so quick?
Perhaps I can find by consulting the files
How step after step added up to miles.
I was sauntering along, my business minding,
When suddenly struck by affection blinding,
Which led to my being a parent nervous
Before they invented the diaper service.
I found myself in a novel pose,
Counting infant fingers and toes.
I tried to be as wise as Diogenes
In the rearing of my two little progenies,
But just as I hit upon wisdom's essence
They changed from infants to adolescents.
I stood my ground, being fairly sure
That one of these days they must mature,
So when I was properly humbled and harried,
They did mature, and immediately married.
Now I'm counting, the cycle being complete,
The toes on my children's children's feet.
Here lies my past, good-by I have kissed it;
Thank you, kids, I wouldn't have missed it.

OLD IS FOR BOOKS

A poet named Robert Browning eloped with a poetess named
    Elizabeth Barrett,
And since he had an independent income they lived in an Italian
    villa instead of a London garret.
He created quite a furor
With his elusive caesura.
He also created a youthful sage,
A certain Rabbi Ben Ezra who urged people to hurry up and age.
This fledgling said, Grow old along with me,
The best is yet to be.
I term him fledgling because such a statement, certes,
Could emanate only from a youngster in his thirties.
I have a friend named Ben Azzara who is far from a fledgling,
Indeed he is more like from the bottom of the sea of life a barnacled
    dredgling.
He tells me that as the years slipped by
He has become utterly dependent on his wife because he has
    forgotten how to tie his tie.
He says he sleeps after luncheon instead of at night.
And he hates to face his shaving mirror because although his
    remaining hair is brown his mustache comes out red and his
    beard comes out white.
Furthermore, he says that last week he was stranded for thirty-six
    hours in his club
Because he couldn't get out of the tub.
He says he was miserable, but when he reflected that the same thing
    probably eventually happened to Rabbi Ben Ezra
It relieved his mizra.

FROM AN ANTIQUE LAND—II

When is a Buick not a Buick?
When it's a Skylark? A Le Sabre? A Wildcat, an Electra, a Riviera?
Is it that a Chevrolet is a Chevrolet is a Chevrolet,
Or that a Chevrolet is a Chevy II is a Chevy II Nova is a Chevelle?
You may know a hawk from a handsaw,
But do you know a Plymouth from a Valiant from a Barracuda from a
    Satellite from a Fury from a Road Runner?
Fooled again; it's all of them.
You've decided to buy a Ford, or perhaps an Oldsmobile, a Mercury,
    Dodge, a Pontiac, a Rambler;
Pick your Rambler, your Pontiac, your Dodge, your Mercury,
    Oldsmobile, Ford from among the following:
Mustang, Comet, Montego, Firebird, Cougar, Bronco,
Charger, Galaxie, Rebel, Tempest, Falcon, Rogue,
Polara and Toronado.
Go ahead, pick the one you want, assuming you can identify it;
Then tell me who made it.
I remember the one-name cars, the cars you could tell apart.
I remember the Panhard, with a sort of lid on legs on top of the
    hood;
Pierce Arrow, its headlights spraddled on the mudguards.
They didn't look like the Mercer, nor the Mercer the Marmon,
The Hupp like the Franklin nor the Franklin like the Reo.
You knew the Pope-Hartford from the Pope-Toledo,
The Simplex from the Stanley, and all from the black Tin Lizzie.
Some were steamers, some air-cooled and some chain-driven.
But each as individual as a fingerprint.
You strained the gas through a chamois rag,
And half the grown-ups had broken wrists from the kick of the
    crank,
And the roadsters looked fine with a collie on the running board.
I see where a fellow paid $45,000 for a 1913 Mercer Runabout.
I wonder how old he was . . .

THEY WON'T BELIEVE, ON NEW YEAR'S EVE,
THAT NEW YEAR'S DAY WILL COME WHAT MAY

How do I feel today? I feet as unfit as an unfiddle,
And it is the result of a certain turbulence in the mind and an
    uncertain burbulence in the middle.
What was it anyway, that angry thing that flew at me?
I am unused to banshees crying Boo at me.
Your wife can't be a banshee,
Or can she?
Of course, some wives become less fond
When you're bottled in bond.
My Uncle George, in lavender-scented Aunt Edna's day,
If he had a glass of beer on Saturday night, he didn't dare come
    home till the following Wednesday.
I see now that he had hit upon the ideal idea,
The passage of time, and plenty of it, is the only marital panacea.
Ah, if the passage of time were backward, and last night I'd been a
    child again, this morning I'd be fragrant with orange juice,
Instead of reeking of pinch-bottle foreign juice;
But if I should turn out to be a child again, what would life hold for
    me?
The woman I love would be too old for me.
There's only one solution to my problem, a hair of the dog, or maybe
    a couple of hairs,
Then if she doesn't get mad at me life will be peaceful, and if she
    does, it will show she really cares.

LET'S NOT CLIMB THE WASHINGTON
MONUMENT TONIGHT

Listen, children, if you'll only stop throwing peanuts and bananas
    into my cage,
I'll tell you the facts of middle age.
Middle age is when you've met so many people that every new
    person you meet reminds you of someone else,
And when golfers' stomachs escape either over or under their belts.
It is when you find all halfbacks anthropoidal
And all vocalists adenoidal.
It is when nobody will speak loud enough for you to hear,
And you go to the ball game and notice that even the umpires are
    getting younger every year.
It's when you gulp oysters without bothering to look for pearls,
And your offspring cannot but snicker when you refer to your
    classmates as boys and your bridge partners as girls.
It is when you wouldn't visit Fred Allen or the Aga Khan if it meant
    sleeping on a sofa or a cot,
And your most exciting moment is when your shoelace gets tangled
    and you wonder whether if you yank it, it will come clean or
    harden into a concrete knot.
Also, it seems simpler just to go to bed than to replace a fuse,
Because actually you'd rather wait for the morning paper than listen
    to the eleven o'clock news,
And Al Capone and Babe Ruth and Scott Fitzgerald are as remote
    as the Roman emperors,
And you spend your Saturday afternoons buying wedding presents
    for the daughters of your contemporers.
Well, who wants to be young anyhow, any idiot born in the last forty
    years can be young, and besides forty-five isn't really old, it's
    right on the border;
At least, unless the elevator's out of order.

EHEU! FUGACES
or
WHAT A DIFFERENCE A LOT OF DAYS MAKE

When I was seventeen or so,
I scoffed at money-grubbers.
I had a cold contempt for dough,
And I wouldn't wear my rubbers.
No aspirin I took for pains,
For pests no citronella,
And in the Aprilest of rains
I carried no umbrella.

When I was young I was Sidney Carton,
Proudly clad in a Spartan tartan.
Today I'd be, if I were able,
Just healthy, wealthy, and comfortable.

When I was young I would not yield
To comforters and bed socks,
In dreams I covered center field
For the Giants or the Red Sox.
I wished to wander hence and thence,
From diamond mine to gold field,
Or piloting, a Blitzen Benz,
Outdistance Barney Oldfield.

When I subscribed to *The Youth's Companion*
I longed to become a second D'Artagnan.
Today I desire a more modest label:
He's healthy, wealthy, and comfortable.

When I was pushing seventeen,
I hoped to bag a Saracen;
Today should one invade the scene,
I'd simply find it embaracen.

Ah, Postumus, no wild duck I,
But just a waddling puddle duck,
So here's farewell to the open sky
From a middle-aged fuddy-duddle duck.

When I was young I was Roland and Oliver,
Nathan Hale and Simón Bolívar.
Today I would rather side step trouble,
And be healthy, wealthy, and comfortubble.

LINES ON FACING FORTY

I have a bone to pick with Fate.
Come here and tell me, girlie,
Do you think my mind is maturing late,
Or simply rotted early?

A MAN CAN COMPLAIN, CAN'T HE?
(A LAMENT FOR THOSE WHO THINK OLD)

Pallid and moonlike in the smog,
Now feeble Phoebus 'gins arise;
The upper floors of Empire State
Have vanished into sooty skies.
Half missing, like the shrouded tower,
Lackluster, like the paten solar,
I draw reluctant waking breath;
Another day, another dolor.

That breath I draw was first exhaled
By diesel and incinerator;
I should have wakened not at all,
Or, were it feasible, even later.
Walls of the world close in on me,
Threats equatorial and polar;
Twixt pit and pendulum I lie;
Another day, another dolor.

Here's news about the current strike,
The latest, greatest test of fission,
A fatal mugging in the park,
An obit of the Geneva mission.
One envelope yields a baffling form
Submitted by the tax comptroller;
A jury summons completes my mail;
Another day, another dolor.

Once eager for, I've come to dread,
The nimble fingers of my barber;
He's training strands across my scalp
Like skimpy vines across an arbor.
The conversation at the club
Is all intestinal or molar;
What dogs the Class of '24?
Another day, another dolor.

Between the dotard and the brat
My disaffection veers and varies;
Sometimes I'm sick of clamoring youth,
Sometimes of my contemporaries.
I'm old too soon, yet young too long;
Could Swift himself have planned it droller?
Timor vitae conturbat me;
Another day, another dolor.

CROSSING THE BORDER

Senescence begins
And middle age ends
The day your descendants
Outnumber your friends.

THE VOLUBLE WHEEL CHAIR

When you roll along admiring the view,
And everyone drives too fast but you;
When people not only ignore your advice,
But complain that you've given it to them twice;
When you babble of putts you nearly holed,
By gad, sir,
You are getting old.

When for novels you lose your appetite
Because writers don't write what they used to write;
When by current art you are unbeguiled,
And pronounce it the work of an idiot child;
When cacophonous music leaves you cold,
By gad, sir,
You are getting old.

When you twist the sheets from night to morn
To recall when a cousin's daughter was born;
When youngsters mumble and won't speak up,
And your dog dodders, who was a pup;
When the modern girl seems a hussy bold,
By gad, sir,
You are getting old.

When you scoff at feminine fashion trends;
When strangers resemble absent friends;
When you start forgetting the neighbors' names
And remembering bygone football games;
When you only drop in at the club to scold,
By gad, sir,
You are getting old.

But when you roar at the income tax,
And the slippery bureaucratic hacks,
And the ancient political fishlike smell,
And assert that the world is going to hell,
Why you are not old at all, at all;
By gad, sir,
You are on the ball.

BIRTHDAY ON THE BEACH

At another year
I would not boggle,
Except that when I jog
I joggle.

TIME MARCHES ON

You ask me, brothers, why I flinch.
Well, I will tell you, inch by inch.
Is it not proper cause for fright
That what is day will soon be night?
Evenings I flinch the selfsame way,
For what is night will soon be day.
At five o'clock it chills my gore
Simply to know it isn't four.
How Sunday into Monday melts!
And every month is something else.
If Summer on the ladder lingers,
Autumn tramples upon her fingers,
Fleeing before the jostling train
Of Winter, and Spring, and Summer again.
Year swallows year and licks its lips,
Then down the gullet of next year slips.
We chip at Time with clocks and watches;
We flee him in love and double scotches;
Even as we scatter in alarm
He marches with us, arm in arm;
Though while we sleep, he forward rides,
Yet when we wake, he's at our sides.
Let men walk straight or let them err,
He never leaves them as they were.
While ladies draw their stockings on
The ladies they were are up and gone,
I pen my lines, I finish, I scan them,
I'm not the poet who began them.
Each moment Time, the lord of changers,
Stuffs our skins with ephemeral strangers.
Good heavens, how remote from me
The billion people I used to be!
Flinch with me, brothers, why not flinch,
Shirts caught in the eternal winch?

Come, let us flinch till Time stands still;
Although I do not think he will.
Hark brothers, to the dismal proof:
The seconds spattering on the roof!

NEXT!

I thought that I would like to see
The early world that used to be,
That mastodonic mausoleum,
The Natural History Museum.
At midnight in the vasty hall
The fossils gathered for a ball.
High above notices and bulletins
Loomed up the Mesozoic skeletons.
Aroused by who knows what elixirs,
They ground along like concrete mixers.
They bowed and scraped in reptile pleasure,
And then began to tread the measure.
There were no drums or saxophones,
But just the clatter of their bones,
A rolling, rattling carefree circus
Of mammoth polkas and mazurkas.
Pterodactyls and brontosauruses
Sang ghostly prehistoric choruses.
Amid the megalosauric wassail
I caught the eye of one small fossil.
Cheer up, old man, he said, and winked—
It's kind of fun to be extinct.

LINES TO BE SCRIBBLED ON SOMEBODY ELSE'S THIRTIETH MILESTONE

Thirty today? Cheer up, my lad!
The good old thirties aren't so bad.
Life doesn't end at twenty-nine,
So come on in, the water's fine.
I, too, when thirty crossed my path,
Turned ugly colors with shame and wrath.
I kicked, I scratched, I bit my nails,
I indulged in tantrums the size of whales,
I found it hard to forgive my mater
For not having had me ten years later.
I struggled with reluctant feet
Where dotage and abdomens meet.
Like the tongue that seeks the missing tooth
I yearned for my extracted youth.
Since then some years have ambled by
And who so satisfied as I.
The thirties are things I wallow among,
With naught but pity for the young.
The less long ago that people were born
The more I gaze on them with scorn,
And each Thanksgiving I Thanksgive
That I'm slowly learning how to live.
So conquer, boy, your grief and rage,
And welcome to the perfect age!
I hope good fairies your footsteps haunt,
And bring you everything you want,
From cowboy suits and Boy Scout knives,
To beautiful, generous, wealthy wives.
If you play the horses, may you play good horses,
If you want divorces, may you get divorces,
Be it plenty of sleep, or fortune, or fame,
Or to carry the ball for Notre Dame,

Whatever it is you desire or covet,
My boy, I hope you get it and love it.
And you'll use it a great deal better, I know,
Than the child that you were a day ago.

IS THIS SEAT TAKEN? YES
or
MY NECK IS STICKING IN

I hope that in my eldering age I'm not becoming noticeably
    querulous,
But I feel that conversations with strangers can be perilous.
Consider the case of the two strangers who met in a hotel dining
    room in Alabama,
And the menu was rather less than a panorama,
Indeed, it was as repetitious as a snore,
And the first stranger said, I'm a little sick of corn pone, and the
    second stranger, who was tall, tan, and turbaned, said, Glad
    to know you, I'm Mohammed Khan, a big Sikh of Cawnpore.
I am also disturbed by accounts of the two strangers, one male and
    one female, who met on the banks of the Congo and shared a
    bowl of semolina,
And presently he said, You've got eyes like a gazelle, and she
    giggled and said, Eyes like a gazelle? And he said, No, you's
    like a hyena.
This is the sort of experience for which I do not hanker,
So if you will excuse me, I shall now run over to the Banker's Trust
    Company and trust a banker.

THE CALENDAR-WATCHERS
or
WHAT'S SO WONDERFUL ABOUT BEING A PATRIARCH?

I'm like a backward berry
Unripened on the vine,
For all my friends are fifty
And I'm only forty-nine.

My friends are steeped in wisdom,
Like senators they go,
In the light of fifty candles,
And one on which to grow.

How can I cap their gallion,
Or top their taste in wine?
Matched with the worldly fifties,
What chance has forty-nine?

Behold my old companions,
My playmates and my peers,
Remote on the Olympus
Of half a hundred years!

These grave and reverend seniors,
They call me Little Man,
They pat my head jocosely
And pinch my cheek of tan.

Why must I scuff my loafers
And grin a schoolboy grin?
Is not my waist as ample?
Is not my hair as thin?

When threatened with a rumba,
Do I not seek the bar?
And am I not the father
Of a freshman at Bryn Mawr?

O, wad some pawky power
Gie me a gowden giftie,
I'd like to stop at forty-nine,
But pontificate like fifty.

THE BARGAIN

As I was going to St. Ives
I met a man with seven lives;
Seven lives,
In seven sacks,
Like seven beeves
On seven racks.
These seven lives
He offered to sell,
But which was best
He couldn't tell.
He swore that with any
I'd be happy forever;
I bought all seven
And thought I was clever,
But his parting words
I can't forget:
Forever
Isn't over yet.

THE PARTY

Come Arabella, fetch the cake,
On a dish with silver handles.
Oh mercy! Feel the table shake!
Lucinda, light the candles.

For Mr. Migg is thir-ty,
Is thir—ty,
Is thir——ty.
The years are crawling over him
Like wee red ants.
Oh, three times ten is thir-ty,
Is for—ty,
Is fif——ty.
The further off from England
The nearer is to France.

The little flames they bob and jig
The dining hall is breezy.
Quick! puff your candles, Mr. Migg,
The little flames die easy.
For Mr. Migg is for-ty,
Is for—ty,
Is for——ty.
The years are crawling over him
Like wee red ants.
Oh four times ten is for-ty,
Is fif—ty,
Is six——ty,
And creeping through the icing,
The other years advance.

Why, Arabella, here's a ring!
Lucinda, here a thimble!
For Mr. Migg there's not a thing—
'Tis not, I trust, a symbol!

For Mr. Migg is fif-ty,
Is fif–ty,
Is fif—ty.
The years are crawling over him
Like wee red ants.

Oh, five times ten is fif-ty,
Is six–ty,
Is seven—ty.
Lucinda, put the cake away,
We're going to the dance.

THE SCREEN WITH THE FACE WITH THE VOICE

How long
Is a song?
O Lord,
How long?
A second?
A minute?
An hour?
A day?
A decade?
A cycle of Cathay?
Press the ears
With occlusive fingers;
The whining melody
Lingers, lingers;
The mouthing face
Will not be hid,
But leers at the eye
From the inner lid.
With the sure advance of ultimate doom
The moaning adenoids larger loom;
The seven-foot eyebrows fall and rise
In roguish rapture or sad surprise;
Eyeballs roll with fine emotion,
Like buoys rocked by a treacle ocean;
Tugged like the bell above the chapel,
Tosses the giant Adam's apple;
Oozes the voice from the magic screen,
A slow Niagara of Grenadine;
A frenzy of ripe orgiastic pain,
Niagara gurgling down a drain.

How long
Is a song?
O Lord,
How long?
As long as Loew,
And Keith,
And Albee;
It Was,
And Is,
And Always Shall Be.
This is the string Time may not sever,
This is the music that lasts forever,
This is the Womb,
This is the Tomb,
This is Alpha, Omega, and Oom!
The eyes, the eyes shall follow you!
The throat, the throat shall swallow you!
Hygienic teeth shall wolf you!
And viscous voice engulf you!
The lolloping tongue itself answer your question!
The Adam's Apple dance at your ingestion!
And you shall never die, but live to nourish the bowels
Of deathless celluloid vowels.

8

THE GREAT(?) OUTDOORS

*"Oh, I must go down to the beach, my lass
And step on a piece of broken glass."*

LINES TO BE MUTTERED THROUGH CLENCHED TEETH AND QUITE A LOT OF LATHER, IN THE COUNTRY

"Hark! Hark! The lark at Heaven's gate sings—"
Shut up, lark!
"And Phoebus 'gins arise—"
Sit down, Phoebus, before I knock you down!

Larks barking like beagles around a person's windows,
Sun-gods sneaking in at dawn and socking a person in the eye—
Why doesn't Nature go back to the Orient where it came from and
     bother the Mohammedans and Hindows
Instead of turning night into day every morning in Westchester
     County, N.Y.?

I speak for a community of commuters who toil for a pittance per
     diem—
Who spend 12½ percent of their waking lives on the N.Y., N.H., &
     H.—
Who would swap a billion shiny new A.M.'s for a secondhand P.M. —
I do not presume to speak for late risers such as Mr. Shubert and
     Mr. Winchell and Mr. Bache.

Why do we submit to a regime so tyrannical and despotic?
Why don't we do something about getting a lot less dawn and a lot
     more dusk?
I mean seriously, without any cracks about six months of night in the
     Arctic—
Because I think if it could be arranged life would be not nearly so
     grotusque.

Daybreak is one of the greatest disadvantages of living under the
     solar system:
It means having to get up almost the very minute you go to bed,
And bathe and shave and scrub industriously at your molar system
And catch a train and go to the office and try to earn some bread.

Come, let us leave the flowers and the birds and the beasts to their
  sun-worship,
All of us human beings ought to be more skeptical than a flower or a
  bird or a beast,
And a little serious thought should convince us that sunshine is
  something to unworship
And that if we want to salute the daybreak we should say not
  "Goodie goodie" but "Ah Cheest."

HE DIGS, HE DUG, HE HAS DUG

Say not Eve needed Adam's pardon
For their eviction from the Garden;
I only hope some power divine
Gets round to ousting me from mine.
On bended knee, perspiring clammily,
I scrape the soil to feed my family,
Untaught, unteachable, undramatic,
A figure sorry and sciatic.
Although I've done the best I could,
Nothing comes up the way it should.
They're making playshoes of my celery,
It's rubbery, and purple-yellery,
My beets have botts, my kale has hives,
There's something crawly in my chives,
And jeering insects think it cute
To swallow my spray and spit out my fruit.
My garden will never make me famous,
I'm a horticultural ignoramus,
I can't tell a stringbean from a soybean,
Or even a girl bean from a boy bean.

PRETTY HALCYON DAYS

How pleasant to sit on the beach,
On the beach, on the sand, in the sun,
With ocean galore within reach,
And nothing at all to be done!
No letters to answer,
No bills to be burned,
No work to be shirked,
No cash to be earned.
It is pleasant to sit on the beach
With nothing at all to be done.

How pleasant to look at the ocean,
Democractic and damp; indiscriminate;
It fills me with noble emotion
To think I am able to swim in it.
To lave in the wave,
Majestic and chilly,
Tomorrow I crave;
But today it is silly.
It is pleasant to look at the ocean;
Tomorrow, perhaps, I shall swim in it.

How pleasant to gaze at the sailors,
As their sailboats they manfully sail
With the vigor of vikings and whalers
In the days of the viking and whale.
They sport on the brink
Of the shad and the shark;
If it's windy they sink;
If it isn't, they park.
It is pleasant to gaze at the sailors,
To gaze without having to sail.

How pleasant the salt anaestheic
Of the air and the sand the the sun;
Leave the earth to the strong and athletic,
And the sea to adventure upon.
But the sun and the sand
No contractor can copy;
We lie in the land
Of the lotus and poppy
We vegetate, calm and aesthetic,
On the beach, on the sand, in the sun.

A WORD ON WIND

Cows go around saying Moo,
But the wind goes around saying Woooo.
Ghosts say Woooo to you, too,
And sometimes they say Boo to you, too,
But everybody has heard the wind and few people have heard a
    ghost,
So it is commonly supposed that the wind says Woooo the most.
Scientists try to tell us that wind is caused by atmospheric
    conditions at the North Pole or over distant Canadian
    ranches,
But I guess scientists don't ever get to the country because
    everybody who has ever been in the country knows that wind
    is caused by the trees waggling their branches.
On the ocean, where there are no trees, they refer to the wind as
    gales,
And it is probably caused by whales,
And the Sahara, where there are no trees or whales either, they call
    the wind a simoom or something,
And it is the result of the profanation of Tutankhamen's tomb or
    something.
Ill winds blow nobody good and they also blow new hats into mud
    puddles and voracious clouds of mosquitoes into propinquity
    with your hide,
And they make your cigarette burn down on just one side.
Some people are very refined,
And when they recite poetry or sing songs they pronounce wind,
    wined.
Well, dear wined, every time you say Wooooo,
Why I wish you would say it to people who say wined, right after you
    have said it somewhere where somebody is making fertilizer
    or glue.

NINE MILES TO THE RAILROAD

The country is a funny place,
I like to look it in the face.

And everywhere I look I see
Some kind of animal or tree.

Indeed, I frequently remark
The country is rather like a park.

The country cows give milk, and moo,
Just like their sisters in the zoo.
The rural squirrel in his rage
Chirks like a squirrel in a cage.

Animals, in their joys and passions,
Like women, follow city fashions.

The horses here pull plows and carts
All day until the sun departs.
In summer, or when fields are frosted,
They work until they are exhausted.

Next, to the track themselves they hie
To be bet upon by the likes of I.

As through the countryside you pass
You look at grass and still more grass.
Grass leers at you where'er you turn
Until your tired eyelids burn.

They ought to break it up, or soften it,
With pretty signs saying, please keep offen it.

I like the country very much.
It's good to hear and smell and touch.
It makes you feel akin with Nature,
Though wobbly on her nomenclature.

I'd free my lungs of city air
If I didn't feel much more important there.

MAX SCHLING, MAX SCHLING, LEND
ME YOUR GREEN THUMB

A TRAVELOGUE OF FLOWERY CATALOGUES
Bobolink!
Bobolink!
Spink!
Spank!
Spink!
Bobbink!
Atkink!
Sprink!

Burpee.

NOT EVEN FOR BRUNCH

When branches bend in fruitful stupor
Before the woods break out in plaid,
The super-market talks more super,
The roadside stands go slightly mad.
What garden grew this goblin harvest?
Who coined these words that strike me numb?
I will not purchase, though I starvest,
The cuke, the glad, the lope, the mum.

In happier days I sank to slumber
Murmuring names as sweet as hope:
Fair gladiolus, and cucumber,
Chrysanthemum and cantaloupe.
I greet the changelings that awoke me
With warmth a little less than luke,
As farmer and florist crowd to choke me
With glad and lope, with mum and cuke.

Go hence, far hence, you jargon-mongers,
Go soak your head in boiling ads,
Go feed to cuttlefish and congers
Your mums and lopes, your cukes and glads.
Stew in the whimsy that you dole us;
I roam where magic casements ope
On cantemum spiced, and cuciolus,
On chrysanthecumber, and gladaloupe.

MARTHA'S VINEYARD

I live at the top of old West Chop
In a house with a cranky stove,
And when I swim I risk life and limb
On the pebbles that line the cove—
Where the waves wish-wash, and the foghorn blows,
And the blowfish nibble at your toes-oes-oes,
The blowfish nibble at your toes.

I lunch and sup on schrod and scup,
And once in a while on beans,
And the only news that I get to peruse
Is in the last year's magazines—
Where the waves wish-wash, and the foghorn blows,
And the blowfish nibble at your toes-oes-oes,
The blowfish nibble at your toes.

When the sea gulls shout the lights go out,
And whenever the lights go on
I pursue the moth with a dusting cloth
Till the Bob White brings the dawn—
Where the waves wish-wash, and the foghorn blows,
And the blowfish nibble at your toes-oes-oes,
The blowfish nibble at your toes.

But when the breeze creeps through the trees
And the small waves shiver and shake,
Oh, I wouldn't swap my old West Chop
For a sizzling Western steak—
I want to wish-wash where the foghorn blows,
And the blowfish nibble at your toes-oes-oes,
The blowfish nibble at your toes.

A BEGINNER'S GUIDE TO THE OCEAN

Let us now consider the ocean.
It is always in motion.
It is generally understood to be the source of much of our rain,
And ten thousand fleets are said to have swept over it in vain.
When the poet requested it to break break break on its cold gray
        rocks it obligingly broke broke broke,
Which as the poet was Alfred Lord Tennyson didn't surprise him at
        all but if it had been me I would probably have had a stroke.
Some people call it the Atlantic and some the Pacific or the
        Antarctic or the Indian or the Mediterranean Sea,
But I always say what difference does it make, some old geographer
        mumbling a few words over it, it will always be just the
        Ocean to me.
There is an immortal dignity about something like the Atlantic,
Which seems to drive unimmortal undignified human beings
        frustratedly frantic.
Just give them one foot on the beach and people who were perfectly
        normal formerly, or whilom,
Why, they are subject to whoops and capers that would get them
        blackballed from an asylum;
Yet be they never so rampant and hollerant,
The ocean is tolerant,
Except a couple of times a day it gives up in disgust and goes off by
        itself and hides,
And that, my dears, accounts for the tides.

KIPLING'S VERMONT

The summer like a rajah dies,
And every widowed tree
Kindles for Congregational eyes
An alien suttee.

A WATCHED EXAMPLE NEVER BOILS

The weather is so very mild
That some would call it warm.
Good gracious, aren't we lucky, child?
Here comes a thunderstorm.

The sky is now indelible ink,
The branches reft asunder;
But you and I, we do not shrink;
We love the lovely thunder.

The garden is a raging sea,
The hurricane is snarling;
Oh happy you and happy me!
Isn't the lightning darling?

Fear not the thunder, little one.
It's weather, simply weather;
It's friendly giants full of fun
Clapping their hands together.

I hope of lightning our supply
Will never be exhausted;
You know it's lanterns in the sky
For angels who are losted.

We love the kindly wind and hail,
The jolly thunderbolt,
We watch in glee the fairly trail
Of ampere, watt, and volt.

Oh, than to enjoy a storm like this
There's nothing I would rather.
Don't dive beneath the blankets, Miss!
Or else leave room for Father.

WHO TAUGHT CADDIES TO COUNT?
or
A BURNT GOLFER FEARS THE CHILD

I have never beheld you, O pawky Scot,
And I only guess your name,
Who first propounded the popular rot
That golf is a humbling game.
You putted perhaps with a mutton bone,
And hammered a gutty ball;
But I think that you sat in the bar alone,
And never played at all.

Ye hae spoken a braw bricht mouthfu', Jamie,
Ye didna ken ye erred;
Ye're richt that golf is a something gamie,
But humble is not the word.
Try arrogant, insolent, supercilious,
And if invention fades,
Add uppitty, hoity-toity, bilious,
And double them all in spades.

Oh pride of rank is a fearsome thing,
And pride of riches a bore;
But both of them bow on lea and ling
To the Prussian pride of score.
Better the beggar with fleas to scratch
Than the unassuming dub
Trying to pick up a Saturday match
In the locker room of the club.

The Hollywood snob will look you through
And stalk back into his clique,
For he knows that he is better than you
By so many grand a week;
And the high-caste Hindu's fangs are bared
If a low-caste Hindu blinks;
But they're just like one of the boys, compared
To the nabobs of the links.

Oh where this side of the River Styx
Will you find an equal mate
To the scorn of a man with a seventy-six
For a man with a seventy-eight?
I will tell you a scorn that mates it fine
As the welkin mates the sun:
The scorn of him with a ninety-nine
For him with a hundred and one.

And that is why I wander alone
From tee to green to tee,
For every golfer I've ever known
Is too good or too bad for me.
Indeed I have often wondered, Jamie,
Hooking into the heather,
In such an unhumble, contemptful gamie
How anyone plays together.

SEASIDE SERENADE

It begins when you smell a funny smell,
And it isn't vanilla or caramel,
And it isn't forget-me-nots or lilies,
Or new-mown hay, or daffy-down-dillies,
And it's not what the barber rubs on Father,
And it's awful, and yet you like it rather.
No, it's not what the barber rubs on Daddy,
It's more like an elderly finnan haddie,
Or, shall we say, an electric fan
Blowing over a sardine can.
It smells of seaweed, it smells of clams,
It's as fishy as ready-made telegrams,
It's as fishy as millions of fishy fishes,
In spite of which you find it delishes,
You could do with a second helping, please,
And that, my dears, is the ocean breeze.
And pretty soon you observe a pack
Of people reclining upon their back,
And another sight that is very common
Is people reclining upon their abdomen.
And now you lose the smell of the ocean
In the sweetish vapor of sunburn lotion,
And the sun itself seems paler and colder,
Compared to vermilion face and shoulder.
The beach is peppered with ladies who look
Like pictures out of a medical book.
Last, not least, consider the kiddies,
Chirping like crickets and Katydiddies,
Splashing, squealing, slithering, crawling,
Cheerful, tearful, boisterous, bawling,
Kiddies in clamorous crowds that swarm
Heavily over your prostrate form,
Callous kiddies who gallop in myriads
Twixt ardent Apollos and eager Nereids,

Kiddies who bring, as a priceless cup,
Something dead that a wave washed up.
Oh, I must go down to beach, my lass,
And step on a piece of broken glass.

I DIDN'T GO TO CHURCH TODAY

I didn't go to church today,
I trust the Lord to understand.
The surf was swirling blue and white,
The children swirling on the sand.
He knows, He knows how brief my stay,
How brief this spell of summer weather,
He knows when I am said and done
We'll have a plenty of time together.

THE HUNTER

The hunter crouches in his blind
'Neath camouflage of every kind,
And conjures up a quacking noise
To lend allure to his decoys.
This grown-up man, with pluck and luck,
Is hoping to outwit a duck.

9

SEASONS AND VERY SPECIAL DAYS

"The year's adolescent!
The air's effervescent!"

COEFFICIENTS OF EXPANSION
(A GUIDE TO THE INFANT SEASON)

What happened in the Hot Stove League last winter?

Well, baseball got a new Commissioner, and the Senators, who are
still the same old Senators although not the original Senators
because the original Senators are now the Twins, got a new
manager, the Splendid Splinter.

Pitchers have been ordered to deliver the ball more allegro and less
adagio.

And if you are wondering about the Royals, well, the Royals used to
be Montreal but now Montreal is the Expos, and Kansas City,
which was the A's, is the Royals, and the A's, which were first
Philadelphia and later Kansas City, are Oakland, under the
partial aegis of Joe DiMaggio.

In lower California, confusion is rife around the pot spots and hot-
rodderies;

No one is able to differentiate between San Diego's twice-born
Padres and the Padres' reborn Johnny Podres.

And, apropos newly launched satellites,

The disappearance of Mickey Mantle was hardly compensated for by
the appearance of something called the Pilots, except
perhaps to a few Seattleites.*

The mound has been lowered because the hitters complained that
the pitchers were too parsimonious and pawky,

And Satchel Paige pitched two scoreless exhibition innings for the
Braves of Atlanta, formerly the Braves of Boston and
Milwaukee.

Finally, at least one sportscaster has added a phrase to his cargo of
argot, and I quote him verbatim:

When a batter leaves a runner stranded on third, he has "failed to
plate him."

So, that's how it went.

This wrapup has been brought to you through the authority of the
undersigned Lifelong Fan, and is not intended in any way to
express for the aforementioned expansion said Lifelong Fan's
enthusiasm, approval, or written consent.

*Since removed to Milwaukee and renamed the Brewers.

SEPTEMBER IS SUMMER, TOO
or
IT'S NEVER TOO LATE TO BE UNCOMFORTABLE

Well, well, well, so this is summer, isn't that *mirabile dictu*,
And these are the days when whatever you sit down on you stick to.
These are the days when those who sell four ounces of synthetic
      lemonade concocted in a theater basement for a quarter enter
      into their inheritance,
And Rum Collinses soak through paper napkins onto people's
      Hepplewhites and Sheratons,
And progressive-minded citizens don their most porous finery and
      frippery.
But it doesn't help, because underneath they are simultaneously
      sticky and slippery.
And some insomniacs woo insomnia plus pajamas and others minus,
And everybody patronizes air-conditioned shops and movies to get
      cool and then complains that the difference in temperature
      gives them lumbago and sinus,
And people trapped in doorways by thunderstorms console
      themselves by saying, Well, anyway this will cool it off while
      we wait,
So during the storm the mercury plunges from ninety-four to ninety-
      three and afterwards climbs immediately to ninety-eight,
And marriages break up over such momentous questions as Who ran
      against Harding—Davis or Cox?
And when you go to strike a match the head dissolves on the box,
But the estival phenomena amaze me not,
What does amaze me is how every year people are amazed to
      discover that summer is hot.

THERE ARE MORE WAYS TO ROAST A PIG
THAN BURNING THE HOUSE DOWN
or
YOU CAN ALWAYS STICK YOUR HEAD
IN A VOLCANO

Poring over calendars is apt to give people round shoulders and a
    squint, or strabismus,
So I am perhaps fortunate in not needing a calendar to tell me when
    it's my birthday or Christmas.
I know that a year has rolled around once more
When I find myself thumbing a crisp new cigarette lighter just like
    the cover of other cigarette lighters strewn on a shelf in the
    garage along with the broken tire chains and the license
    plates for 1934.
It is only for myself that I presume to speak,
But I can light cigarettes with a cigarette lighter for exactly one
    week,
And then on the eighth day something comes up for renewal,
And sometimes it's the flint, and maybe the powder horn or ramrod,
    and sometimes the fuel,
And if it's the flint you unscrew the little jigger at the bottom and
    the insides jump out at you like a jack-in-the-box and you
    can't get them back in without the services of an engineer
    and a gunsmith and a vet,
And if it's the fuel it gets everywhere except into the tank and when
    you spin the wheel the whole thing including your hand flares
    up like a crêpe Suzette.
Well, enough is enough,
And many less ingenious persons would turn to chewing cut plug, or
    sniffing snuff,
But in between birthdays and Christmases I have figured out a way
    to light cigarettes indoors and out in any kind of weather;
I just rub a match and a matchbox together.

A WORD ABOUT WINTER

Now the frost is on the pane,
Rugs upon the floor again,
Now the screens are in the cellar,
Now the student cons the speller,
Lengthy summer noon is gone,
Twilight treads the heels of dawn,
Round-eyed sun is now a squinter,
Tiptoe breeze a panting sprinter,
Every cloud a blizzard hinter,
Squirrel on the snow a printer,
Rain spout sprouteth icy splinter,
Willy-nilly, this is winter.

Summer-swollen doorjambs settle,
Ponds and puddles turn to metal,
Skater whoops in frisky fettle,
Golf-club stingeth like a nettle,
Radiator sings like a kettle,
Hearth is Popocatepetl.

Runneth nose and chappeth lip,
Draft evadeth weather strip,
Doctor wrestleth with grippe
In never-ending rivalship.
Rosebush droops in garden shoddy,
Blood is cold and thin in body,
Weary postman dreams of toddy,
Head before the heart grows noddy.

On the hearth the embers gleam,
Glowing like a maiden's dream,
Now the apple and the oak
Paint the sky with chimney smoke,
Husband now, without disgrace,
Dumps ash trays in the fireplace.

CHANT AT THE END OF A BEGINNINGLESS SUMMER

The sky is overcast and I am undercast and the fog creeps in on
    little iceberg feet,
And there is no retreat.
I would don my Job-like false-whiskers and my straggly King Lear
    wig;
I shake them, and out drops an earwig.
Oh dank, dank, dank, there is no chill in the martini nor warmth in
    the toddy.
The aura of the house is that of a damp demd moist unpleasant
    body.
You will note that I cannot even quote Dickens correctly, as once I
    used,
In this weather, all my Dickens have gone back to Proust.
In this weather, in this weather
One hundred six-cent stamps and fifty air-mails have become
    permanently glued together.
At night eaves drip and foghorn moans in tuneless timeless
    antiphony,
I have not seen the moon since the second Sunday after Epiphany.
Strangely, I find I miss the moon no whit,
Nor have I since the two U.S.'s have changed her from "she" to "it."
I want to return to the womb,
No matter of whom.
Respect my gloom, my gloom is lodged in my craw,
Do not mark, fold, tear or staple my gloom, it is recommended for
    mature audiences, it is void where prohibited by law.
Summer that never was, of seeing yoursel as others see ye I'll gie ye
    the giftie;
No maiden of bashful fifteen like other summers hae ye been, but
    unco like, as Richard Brinsley Sheridan almost said,
A weirdo of fifty.

HYMN TO THE SUN AND MYSELF

Well! Well!
The day's at the morn!
Dandy old day!
Dandy old morn!
Oh! Look!
The hillside's dew-pearled!
Nicely old hillside!
Nicely dew-pearled!
And oh! Look!
The snail's on the thorn!
Lucky old snail!
Lucky old thorn!
Well! Well!
All's right with the world!
Hurrah for the right!
Hurrah for the world!

For oh! what a day it is today, my lads!
Oh! my lads, what a day it is today!
At 11:07 a.m. I'll be 27¾ years old.
An age dear to me because it was once passed through by Edna St.
        Vincent Millay.
Oh what fun to be young and healthy and alive
And privileged to do some of the work of the world from nine to five!
Oh let me be truly thankful for every one of those 27¾ years;
For not having been run over by the Lexington Avenue Express or
        gored by runaway steers;
For not having been able to afford a passage on the *Titanic*,
And for not having had any money to lose in the recent stock market
        panic;
For never having written a best-seller, only to be wounded by the
        critics;
For never having gotten impeached for making millions in dirty
        politics;

For never having made any enemies by getting ahead too speedily;
For not finding the world at my feet while still as young as
      Lindbergh or Gertrude Ederle;
For not having tried to impress my girl but being naturaler with her
      and naturaler;
So that now instead of having to marry and all that I can continue to
      be a careless baturaler;
Above all let me be thankful for something rarer than gold—
Viz: that at 11:07 a.m. I'll be 27 ¾ years old.
Oh let my future be as lucky as my past!
Oh let every day for a long time not be my last!

PUT BACK THOSE WHISKERS, I KNOW YOU

There is one fault that I must find with the twentieth century,
And I'll put it in a couple of words: Too adventury.
What I'd like would be some nice dull monotony
If anyone's gotony.
People have gone on for years looking forward hopefully to the
      beginning of every fresh anno Domini,
Full of more hopes that there are grits in hominy,
Because it is their guess that the Old Year has been so bad that the
      New Year cannot help being an improvement, and may I say
      that they would never make a living as guessers,
Because what happens, why the New Year simply combines and
      elaborates on the worst features of its predecessors.
Well, I know what the matter is, it stands out as clear as a chord in a
      symphony of Sibelius's,
The matter is that our recent New Years haven't been New Years at
      all, they have just been the same Old Year, probably 1914 or
      something, under a lot of different aliases.
In my eagerness to encounter a New Year I stand ahead of most,
But only if it's a true New Year, not if it's merely the same Old Year
      with its beard shaved off and wearing a diaper labeled New
      Year just to get on the cover of the *Saturday Evening Post.*

THE RETURN

Early is the evening,
Reluctant the dawn;
Once there was summer;
Sudden it was gone.
It fell like a leaf,
Whirled downstream.
Was there ever summer,
Or only a dream?
Was ever a world
That was not November?
Once there was summer.
And this I remember,

Cornflowers and daisies,
Buttercups and clover,
Black-eyed Susans, and Queen Anne's lace,
A wide green meadow,
And the bees booming over,
And a little laughing girl with the wind in her face.

Strident are the voices
And hard lights shine;
Feral are the faces;
Is one of them mine?
Something is lost now;
Tarnished the gleam;
Was there ever nobleness,
Or only a dream?
Yes, and it lingers,
Lost not yet;
Something remains
Till this I forget,

Cornflowers and clover,
Buttercups and daisies,
Black-eyed Susans under blue and white skies;
And the grass waist-high
Where the red cow grazes,
And a little laughing girl with faith in her eyes.

TRICK OR TREK

If my face is white as a newmade sail,
It's not that it's clean, it's simply pale.
The reason it's pale as well as clean:
I'm a shaken survivor of Halloween.
The little ones of our community
This year passed up no opportunity;
You should have seen the goblins and witches;
At our expense, they were all in stitches.
They shook with snickers from warp to woof
When our doormat landed on the roof.
And take a look at our garden's format—
It now resembles the missing dormat.
The doorbell got torn out by the roots,
So our guests announce themselves tooting flutes.
Don't blame me if I wince or flinch,
They tore the fence down inch by inch.
Forgive me if I flinch or wince,
We haven't seen our mailbox since,
And we can't get into our own garage
Since they gave the door that Swedish massage.
All this perhaps I could forgive,
In loving kindness I might live,
But on every window they scrawled in soap
Those deathless lines, *Mr. Nash is a dope.*
At the very glimpse of a Jack-o'-lantern
I've got one foot on the bus to Scranton.
When Halloween next delivers the goods,
You may duck for apples—I'll duck for the woods.

I ALWAYS SAY THERE'S NO PLACE
LIKE NEW YORK IN THE SUMMER
or
THAT COTTAGE SMALL BY A WATERFALL
WAS SNAPPED UP LAST FEBRUARY

Estivation means passing the summer in a torpid condition, which is
    why I love to estivate,
But I find that planning my estivation is as chaotic as the
    nightmares caused by that fried lobster with garlic sauce
    which I when restive and indigestive ate.
When icicles hang by the wall and people smear Chap Stick on their
    faces
I can't seem to take it in that the hounds of Spring are actually on
    Winter's traces.
The subfreezing months are what my wits are frozen and subhuman
    in;
Sing cuccu never so lhude, cuccu cannot convince me that Sumer is
    icumen in.
And when he tosses his chewing gum wrappers at the wastebasket,
    he hits it three times out of five.
The economics of housewifery are beyond his scope;
After he has washed his hands, you find he has used three fresh
    towels and two new cakes of soap.
Yes, Mr. Nagle is the housewife's pet.
He can mess up half a dozen clean ash trays with one regular-size
    cigarette.
Sometimes he goes to the opposite pole,
He puts dead matches back in the matchbox, and cracks nuts and
    puts the shells back in the bowl.
No matter how deeply you are planted in a peaceful day at home,
    Mr. Nagle can uproot you;
Scots wha' hae wi' wallydraigles bled, I salute you.

PIPE DREAMS

Many people have asked me what was the most beautiful sight I saw
     during the recent summer,
And I think the most beautiful sight was the day the water wouldn't
     stop running and in came the plumber,
Because your cottage may be very cunning,
But you don't appreciate it when the water won't stop running,
And you would almost rather submit to burgling
Than to consistent gurgling.
And then the other most beautiful sight I saw during the summer
Was the day the water wouldn't run at all and in came the plumber,
Because one thing even less enticing than a mess of pottage
Is a waterless cottage,
So apparently all my beautiful memories of the summer
Are beautiful memories of the plumber,
And I am sorry they aren't more romantic,
I am sorry they are not memories of the moonlight rippling on the
     Atlantic,
On my yes, what wouldn't I give for some beautiful memories of the
     fields and the sky and the sea,
But they are not for the likes of me,
Nay, if you want to have beautiful memories of the summer,
Why the thing to do is to be a plumber,
Because then you can have some really beautiful beauties to
     remember,
Because naturally plumbers wouldn't think plumbers were the most
     beautiful thing they saw between June and September.
And that's the great advantage plumbers have over me and you,
They don't have to think about plumbers, so they can concentrate on
     the view.

I REMEMBER YULE

I guess I am just an old fogey
I guess I am headed for the last roundup, so come along little dogey.
I can remember when winter was wintery and summer was estival;
I can even remember when Christmas was a family festival.
I can even remember when Christmas was an occasion for fireside
 rejoicing and general good will,
And now it is just the day that it's only X shopping days until.
What, five times a week at 8:15 p.m., do the herald angels sing?
That a small deposit now will buy you an option on a genuine
 diamond ring.
What is the message we receive with Good King Wenceslaus?
That if we rush to the corner of Ninth and Main we can get that pink
 mink housecoat very inexpenceslaus.
I know what came upon the midnight clear to our backward parents,
 but what comes to us?
A choir imploring us to Come all ye faithful and steal a 1939
 convertible at psychoneurotic prices from Grinning Gus.
Christmas is a sitting duck for sponsors, it's so commercial,
And yet so noncontroversial.
Well, you reverent sponsors redolent of frankincense and myrrh,
 come smear me with bear-grease and call me an un-
 American hellion,
This is my declaration of independence and rebellion.
This year I'm going to disconnect everything electrical in the house
 and spend the Christmas season like Tiny Tim and Mr.
 Pickwick;
You make me sickwick.

HAND ME DOWN MY OLD SCHOOL
SLIDING PADS
or
THERE'S A HINT OF STRAWBERRY
LEAVES IN THE AIR

This is the outstretched, tentative toe,
The placid paddling into dotage:
To complement the radio
With the library of a summer cottage.

What calmer joy can life afford,
What more can fortune offer, or fame,
Than reading Mrs. Humphry Ward
While listening to the baseball game?

A glimpse of ducal silhouettes,
A flash of electronic science,
As kind hearts clash with coronets—
Also the Cardinals with the Giants.

The heroine's birth is most unusual—
It's three and two on Enos Slaughter.
What would she think of Stanley Musial,
And he of Lady Rose's daughter?

The code of stout King Edward's reign
Conceals outstanding hanky-panky,
Suggesting time and time again
The hidden ball of Eddie Stanky.

Beware, fair child, of how you stray;
Warkworth, that cad, is far too cuddly!
Ah! In the ninth, with two away,
She's rescued by the Duke of Chudleigh!

In a world where even umpires err,
Why scorn the Duchess's stumbling start?
"When she learned at last he needed her,
The dear knowledge filled and tamed her heart."

Oh, bury me where the blue begins,
Where ball meets bat as lord meets lord,
Out where the home team always wins
And virtue is its Humphry Ward.

HERE WE GO QUIETLY NUTS IN MAY

Do you hanker for April showers,
Or a rarefied day in June?
Give me a grade-A May day,
And please deliver it soon.
I am weary of branches naked,
Creaking like lovelorn cats;
The earth underfoot mud-cakèd,
And the sun overhead ersatz.
Send me a balmy zephyr
To play me a rigadoon,
And I'll gulp of my grade-A May day
Till my hiccups hammer the moon.

SPRING SONG

Listen, buds, it's March twenty-first;
Don't you know enough to burst?
Come on, birds, unlock your throats!
Come on, gardeners, shed your coats!
Come on zephyrs, come on flowers,
Come on grass, and violet showers!
And come on, lambs, in frisking flocks!
Salute the vernal equinox!
Twang the cheerful lute and zither!
Spring is absolutely hither!
Yester eve was dark despair,
With winter, winter, everywhere;
Today, upon the other hand,
'Tis spring throughout this happy land.
Oh, such is Nature's chiaroscuro,
According to the Weather Bureau.

Then giddy-ap, Napoleon! Giddy-ap, Gideon!
The sun has crossed the right meridian!
What though the blasts of Winter sting?
Officially, at least, it's Spring,
And be it far from our desire
To make the Weather Man a liar!

So, blossom, ye parks, with cozy benches,
Occupied by blushing wenches!
Pipe, ye frogs, while swains are sighing,
And furnaces unwept are dying!
Crow, ye cocks, a little bit louder!
Mount, ye sales of paint and powder!
Croon, ye crooner, yet more croonishly!
Shine, ye moon, a lot more moonishly!
And oh ye brooklets, burst your channels!
And oh ye camphor, greet ye flannels!
And bloom, ye clothesline, bloom with wash,
Where erstwhile squudged the grim galosh!
Ye transit lines, abet our follies
By turning loose your open trolleys!
And ye, ye waking hibernators,
Drain anti-freeze from your radiators!
While ye, ye otherwise useless dove,
Remember, please, to rhyme with love.

Then giddy-ap, Napoleon! Giddy-ap, Gideon!
The sun has crossed the right meridian!
What though the blasts of Winter sting?
Officially, at least, it's Spring!

MIDSUMMER'S DAYMARE

Mumbo jumbo, what have we here?
Why we have the longest day in the year.
This is the rarest day of June,
And it's weeks and weeks from dawn to noon.
This is the calendar's blazing highlight,
It's months and months from noon to twilight.
Lucky are they who retain their friends
Through the day that seldom if ever ends.
Take a modest date, like December twenty,
And still the telephone jangles plenty,
Still you encounter bores enough,
Obligations and chores enough,
Visitors to avoid enough
Like something out of Freud enough,
Creditors, editors, tears and combats,
Newsreel beauties embracing wombats,
Feeble coffee and vanishing waiters,
Newsreel girls riding alligators,
Traffic and taxes and dues and duties
And candidates kissing newsreel beauties.
Oh, man has need of all his strength
To survive a day of medium length;
What wonder, then, that man grows bitter
On a day that sits like a flagpole-sitter?
Mumbo jumbo, noon infernal
This, my dears, is the day eternal.
You toil for a dollar or two per diem,
You mope and hope for the blessed p.m.,
You look at the clock, you're ready for mayhem;
Is it p.m. yet? No, it's still the a.m.!
On farm and field, in office and park,
This is the day that won't get dark.
Dusk is an exile, night has fled,
Never again shall we get to bed,

The sun has swallowed the moon and stars,
Midnight lies with the buried Czars.
This is the guerdon of prayer and fasting:
Glorious day, day everlasting!

SUMMER SERENADE

When the thunder stalks the sky,
When tickle-footed walks the fly,
When shirt is wet and throat is dry,
Look, my darling, that's July.

Though the grassy lawn be leather,
And prickly temper tug the tether,
Shall we postpone our love for weather?
If we must melt, let's melt together!

EPILOGUE TO MOTHER'S DAY, WHICH IS TO BE PUBLISHED ON ANY DAY BUT MOTHER'S DAY

Mothers! Mothers! It was visions of mothers that had been
    relentlessly haunting me,
Wherever I turned I saw misty mothers sitting around taunting me.
It was battalions of irritated spectres that blanched my face and
    gave me this dull and lustre-lack eye,
Night and day I was surrounded by mothers, from Mrs. Whistler,
    Senior, to Mrs. Dionne and from Yale the mother of men to
    Niobe and the mother of the Gracchi.
I resented this supernatural visitation, these are not the dark ages,
    these are the days of modernity,
I wilted before this intrusion of miasmic maternity.
Mothers, I cried, oh myriads of mothers, I can stand it no longer,
    what can I do for you?
Do you want me to have you exorcised, do you want me to pray for
    you, do you want me to say Boo for you?
I know you are major figures in history's Who's Whom,
But I wish you would go away because your company is flattering
    but I would rather have your room.

Then they replied in hollow chorus,
We have thought of something that we want to have published but
      we can't write so you will have to write it for us,
And if you write it we will leave you alone,
And if you don't write it we will haunt you brain from skull and flesh
      from bone,
So I acquiesced and the ghastly horde dictated to me and I wrote it,
And a promise is a promise and an army of ghostly mothers is an
      army of ghostly mothers, so I quote it:—
M is for the preliminary million-dollar advertising appropriation,
O means that she is always white-haired, bespectacled and at least
      eighty-five years old,
T is for Telegraph message number 31B which contains a tastefully
      blended expression of sentiment and congratulation,
H is for the coast-to-coast questionnaire which proved conclusively
      that seven-and-one-half citizens out of every ten with
      incomes of $5000 a year or better would rather have their
      mother than gold.
E is for the Elephants which everybody is very glad didn't sit down
      on their mothers,
R is for Rosemary which is for Remembrance of the fact that a
      mother is one thing that you will never have more than one
      of,
Put them all together and before you can say H. Wellington
      Carruthers, they spell what everybody who loves their mother
      only once a year and then only at the instigation of the
      Chamber of Commerce is a son of.

THE STRANGE CASE OF MR. BALLANTINE'S
VALENTINE

Once upon a time there was an attorney named Mr. Ballantine.

He lived in the spacious gracious days of the nineteenth century.

Mr. Ballantine didn't know they were spacious and gracious.

He thought they were terrible.

The reason he thought they were terrible was that love had passed him by.

Mr. Ballantine had never received a valentine.

He said to his partner, My name is Mr. Ballantine and I have never received a valentine.

His partner said, Well my name is Mr. Bogardus and I have received plenty of valentines and I just as soon wouldn't.

He said Mr. Ballantine didn't know when he was well off.

Mr. Ballantine said, I know my heart, I know my mind, I know I long for a valentine.

He said here it was St. Valentine's day and when he sat down at his desk what did he find?

Valentines?

No.

I find affidavits, said Mr. Ballantine.

That's the kind of valentine I get, said Mr. Ballantine.

Mr. Bogardus said that affidavit was better than no bread.

Mr. Ballantine said that affidavit, affidavit, affidavit onward, into the valley of death rode the six hundred.

Mr. Bogardus said that any man who would rhyme "onward" with "six hundred" didn't deserve any affidavits at all.

Mr. Ballantine said coldly that he was an attorney, not a poet, and Mr. Bogardus had better take the matter up directly with Lord Tennyson.

Mr. Bogardus said Oh all right, and speaking of lords, he couldn't remember who was the king before David, but Solomon was the king affidavit.

Mr. Ballantine buried Mr. Bogardus in the cellar and went out in search of love.

Towards evening he encountered a maiden named Herculena, the Strongest Woman in the World.

He said, Madam my name is Mr. Ballantine and I have never received a valentine.

Herculena was delighted.

Mr. Ballantine nearly burst with joy.

Herculena nearly burst with pride.

She flexed her biceps.

She asked Mr. Ballantine to pinch her muscle.

Mr. Ballantine recovered consciousness just in time to observe the vernal equinox.

He thought she said bustle.

She said, My name is Herculena the Strongest Woman in the World, and I have never received a valentine either.

Mr. Ballantine and Herculena decided to be each other's valentine.

All was merry as a marriage bell.

THE ETERNAL VERNAL
or
IN ALL MY DREAMS MY FAIR FACE BEAMS

Forgive this singsong,
It's just my spring song.
All winter like the blossoms
I've been playing possums,
But with April adjacent
I'm a possum renascent.
I'm the Renaissance
In gabardine pants,
I'm a gossoon once more,
Not forty-five, but forty-four,
I drink my kumiss
With pepper and pumice,
I swim where the herring do
In search of derring-do,
I crouch in a pergola
To catch me a burgola,
I'm Gustavus Adolphus
Among tennis players and golphus,
Compared to me they're a tortoise
With advanced rigor mortis,
I combine the music of Götterdämmerung
With the words of the Decamerrung,
I woo nymphs like billy-o
With my well-known punctilio,
Which unless I've progressed
Is the punkest tilio by actual test,
I roll a one and a two at dice and consider them better than a good
        cook or a good wife are,
Because one and two is free, and that's what the best things in life
        are,
And if anyone disagrees they might just as well not have done it,

Because I know this business backwards and that's the way I
    propose to run it.
In a word, it is spring,
And I can do any thing.

ALWAYS MARRY AN APRIL GIRL

Praise the spells and bless the charms,
I found April in my arms.
April golden, April cloudy,
Gracious, cruel, tender, rowdy;
April soft in flowered languor,
April cold with sudden anger,
Ever changing, ever true—
I love April, I love you.

JANGLE BELLS

Man is said to want but little here below,
And I have an idea that what he wants littlest of is snow.
Snow is all right while it is snowing;
It is like inebriation because it is very pleasing when it is coming,
      but very unpleasing when it is going,
But any further resemblance between the two has escaped this Old
      Master,
Because certainly everybody would rather be sozzled than
      snowbound, except maybe Mrs. Ella Boole and Lady Astor.
Snow is what you are up to your neck in when people send you post
      cards from Florida saying they wish you were there, and I
      wish they might sit on a burr,
Because they don't wish anything of the kind, no, they are secretly
      glad you are not there, otherwise they couldn't send the post
      card saying they wish you were.

HERE USUALLY COMES THE BRIDE

June means weddings in everyone's lexicon,
Weddings in Swedish, weddings in Mexican.
Breezes play Mendelssohn, treeses play Youmans,
Birds wed birds, and humans wed humans.
All year long the gentlemen woo,
But the ladies dream of a June "I do."
Ladies grow loony, and gentlemen loonier;
This year's June is next year's Junior.

SUMMERGREEN FOR PRESIDENT

Winter comes but once a year but it lasts for most of it,
And you may think there is a chance it may be a mild one, but there
    isn't a ghost of it.
Some people still say ice is nicer than slush,
And to those people I say Hush.
Some people still say snow is nicer than rain,
Which is like being still unreconciled to the defeat of James G.
    Blaine.
Some people still say a freeze is nicer than a thaw,
And I hope they find cold storage Japanese beetles in their slaw.

Slush is much nicer than ice because when you step in it you simply
    go splash, instead of immediately depositing either your
    posterior or your pate on it,
And also you don't have to skate on it.
Rain is much nicer than snow because you don't have to have rain
    plows piling rain up in six-foot piles exactly where you want
    to go,
And you don't have to build rain-men for the kiddies and frolic in
    sleighs and sleds, and also rain is nicer because it melts the
    snow.
A thaw is obviously much nicer than a freeze,
Because it annoys people with skis.
And in all my life I have only known one man who honestly liked
    winter better than summer,
Because every summer he used to have either his tonsils or his
    appendix or something out, and every winter he was a
    plumber.

THE MIDDLE OF THE MONTH

Oh, some people grieve for New Year's Eve,
And some for the dog days fiddle;
My moment sublime is the restful time
When the month is at the middle.

Sing tirra lirra loo for the middle of the month,
Which wipes out woes like chamois!
The middle of the month is honey and milk!
The middle of the month is mammy!
Now let us exult,
For the bills of ult.
Are limbo's laughing stocks;
At Fate we scoff,
For a fortnight off
Are the impotent bills of prox.
The first of the month is oyster-gray,
The last of the month is clammy,
But it's tirra lirra loo for the middle of the month,
For the middle of the month is mammy!

Time, fly not back upon they track!
The past is merely tedium,
And the future, too, so stand still, do,
While the month is at the medium!

Then tirra lirra loo for the middle of the month
And gambol it in like May Day!
The ravenous wolves are toothless now,
The lambs are in their heyday.

Now turn not pale
At the morning mail
Nor shrink when the telephone shrills,
No evil betides
On the blessed Ides,
The lull between the bills!
Oh, the first of the month is oyster-gray
And the last of the month is clammy,
But it's tirra lira loo for the middle of the month,
For the middle of the month is mammy!

GOOD RIDDANCE, BUT NOW WHAT?

Come children, gather round my knee;
Something is about to be.

Tonight's December thirty-first,
Something is about to burst.

The clock is crouching, dark and small,
Like a time bomb in the hall.

Hark, it's midnight, children dear.
Duck! Here comes another year!

RAVEN, DON'T STAY AWAY FROM MY DOOR
—A CHANT FOR APRIL FIRST

What pleasanter task for All Fools' Day than going over all the
    things you have done before
And don't want to do again never no more, never no more, never no
    more?
Oh softer than the lap of ripples on Innisfree's poetically described
    shore
Is never no more.
Sweeter than the prospect of encountering a dozen ladies each as
    exquisite as Mr. Poe's lost Lenore
Is never no more.
More alluring than an invitation to visit rich and charming friends
    on the Côte d'Or
Is never no more.
Oh let us toy with the comforting but untrue tenet that the burnt
    child dreads the fire that burned him;
Let us each of us dream that the last lesson he had was a lesson that
    really learned him.
I at least refuse to be dissudaded by anyone, even Mrs. Luce or Mrs.
    Post or Dorothy Dix or Petrarch's Laura;
On this day of days I shall be a hard-shell, shouting fundamentalist
    never no maura.
Never no more will I escort a lady home downtown when I am sleepy
    and want to go up;

Or drink buttermilk, or sauerkraut juice; or anything at all out of a
    paper cup;
Or see anybody off on a boat;
Or expect anybody else to like a book or a play on which I happen
    to particularly dote.
Or underestimate a Slav;
Or say politely No I haven't heard a story, when as a matter of fact I
    have;
Or let any parent tell me what Sister said to Sonny;
Or play bridge for love, or if it comes to that, for money;
Or get flustered into accepting an invitation I don't want to accept
    just because I can't think quickly at the telephone;
Or believe that something is better than something else just because
    it's wrapped in cellophane.
Also, commuting and eating out of doors—
These belong on any list of ideal never no mores.
In conclusion may I say that if this were not a song for the First of
    April I'd feel very guilty
At daring even to contemplate such a devastatingly delightful
    impossibility.

PLEASE LEAVE FATHER ALONE

Mother's Day is a very fine day,
And mothers are very fine people,
And the human race by them is crowned
As the church is crowned by the steeple.
We often refer to mother love;
To mother hate, less often;
To fathers we hardly refer at all,
But once a year we soften.

It's Father's Day, it's Father's Day,
The eager mothers cry.
And what of that? And what of that?
The fathers make reply.
Well, here's a collar, and here's a stud,
The mothers murmur low,
And fathers avoid each other's glance,
Meaning, I told you so.

Oh, Mother's Day is a very fine day,
And not alone for mothers.
The florist finds it to his taste,
And so do a lot of others.
The candy people jump for joy,
The jeweller rubs his hands,
And the new coupé is shining proof
That Father understands.

It's Mother's Day, it's Mother's Day,
The eager fathers cry,
And, Red-hot diggety ziggety dog,
The mothers make reply.
Well, here's a wrap of sable fur,
The fathers murmur low,
And mothers catch each other's glance,
Meaning, I told you so.

Oh, Father's Day is a dreadful day,
And therefore fathers dread it;
For better a cycle of calm neglect
Than a day of grudging credit.
Oh why not leave the fathers be?
Their point of view is stoic;
So let them lurk in their niche in life,
Essential but not heroic.

NOT GEORGE WASHINGTON'S, NOT
ABRAHAM LINCOLN'S, BUT MINE

Well, here I am thirty-eight,
Well, I certainly thought I'd have longer to wait.
You just stop in for a couple of beers,
And gosh, there go thirty-seven years.
Well, it has certainly been fun,
But I certainly thought I'd have got a lot more done.
Why if I had been really waked up and alive,
I could have been a Congressman since I was twenty-one or
President since I was thirty-five.
I guess I know the reason my accomplishments are so measly:
I don't comprehend very easily.
It finally dawned on me that in life's race I was off to a delayed start
When at the age of thirty-three I had to be told that I could swim
faster if I'd keep my fingers together instead of spreading
them apart,
And I was convinced that precociousness was not the chief of my
faults
When it was only last winter that I discovered that the name of that
waltz that skaters waltz to is "The Skaters' Waltz."
After thirty-seven years I find myself the kind of man that anybody
can sell anything to,
And nobody will ever tell anything to.
Whenever people get up a party of which I am to be a member to
see some picture which I don't want to see because I am
uninterested in the situation that Scarlett and Mr. Chips are
estranged over,

Why my head is what it is arranged over.

Contrariwise, I myself not only can't sell anybody anything,

I can't even ever tell anybody anything.

I have never yet had a good gossip bomb all poised and ready to
burst

That somebody hasn't already told everybody first.

Yes, my career to date has certainly been a fiasco;

It would not have made a thrilling dramatic production for the late
Oliver Morosco or the late David Belasco.

But in spite of the fact that my career has been a fiasco to date,

Why I am very proud and happy to be thirty-eight.

A CAROL FOR CHILDREN

God rest you, merry Innocents,
Let nothing you dismay,
Let nothing wound an eager heart
Upon this Christmas day.

Yours be the genial holly wreaths,
The stockings and the tree;
An aged world to you bequeaths
Its own forgotten glee.

Soon, soon enough come crueler gifts,
The anger and the tears;
Between you now there sparsely drifts
A handful yet of years.

Oh, dimly, dimly glows the star
Through the electric throng;
The bidding in temple and bazaar
Drowns out the silver song.

The ancient altars smoke afresh,
The ancient idols stir;
Faint in the reek of burning flesh
Sink frankincense and myrrh.

Gaspar, Balthazar, Melchior!
Where are your offerings now?
What greetings to the Prince of War,
His darkly branded brow?

Two ultimate laws alone we know,
The ledger and the sword—
So far away, so long ago,
We lost the infant Lord.

Only the children clasp his hand;
His voice speaks low to them,
And still for them the shining band
Wings over Bethlehem.

God rest you, merry Innocents,
While innocence endures.
A sweeter Christmas than we to ours
May you bequeath to yours.

GOOD-BY, OLD YEAR, YOU OAF
or
WHY DON'T THEY PAY THE BONUS?

Many of the three hundred and sixty-five days of the year are
      followed by dreadful nights but one night is by far, oh yes, by
      far the worst,
And that, my friends, is the night of December the thirty-first.
Man can never get it through his head that he is born to be not a
      creditor but a debtor;
Man always thinks the annual thought that just because last year
      was terrible next year is bound to be better.
Man is a victim of dope
In the incurable form of hope;
Man is a blemishless Pollyanna,
And is convinced that the advent of every New Year will place him
      in possession of a bumper crop of manna.
Therefore Man fills himself up with a lot of joie de vivre
And goes out to celebrate New Year's Ivre;
Therefore millions of respectable citizens who just a week before
      have been perfectly happy to sit at home and be cozily
      Christmas carolized
Consider it a point of honor to go out on the town and get themselves
      paralyzed;
Therefore the whistles blow toot toot and the bells ring ding ding
      and the confetti goes confetti confetti at midnight on the
      thirty-first of December,
And on January first the world is full of people who either can't and
      wish they could, or can and wish they couldn't remember.

They never seem to learn from experience;
They keep on doing it year after year from the time they are puling
    infants till they are doddering octogenerience.
My goodness, if there's anything in heredity and environment
How can people expect the newborn year to manifest any culture or
    refironment?
Every New Year is the direct descendant, isn't it, of a long line of
    proven criminals?
And you can't turn it into a philanthropist by welcoming it with
    cocktails and champagne any more successfully than with
    prayer books and hyminals.
Every new year is a country as barren as the old one, and it's no use
    trying to forage it;
Every new year is incorrigible; then all I can say is for Heaven's
    sakes, why go out of your way to incorrage it?

EPSTEIN, SPARE THAT YULE LOG!

When I was but a boy,
'Twas my once-a-yearly joy
To arise of a Yuletide morning,
And eagerly behold
The crimson and the gold
Of the messages the mantelpiece adorning.
There were angels, there were squires,
There were steeples, there were spires,
There were villagers, and mistletoe and holly,
There were cozy English inns
With the snow around their chins,
And I innocently thought them rather jolly.
I blush for me, but by your leave,
I'm afraid that I am still naïve.

Oh, give me an old-fashioned Christmas card,
With mistletoe galore, and holly by the yard,
With galumptious greens and gorgeous scarlets,
With crackling logs and apple-cheeked varlets,
With horses prancing down a frosty road,
And a stagecoach laden with a festive load,
And the light from the wayside windows streaming,
And a white moon rising and one star gleaming.

Departed is the time
Of Christmases sublime;
My soprano is now a mezzo-basso;
And the mantelpiece contains
The angular remains
Of a later representative Picasso.
There are circles, there are dots,
There are corners, there are spots,
There are modernistic snapshots of the city;
Or, when the artist lags,
They are livened up with gags.
You must choose between the arty and the witty.
I blush for me, but I must say
I wish you'd take them all away.

Oh, give me an old-fashioned Christmas card,
With hostlers hostling in an old inn yard,
With church bells chiming their silver notes,
And jolly red squires in their jolly red coats,
And a good fat goose by the fire that dangles,
And a few more angels and a few less angles.
Turn backward, Time, to please this bard,
And give me an old-fashioned Christmas card.

ADVICE OUTSIDE A CHURCH

Dear George, behold the portentous day
When bachelorhood is put away.
Bring camphor balls and cedarwood
For George's discarded bachelorhood;
You, as the happiest of men,
Wish not to wear it ever again.
Well, if you wish to get your wish,
Mark well my words, nor reply Tush-pish.
Today we fly, tomorrow we fall,
And lawyers make bachelors of us all.
If you desire a noisy nursery
And a golden wedding anniversary,
Scan first the bog where thousands falter:
They think the wooing ends at the altar,
And boast that one triumphant procession
Has given them permanent possession.
They simply desist from further endeavor,
And assume that their brides are theirs forever.
They do not beat them, they do no wrong to them,
But they take it for granted their brides belong to them.
Oh, every trade develops its tricks,
Marriage as well as politics,
Suspense is silk and complacence is shoddy,
And no one belongs to anybody.
It is pleasant, George, and necessary
To pretend the arrangement is temporary.
Thank her kindly for favors shown;
She is the lender, and she the loan;
Nor appear to notice the gradual shift
By which the loan becomes a gift.
Strong are the couples who resort
More to courtship and less to court.
And I warn you, George, for your future good,
That ladies don't want to be understood.

Women are sphinxes, Woman has writ it;
If you understand her, never admit it.
Tell her that Helen was probably beautifuller,
Call, if you will, Penelope dutifuller,
Sheba charminger, Guinevere grander
But never admit that you understand her.
Hark to the strains of Lohengrin!
Heads up, George! Go in and win!

CONFOUND YOU, DECEMBER TWENTY-SIXTH, I APOLOGIZE

December twenty-fifth is an exciting day because it is what people
 refer to when Merry Christmas they wish you;
But December twenty-sixth is just the day you spend tripping over
 ribbons and wading through green and scarlet tissue.
It is a day of such anticlimax as to frustrate the most ambitious,
It is lined with gray satin like a medium-priced casket, its
 atmosphere is faintly morticious.
It is a day oppressive as asthma,
A day on which you want to call up the blood bank and ask them to
 return your plasma.
Its hours are dilatory
As a ten-cent depilatory.
Indeed it is a day subject to such obsecration and obloquy
That I am beginning to feel sorry for it, my knees are getting
 wobloquy as I strangle a sobloquy.
I am regretful that in discussing the reputation of December twenty-
 sixth I may have said anything to jeopardize it,
So by way of making amends I suggest that from now on we not
 necessarily lionize it, but couldn't we maybe just leopardize
 it?

APRIL YULE, DADDY!

Roses are things which Christmas is not a bed of them,
Because it is the day when parents finally realize that their children
    will always be a jump ahead of them.
You stay up all night trimming the tree into a veritable fairyland and
    then in the joyous morn you spring it on the children in a
    blaze of glory, and who says Ooh!?
You.
And you frantically point out the dictator's ransom in building sets
    and bicycles and embarrassingly lifelike dolls with which the
    room is checkered,
And the little ones pay about as much attention to them as they
    would to the punctuation in the *Congressional Record*,
Because they are fully occupied in withdrawing all the books from
    the bookcase to build a house to house the pup in,
Or pulling down the curtains to dress up in,
And you stand hangdoggedly around because you haven't any place
    to go,
And after a while they look casually over at the dictator's ransom
    and say, "Are those the presents? Oh."
And you console yourself by thinking Ah happy apathy, as long as
    we haven't had an emotional climax maybe we won't have an
    emotional anticlimax, maybe we'll get through the day
    without hysterics, ah happy apathy,
Ah may this Yuletide indeed turn out to be Yuletide without
    mishapathy.
Ah could this sensational lull but be permanent instead of pro tem;
Ah and doubly ah, if Christmas day could but end at eleven a.m.!—
But it doesn't, but the lull does, and here's something else you
    discover as you keep on living,
Which is that Christmas doesn't end for about two weeks after
    Christmas, but it starts all over again right after the following
    Thanksgiving.

BEWARE OF EASTER MONDAY

Comes a feast day and I am a fair to middling feaster,
I even go as far as to finish off the cloves in the ham at Easter.
My plate is clean enough to be eaten off by Amy Vanderbilt or Mrs.
    Grundy;
But what about Easter Monday?
On Thanksgiving, naturally, it's turkey and cranberry,
This you can count on from coast to coast, from Seattle to Danbury.
The same at Christmas, though somewhat more indigestible,
Because of that seasonal additive, plum pudding, the popular
    combustible comestible.
Nevertheless, a pretty dish to set before a queen, as Catherine de
    Médicis remarked to the Prince de Condé,
But what about Easter Monday?
Less mouth-watering is Saint Andrew's Day, noted for haggis, a dish
    of which only a Scotsman could be a condoner,
Since it consists of the heart and liver of a sheep or calf mixed with
    oatmeal and suet, boiled in the stomach of the original owner.
But it's another story on another saint's day, that of Saint Patrick, not
    to be confused with Saint Thomas Aquinas,
When we can dig into corned beef and cabbage that instead of
    parsley is decorated with shamrocks, scientifically known as
    Trifolium minus.
Yes, most feast days provide a fascinating salmagundi,
But again, what about Easter Monday?
Oh, Easter Monday is the day when you long for a magic compound
    with which your taste buds to inoculate
Because all that's left in the larder is a naked ham bone and a mess
    of jelly beans and a couple of dozen eggs either hard-boiled
    and dyed or runny synthetic choculate.
This is a prospect fearsome enough to kill the appetite of a hungry
    sailor adrift in the Bay of Fundy,
Which is why I call the day after Easter the truly blue, or *sic transit
    gloria,* Monday.

10

ILLS AND CHILLS

"A good deal of superciliousness
Is based on biliousness."

WINTER COMPLAINT

Now when *I* have a cold
I am careful with my cold,
I consult my physician
And I do as I am told.
I muffle up my torso
In woolly woolly garb,
And I quaff great flagons
Of sodium bicarb.
I munch on aspirin,
I lunch on water,
And I wouldn't dream of osculating
Anybody's daughter,
And to anybody's son
I wouldn't say howdy,
For I am a sufferer
Magna cum laude.
I don't like germs,
But I'll keep the germs I've got.
Will I take a chance of spreading them?
Definitely not.
I sneeze out the window
And I cough up the flue,
And I live like a hermit
Till the germs get through.
And because I'm considerate,
Because I'm wary,
I am treated by my friends
Like Typhoid Mary.

Now when *you* have a cold
You are careless with your cold,
You are cocky as a gangster
Who has just been paroled.
You ignore your physician,

You eat steaks and oxtails,
You stuff yourself with starches,
You drink a lot of cockstails,
And you claim that gargling
Is of time a waste,
And you won't take soda
For you don't like the taste,
And you prowl around parties
Full of selfish bliss,
And you greet your hostess
With a genial kiss.
You convert yourself
Into a deadly missile,
You exhale Hello's
Like a steamboat whistle.
You sneeze in the subway
And you cough at dances,
And let everybody else
Take their own good chances.
You're a bronchial boor,
A bacterial blighter,
And you get more invitations
Than a gossip writer.

Yes, your throat is froggy,
And your eyes are swimmy,
And your hand is clammy,
And your nose is brimmy,
But you woo my girls
And their hearts you jimmy
While I sit here
With the cold you gimmy.

THIS IS GOING TO HURT JUST A LITTLE BIT

One thing I like less than most things is sitting in a dentist chair
    with my mouth wide open,
And that I will never have to do it again is a hope that I am against
    hope hopen.
Because some tortures are physical and some are mental,
But the one that is both is dental.
It is hard to be self-possessed
With your jaw digging into your chest,
So hard to retain your calm
When your fingernails are making serious alterations in your life
    line or love line or some other important line in your palm;
So hard to give your usual effect of cheery benignity
When you know your position is one of the two or three in life most
    lacking in dignity.
And your mouth is like a section of road that is being worked on,
And it is all cluttered up with stone crushers and concrete mixers
    and drills and steam rollers and there isn't a nerve in your
    head that you aren't being irked on.
Oh, some people are unfortunate enough to be strung up by thumbs,
And others have things done to their gums,
And your teeth are supposed to be being polished,
But you have reason to believe they are being demolished,
And the circumstance that adds most to your terror
Is that it's all done with a mirror,
Because the dentist may be a bear, or as the Romans used to say,
    only they were referring to a feminine bear when they said it,
    an *ursa*,
But all the same how can you be sure when he takes his crowbar in
    one hand and mirror in the other he won't get mixed up, the
    way you do when you try to tie a bow tie with the aid of a
    mirror, and forget that left is right and *vice versa*?

And then at last he says That will be all; but it isn't because he then
      coats your mouth from cellar to roof
With something that I suspect is generally used to put a shine on a
      horse's hoof,
And you totter to your feet and think, Well it's all over now and after
      all it was only this once,
And he says come back in three monce.
And this, O Fate, is I think the most vicious circle that thou ever
      sentest,
That Man has to go continually to the dentist to keep his teeth in
      good condition when the chief reason he wants his teeth in
      good condition is so that he won't have to go to the dentist.

OH TO BE ODD!

Hypochondriacs
Spend the winter at the bottom of Florida and the summer on top of
      the Adirondriacs.
You go to Paris and live on champagne wine and cognac
If you're a dipsomognac.
If you're a manic-depressive
You don't go anywhere where you won't be cheered up, and people
      say "There, there!" if your bills are excessive.
But you stick around and work day and night and night and day with
      your nose to the sawmill
If you're normal.

NO WOE IS GOSSAMER TO MR. BESSEMER

Perhaps Mr. Bessemer is not a pessimist but, last and first,
He expects the worst.
It could be aptly put
That Mr. Bessemer got out of the cradle on the wrong foot.
He suspects that any dish prepared outside the home and many
    prepared inside the home will break him out in purple spots
    and red spots,
And that the Federal Communications Commission anticipates
    where he is going to place his radio and TV and rushes ahead
    to fill his air with dead spots;
He is certain that the train he must catch will leave early, and that,
    once caught, it will arrive late,
And, as a Michigan alumnus, that the Big Ten title will go to Ohio
    State.
But it is on the subject of the weather
That his forebodings really get together.
Mr. Bessemer is the holidaymakers' bane;
His ears are filled with ancestral voices prophesying rain.
Be the sunset garish as a festival in Spain,
Mr. Bessemer predicts rain;
Be the sunrise cheery as Mr. Wodehouse's fiction,
Rain is his prediction;
While if on the eve of a three-day week end the skies be runny,
He conjures up a northeaster; in fact, some people call him the
    North Easter bunny.
Yes, Mr. Bessemer has predicted rain under all circumstances
    except one,
And that was during a drought in Texas, and a big cloud came up,
    and he predicted sun.

ALLERGY IN A COUNTRY CHURCHYARD

Once there was a man named Mr. Weaver,
And he had a lot of hay but he didn't have any hay fever,
So he ran an advertisement which he wanted to charge, but for
      which he was compelled to pay,
And he advertised that he would like to meet up with somebody who
      had a lot of hay fever but didn't have any hay,
So along came a man and he said he had seen his ad in the paper,
And was the proposition serious or merely a prankish caper,
And Mr. Weaver said it was as serious as the dickens,
Because to his mind hay fever was to the human race what
      bumblefoot, limber neck and edema of the wattles were to
      chickens,
And he said he was the most modest of men,
But never having had hay fever he felt very irked at being
      outexperienced by any passing bumblefooted hen,
And the man said I can describe hay fever for you so you'll know all
      about it but first how much are you prepared to pay?
And Mr. Weaver said, "Can I charge it?" and the man said No, so
      Mr. Weaver said he would give him all his hay,
So the man said All right and threw pepper in Mr. Weaver's eyes,
And Mr. Weaver said, "What are you doing?" and the man said
      "Never mind, just kindly answer the following questions with
      the correct replies,
What's the kind of nut you put back in the dish at cocktail parties,"
      and Mr. Weaver said "A cashew," and the man said
      "Gesundheit. What material do politicians say their
      opponents' lies are composed of?" and Mr. Weaver said "The
      whole cloth," and the man said "No no try again," and Mr.
      Weaver said "A tissue," and the man said "Gesundheit.
      What's a filmy collar often worn by women?" and Mr. Weaver
      said "A fichu," and the man said "Gesundheit. Now you
      know all about hay fever,"
So he went off with Mr. Weaver's hay, but first he telephoned an old
      schoolmate in Vancouver and charged the call to Mr. Weaver.

WHAT THE WELL-READ PATIENT IS TALKING ABOUT
or
LOOK, MA, WHAT I GOT!

The more I leaf through the dictionary in my physician's waiting
    room the more my ego grows;
I feel rather like the man who was delighted to find that all his life
    he had been speaking prose,
Because I discover that my modest minor ailments,
Why, when expressed in scientific terminology, they are major
    physical derailments.
What I thought were merely little old mumps and measles turn out
    to have been parotitis and rubella,
And chicken pox, that's for the birds, have I told you about my
    impressive varicella?
I apologize for my past solecisms, which were heinous,
Never again shall I mention flat feet or bunions when referring to the
    hallux valgus on my pes planus.
It projects me into a state of hypnosis
To reflect that a watched pot never boils, it furunculosis.
Once my internal rumblings at parties caused me to wish I could
    shrink to nothing, or at least to a pigmy,
But now I proudly inquire, Can everybody hear my borborygmi?
My one ambition is to become as rich as Croesus.
So that instead of this bourgeois backache I can afford some
    spondylolisthesis,
Although then I suppose I would look back on my impecunious days
    with acute nostalgia
Because my headaches would also have progressed from rags to
    riches, or from Horatio Alger to cephalalgia.
I have certainly increased my learning by more than a smidgin,
Now I know that that specifically projecting Hollywood starlet is not
    a squab, she's a steatopigeon.
Indeed, I know so much that it would be truly tragic were I to be
    afflicted with aphasia,
And if you can't swallow that statement it is my diagnosis that you
    are suffering from achalasia.

CAN I GET YOU A GLASS OF WATER?
or
PLEASE CLOSE THE GLOTTIS AFTER YOU

One trouble with a cough,
It never quite comes off.
Just when you think you're through coughing
There's another cough in the offing.
Like the steps of a moving stair
There is always another cough there.
When you think you are through with the spasm
And will plunge into sleep like a chasm,
All of a sudden, quickly,
Your throat gets tickly.
What is this thing called a cough
That never quite comes off?
Well, the dictionary says it's an expulsion of air from the lungs with
      violent effort and noise produced by abrupt opening of the
      glottis,
To which I can only reply, Glottis—schmottis!
Not that I reject the glottis theory, indeed I pride myself on the
      artistry
Of my glottistry,
But there is a simpler definition with which I freely present you:
A cough is something that you yourself can't help, but everybody
      else does on purpose just to torment you.

I'M TERRIBLY SORRY FOR YOU, BUT I CAN'T HELP LAUGHING

Everybody has a perfect right to do what they please,
But one thing that I advise everybody not to do is to contract a
    laughable disease.
People speak of you respectfully if you catch bubonic,
And if you get typhus they think you have done something positively
    mastodonic;
One touch of leprosy makes the whole world your kin,
And even a slight concussion earns you an anxious inquiry and not
    a leering grin.
Yet, as long as people are pretty sure you have something you are
    going to be removed by,
Why they are very sympathetic, and books and flowers and visits
    and letters are what their sympathy is proved by.
But unfortunately there are other afflictions anatomical,
And people insist on thinking that a lot of them are comical,
And if you are afflicted with this kind of affliction people are
    amused and disdainful,
Because they are not bright enough to realize that an affliction can
    be ludicrous and still be ominous and painful.
Suppose for instance you have a dreadful attack of jaundice, what
    do they do?
They come around and smile and say Well well, how are you today,
    Dr. Fu-Manchu?
The early martyrs thought they knew what it was to be taken over
    the jumps,
But no martyr really ought to get his diploma until he has undergone
    his friends' witticisms during his mumps.
When you have laryngitis they rejoice,
Because apparently the funniest thing in the world is when you can't
    chide them for laughing at your lost voice, because you have
    lost your voice.

So I advise you, at the risk of being pedantic,
If you must be sick, by all means choose a sickness that is
        preferably fatal and certainly romantic,
Because it is much better to have that kind of sickness and be sick
        unto death or anyway half to death,
Than to have the other kind and be laughed to death.

OLD DR. VALENTINE
TO HIS SON

Your hopeless patients will live,
Your healthy patients will die.
I have only this word to give
Wonder, and find out why.

MAN BITES DOG-DAYS

In this fairly temperate clime
Summertime is itchy time.
O'er rocks and stumps and ruined walls
Shiny poison ivy crawls.
Every walk in woods and fields
Its aftermath of itching yields.
Hand me down my rusty hatchet;
Someone murmured, Do not scratch it.

Reason permeates my rhyme:
Summertime is itchy time.
Beneath the orange August moon
Overfed mosquitoes croon.
After sun-up, flies and midges
Raise on people bumps and ridges.
Hand me down my rusty hatchet;
Someone murmured, Do not scratch it.

Lo, the year is in its prime;
Summertime is itchy time.
People loll upon the beaches
Ripening like gaudy peaches.
Friends, the beach is not the orchard,
Nor is the peach by sunburn tortured.
Hand me down my rusty hatchet;
Someone murmured, Do not scratch it.

Now the menu is sublime;
Summertime is itchy time.
Berries, clams, and lobsters tease
Our individual allergies.
Rash in rosy splendor thrives,
Running neck-and-neck with hives.
Hand me down my rusty hatchet;
Someone murmured, Do not scratch it.

The bluebells and the cowbells chime;
Summertime is itchy time.
Despite cold soup, and ice, and thermoses
Garments cling to epidermises.
That fiery-footed centipede,
Prickly heat prowls forth to feed.
Hand me down my rusty hatchet;
Someone murmured, Do not scratch it.

Hatchet-killings ain't a crime:
Summertime is itchy time.

THE GERM

A mighty creature is the germ,
Though smaller than the pachyderm.
His customary dwelling place
Is deep within the human race.
His childish pride he often pleases
By giving people strange diseases.
Do you, my poppet, feel infirm?
You probably contain a germ.

I'M A PLEASURE TO SHOP FOR

Mine is a dauntless spirit, meaning a spirit that is hard to daunt;
Therefore, since nobody gives me Christmas presents any more, I
    shall console myself by compiling a list of Christmas presents
    that I do not want.
I do not want a lamp made out of an umbrella stand, or a coffee
    table made out of an old wagon wheel, or a fire screen made
    out of a leftover piece of trellis,
Or, indeed, anything made out of, or to look like, anything ellis.
I do not want a novel written by a young genius in the earnest belief
    that nothing awful has ever happened before to anyone but
    him, certainly not to us dowdy duffers and stodgy codgers,
Nor tickets to the new musical by the smart boys who think they
    have discovered the secret of Hammerstein and Rodgers.
Since I am crazy about harshness and unpleasant aftertaste, I do not
    want a milder, less irritating cigarette, no matter how
    scientific the tests,
Nor an evening with friends watching the TV personality girls whom
    I can only think of irreverently as Community Chests.
I do not want a squirrel tail or a Confederate flag to dangle from the
    aerial of my car,
Or a picture window through which better to view my neighbor's
    picture window or the adjacent abattoir.
For me, please, no bottled Martinis,
No sweetbreads, no cottage cheese with or without chives, no blinis
    in sour cream, indeed, neither sour cream no blinis.
If you will just not come across with any one of the above, and make
    it snappy,
You will also make one dear old gentleman's Christmas very, very
    happy.

FAHRENHEIT *GESUNDHEIT*

Nothing is glummer
Than a cold in the summer.
A summer cold
Is to have and to hold.
A cough in the fall
Is nothing at all,
A winter snuffle
Is lost in the shuffle,
And April sneezes
Put leaves on the treeses,
But a summer cold
Is to have and to hold.
Though golf course and beach
Slip beyond your reach,
By a fate grotesque
You can get to your desk,
And there is no rescue
From these germ grotesque.
You can feel it coming
In your nasal plumbing,
But there is no plumber
For a cold in the summer.
Nostrilly, tonsilly,
It prowls irresponsilly;
In your personal firmament
Its abode is permanent.
Oh, would it were curable
Rather than durable;
Were it Goering's or Himmler's,
Or somebody simlar's!
O Laval, were it thine!
But it isn't, it's mine.
A summer cold
Is to have and to hold.

THE COMMON COLD

Go hang yourself, you old M.D.!
You shall no longer sneer at me.
Pick up your hat and stethoscope,
Go wash your mouth with laundry soap;
I contemplate a joy exquisite
In never paying you for your visit.
I did not call you to be told
My malady is a common cold.

By pounding brow and swollen lip;
By fever's hot and scaly grip;
By these two red redundant eyes
That weep like woeful April skies;
By racking snuffle, snort, and sniff;
By handkerchief after handkerchief;
This cold you wave away as naught
Is the damnedest cold man ever caught.

Give ear, you scientific fossil!
Here is the genuine Cold Colossal;
The Cold of which researchers dream,
The Perfect Cold, the Cold Supreme.
This honored system humbly holds
The Super-cold to end all colds;
The Cold Crusading for Democracy;
The Führer of the Streptococcracy.

Bacilli swarm within my portals
Such as were ne'er conceived by mortals,
But bred by scientists wise and hoary
In some Olympian laboratory;
Bacteria as large as mice,
With feet of fire and heads of ice
Who never interrupt for slumber
Their stamping elephantine rumba.

A common cold, forsooth, gadzooks!
Then Venus showed promise of good looks;
Don Juan was a budding gallant,
And Shakespeare's plays show signs of talent;
The Arctic winter is rather coolish,
And your diagnosis is fairly foolish.
Oh what derision history holds
For the man who belittled the Cold of Colds!

PLATITUDINOUS REFLECTION

A good deal of superciliousness
Is based on biliousness.
People seem to be proud as peacocks
Of any infirmity, be it hives or dementia praecox.

A BULLETIN HAS JUST COME IN

The rabbit's dreamy eyes grow dreamier
As he quietly gives you tularemia.

The parrot clashes his hooked proboscis
And laughs while handing you psittacosis.

In every swamp or wooded area
Mosquito witches brew malaria.

We risk at every jolly picnic
Spotted fever from a tick nick.

People perish of bubonic;
To rats, it's better than a tonic.

The hog converted into pork
Puts trichinosis on your fork.

The dog today that guards your babies
Tomorrow turns and gives them rabies.

The baby, once all milk and spittle,
Grows to a Hitler, and boy, can he hittle!

That's our planet, and we're stuck with it.
I wish its inheritors the best of luck with it.

MS. FOUND IN A QUAGMIRE

Up, up, lad, time's a-wastin', press the ignition.
If relief is not forthcoming, consult your physician.
Winnow your symptoms, but never discard the chaff,
And consult your physician, your physician deserves a laugh.
Explain that when you swallow so much as a coddled egg it sticks
      like a fishbone
Somewhere behind your wishbone;
Inquire why your eyes of a sudden refuse to be focused,
And what is the sound in your ears like a courting locust.
Your physician's a man of talents;
Ask him whatever became of your sense of balance.
Don't be irked by his suavity;
Tell how you walk with your legs braced wide lest you trip over
      gravity;
Tell him, too, that your gaze is fixed on your shoes as you walk, and
      better to tell him why:
That a too long upward glance would send you headlong into the
      sky.
Tell him straight that on such and such a day
They took the difference between down and up away.
Give him your problem to solve,
Ask him what to hold onto when under your feet you can feel the
      earth revolve;
Every molehill a mountain, every wormhole a crater,
And every step like the step at the top of the escalator,
And don't forget
To reveal your discovery that hair can sweat.
Go ahead, tell him;
Release the cat from the bag, let the doctor bell him.
Give the doctor the chart, show him the map and the graph;
If relief is not forthcoming, it says right here on the label, consult
      your physician, your physician deserves a laugh.

TABOO TO BOOT

One bliss for which
There is no match
Is when you itch
To up and scratch.

Yet doctors and dowagers deprecate scratching,
Society ranks it with spitting and snatching,
And medical circles consistently hold
That scratching's as wicked as feeding a cold.
Hell's flame burns unquenched 'neath how many a stocking
On account of to scratch in a salon is shocking!

'Neath tile or thatch
That man is rich
Who has a scratch
For every itch.

Ho, squirmers and writhers, how long will ye suffer
The medical tyrant, the social rebuffer!
On the edge of the door let our shoulder blades rub,
Let the drawing room now be as free as the tub!

I'm greatly attached
To Barbara Frietchie.
I bet she scratched
When she was itchy.

WHEN THE DEVIL WAS SICK COULD HE PROVE IT?

Few things are duller
Than feeling unspecifically off-color,
Yes, you feel like the fulfilment of a dismal prophecy,
And you don't feel either exercisey or officey,
But still you can't produce a red throat or a white tongue or uneasy
      respiration or any kind of a symptom,
And it is very embarrassing that whoever was supposed to be
      passing out the symptoms skymptom,
Because whatever is the matter with you, you can't spot it
But whatever it is, you've got it,
But the question is how to prove it,
And you suck for hours on the mercury of the thermometer you
      finally sent out for and you can't move it,
And your entire system may be pneumococci'd or streptococci'd,
But the looks you get from your loved ones are simply skepticocci'd,
And Conscience glares at you in her Here comes that bad penny
      way,
Crying There's nothing the matter with you, you're just trying to get
      out of doing something you never wanted to do anyway,
So you unfinger your pulse before Conscience can jeer at you for a
      fingerer,
And you begin to believe that perhaps she is right, perhaps you are
      nothing but a hypochondriacal old malingerer,
And you take a farewell look at the thermometer,
And that's when you hurl the bometer.
Yes sir, it's as good as a tonic,
Because you've got as pretty a ninety-nine point one as you'd wish
      to see in a month of bubonic.
Some people hold out for a hundred or more before they collapse,
But that leaves too many gaps;
As for me,
I can get a very smug Monday, Tuesday, Wednesday, Thursday, or
      Friday in bed out of a tenth of a degree.
It is to this trait that I am debtor
For the happy fact that on week ends I generally feel better.

TELL IT TO THE ESKIMOS
or
TELL IT TO THE ESQUIMAUX

Jonathan Jukes is full of health,
And he doesn't care who knows it.
Others may exercise by stealth,
But he with a cry of *Prosit!*
Others put up with coated tongues,
And shoulders narrow and droopy;
Jonathan overinflates his lungs
With a thundering shout of Whoopee!
Jonathan's noise is healthy noise,
Jonathan's joys are healthy joys,
Jonathan shuns the primrose path,
And starts the day with an icy bath.

I might forgive the super-physique
Contained in the Jukes apparel;
The apple glowing in either cheek;
The chest like an oyster barrel;
The muscles that flow like a mountain stream
And the nose that needs no Kleenex,
The rigorous diet, the stern régime
Of arduous calistheenex;
I can pardon most of the healthy joys,
I can pardon most of the healthy noise,
But Heaven itself no pardon hath
For the man who boasts of an icy bath.

If the Missing Links were vigorous chaps
And their manly deeds were myriad,
Must civilization then relapse
Back to the glacial period?
Humanity learns at a fearful price;
Must the lessons all be lost?

Does the locomotive feed on ice?
Is the liner propelled by frost?

One constant truth mankind has found
Through fire and flood and slaughter:
The thing that makes the wheels go round
Is plenty of good hot water.
And therefore, therefore, Jonathan Jukes,
You deserve the harshest of harsh rebukes;
You and your frigid daily bath
Are blocking civilization's path.
You think of yourself as Spartan and spunky?
So, Jonathan, is the old brass monkey.

COUSIN EUPHEMIA KNOWS BEST
or
PHYSICIAN, HEAL SOMEBODY ELSE

Some people don't want to be doctors because they think doctors
     don't make a good living,
And also get called away from their bed at night and from their
     dinner on Christmas and Thanksgiving,
And other people don't want to be doctors because a doctor's friends
     never take their symptoms to his office at ten dollars a throw
     but insert them into a friendly game of gin rummy or
     backgammon,
And ask questions about their blood count just as the doctor is
     lining up an elusive putt or an elusive salmon.
These considerations do not influence me a particle;
I do not want to be a doctor simply because somewhere in the family
     of every patient is a female who has read an article.
You remove a youngster's tonsils and the result is a triumph of
     medical and surgical science,
He stops coughing and sniffling and gains eleven pounds and gets
     elected captain of the Junior Giants,
But his great-aunt spreads the word that you are a quack,
Because she read an article in the paper last Sunday where some
     Rumanian savant stated that tonsillectomy is a thing of the
     past and the Balkan hospitals are bulging with people
     standing in line to have their tonsils put back.
You suggest calamine lotion for the baby's prickly heat,
And you are at once relegated to the back seat,
Because its grandmother's cousin has seen an article in the
     "Household Hints" department of *Winning Parcheesi* that
     says the only remedy for prickly heat is homogenized
     streptomycin,
And somebody's sister-in-law has seen an article where the
     pathologist of *Better Houses and Trailers* says calamine lotion
     is out, a conscientious medicine man wouldn't apply
     calamine lotion to an itching bison.

I once read an unwritten article by a doctor saying there is only one
      cure for a patient's female relative who has read an article:
A hatpin in the left ventricle of the hearticle.

THE SNIFFLE

In spite of her sniffle,
Isabel's chiffle.
Some girls with a sniffle
Would be weepy and tiffle;
They would look awful,
Like a rained-on waffle,
But Isabel's chiffle
In spite of her sniffle.
Her nose is more red
With a cold in her head,
But then, to be sure,
Her eyes are bluer.
Some girls with a snuffle,
Their tempers are uffle,
But when Isabel's snivelly
She's snivelly civilly,
And when she is snuffly
She's perfectly luffly.

The bubbles soar and die in the sterile bottle
Hanging upside down on the bedside lamppost.
Food and drink
Seep quietly through the needle strapped to the hand.
The arm welcomes the sting of mosquito hypodermic—
Conveyor of morphia, the comforter.
Here's drowsiness, here's lassitude, here's nothingness,
Sedation *in excelsis.*
The clouded mind would stray into oblivion
But for the grackle-squawk of the box in the hall,
The insistent call for a faceless goblin horde
Of sorcerers, vivisectionists, body-snatchers.
Dr. Polyp is summoned,
Dr. Gobbo and Dr. Prodigy,
Dr. Tortoise, Dr. Sawdust, and Dr. Mary Poppins,
La belle dame sans merci.
Now it's Dr. Bandarlog and Dr. Bacteria,
And last of all, the terrifying one,
Dodger Thomas.
And there is no lock on the door.
On the third day, the goblins are driven off
To the operating room beneath the hill.
Dr. Vandeleur routs gibbering Bandarlog,
Bacteria flees before swarthy Dr. Bagderian.
Sawdust and Polyp yield to Saunders and Pollitt,
And it's Porter instead of Tortoise who knocks at the door.
He will test the blood, not drain it.
The eerie impostors are gone, all gone but one—
Dodger Thomas.
I know he is lurking somewhere in a shadow.
Dodger Thomas.
I've never met him, but old friends have.
I know his habit:
He enters without knocking.

VISITORS LAUGH AT LOCKSMITHS, OR, HOSPITAL DOORS HAVEN'T GOT LOCKS ANYHOW

Something I should like to know is, which would everybody rather
        not do:
Be well and visit an unwell friend in the hospital, or be unwell in
        the hospital and have a well friend visit you?
This is a discussion which I am sorry that I ever commenced it,
For not only does it call up old unhappy memories, but each choice
        has so much to be said against it.
Take the sight of a visitor trying to entertain a patient or a patient
        trying to entertain a visitor,
It would bring joy to the heart of the Grand Inquisitor.
The patient either is too ailing to talk or is panting to get back to the
        chapter where the elderly spinster is just about to reveal to
        the Inspector that she now thinks she can identify the second
        voice in that doom-drenched quarrel,
And the visitor either has never had anything to say to the patient
        anyway or is wondering how soon it would be all right to
        depart for Belmont or Santa Anita or Laurel,
And besides, even if both parties have ordinarily much to discuss
        and are far from conversational mediocrities,
Why, the austere hygienic surroundings and the lack of ashtrays
        would stunt a dialogue between Madam de Staël and
        Socrates,
And besides, even if anybody did get to chatting glitteringly and
        gaudily,
They would soon be interrupted by the arrival of a nurse or an
        orderly.
It is a fact that I must chronicle with distress
That the repartee reaches its climax when the visitor finally spots
        the handle on the foot of the bed and cranks the patient's
        knees up and down and says, "That certainly is ingenious,"
        and the patient answers Yes.

How many times a day do I finger my pulse and display my tongue
to the mirror while waiting for a decision to be elicited:
Whether to ignore my host of disquieting symptoms and spend my
days visiting friends who have surrendered to theirs, or to
surrender to my own and spend my days being visited.

ONE THIRD OF A CALENDAR

In January everything freezes.
We have two children. Both are she'ses.
This is our January rule:
One girl in bed, and one in school.

In February the blizzard whirls.
We own a pair of little girls.
Blessings upon of each the head—
The one in school and the one in bed.

March is the month of cringe and bluster.
Each of our children has a sister.
They cling together like Hansel and Gretel,
With their noses glued to the benzoin kettle.

April is made of impetuous waters
And doctors looking down throats of daughters.
If we had a son too, and a thoroughbred,

We'd have a horse,
And a boy,
And two girls
In bed.

SONG FOR A TEMPERATURE OF A HUNDRED AND ONE

Of all God's creatures give me man
For impractical uniqueness,
He's hardly tenth when it comes to strenth,
But he leads the field in weakness.
Distemper suits the ailing dog,
The chicken's content with pip,
But the human race, which sets the pace,
Takes nothing less than Grippe.

THEN, hey for the grippe, for the goodly la grippe!
In dogs it's distemper, in chickens it's pip;
But the lords of creation insist at the least
On the germ that distinguishes man from the beast.

The mule with mange is satisfied,
They tell me in the South;
And the best-bred cows with drowse and browse,
Content with hoof-and-mouth;
Bubonic cheers the humble rat
As he stealthily leaves the ship;
When the horse gets botts he thinks it's lots,
But people hold out for grippe.

THEN, hey for the grippe, for the goodly la grippe,
For the frog in the throat and the chap on the lip;
For the ice on the feet and the fire on the brow,
And the bronchial tubes that moo like a cow.

And hey for the ache in the back of the legs,
And the diet of consommé, water and eggs,
For the mustard that sits on your chest like a cactus,
For the doctor you're kindly providing with practus;
And hey for the pants of which you're so fond,
And the first happy day they're allowed to be donned;

For the first day at work, all bundled in wraps,
And last but not least, for the splendid relapse.
So let man meet his Maker, a smile on his lip,
Singing hey, double hey, for the goodly la grippe.

11

TRAVELS AND TRAVAILS

"Oh, what in the world could be more fun
Than to have your holiday over and done?"

NO, YOU BE A LONE EAGLE

I find it very hard to be fair-minded
About people who go around being air-minded.
I just can't see any fun
In soaring up up up into the sun
When the chances are still a fresh cool orchid to a paper geranium
That you'll unsoar down down down onto your (to you) invaluable
      cranium.
I know the constant refrain
About how it's safer up in God's trafficless heaven than in an
      automobile or a train
But—
My God, have you ever taken a good look at a strut?
Then that one about how you're in Boston before you can say
      antidisestablishmentarianism
So that preferring to take five hours by rail is a pernicious example
      of antiquarianism.
At least when I get on the Boston train I have a good chance of
      landing in the South Station
And not in that part of the daily press which is reserved for victims
      of aviation.
Then, despite the assurance that aeroplanes are terribly comfortable
      I notice that when you are railroading or automobiling
You don't have to take a paper bag along just in case of a funny
      feeling.
It seems to me that no kind of depravity
Brings such speedy retribution as ignoring the law of gravity.
Therefore nobody could possibly indict me for perjury
When I swear that I wish the Wright brothers had gone in for silver
      fox farming or tree surgery.

PARADISE FOR SALE

DORSET—8 miles Dorchester
In the valley of the River Piddle.
Kiddles Farm, Piddletrenthide
   A Small Mixed Farm
With Small Period Farmhouse
Dining/Living Room, Kitchen
   3 Bed Rooms, Bathroom
         —Adv. in *Country Life*

Had I the shillings, pounds, and pence,
I'd pull up stakes and hie me hence;
I'd buy that small mixed farm in Dorset,
Which has an inglenook and faucet—
Kiddles Farm,
Piddletrenthide,
In the valley of the River Piddle.

I'd quit these vehement environs
Of diesel fumes and horns and sirens,
This manic, fulminating ruction
Of demolition and construction,
For Kiddles Farm,
Piddletrenthide,
In the valley of the River Piddle.

Yes, quit for quietude seraphic
Con Edison's embrangled traffic,
To sit reflecting that the skylark,
Which once was Shelley's, now is my lark,
At Kiddles Farm,
Piddletrenthide,
In the valley of the River Piddle.

I'm sure the gods could not but bless
The man who lives at that address,
And revenue agents would wash their hands
And cease to forward their demands
To Kiddles Farm,
Piddletrenthide,
In the valley of the River Piddle.

Oh, the fiddles I'd fiddle,
The riddles I'd riddle,
The skittles I'd scatter,
The winks I would tiddle!
Then hey diddle diddle!
I'll jump from the griddle
And live out my days
To the end from the middle
On Kiddles Farm,
Piddletrenthide,
in the valley of the River Piddle.

THE BACK OF MINE HAND TO MINE HOST

Once there was a pawnbroker who got stuck with a batch of
      unredeemed slots for used razor blades, and he said, "Well,
I guess I've got the beginnings of a hotel.
So far as I am aware of,
All I need now is no hooks and some dummy taps marked 'Ice
      Water' and the bathrooms are taken care of."
He also didn't need any bureaus—just those combination desk and
      dressing tables that your knees won't fit under, so you can
      neither write nor primp, and they have another feature
      equally fell:
You have to leave your shirts in your suitcase, because the two lower
      drawers are filled with blankets and the top one with
      telegraph forms and picture postcards of the hotel.
He got a mad inventor to invent a bedside lamp with a three-way
      switch so that when you finish your paperback thriller, either
      American or Britannian,
Why, you can't turn out your light without turning on that of your
      slumbering companion.
He employed one maid for bedmaking and fifty maids who excel at
      the sole duty he assigned them,
Which is to wait until you are in a state of extreme dishabille and
      then burst into your room and cry "Just checking!" and
      vanish in a puff of smoke, leaving a smell of sulphur behind
      them.
I would recommend this hotel to you if you have a lot of old razor
      blades you have been meaning to get rid of because you can't
      afford to have them gold-plated or silverized,
Particularly if you regard the cardboard bosoms with which your
      sameday laundered shirts are stuffed as an adequate
      substitute for the buttons which have been pulverized.

WHO'LL BUY MY LINGUAL?
OR
YOU PRONOUNCE PLUIE, LOUIE

I wander through a Paris shower,
Off to inspect a flat *à louer*.

The water pours as from a pitcher
On walls inscribed *Défense d'afficher*.

If I have splashed through such a pond,
I don't remember *ou* or *quand*.

With raindrops glistening on my garment,
I reach my goal, I don't know *comment*.

I ring, I do not wish to trespass,
For trespassing is naughty, *n'est-ce pas?*

The stairway irks my fallen arch,
Because one learns *l'ascenseur ne marche*.

I like the flat; with cheerful mien
I murmur to the man, '*Combien?*'

He mentions his idea of payment,
I say that it's exorbitant, *vraiment*—

Have I misunderstood his statement?
I do not speak the French *parfaitement*.

He mentions a reduced emolument,
I cry that it's a deal, *absolument*.

And now I think a glass of wine
Would not be too unpleasant, *hein?*

SO I RESIGNED FROM THE CHU CHIN CHOWDER AND MARCHING CLUB

The thing about which I know the least
Is the inscrutable East.
Neither is my ignorance immutable,
I find that every hour the East grows more inscrutable.
Day by day
I memorize pithy witticisms beginning "Confucius say."
I retire to leafy bowers
And immerse myself in *Kai-Lung's Golden Hours*,
In the evening I beat assiduously on a gong,
Picking out "Slow Boat to China" and "Why Did I Tell You I
        Was Going to Shanghai?" and "Chong He Come from
        Hong Kong."
In a valiant effort the inscrutable Oriental mind to explore
I have lost a fortune at mah-jongg to an inscrutable Pekingese
        puppy who lives next door,
All to no avail;
Scrutably speaking, I am beyond the pale.
I have only one accomplishment about which I would write home to
        Mother:
I can tell at least one Celestial from at least one other;
I can tell you, for a modest price,
The difference between a mandarin waving his hat over a prostrate
        palanquin bearer and a mandarin sitting on a cake of ice.
Do you want to know, really and truly?
Well, the first mandarin is fanning his coolie.

THE BUSES HEADED FOR SCRANTON

The buses headed for Scranton travel in pairs.
The lead bus is the bolder,
With the taut appearance of one who greatly dares;
The driver glances constantly over his shoulder.

The buses headed for Scranton are sturdy craft,
Heavy-chested and chunky;
They have ample vision sideways and fore and aft;
The passengers brave, the pilots artful and spunky.

Children creep hand in hand up gloomy stairs;
The buses headed for Scranton travel in pairs.

They tell of a bus that headed for Scranton alone;
It dwindled into the West.
It was later found near a gasoline pump—moss-grown,
Deserted, abandoned, like the *Mary Celeste*.

Valises snuggled trimly upon the racks,
Lunches in tidy packets,
Twelve *Daily Newses* in neat, pathetic stacks,
Thermoses, Chiclets, and books with paper jackets.

Some say the travelers saw the Wendigo,
Or were eaten by bears.
I know not the horrid answer, I only know
That the buses headed for Scranton travel in pairs.

IT WOULD HAVE BEEN QUICKER TO WALK
or
DON'T TELL ME WE'RE THERE ALREADY

Let us call her Mrs. Mipping, but her name is legion,
And she is to be found in any taxi helping to congest any congested
region.
Human experience largely consists of surprises superseding
surmises,
And most surprises are unpredictable, which is why they come as
surprises,
There is one surprise, however, that is as predictable as a statement
by a Republican or Democratic national chairman or a
picture window in a pre-fab,
And that is the surprise of Mrs. Mipping when she gets to where she
was going in a cab.
In fact, she gets two surprises at a clip:
The first, that she has reached her destination, and the second, that
she is expected to pay for the trip.
If she is heading down to 5th Avenue and 52nd Street she doesn't
start to assemble her packages at 57th or 55th or even 53rd,
But when the cab pulls up at her corner she flutters like a
bewildered bird,
And she proceeds to gather up her impedimenta
While the faces of the several dozen drivers blocked behind her turn
magenta,
And only then does she realize that a figure has been registered on
the meter,
And she is thunderstruck as by an explosion of gunpowder, which is
largely composed of sulphur, charcoal and saltpeter.
Down go the packages on the seat again,

And she fumbles in her bag for her purse and fumbles in her purse
    for change and finally hands the driver a ten.
By the time the transaction is completed it is growing dark,
And traffic is backed up all the way to Central Park.
I believe that the Traffic Commissioner could soon iron out the
    situation as smooth as silk
Simply by opening charge accounts with the taxi companies for
    Mrs. Mipping and her addlepated ilk.

IS IT TRUE WHAT THEY SAY ABOUT DIXIE
OR
IS IT JUST THE WAY THEY SAY IT?

Our country, south and west of Hatteras,
Abounds in charming feminine flatteras.
Sweet talk is scant by Lake Cayuga,
But in Tennessee, they chatta nougat.

THE NAME IS TOO FAMILIAR

You go away for a trip, either business or pleasure,
And you think to settle down to a little anonymous leisure,
And the first thing you see on the train is a sign bearing the name of
      the porter,
And his name is Lafcadio Pauncefoote so you can't call him Boy or
      George, which eventually worries you into giving him an
      extra quarter,
And you go into the dining car a little later,
And there you are confronted with signs confiding to you the names
      of the steward and the waiter,
And the steward hovers over you like a hospitable owl,
And you can't call him Steward because now you think of him as
      Mr. Feeney your host, so when he asks you how your steak is
      you say Splendid instead of Foul,
And you get off the train and into a taxi,
And there's a picture to tell you that the driver's name is Maxie,
And you don't want to be hemmed in by names, you want to be
      alone,
But you think, At least it's other people's names that are hounding
      me and not my own,
And you go and register at a hotel and up comes the third assistant
      manager with a third assistant managerial gurgle,
And he looks at the register and then shakes hands and says We're
      mighty glad to have you with us, Mr. Alf B. Murgle,
We certainly hope you enjoy your stay, Mr. Murgle,
And the bellboy gets the idea and says Right this way, Mr. Murgle,
And the elevator boy gets the idea and says This is your floor, Mr.
      Murgle,
And the floor clerk gets the idea and says Good morning Mr. Murgle,
      there's your door, Mr. Murgle,
And the telephone girl gets the idea and says, Good morning Mr.
      Murgle, okay Plaza 3-8362, Mr. Murgle,
And the waiter gets the idea and says Will that be all, Mr. Murgle?
      Thank you, Mr. Murgle,

So your private life in the hotel is about as private as the private life
     of the Dionnes, but at first you are slightly flattered because
     you think Somebody important must have sent them word of
     you,
And after they have Mr. Murgled you for the thousandth time you try
     to cash a two-dollar check and you discover they have never
     heard of you,
Yes, it's all a figure of speech,
Because they not only know you, but also don't know you, and
     combine the worst features of each.
That's the beauty about a name, whenever we want to anonymously
     relax it pops up and prevents us,
And it is certainly nice to get home again and settle down as an
     obscure statistic in the census.

SCRAM, LION!

Gentlemen, I give you the British Empire,
And the late Queen Victoria, by no means a vampire.
Britain and Britons I far from excoriate,
I deeply admire their Poet Laureate,
I prefer an evening with A. P. Herbert
To a sail in the moonlight sipping sherbert,
And I'd rather hear a Savoy opera
Than loll in the tropics cornering copra,
And I think Miss Lillie is quite a card
And I'm all agog over Scotland Yard.
I'm impressed by squires who run for Parliament
And serve their country for a modest emolument.
Yes, I praise their peers and I praise their commoners,
Their fogs and faces and other phenomenas;
I'm even sufficiently flibberty-gibberty
To praise their premise of personal liberty.
But bo, I'll hand you the whole shebang
When they start to sling Amurrican slang,
And calculate you will lose your lunch
When you glim an Amurrican joke in *Punch*,
For Piccadilly is less spectacular
Than its torture of Transatlantic vernacular.
Then, Bravo, Britain! and Long Live George!
Away with Yorktown and Valley Forge;
I've a spilth of open-mouthed admiration
For a top-hole pukka sahib nation
But nix on our chatter—it can't be did.
Twenty-three, skiddoo!—Yours,

The Candy Kid.

I know a renegade hotel.
I also know I hate it well.
An inn so vile, an inn so shameless,
For very disgust I leave it nameless,
Loathing the name I will not utter,
Whose flavor reeks of rancid butter.
Five stories tall this mantrap stands,
With steps outstretched like welcoming hands,
And travelers, weary of their mileage,
Respond to its bright electric smileage.
They park their cars, and praise the Lord
For downy bed and toothsome board.
They pass unwary through its portals,
And every imp in Hades chortles.
Behold the regulars in the lobby;
Expectoration is their hobby.
Behold the loftiest of clerks:
He's manicuring as he works,
And bridles into dapper wrath
At a mild request for a room and bath.
Behold the niftiest of collars
Which murmurs, "That will be sixteen dollars,"
The leer with innuendo rife,
Which says your wife is not your wife.
The doddering, halting elevator,
A contemporary of Poe or Pater.
The impudent boy with step that lags
Who snatches your coins and hides your bags;
The ill-fitting door to the musty room
That smells like a fairly empty tomb;
The bath you crave, being cramped and dusty
And the hot that turns out to be cold and rusty,
The towels clammy, the basin black,
And the bed that sags like a postman's back.
The dinner (ten dollars and a quarter)

For the porterhouse that tastes like the porter.
The sleepy ascent to the room once more,
And the drunken Lothario next door.
You see that the beds are not turned down,
And you know the bedclothes are dank and brown,
And there isn't a thing to bang your clothes on,
And the sheet you shudder to place your toes on.
You search in vain for a bedside lamp,
You lose your slippers, the rug is damp,
The bulb in the ceiling is all in all,
And the switch is set in the furtherest wall.
A century later the night is past,
And you stagger down to break your fast.
Fossil bacon and powdery eggs
And a cup of tepid water and dregs,
And you reach the desk and surrender your keys,
And the clerk sneers "Thirty-one dollars, please.
Fifteen for meals and sixteen for the room,
Do you know to who you are speaking to whom?
You can fry in Hell so long as you pay;
Stop in again when you pass our way!"
I know a renegade hotel.
I also know I hate it well.
To name its name I can't be induced
Because I'm sure it considers every knock a boost.

RIDING ON A RAILROAD TRAIN

Some people like to hitch and hike;
They are fond of highway travel;
Their nostrils toil through gas and oil,
They choke on dust and gravel.
Unless they stop for the traffic cop
Their road is a fine-or-jail road,
But wise old I go rocketing by;
I'm riding on the railroad.

I love to loll like a limp rag doll
In a peripatetic *salon*;
To think and think of a long cool drink
And cry to the porter, *allons*!
Now the clickety clack of wheel on track
Grows clickety clackety clicker:
The line is clear for the engineer
And it mounts to his head like liquor.
With a farewell scream of escaping steam
The boiler bows to the Diesel;
The Iron Horse has run its course
And we ride a chromium weasel;
We draw our power from the harnessed shower,
The lightning without the thunder,
But a train is a train and will so remain
While the rails glide glistening under.

Oh, some like trips in luxury ships,
And some in gasoline wagons,
And others swear by the upper air
And the wings of flying dragons.
Let each make haste to indulge his taste,
Be it beer, champagne or cider;
My private joy, both man and boy,
Is being a railroad rider.

HAVE A SEAT BEHIND THE POTTED
PALM, SIR

I'm just an untutored traveling man,
And I only know as much as I can,
But ask me about itineraries,
And I'll tell you one factor that never varies:
All of the overnight trains arrive
In the dim-lit neighborhood of five.
Wherever you come, from wherever you've gone,
You always get into town at dawn.
You're reluctant to sway to the washroom once more
Between quivering curtain and quavering snore;
Why should one, when one in one's pocket hath
A hotel reservation for room and bath?
Detroit, Seattle, Dubuque, New Haven,
You descend at sunrise unbuttoned, unshaven,
In yesterday's socks and yesterday's shirt,
And yesterday's city's pervasive dirt,
But only a jiffy, you fondly suppose,
From a bath and a nap and a change of clothes,
Seeing you hold what is laughingly termed
A hotel reservation, confirmed.
You approach the desk with footstep glad,
And your reservation ironclad.
The clerk offhandedly waves you aside;
Your room is there, but it's occupied.
No use to wheedle, nobody to placate;
You're marooned till the squatter decides to vacate.
You retire to a crowded bench in the lobby,
And pretend that your beard is a lovable hobby.
By noon you're a vagrant, offensive and jailable;
You're finally told that your room is available.
You ascend to your castle among the stars,

And what do you find? Four dead cigars,
Towels and sheets in a crumpled bunch,
And word that the maid is out to lunch.
By confirmed reservations I'm stymied and bunkered;
I'd just as soon trust a confirmed drunkard.

THE UNWINGED ONES

I don't travel on planes.
I travel on trains.
Once in a while, on trains,
I see people who travel on planes.
Every once in a while I'm surrounded
By people whose planes have been grounded.
I'm enthralled by their air-minded snobbery,
Their exclusive hobnobbery.
They feel that they have to explain
How they happen to be on a train,
For even in Drawing Room A
They seem to feel déclassé.
So they sit with portentous faces
Clutching their attaché cases.
They grumble and fume about how
They'd have been in Miami by now.
By the time that they're passing through Rahway
They should be in Havana or Norway,
And they strongly imply that perhaps,
Since they're late, the world will collapse.
Sometimes on the train I'm surrounded
By people whose planes have been grounded.
That's the only trouble with trains;
When it fogs, when it smogs, when it rains,
You get people from planes.

Once upon a time there was an Italian,
And some people thought he was a rapscallion,
But he wasn't offended,
Because other people thought he was splendid,
And he said the world was round,
And everybody made an uncomplimentary sound,
But his only reply was Pooh,
He replied, Isn't this fourteen ninety-two?
It's time for me to discover America if I know my chronology,
And if I discover America you owe me an apology,
So he went and tried to borrow some money from Ferdinand
But Ferdinand said America was a bird in the bush and he'd rather
      have a berdinand,
But Columbus' brain was fertile, it wasn't arid,
And he remembered that Ferdinand was unhappily married,
And he thought, there is no wife like a misunderstood one,
Because her husband thinks something is a terrible idea she is
      bound to think it a good one,
So he perfumed his handkerchief with bay rum and citronella,
And he went to see Isabella,
And he looked wonderful but he had never felt sillier,
And she said, I can't place the face but the aroma is familiar,
And Columbus didn't say a word,
All he said was, I am Columbus, the fifteenth-century Admiral Byrd,
And just as he thought, her disposition was very malleable,
And she said, Here are my jewels, and she wasn't penurious like
      Cornelia the mother of the Gracchi, she wasn't referring to
      her children, no, she was referring to her jewels, which were
      very very valuable,
So Columbus said, somebody show me the sunset and somebody did
      and he set sail for it
And he discovered America and they put him in jail for it,
And the fetters gave him welts,

And they named America after somebody else,
So the sad fate of Columbus ought to be pointed out to every child
and every voter,
Because it has a very important moral, which is, Don't be a
discoverer, be a promoter.

CHANGE HERE FOR WICHITA FALLS
or
HAS ANYBODY SEEN MY WANDERLUST?

Luxury travel is something for which I pant;
But can I afford it? No, I can't.
Would I had studied Oriental languages as a pup;
I am always going to places where the timetable says Read UP.
Trains that me back to ole Virginny or ole Indianny carry,
They have always just dropped off the diner at Harrisburg or
Wilkes-Barre, which I always get confused with John Wilkes-
Barre.
Of streamliners and stratodomers I have heard gladsome tidings,
But to me they are simply blinding streaks to make way for which I
have spent innumerable hours on rusty sidings.
To some people travel conjures up a picture of luggage plastered
with glamorous labels and tags;
To me it is a picture of a remote station platform with no porters and
taxis, just me and my sacroiliac and three heavy bags.
I am told that the comforts in modern hotels are stunning;
My experience is that a hotel is a place with the elevator out of
order where you can only wash one hand at a time because
there is no stopper for the drain and you have to keep
squeezing the handles of the faucet to keep the water
running.
That is the hard way to get an ablution;
It reminds me of the visitor to the Chinese zoo who asked what
language the aquatic carnivora talked, Pidgin English? and
the keeper replied, No, Otter Confucian.

I have just returned from a foreign tour,
But ask me not what I saw, because I am not sure.
Not being a disciplinarian like Father Day,
I saw everything the wrong way,
Because of one thing about Father Day I am sure,
Which is that he would not have ridden backwards so that the little
 Days could ride forwards on their foreign tour.
Indeed I am perhaps the only parent to be found
Who saw Europe, or eporuE, as I think of it, the wrong way round.
I added little to my knowledge of the countryside but much to my
 reputation for docility
Riding backwards through ecnarF and ylatI.
I am not quite certain,
But I think in siraP I saw the ervuoL, the rewoT leffiE, and the
 Cathedral of emaD ertoN.
I shall remember ecnerolF forever,
For that is where I backed past the house where etnaD wrote the
 "onrefnI,' or ydemoC eniviD, and twisted my neck admiring
 the bridges across the onrA reviR.
In emoR I glimpsed the muroF and the nacitaV as in a mirror in the
 fog,
While in ecineV I admired the ecalaP segoD as beheld from the
 steerage of an alodnoG.
So I find conditions overseas a little hard to judge,
Because all I know is what I saw retreating from me as I rode
 backwards in compartments in the niart and in carriages
 sitting on the taes-pmuj.

EVERYBODY WANTS TO GET INTO
THE BAEDEKER

Most travelers eavesdrop
As unintentionally as autumn leaves drop,
Which brings up a question that confronts every conscientious
    traveler:
Should he, or should he not, of overheard misinformation be an
    unraveler?
The dear little old lady in front of you asks, What river is that, is it
    the Swanee or the Savannah?
And somebody who has no idea firmly says, It's the Potomac. It
    happens to be the Susquehanna.
The visiting Englishman asks, What is that mountain, and somebody
    yells, Pike's Peak! into his ear.
It isn't. It's Mt. Rainier.
Can one oneself of responsibility disembarrass
When one hears a fellow passenger being assured that the *Île de
    France* sails right up the Seine to Paris?
What is the etiquette
When one hears an eager sight-seer being informed that Greenwich
    Village is in Connecticut?
It is my experience that people who volunteer information are
    people who don't know the Eiffel Tower from the Tower of
    Pisa,
Or Desdemona from the Mona Lisa.
I am convinced that they have learned their geography through
    drawing mustaches on girls on travel posters,
And have done their own traveling exclusively on roller coasters.
*What is that, madam? How do you get from 42nd Street and
    Broadway to Times Square?*
Sorry, madam, but it's impossible to get from here to there.

THE CITY

This beautiful ditty
Is, for a change, about the city,
Although ditties aren't very popular
Unless they're rural and not metropular.

Sentimentalists object to towns initially
Because they are made artificially,
But so is vaccination,
While smallpox is an original creation.

Artists speak of everything urban
As the W.C.T.U. speaks of rye and bourbon,
And they say cities are only commercial marts,
But they fail to realize that no marts, no arts.

The country was made first,
Yes, but people lived in it and rehearsed,
And when they finally got civilization down,
Why, they moved to town.

Take country people, they suffer stoically,
But city people prefer to live unheroically;
Therefore city dentistry is less painful,
Because city dentists find it more gainful.

City people are querulous and queasy,
And they'd rather die than not live easy

And if they did die, they'd find fault
If they weren't put in an air-conditioned vault.

Yes, indeed, they are certainly sissies,
Not at all like Hercules or Ulysses,
But because they are so soft,
City life is comfortable, if not perpetually, at least oft.

ENGLAND EXPECTS

Let us pause to consider the English,
Who when they pause to consider themselves they get all reticently
      thrilled and tinglish,
Englishmen are distinguished by their traditions and ceremonials,
And also by their affection for their colonies and their
      condescension to their colonials.
When foreigners ponder world affairs, why sometimes by doubts
      they are smitten,
But Englishmen know instinctively that what the world needs most
      is whatever is best for Great Britain.
English people disclaim sparkle and verve,
But speak without reservations of their Anglo-Saxon reserve.
After listening to little groups of English ladies and gentlemen at
      cocktail parties and in hotels and Pullmans, of defining
      Anglo-Saxon reserve I despair,
But I think it consists of assuming that nobody else is there.
All good young Englishmen go to Oxford or Cambridge and they all
      write and publish books before their graduation,
And I often wondered how they did it until I realized that they have
      to do it because their genteel accents are so developed that
      they can no longer understand each other's spoken words so
      the written word is their only means of intercommunication.
England is the last home of the aristocracy, and the art of protecting
      the aristocracy from the encroachments of commerce has
      been raised to quite an art,
Because in America a rich butter-and-egg man is only a rich butter-
      and-egg man or at most an honorary LL.D. of some hungry
      university, but in England why before he knows it he is Sir
      Benjamin Buttery, Bart.
Anyhow, I think the English people are sweet,
And we might as well get used to them because when they slip and
      fall they always land on their own or somebody else's feet.

EVERYBODY'S MIND TO ME A KINGDOM IS
or
A GREAT BIG WONDERFUL WORLD IT'S

Some melodies are popular as well as classical, which I suppose
    makes them popsicles,
And some poems are part William Cullen Bryant and part Nick
    Kenny which makes them thanatopsicles,
And to some people Wisconsin is what Guinevere was to Launcelot,
And if they are away from it they are Wisconsolate.
Some naturalists know why the sphinx is sphinxlike and the griffin
    is griffiny,
And some couples are so wealthy that even their tiffs are from
    Tiffany.
Some Angeleno socialites fine each other a dollar
If they say La Jolla,
And give each other a Picasso or a Goya
For pronouncing it La Hoya.
Why should not I pick up a masterpiece or a coin?
I will not longer say Des Moines,
I shall sail into the C. B. & Q. ticket office like a swan,
And ask for a lower to Day Mwahn.
This I shall do because I am a conscientious man, when I throw
    rocks at sea birds I leave no tern unstoned,
I am a meticulous man, and when I portray baboons I leave no stern
    untoned,
I am a man who values the fitness of things above notoriety and pelf,
Which is why I am happy I heard the cockney postmaster say to a
    doctor who was returning a leprechaun to Glocca Morra in an
    open envelope, Physician, seal thy h'elf.

GRIN AND BEAR LEFT

I don't want to be classed among the pedantics,
But next time I visit friends who have moved to the country I want to
 get together with them on terminology, or semantics.
When you ask them on the telephone how to get there they smilingly
 cry that it is simple,
In fact you can practically see them dimple,
You just drive on Route 402 to Hartley and then bear left a couple
 of miles till you cross a stream,
Which they imply is alive with tench, chub, dace, ide, sturgeon and
 bream,
And you go on till you reach the fourth road on the right,
And you can't miss their house because it is on a rise and it is
 white.
Well it's a neighborhood of which you have never been a frequenter,
But you start out on 402 and soon find yourself trying to disentangle
 Hartley from East Hartley, West Hartley, North and South
 Hartley, and Hartley Center,
And you bear left a couple of miles peering through the windshield,
 which is smattered with gnats and midges,
And suddenly the road is alive with bridges,
And your tires begin to scream
As you try to decide which bridge spans a rill, which a run, which a
 branch, which a creek, which a brook or river, and which
 presumably a stream;
And having passed this test you begin to count roads on the right,
 than which no more exhausting test is to be found,
For who is to say which is a road, which a lane, which a driveway
 and which just a place where somebody backed in to turn
 around?
But anyhow turning around seems a good idea so there is one thing I
 don't know still:
Whether that white house where the cocktails are getting warm and
 the dinner cold is on a ridge, a ledge, a knoll, a rise, or a hill.

FIRST FAMILIES, MOVE OVER!

Carry me back to Ole Virginny,
And there I'll meet a lot of people from New York,
There the Ole Marsa of the Hounds is from Smithtown or Peapack or
    Millbrook,
And the mocking bird makes music in the sunshine accompanied by
    the rattling shaker and the popping cork.

All up and down the old plantation
Socialites are riding hell-for-leather like witches and warlocks,
And there is only one thing that keeps the squirearchy from being a
    genuine reproduction,
Which is that the peasantry's hair is kinky so they haven't any
    forelocks so they can't tug their forelocks.

In the evening by the bright light you can hear those darkies
    singing,
How the white folks do enjoy it and call the attention of their friends
    from Piping Rock to the natural musical talent of the dusky
    proletariat.
You can hear those banjos ringing because the hands have been
    ordered to exchange their saxophones for banjos,
And they wish they were singing Lookie lookie lookie, here comes
    Cookie, but their instructions are to sing Swing Low Sweet
    Chariot.

Oh what is more beautiful and more Southern than a Southern
    beauty from Philadelphia or Rumson,
And indeed where was Southern beauty before the advent of
    Rubinstein and Elizabeth Arden?
And what is more gracious than a hostess calling you you-all in the
    singular and plural indiscriminately,
And what has more local color than a lovely girl in jodhpurs telling
    you about her gyarrrden?

Oh the long happy days spent huntin' or shootin' or fishin',
Or in any other sport provided it's lackin' in g's!
Oh the long happy evenings spent sniffing jasmine and poring over
the shiny new family Bible,
And figuring out that after all this is really your home because great
grandmother Wilkins was a Filkins and the Filkinses were
related by marriage to the Randolphs or the Lees!

So please somebody carry me back to Ole Virginny,
Where gentlemen are gentlemen and a lady is known by the product
she endorses,
Where the atmosphere is as Southern as an advertisement for a
medium-priced rye whiskey,
And where the Virginians from Virginia have to ride automobiles
because the Virginians from Long Island are the only ones
who can afford to ride horses.

ON WAKING TO THE THIRD RAINY
MORNING OF A LONG WEEK END

Well, what shall I do today?
Shall I spend the day in the hay?
Shall I cover my head with the sheet,
Or go downstairs and eat?

If I leave my cozy nest
I will meet a fellow guest,
Or, what would irk me most,
I would meet my hostess and host,
While, if I stay upstairs,
My troubles are mine, not theirs.

I refuse to play Lotto or euchre
For either love or lucre;
I'm tired of discussing the arts,
And I've got bursitis from darts.
I am sick of people appearing
To announce that it looks like clearing;
Of games with pencil and paper,
And the girl who does Ruth Draper.

Today it would be as well,
I think, to lurk in my cell.
I'll refuse to speak to outsiders,
And only make friends with spiders;
I'll count the cracks in the floor,
And the steps between window and door;
I'll identify several stars
At night as I peer through the bars,

And when pastimes like these I exhaust,
I'll memorize *Paradise Lost*.

In closing, I'll mention, dear Auntie,
That the food here is wholesome but scanty;
If you'll send me a pie, when I open it
I'll hope for a file and a rope in it.

YOU BET TRAVEL IS BROADENING

Doctors tell me that some people wonder who they are, they don't
    know if they are Peter Pumpkin-eater or Priam,
But I know who I am.
My identity is no mystery to unravel,
Because I know who I am, especially when I travel.
I am he whom the dear little old ladies who have left their
    pocketbooks on the bureau at home invariably approach,
And he whom the argumentative tippler oozes in beside though
    there are thirty empty seats in the coach.
I am he who finds himself reading comics to somebody else's
    children while the harassed mother attends to the youngest's
    needs,
Ending up with candy bar on the lapel of my previously faultless
    tweeds.
I am he in the car full of students celebrating victory with
    instruments saxophonic and ukulelean,
And he who, speaking only English, is turned to for aid by the non-
    English-speaking alien.
I am he who, finding himself the occupant of one Pullman space that
    has been sold twice, next finds himself playing Santa,
Because it was sold the second time to an elderly invalid, so there is
    no question about Who is going to sit in the washroom from
    Philadelphia to Atlanta.
I guess I am he who if he had his own private car
Would be jockeyed into sharing the master bedroom with a man with
    a five-cent cigar.

I WILL ARISE AND GO NOW

In far Tibet
There live a lama,
He got no poppa,
Got no momma,

He got no wife,
He got no chillun,
Got no use
For penicillun,

He got no soap,
He got no opera,
He don't know Irium
From oopra,

He got no songs,
He got no banter,
He don't know Hope,
He don't know Cantor,

He got no teeth,
He got no gums,
Don't eat no Spam,
Don't need no Tums.

He love to nick him
When he shave;
He also got
No hair to save.

Got no distinction,
No clear head,
Don't call for Calvert;
Drink milk instead.

He use no lotions
For allurance,
He got no car
And no insurance,

No Alsop warnings,
No Pearson rumor
For this self-centered
Nonconsumer.

Indeed, the
Ignorant Have-Not
Don't even know
What he don't got.

If you will mind
The box-tops, comma,
I think I'll go
And join that lama.

SEPTEMBER MORN

Oh, what in the world could be more fun
Than to have your holiday over and done;
Than to stand in a rural railway station
With fifty weeks till your next vacation!
Ah me, what jovial words are spoken
When you find the suitcase handle is broken.
You juggle golf bags and tennis rackets,
And ludicrous bulging paper packets,
You count your paraphernalia twice
From the children themselves to their milk and ice.
A whistle announces the train is coming;
You drop the children's portable plumbing;
The train draws up with a jerk and a wiggle
From the engineer's convulsive giggle,
And every window flattens the nose
Of a passenger reveling in your woes,
And the only car with an open door
Is a hundred yards behind or before.
Heave up the bags, the ice, the milk,
Heave up your struggling youthful ilk!
Heave up, heave up, and keep on heaving;
This good old train will soon be leaving.
The grim conductor, watch in hand,
Glares angrily on your hapless band.
Oh when was order e'er restored
By disgusted cries of All aboard?
This luggage on the platform piled
May well conceal a favorite child.
Conductor, cease your cry disgusted;
Distracted parents can't be trusted,
In times of stress they have been known
To ship their offspring off alone;
Not unprotected, not at large,
But in the kind conductor's charge.
Farewell, farewell to the sand and foam,

You are getting yourself and your family home.
Oh, I think there is no such capital fun
But having your teeth out one by one.

A BRIEF GUIDE TO NEW YORK
———————

In New York beautiful girls can become more beautiful by going to
    Elizabeth Arden
And getting stuff put on their faces and waiting for it to harden,
And poor girls with nothing to their names but a letter or two can get
    rich and joyous
From a brief trip to their loyous.
So I can say with impunity
That New York is a city of opportunity.
It also has many fine theaters and hotels,
And a lot of taxis, buses, subways and els,
Best of all, if you don't show up at the office or at a tea nobody will
    bother their head,
They will just think you are dead.
That's why I really think New York is exquisite,
And even nicer to live in than to visit.

THE STRANGE CASE OF MR. NIOBOB'S
TRANSMOGRIFICATION

Listen motorists, and learn:

Once there was a motorist named Mr. Niobob who took a trip from
which he didn't return.

His first five miles were simply seraphic

Because he was on a dual highway and there wasn't even a
smattering of traffic

But then he had to leave the dual highway because his destination
was merely New York,

And dual highways never go to anybody's destination, they all lead
to a deserted traffic circle in Yoakum Corners or Medicine
Fork,

So Mr. Niobob turned off the trafficless dual highway and with his
usual luck,

Well yes, he immediately found himself behind a truck,

And whenever to pass it he mustered his nerve

Well, naturally, they came to a curve,

And it also bored him

That whenever the road straightened out and he edged over for a
dash there would be another truck clattering toward him,

And he wished he had picked up a little voodoo on his cruise to
Haiti,

Because while the truck bogged down to three miles per hour on the
way uphill, why when he thought to overtake it on the way
down it accelerated to eighty,

And all of a sudden they again entered a dual highway,

And Mr. Niobob said, "By gum, now I can drive my way,"

And he stepped on the gas with all his might,

And just as he overtook the truck it turned down a side road on the
right.

Poor frustrated Mr. Niobob, his mind slipped quietly over the brink,

He just sat down and cried and cried until a kind Commissioner of
Motor Vehicles took pity on him and transformed him into a
fountain, at which tired truck drivers often pause to drink.

"TOMORROW, PARTLY CLOUDY"

Rainy vacations
Try people's patience.
To expect rain in the autumn
Experience has tautumn,
And rain in the spring and winter
Makes no stories for the printer,
But rain on summer colonies
Breeds misdemeanors and felonies.
Summer cottages are meant just to sleep in,
Not to huddle all day in a heap in,
And whether at sea level or in higher places
There are not enough fireplaces,
And the bookcase stares at you starkly
And seems to be full of nothing but Volume II of the life of
    Rutherford B. Hayes, and *The Rosary*, by Florence M. Barclay,
And everybody wishes they had brought woolens and tweeds instead
    of linens and foulards,
And if you succeed in lining up four for bridge the only deck turns
    out to have only fifty-one cards,
And tennis rackets grow frazzled and golf sticks rusty and bathing
    suits moldy,
And parents grow scoldy,
And on all sides you hear nothing but raindrops going sputter-sput,
    sputter-sput,
And bureau drawers won't open and bathroom doors won't shut,
And all attempts at amusement fail,
Even reading the previous tenants' jettisoned mail,
Although naturally it would never have been jettisoned
If it hadn't been reticent.
But you could stand everything if it wasn't for one malignant
    committee,
Which is the one that turns the sun on again just as you are leaving
    for the city.
Yes indeed, rainy vacations
Certainly try people's patience.

I WANT A DRINK OF WATER, BUT NOT FROM
THE THERMOS

Have you ever lost your early start on a six-hundred-mile trip and
    had to spend the night in an individual wayside slum instead
    of the cozy inn at which you had foresightedly engaged rooms
    because child A couldn't find her absolutely favorite doll,
    and when she did find it, child B hadn't finished plaiting her
    hair yet?
Then you will agree with me that an accurate definition of a
    millionth of a second is the interval between the moment
    when you press the starter as you begin a six-hundred-mile
    trip and the moment when two little tired voices inquire from
    the back seat, "Are we nearly there yet?"
Then again, consider the other millionth of a second which lasts a
    year, when Time stands still, and Eternity in the lap of
    Infinity lingers,
Which is while you sit in helpless paralysis while child B carefully
    slams the door on child A's fingers.
Take the battle royal whose results no bachelor need ever have
    computed,
Which is the struggle to sit nearest to the open window, a struggle
    the prize for which is the privilege of sticking the head and
    arms out in just the right position to be immediately
    amputated.
Yes, for the father of none to thank his stars I think it only
    behooving,
If merely because he has not to contend with little ones who will
    descend from the car only on the traffic side, and preferably
    quite some time before the car but not the traffic has stopped
    moving.
Yes, he can roll along as confident as brass;
No restlessly whirling little leg will knock his spectacles off as he
    confronts a bus, no little hand groping the floor for a vanilla
    ice cream cone with chocolate thingamajigs on it will
    suddenly alight heavily upon the gas.
As the father of two there is a respectful question which I wish to

ask of fathers of five:
How do you happen to be still alive?

NOW YOU SEE IT, NOW I DON'T

Some people look to the future and others look days of yore-wards,
But even they see more eye to eye than two people on a train one of
      whom is riding backwards and the other forwards.
I don't know how it does or when,
But anything interesting described by a forwards rider has vanished
      by the time it should have swum into the backwards rider's
      ken,
While, through a freak twist of the current
The backwards rider gets to see a lot of interesting things that
      should have been there a moment ago for the forwards rider
      to see but somehow they just wurrent.
Travelers have told me and I have believed them,
That such noticeable objects as the Mississippi River and the Sierra
      Nevada mountains have disappeared between the time when
      the forwards rider pointed them out and the backwards rider
      should have perceived them.
There are those who in an effort to explain this phenomenon have
      developed a disturbing knack;
They sit forwards and look back,
While others to whom their vertebræ are dearer
Sit backwards and gaze on the fleeting landscape through a mirror.
But no matter what they describe
Their accounts never jibe.
When I eventually establish my Universal Travel Service and Guide
      Ways
I shall advise all my clients who really want to see anything just to
      sit at home and look sideways.

GOODY FOR OUR SIDE AND YOUR
SIDE TOO

Foreigners are people somewhere else,
Natives are people at home;
If the place you're at is your habitat,
You're a foreigner, say in Rome.
But the scales of Justice balance true,
And tit leads into tat,
So the man who's at home when he stays in Rome
Is abroad when he's where you're at.

When we leave the limits of the land in which
Our birth certificates sat us,
It does not mean just a change of scene,
But also a change of status.
The Frenchman with his fetching beard,
The Scot with his kilt and sporran,
One moment he may a native be,
And the next may find him foreign.

There's many a difference quickly found
Between the different races,
But the only essential differential
Is living different places.
Yet such is the pride of prideful man,
From Austrians to Australians,
That wherever he is, he regards as his,
And the natives there, as aliens.

Oh, I'll be friends if you'll be friends,
The foreigner tells the native,
And we'll work together for our common ends
Like a preposition and a dative.
If our common ends seem mostly mine,
Why not, you ignorant foreigner?

And the native replies contrariwise;
And hence, my dears, the coroner.

So mind your manners when a native, please,
And doubly when you visit
And between us all a rapport may fall
Ecstatically exquisite.
One simple thought, if you have it pat,
Will eliminate the coroner:
You may be a native in your habitat,
But to foreigners you're just a foreigner.

12

MEN AT WORK

"It seems to be very irking
To people at work to see other people not working."

LAMENT ON THE EVE OF PARTING

I shall grieve, I grieve, I am grieving.
Abel is leaving.
Abel, the wise and the clever,
Is leaving, is leaving forever.
He goes to a wealthy tycoon
For an extra five dollars a moon,
Abel, the kind and gentle
Whose faults, if any, were minor and incidental.
North Carolina was his native heath
And the gold in his heart ran all the way up to his teeth.
Abel, the courtly and portly
Is departing shortly.
Never were white shoes whitened or tan shoes tanned
As beneath his caressing hand,
Nor the silver and glass so luminous
As beneath those fingers bituminous.
Did a faucet leak, did the furnace refuse to function?
Abel had straightened it out between breakfast and luncheon.
Did a fuse blow, or a bulb flicker and die like the flame of plum-
    pudding brandy?
He had always a new one handy.
Did a guest request a harpoon, a harp, a tarpaulin, a tarpon, a
    turpentine hipbath, a hymnal, let the guest request what he
    would,
Abel would either produce, or rig up something as good.
He could string a radio aerial
Or lay out a person for burial.
His voice dark honey dripping from an olden golden pitcher,
Only smoother and richer.
Farewell, Abel, good-by.
You recede from my misty eye,
You have left to join your tycoon
For five more dollars a moon.
O Abel, no longer visible,
Abel, I'm misible!

THE QUACK FROWN SOX LUMPS OVEN THE—
or
FAREWELL PHI BETA KAFKA

If my mind is wandery,
Well, I'm in a quandary.
I am recovering from a temporary secretary, a girl from Bennington,
Who neither resembled nor had heard of such dream girls of my
youth as Louise Groody or Ann Pennington.
She came to me under the misapprehension that she could thereby
pick up experience in an easy school, not a hard school,
Which would lead her to producing and directing off-Broadway
plays of the avant-, or prenez-garde school.
Her eyes and her conversation glistened,
But she never listened.
When she encountered such a Nordic name as Georg she carefully
pronounced it Gay-org,
But when transcribing a reference to *The Raven* she typed it *Mr.
Raven*, which led me into fruitless speculation as to what
Thornton Burgess would have named the ape in *Murders in
the Rue Morgue*.
I played Polonius to this pixie, plying her with admonitions both as
a kindly pa and as a harsh pa,
But when I handed her a package for Parcel Post she sent it Marcel
Proust, as I only realized when it eventually returned to me
stamped *Marcel Proust ne marche pas*.
To sum up, let me say that I am at present capable of living, or
viable,
But I am also easily crumbled or reduced to powder, which is
friable.
Being both viable and friable I wish to prolong my existence, not to
wreck it,
And I am now looking for a good listener who just squeaked through
high school in Feeble Bluff, Nebraska, and never heard of
Joyce or Samuel Beckett.

IF HE WERE ALIVE TODAY, MAYHAP, MR. MORGAN
WOULD SIT ON THE MIDGET'S LAP

"Beep-beep.
BANKERS TRUST AUTOMOBILE LOAN
You'll find a banker at Bankers Trust"
—Advertisement in N.Y. *Times*

When comes my second childhood,
As to all men it must,
I want to be a banker
Like the banker at Bankers Trust.
I wouldn't ask to be president,
Or even assistant veep,
I'd only ask for a kiddie car
And permission to go beep-beep.

The banker at Chase Manhattan,
He bids a polite Good-day;
The banker at Immigrant Savings
Cries Scusi! and Olé!
But I'd be a sleek Ferrari
Or perhaps a joggly jeep,
And scooting around at Bankers Trust,
Beep-beep, I'd go, beep-beep.

The trolley car used to say clang-clang
And the choo-choo said toot-toot,
But the beep of the banker at Bankers Trust
Is every bit as cute.
Miaow, says the cuddly kitten,
Baa, says the woolly sheep,
Oink, says the piggy-wiggy,
And the banker says beep-beep.

So I want to play at Bankers Trust
Like a hippety-hoppy bunny,
And best of all, oh best of all,
With really truly money.
Now grown-ups dear, it's nightie-night
Until my dream comes true,
And I bid you a happy boop-a-doop
And a big beep-beep adieu.

MINI-JABBERWOCKY

Most people would find rising unemployment
A source of unenjoyment.
Not so the anonymous presidential advisor
Whose comment might have been wiser.
He has informed the nation
That rising unemployment is merely a statistical aberration.
I don't want to argue or squabble,
But that gook I won't gobble.

THE STRANGE CASE OF THE
LUCRATIVE COMPROMISE

Some people are in favor of compromising, while other people to
     compromise are loath.
I cannot plump for either side, I think there is something to be said
     for both.
But enough of discussion, let us proceed to example,
Of which the experience of Porteous Burnham should be ample.
The infant Burnham was a prodigious phenomenon, a phenomenon
     truly prodigious,
His parents and teachers regarded him with awe verging on the
     religious.
His genius was twofold, it appeared to have no ceiling,
And it was directed toward the science of lexicography and the
     science of healing.
Anatomy and etymology were Pablum to the infant Burnham;
At the age of five he knew that people don't sit down on their
     sternum,
Although he would occasionally say so in jest,
Later explaining that the word derived from the Greek *sternon*,
     meaning chest.
At the age of twenty-one he was an M.D. and a D.Litt., but his
     career hung in the balance,
Because he couldn't choose between his talents,
Until one day he was approached by an advertising agency that had
     heard of his dual gift,
And to work out a compromise they made shift,
And now he is the one who thinks up those frightening pseudo-
     scientific names for all the strange new ailments the
     consumer gets—
That is, if he uses the wrong sponsor's toothpaste or cigarettes;
And he makes a hundred thousand dollars a year, U.S. not Mexican,
Because the compromise landed him in a luxurious penthouse on
     Park Avenue, which is midway between Medicine and
     Lexicon.

ANYBODY FOR MONEY?
or
JUST BRING YOUR OWN BASKET

Consider the banker.

He was once a financial anchor.

To pinch our pennies he would constantly implore us,

And if we wouldn't pinch them ourselves, he would pinch them
      for us.

Down to thrift he was always admonishing us to buckle,

Reminding us that many a mickle makes a muckle.

When with clients he was closeted,

He was attempting to convince them that everything ought to be
      made do, worn out, eaten up, or deposited.

In a word, if you wanted to catch up with the Joneses or bust,

You couldn't do either with the connivance of the First National
      Pablum Exchange & Trust.

Yes, bankers used to be like Scrooge before he encountered the
      ghost of Marley,

But along came TV and now they are Good-Time Charlie.

The jingle of coins multiplying at two per cent per annum has given
      way to the jingle of the singing commercial,

And their advertisements, implying that anyone who doesn't turn in
      his this year's car for a next year's model with all the latest
      excessories and borrow the difference from them is a frugal
      old fogy, range from the supplicatory to the coercial.

The way some people sing whiskily,

Bankers are singing fiscally.

Everything is hey-nonny-nonny,

Come in and get some money.

That bankers have only themselves to blame for the recent wave of
      holdups and embezzlements I think highly probable,

They are behaving so provocatively robbable.

KIND OF AN ODE TO DUTY

O Duty,
Why hast thou not the visage of a sweetie or a cutie?
Why displayest thou the countenance of the kind of conscientious
      organizing spinster
That the minute you see her you are aginster?
Why glitter thy spectacles so ominously?
Why are thou clad so abominously?
Why art thou so different from Venus
And why do thou and I have so few interests mutually in common
      between us?
Why art thou fifty per cent martyr
And fifty-one per cent Tartar?
Why is it thy unfortunate wont
To try to attract people by calling on them either to leave undone the
      deeds they like, or to do the deeds they don't?
Why art thou so like an April post mortem
On something that died in the autumn?
Above all, why dost thou continue to hound me?
Why art thou always albatrossly hanging around me?
Thou so ubiquitous,
And I so iniquitous.
I seem to be the one person in the world thou art perpetually
      preaching at who or to who;
Whatever looks like fun, there art thou standing between me and it,
      calling yoo-hoo.
O Duty, Duty!
How noble a man should I be hadst thou the visage of a sweetie or a
      cutie!
Wert thou but houri instead of hag
Then would my halo indeed be in the bag!
But as it is thou art so much forbiddinger than a Wodehouse hero's
      forbiddingest aunt
That in the words of the poet, When Duty whispers low, Thou must,
      this erstwhile youth replies, I just can't.

THE STRANGE CASE OF THE AMBITIOUS CADDY

Once upon a time there was a boy named Robin Bideawee.

He had chronic hiccups.

He had hay fever, too.

Also, he was learning to whistle through his teeth.

Oh yes, and his shoes squeaked.

The scoutmaster told him he had better be a caddy.

He said, Robin, you aren't cut out for a scout, you're cut out for a caddy.

At the end of Robin's first day as a caddy the caddymaster asked him how he got along.

Robin said, I got along fine but my man lost six balls, am I ready yet?

The caddymaster said No, he wasn't ready yet.

At the end of the second day the caddymaster asked him again how he got along.

Robin said, My man left me behind to look for a ball on the fourth hole and I didn't catch up to him till the eighteenth, am I ready yet?

The caddymaster said No, he wasn't ready yet.

Next day Robin said, I only remembered twice to take the flag on the greens and when I did take it I wiggled it, am I ready yet?

The caddymaster said No, he wasn't ready yet.

Next day Robin said, My man asked me whether he had a seven or an eight on the waterhole and I said an eight, am I ready yet?

The caddymaster said No, he wasn't ready yet.

Next day Robin said, Every time my man's ball stopped on the edge of a bunker I kicked it in, am I ready yet?

The caddymaster said No, he wasn't ready yet.

Next day Robin said, I never once handed my man the club he asked for, am I ready yet?

The caddymaster said No, he wasn't ready yet.

Next day Robin said, I bet a quarter my man would lose and told him so, am I ready yet?

The caddymaster said, Not quite.

Next day Robin said, I laughed at my man all the way round, am I ready yet?

The caddymaster said, Have you still got hiccups, and have you still got hay fever, and are you still learning how to whistle through your teeth and do your shoes still squeak?

Robin said, Yes, yes, a thousand times yes.

Then you are indeed ready, said the caddymaster.

Tomorrow you shall caddy for Ogden Nash.

EVERY DAY IS MONDAY

Monday is the day that everything starts all over again,
Monday is the day when just as you are beginning to feel peaceful
you have to get up and get dressed and put on your old gray
bonnet and drive down to Dover again,
It is the day when life becomes grotesque again,
Because it is the day when you have to face your desk again;
When the telephone rings on Saturday or Sunday you are pleased
because it probably means something pleasing and you take
the call with agility,
But when it rings on any other day it just usually means some
additional responsibility.
And if in doubt,
Why the best thing to do is to answer it in a foreign accent or if you
are a foreigner answer it in a native accent and say you are
out.
Oh, there is not a week-day moment that can't wring a sigh from
you,
Because you are always being confronted with people who want to
sell you something, or if they don't want to sell you
something, there is something they want to buy from you,
And every shining hour swaggers arrogantly up to you demanding to
be improved,
And apparently not only to improve it, but also to shine it, is what
you are behooved.
Oh for a remedy, oh for a panacea, oh for a something, oh yes, oh for
a coma or swoon,
Yes indeed, oh for a coma that would last from nine A.M. on Monday
until Saturday noon.

GRASSHOPPERS ARE VERY INTELLIGENT

Ah woe, woe, woe, man was created to live by the sweat of his brow,

And it doesn't make any difference if your brow was moist yesterday
and the day before, you've still got to get it moist again right
now,

And you know deep in your heart that you will have to continue
keeping it dewy

Right up to the time that somebody at the club says, I suppose we
ought to go to what's-his-name's funeral, who won the fifth at
Bowie?

That's a nasty outlook to face,

But it's what you get for belonging to the human race.

So far as I know, mankind is the only section of creation

That is doomed to either pers- or ex-piration.

Look at the birds flying around, and listen to them as their voices in
song they hoist;

No wonder they sing so much, that haven't got any brows, and if
they had they couldn't be bothered keeping them moist.

And bees don't do anything either, bees just have a reputation for
industry because they are sharp enough to buzz,

And people hear a bee buzzing and don't realize that buzzing isn't
any trouble for a bee so they think it is doing more than it
actually does,

So next time you are about to expend some enthusiasm on the bee's
wonderful industrial powers,

Just remember that that wonderful bee would die laughing if you
asked it to change places with you and get its brow moist
while you went around spending the day smelling flowers.

But if you are humanity, it is far from so,

And that is why I exclaim Woe woe woe,

Because I don't see much good in being the highest form of life

If all you get out of it is a brow moist from perpetual struggle and
strife.

Indeed sometimes when my brow is particularly moist I think I

would rather be a humble amœba
Than Solomon in all his glory entertaining the Queen of Sheba.

SPRING COMES TO MURRAY HILL

I sit in an office at 244 Madison Avenue,
And say to myself You have a responsible job, havenue?
Why then do you fritter away your time on this doggerel?
If you have a sore throat you can cure it by using a good goggeral,
If you have a sore foot you can get it fixed by a chiropodist,
And you can get your original sin removed by St. John the Bopodist,
Why then should this flocculent lassitude be incurable?
Kansas City, Kansas, proves that even Kansas City needn't always
        be Missourible.
Up up my soul! This inaction is abdominable.
The pilgrims settled Massachusetts in 1620 when they landed on a
        stone hummock.
Maybe if they were here now they would settle my stomach.
Oh, if I only had the wings of a bird
Instead of being confined on Madison Avenue I could soar in a jiffy
        to Second or Third.

I YIELD TO MY LEARNED BROTHER
or
IS THERE A CANDLESTICK MAKER IN THE HOUSE?

The doctor gets you when you're born,
The preacher, when you marry,
And the lawyer lurks with costly clerks
If too much on you carry.
Professional men, they have no cares;
Whatever happens, they get theirs.

You can't say When
To professional men,
For it's always When to they;
They go out and golf
With the big bad wolf
In the most familiar way.
Hard times for them contain no terrors;
Their income springs from human errors.

The noblest lord is ushered in
By a practicing physician,
And the humblest lout is ushered out
By a certified mortician.
And in between, they find their foyers
Alive with summonses from lawyers.

Oh, would my parents long ago
Had memorized this motto!
For then might I, their offspring, buy
A Rolls or an Isotto.
But now I fear I never can,
For I am no professional man.

You can't say When
To professional men,
For it's always When to they;
They were doing fine
In '29,
And they're doing fine today.
One beacon doth their paths illumine,
To wit: To err is always humine.

MORE ABOUT PEOPLE

When people aren't asking questions
They're making suggestions
And when they're not doing one of those
They're either looking over your shoulder or stepping on your toes
And then as if that weren't enough to annoy you
They employ you.
Anybody at leisure
Incurs everybody's displeasure.
It seems to be very irking
To people at work to see other people not working,
So they tell you that work is wonderful medicine,
Just look at Firestone and Ford and Edison,
And they lecture you till they're out of breath or something
And then if you don't succumb they starve you to death or
       something.
All of which results in a nasty quirk:
That if you don't want to work you have to work to earn enough
       money so that you won't have to work.

TWO SONGS FOR A BOSS NAMED
MR. LONGWELL

I

Put it there, Mr. Longwell, put it there!
You're a bear, Mr. Longwell, you're a bear!
It's our verdict
That your service is perfect.
You're a regular American crusader
And you'll lick old H. L. Mencken's Armada.
You know life isn't all a picnic
But it hasn't made you a cynic.
From first to last
As the banner goes past
We'll sing our favorite air.
Our choice always narrows
To the man you can't embarrass,
So put it there, Mr. Longwell, put it there!

II

L for loyalty to his grand old firm,
O for his eyes of blue,
N for his ideals and his spirit of co-operation,
G for his influence on me and you.
W for his ability to collect and co-ordinate facts,
E-L-L for the laborsaving card-index system he put through.
Put them all together, they spell LONGWELL,
Which is about what you might expect them to do.

DANCE UNMACABRE

This is the witching hour of noon;
Bedlam breaks upon us soon.
When the stroke of twelve has tolled
What a pageant doth unfold.
Drawers slam on pads of notes,
Eager fingers clutch at coats;
Compact, lipstick, comb and hat,
Here a dab and there a pat;
The vital letter just begun
Can sulk in the machine till one.
Stenographers on clicking heels
Scurry forth in quest of meals;
Secretaries arm in arm
Fill the corridors with charm;
The stolid air with scent grows heavy
As bevy scuttles after bevy;
Like the pipers on the beach,
Calling shrilly each to each,
Sure as arrows, swift as skaters,
Converging at the elevators.
From the crowded lift they scatter
Bursting still with turbulent chatter;
The revolving door in rapture whirls
Its quarters full of pretty girls.
Soignée, comme il faut and *chic*
On forty or forty-five a week.
When One upon the dial looms
They hurry to their office tombs,
There to bide in dust till five,
When they come again alive.

MR. ARTESIAN'S CONSCIENTIOUSNESS

Once there was a man named Mr. Artesian and his activity was
 tremendous,
And he grudged every minute away from his desk because the
 importance of his work was so stupendous;
And he had one object all sublime,
Which was to save simply oodles of time.
He figured that sleeping eight hours a night meant that if he lived to
 be seventy-five he would have spent twenty-five years not at
 his desk but in bed,
So he cut his slumber to six hours which meant he only lost eighteen
 years and nine months instead,
And he figured that taking ten minutes for breakfast and twenty
 minutes for luncheon and half an hour for dinner meant that
 he spent three years, two months and fifteen days at the table,
So that by subsisting solely on bouillon cubes which he swallowed at
 his desk to save this entire period he was able,
And he figured that at ten minutes a day he spent a little over six
 months and ten days shaving,
So he grew a beard, which gave him a considerable saving,
And you might think that now he might have been satisfied, but no,
 he wore a thoughtful frown,
Because he figured that at two minutes a day he would spend thirty-
 eight days and a few minutes in elevators just travelling up
 and down,
So as a final timesaving device he stepped out the window of his
 office, which happened to be on the fiftieth floor,
And one of his partners asked "Has he vertigo?" and the other
 glanced out and down and said "Oh no, only about ten feet
 more."

WILL CONSIDER SITUATION

These here are words of radical advice for a young man looking for a
        job:
Young man, be a snob.
Yes, if you are in search of arguments against starting at the bottom,
Why I've gottom.
Let the personnel managers differ;
It's obvious that you will get on faster at the top than at the bottom
        because there are more people at the bottom than at the top
        so naturally the competition at the bottom is stiffer.
If you need any further proof that my theory works,
Well, nobody can deny that presidents get paid more than vice-
        presidents and vice-presidents get paid more than clerks.
Stop looking at me quizzically;
I want to add that you will never achieve fortune in a job that makes
        you uncomfortable physically.
When anybody tells you that hard jobs are better for you than soft
        jobs be sure to repeat this text to them,
Postmen tramp around all day through rain and snow just to deliver
        people's in cozy air-conditioned offices checks to them.
You don't need to interpret tea leaves stuck in a cup
To understand that people who work sitting down get paid more than
        people who work standing up.
Another thing about having a comfortable job is you not only
        accumulate more treasure;
You get more leisure.
So that when you find you have worked so comfortably that your
        waistline is a menace,
You correct it with golf or tennis.
Whereas if in an uncomfortable job like piano-moving or
        stevedoring you indulge,
You have no time to exercise, you just continue to bulge.
To sum it up, young man, there is every reason to refuse a job that
        will make heavy demands on you corporally or manually,

And the only intelligent way to start your career is to accept a sitting position paying at least twenty-five thousand dollars annually.

TWEEDLEDEE AND TWEEDLEDOOM

Said the Undertaker to the Overtaker,
Thank you for the butcher and the candlestick-maker,
For the polo player and the pretzel-baker,
For the lawyer and the lover and the wife-forsaker,
Thank you for my bulging, verdant acre,
Said the Undertaker to the Overtaker.
Move in, move under, said the Overtaker.

KINDLY UNHITCH THAT STAR, BUDDY

I hardly suppose I know anybody who wouldn't rather be a success
    than a failure,
Just as I suppose every piece of crabgrass in the garden would much
    rather be an azalea,
And in celestial circles all the run-of-the-mill angels would rather
    be archangels or at least cherubim and seraphim,
And in the legal world all the little process-servers hope to grow up
    into great big bailiffim and sheriffim.
Indeed, everybody wants to be a wow,
But not everybody knows exactly how.
Some people think they will eventually wear diamonds instead of
    rhinestones
Only by everlastingly keeping their noses to their ghrinestones,
And other people think they will be able to put in more time at Palm
    Beach and the Ritz
By not paying too much attention to attendance at the office but
    rather in being brilliant by starts and fits.
Some people after a full day's work sit up all night getting a college
    education by correspondence,
While others seem to think they'll get just as far by devoting their
    evenings to the study of the difference in temperament
    between brunettance and blondance.
In short, the world is filled with people trying to achieve success,
And half of them think they'll get it by saying No and half of them
    by saying Yes,
And if all the ones who say No said Yes, and vice versa, such is the
    fate of humanity that ninety-nine per cent of them still
    wouldn't be any better off than they were before,
Which perhaps is just as well because if everybody was a success
    nobody could be contemptuous of anybody else and
    everybody would start in all over again trying to be a bigger
    success than everybody else so they would have somebody to
    be contemptuous of and so on forevermore,

Because when people start hitching their wagons to a star,
That's the way they are.

SECOND LIMICK

A cook named McMurray
Got a raise in a hurry
From his Hindu employer
By favoring curry.

INTROSPECTIVE REFLECTION

I would live all my life in nonchalance and insouciance
Were it not for making a living, which is rather a nouciance.

13

STUFF AND NONSENSE

"In the Vanities
No one wears panities."

HOW PLEASANT TO APE MR. LEAR

A crusader's wife slipped from the garrison
And had an affair with a Saracen.
     She was not oversexed,
     Or jealous or vexed,
She just wanted to make a comparison.

A novelist of the absurd
Has a voice that will shortly be heard.
     I learn from my spies
     He's about to devise
An unprintable three-letter word.

The Pilgrims ate quahaugs and corn yet,
Which gourmets would scorn through a lorgnette.
     For this kind of living
     They proclaimed a Thanksgiving.
I'm thankful I hadn't been born yet.

An exiled Iraqi went back
To his home with a ewe in his pack.
     He said people all knew
     Every Q needs a U
So he put the ewe back in Iraqu.

A Knight of the Garter long hence
Was expelled from that order of gents.
     He was fairly adroit
     When he cried "Honi Soit,"
But he couldn't pronounce "Mal y Pense."

A chuckling tycoon of Fort Worth,
When asked for the cause of his mirth,
     Replied, Houston and Dallas
     Will shore bust a gallus
When they hear I've just purchased the earth.

A male entomologist author
Waxed wrother and wrother and wrother—
He socked his own brother
Who called him a mother
Instead of an eminent mother.

FRAGONARD

There was an old miser named Clarence,
Who simonized both of his parents.
"The initial expense,"
He remarked, "is immense,
But I'll save it on wearance and tearance."

SPECULATIVE REFLECTION

I wonder if the citizens of New York will ever get sufficiently wroth
To remember that Tammany cooks spoil the broth.

WE HAVE MET THE SASSENACHS AND THEY ARE OURS; EVEN THE YEAR IS NOW McMLXIX

Lang syne 'twas only a pair of Mc's
Gaed wimplin' through the town—
Marshall McLuhan and Rod McKuen,
Wi' never an Alec McCowen.

McLuhan shared a braw pint-stowp
Wi' ghaist or deil or Ouija,
Till himsel' nor naebody else could tell
The messages from the meja.

McKuen trolled the quid folk song
Like "Relique of Bishop Percy,"
And frae dine to ilka mornin' sun
Set the bairns all arsy-versy.

But a' things canty maun come in threes
(Sing thistle, heather, and rowan!);
Quo' Rod McKuen to Marshall McLuhan,
"Ca' oot for Alec McCowen!"

"And gie's a hand, my trusty fiere,"
Says McLuhan to McKuen,
"We'll take a right guid willie-waught
In honor of the new one."

Now there's three hae rin about the braes
And pu'd fu' monie a gowan—
Marshall McLuhan and Rod McKuen
And His Holiness Alec McCowen.

SHALL WE DANCE?
BEING THE CONFESSIONS OF A BALLETRAMUS—II

I learned my French by working hard
At listening to Hildegarde.
That's why a word like "*entrechat*"
Is something *je ne comprends pas.*
Is it a stage direction that
Calls for the advent of a cat?
Assume a comma in the center:
Does "*entre, chat*" bid cat to enter?
Let's start again. Does "*entre*" mean
"Among," or possibly "between"?
I find I cannot swallow that;
How do you get between one cat?
Let's forget the tiresome *entrechat*
And watch a *danse du ventrechat.*

MONEY IS EVERYTHING

Better a parvenu
Living luxuriously on Park Arvenu
Than a Schuyler or a Van Rensselaer
Living inexpensselaer.

A DREAM OF INNOCENT ORGIES
or
THE MOST UNFORGETTABLE CHARACTERS
I NEVER MET

I'm glad I wasn't ever a Clyde or a Bonnie,
But I'm sorry I was never a stage-door Johnny.
I'd love to have driven down the Gay White Way
In a hansom cab with a big bouquet
To share a bottle and a Chicken Kiev
With a Mitzi Hajos or a Fritzi Scheff
Or a Trixie Friganza—
To squire such dames as,
Glittering names as,
Mitzi Hajos,
Fritzi Scheff,
Or Trixie Friganza.

Had I been born just a little bit earlier,
When ladies of the chorus were voluptuously girlier,
I'm sure I could have fostered in a manner deft
A brotherly acquaintance with the second from the left.
But I'd rather have waited for a real bonanza
Like a Fritzi Scheff or a Trixie Friganza
Or a Mitzi Hajos—
To spend my patrimony
Skirting matrimony
With a Fritzi Scheff,
A Mitzi Hajos,
Or a Trixi Friganza,

I'd have overtipped the doormen underneath the canopies
Of elegant cafes from Rector's to Bustanoby's.
They'd warn me when a menace appeared upon the premises—
Say, a gentleman name of Harry Thaw or lady name of Nemesis.
When I heard the chimes at midnight with a Mitzi Hajos,
My conduct would have been I hope outrajos. . .

Through all my salad days,
Mardi Gras gala days,
With a Mitzi Hajos,
A Fritzi Scheff,
Or a Trixie Friganza.

Had I only been twenty instead of ten
I'd have been a legend in Manhattan then,
But temptation was thwarted by the simple truth:
I was just too young to misspend my youth
With a Fritzi Scheff,
A Mitzi Hajos,
A Trixie Friganza,
Or even a Floradora girl.

EDOUARD

A bugler named Dougal MacDougal
Found ingenious ways to be frugal.
He learned how to sneeze
In various keys,
Thus saving the price of a bugle.

HARK, HARK, THE LARKS DO BARK

Every schoolboy knows a wallaby from a wombat,
But only bright schoolboys know that the lark fight and not the dog
      fight is the most personal form of aerial combat.
Take the duel between those two rivals for the heart of a frivolous
      lady lark who to each had beckoned:
Percy B. Shelley's lark and the lark celebrated in *Sound of Music* by
      Oscar Hammerstein II.
The Shelley lark was from heaven or near it amorously pouring its
      full heart,
And the comments of the Hammerstein lark were jealous and tart.
Its very salutation was pert:
"Hail to thee, whatever thou mayst be, because it's on record that
      bird thou never wert.
Thou wert never even a gnatcatcher or a goatsucker or a godwit or
      yet a skua bird."
And the Shelley lark said, "I am too a bird!"
And the Hammerstein lark said, "I will argue to and fro not,
Shelley himself admits that what thou art we know not.
He said that maybe thou wast a highborn maiden in a palace tower,
      or perhaps a glowworm golden in a bed of dew.
Does that sound like a bird to you?"
And the Shelley lark said, "Shelley says, what says Shelley, let
      Shelley say!
What says Oscar Hammerstein II? He says only that you are still
      learning to pray.
A fine claim you have to be famous!
At your age I not only knew all of 'Now I Lay Me,' but also I could
      whistle 'Lead Kindly Light' and 'Venite Adoremus.'"
Here the lady lark, who had been yawning, exclaimed, "Oh, skip it!"
And went off with a tone-deaf pipit.

TALLYHO-HUM

Have you ever gone visiting for a weekend of ravelry
Only to find yourself surrounded by the Cavalry?
Not regular cavalry like Hussars or Lancers or Northwest Mounted
     Police,
But people who actually ride horses for pleasure in times of peace.
People who expose themselves gratis to risks for which we pay the
     Lancer, the Hussar and the Mountie,
People who recover from a broken rib at Meadowbrook in time to
     fracture a vertebra at Peapack which will just be knitting
     when they split a collarbone in Harford County,
People who otherwise may be cynics and stoics,
But go yowling berserk whenever the cheerleader says "Yoicks!"
Well, you can take the word of an old mossback
Who's never been on hossback,
It's very hard to chat
With people like that,
Because they are not very interested in talking about the screen or
     the stage or the latest best-selling book or dud book,
All they want to talk about is the Stud Book,
And willy nilly
You've got to hear about the children of the ch. f.,
And if you think you can safely join in a family conversation, Dear
     me,
The mirth that you provoke when you ask after the children of the
     b.g.
On such seas you are indeed a ship without a rudder
If like myself you do not know a hock from a girth or a wither from
     an udder.
And you will feel about horses, even those born and bred in Old
     Kentucky,
Much as you do about streptocucci.

HOW MANY MILES TO BABYLON?

How many miles to Babylon?
Love-in-a-mist and Bovril.
Are there more Sitwells than one?
Oh yes, there are Sacheverell.

REFLECTION ON THE PASSAGE OF TIME, ITS INEVITABILITY AND ITS QUIRKS

In nineteen hunderd
Jeunes filles wondered.

FOURTH LIMICK

Three young Tennesseans
Whom snobs called plebeians
Cried, What do you mean?
We's married to we-uns.

YOU'LL DRINK YOUR ORANGE JUICE
AND LIKE IT, COMRADE

Soviet Union agrees to absorb quantities of citrus
fruits to relieve Cyprus surplus.

—Newspaper item

There's a Cyprus citrus surplus,
Citrus surplus Cypriotic.
No Sicilian citrus surplus
But a Cyprus citrus surplus,
Not a Cyprus citron surplus
But a Cyprus citrus surplus,
Not a Cyprus citrus circus
But a Cyprus citrus surplus.
It's a special citrus surplus,
Cyprus citrus super surplus.
"Just a surface citrus surfeit,"
Says a cryptic Coptic skeptic.
But the bishop in his surplice
Certifies the surfeit citrus—
In his surplus Sunday surplice,
Certifies the citrus surfeit,
Who'll assimilate the surplus,
Siphon off the Cyprus citrus?
Sipping at the citrus cistern,
Who'll suppress the Cyprus surplus?
Says the Soviet to Cyprus,
"Send us all your surplus citrus;
This is just a simple sample
Of Socialist assistance.
Should you show a similar surplus
In the simmering summer solstice,
Send a summons to the Soviet
For surplus citrus solace."

Now on Cyprus they're all reading
Victory, by Joseph Comrade.

ALL QUIET ALONG THE POTOMAC,
EXCEPT THE LETTER G

The table talk in Washington
I hear by special messenger,
Is brightened by the presence there
Of Kiplinger and Kissinger.

The anecdotes are wittier,
The chitterchat flows ripplinger,
As of the moment on the bus
When Kissinger met Kiplinger.

"My name is Mr. Kiplinger,"
Said Kiplinger to Kissinger.
"And I'm Professor Kissinger,"
Replied his fellow passenger.

"You'll kindly note my *g* is hard,"
Said Kiplinger to Kissinger;
"Some people call me Kiplinjer,
And nothing is depressinjer."

"Hard *g* to me," said Kissinger,
"Is sentimental goo.
Kissing-er means more osculant.
More osculant than who?"

"One dowager," said Kiplinger,
"She goes beyond Kiplinjery.
She dragged me to the opera
To add Yseult to injury."

Kiplinger grew progressively pressinger;
"Do you know my good friend Arthur Schlesinger?"
Kissinger answered his fellow passenger,

"No, but I know an Arthur Schlesinger.
In a city named for George or Martha.
How odd that we each should know an Arthur!
Let's have a foursome at Burning Tree,
Your Arthur and you against mine and me."

LATHER AS YOU GO

Beneath this slab
John Brown is stowed.
He watched the ads,
And not the road.

GEOGRAPHICAL REFLECTION

The Bronx?
No, thonx!

RAPUNZEL, RAPUNZEL, LET'S LET DOWN
OUR HAIR

Once there was a fair young damsel and she early went, from an
          inferiority complex, out of her wits,
Because her friends at Wolfcroft were Miss Diana Fitz-James,
          Miss Perdita Fitz-Clarence, and the Honorable Miss Mavis
          Fitz-Something-or-other, and she herself was only Miss
          Rapunzel-Fitts.
Rapunzel went around singing that mares and does won't eat ivy,
          but little lambs 'll,
So she was really more a dumsel than a damsel.
She had another song for festive occasions, when none was so festive
          as she;
She sang "Marilyn Monrollalong o'er the Debussy."
She was a joy to behold, but her mind worked clumsily,
Or, shall we say, dumsily.
After three semesters of *Hamlet* she still couldn't tell handsaws from
          hawks,
And she thought the Gunpowder Plot involved poisoning the
          Parliament with toadstools because she had learned on a
          nature-walk that fungus was made before Fawkes.

In a Scandinavian fjord where she visited her friend Miss
          Fjitz-ffjoulkes on a rocky islet
She responded, when asked if her brother in the Air Force was a
          pilot yet, No, he's a yet pilot.
The last I heard of her, she had married a realtor, name of Babbitt,
And she was at a dinner with her mind on green peas, sitting beside
          another realtor who said, I'm from Cedar Rapids, and she
          thought he said, I'm Peter Rabbit.
This episode was on Rapunzel's memory permanently etched,
And she has grown old wondering whether he really was Peter
          Rabbit, or whether he was just a little bit tetched.

YOUR LEAD, PARTNER, I HOPE
WE'VE READ THE SAME BOOK

When I was just a youngster,
Hardly bigger than a midge,
I used to join my family
In a game of auction bridge.
We were patient with reneging,
For the light was gas or oil,
And our arguments were settled
By a reference to Hoyle.
Auction bridge was clover;
Then the experts took it over.
You could no longer bid by the seat of your pants,
The experts substituted skill for chance.

The experts captured auction
With their lessons and their books,
And the casual week-end player
Got a lot of nasty looks.
The experts captured auction
And dissected it, and then
Somebody thought up contract,
And we played for fun again.
It was pleasant, lose or win,
But the experts muscled in,
And you couldn't deal cards in your own abode
Without having memorized the latest code.

We turned to simpler pastimes
With our neighbors and our kin;
Oklahoma or canasta,
Or a modest hand of gin.
We were quietly diverted
Before and after meals,

Till the experts scented suckers
And came yapping at our heels.
Behold a conquered province;
I'm a worm, and they are robins.
On the grandchildren's table what books are displayed?
Better Slapjack, and *How to Win at Old Maid.*

In a frantic final effort
To frivol expert-free,
I've invented Amaturo
For just my friends and me.
The deck has seven morkels
Of eleven guzzards each,
The game runs counterclockwise,
With an extra kleg for dreech,
And if you're caught with a gruice,
The score reverts to deuce.
I'll bet that before my cuff links are on the bureau
Some expert will have written *A Guide to Amaturo.*

DRUSILLA

There was an old man of Scholairie
Who settled himself in a quarry.
And those who asked why
Got the candid reply,
"Today is the day of the soirée."

TO EE IS HUMAN

Once there were two men named Mr. Webster and Mr. Merriam,

And they had many differences but in the face of a common danger
they decided to bury 'em.

Some people, vouchsafed Mr. Webster, can't see the wood for the
trees,

But I can't see the language for the rising tide of double e's.

I know, vouched Mr. Merriam even more safely, that jargon will
someday overwhelm our mother tongue, but I can remember
before it had begun to,

And the suffix *er* denoted who did it and suffix *ee* denoted who it was
done to.

In my day, barked Mr. Webster, an employer employed an employee,
and a trustee was one who was trusted,

Which, bowwowed Mr. Merriam, although beside the point, is why
many trusters went busted.

Who, rapped Mr. Webster, escapes an escapee?

That, knock-knocked Mr. Merriam, is what puzzles me.

Has the moment come, rapiered Mr. Webster, to abjectly surrender
to journalese?

On that, riposted Mr. Merriam, you may bet not only your shirt but
also your jacket and trousers, I mean trousees.

Well, epitaphed Mr. Webster, none so blind as those who will not
see;

In the future please address me not as Mr. Webster but as Mr.
Webstee.

FIRST LIMICK

An old person of Troy
Is so prudish and coy
That it doesn't know yet
If it's a girl or a boy.

LEGAL REFLECTION

The postal authorities of the United States of America
Frown on Curiosa, Erotica and Esoterica,
Which is a break, I guess,
For stockholders of the American Railway Express.

THIRD LIMICK

Two nudists of Dover,
Being purple all over,
Were munched by a cow
When mistaken for clover.

I CAN HARDLY WAIT FOR THE SANDMAN

There are several differences between me and Samuel Taylor
       Coleridge, whose bust I stand admiringly beneath;
He found solace in opium, I found it in Codman's Bayberry Chewing
       Gum, at least until it started loosening my teeth.
Another difference between me and Samuel Taylor Coleridge is
       more massive in design:
People used to interrupt him while he was dreaming his dreams, but
       they interrupt me while I am recounting mine.
Now, if anybody buttonholes you to tell you about how they dreamt
       they were falling, or flying, or just about to die and they
       actually would have died if they hadn't woken up abruptly,
Well, they deserve to be treated interruptly,
But when somebody with a really interesting dream takes the floor,
I don't think people ought to break away and start listening to the
       neighborhood bore.
Therefore I feel I need offer no apology
For having gathered a few of my more representative dreams into a
       modest anthology.
Once I dreamt I was in this sort of, you know, desert with cactuses
       only they were more like caterpillars and there were skulls
       and all the rest,
And right in the middle of this desert was a lifeboat with the name
       Mary Celeste,
And if I hadn't woken up because the heat was so blistery,
Why, I bet I would have solved this mystery of nautical history.
Another time I dreamt I was climbing this mountain although
       actually it was more like a beach,
And all of a sudden this sort of a merry-go-round I forgot to tell you
       about turned into a shack with a sign saying, LEDA'S PLACE,
       SWANBURGERS 10¢ EACH.
I hope you will agree that of dreams I am a connoisseur,
And next time I will tell you about either how I dreamt I went down
       the rabbit hole or through the looking glass, whichever you
       prefer.

HOW TO BE MARRIED WITHOUT A SPOUSE
or
MR. KIPLING, WHAT HAVE YOU DONE WITH MR. HAUKSBEE?

Do any of you old fogies remember Mrs. Hauksbee? Without Mrs.
    Hauksbee, Simla and Poona
Would have been just like Altoona.
At Mrs. Hauksbee's burra khanas
Nabobs pinned tails on donkeys and viceroys bobbed for bananas.
Mrs. Hauksbee disentangled subalterns and aides-de-camp
From shopworn maids-de-camp.
Under the deodars, whatever they may be, Mrs. Hauksbee was in
    her glory,
But this is another story.
Mrs. Hauksbee was attended by a faithful old *amah*,
Which is the equivalent of in Alabama a faithful old *mamah*,
And this now *amah* was a conservative reactionary Hindu,
And she got tired of Mrs. Hauksbee all the time shifting her hemline
    and her hair-do and her skin-do,
And finally she asked Mrs. Hauksbee why she had dyed her hair
    again and she got one of the usual answers.
Mrs. Hauksbee said she was changing her style to reform young
    Slingsby of the Umpteenth Lancers,
And the *amah* (she had surreptitiously attended the Sorbonne)
Murmured, "*Plus ça change, plus c'est la memsahib,*" and wandered
    on.

THE MERMAID

Say not the mermaid is a myth,
I knew one once named Mrs. Smith.
She stood while playing cards or knitting;
Mermaids are not equipped for sitting.

WHAT'S THE USE?

Sure, deck your lower limbs in pants;
Yours are the limbs, my sweeting.
You look divine as you advance
Have you seen yourself retreating?

THE CHERUB

I like to watch the clouds roll by,
And think of cherubs in the sky;
But when I think of cherubim,
I don't know if they're her or him.

THE DROP OF A HAT

Darling, what is that?
That, angel, is a hat.
Are you positive? Are you certain?
Are you sure it's not a curtain?
Shall you really place your head in it?
How's for keeping cake or bread in it?
Do not wear it on your head;
Find some other use instead.
Say a cloth for drying dishes,
Or a net for catching fishes.
Darling, what is that?
Are you sure it is a hat?
And if so, what was the matter
With the hatter?
Was he troubled? Was he ill?
Was he laughing fit to kill?
Oh, what was on his mind
As he designed?
Had he gone without his supper?
Was he dressing in an upper?
Did he plot a wily plan
To annoy his fellow man?
Is its aspect, rear and frontal,
Intended to disgruntle,
Or was it accidental
And is he now repental?
Are memories of the brim
Now agony to him?
Do visions of the crown
Drag his spirits down?
Oh, may the Furies batter
That eleven-fingered hatter!
May doom and gloom enswaddle

The creator of this model!
I hope he made a lot of them,
That dozens he has got of them;
I hope he has a harem,
And all his spouses warem.

MY MY

I. MY DREAM

Here is a dream.
It is my dream—
My own dream—
I dreamt it.
I dreamt that my hair was kempt,
Then I dreamt that my true love unkempt it.

2. MY CONSCIENCE

I could of
If I would of,
But I shouldn't,
So I douldn't.

SHRINKING SONG

Woollen socks, woollen socks!
Full of color, full of clocks!
Plain and fancy, yellow, blue,
From the counter beam at you.
O golden fleece, O magic flocks!
O irresistible woollen socks!
O happy haberdasher's clerk
Amid that galaxy to work!
And now it festers, now it rankles
Not to have them round your ankles;
Now with your conscience do you spar;
They look expensive, and they are;
Now conscience whispers, You ought not to,
And human nature cries, You've got to!
Woollen socks, woollen socks!
First you buy them in a box.
You buy them several sizes large,
Fit for Hercules, or a barge.
You buy them thus because you think
These lovely woollen socks may shrink.
At home you don your socks with ease,
You find the heels contain your knees;
You realize with saddened heart
Their toes and yours are far apart.
You take them off and mutter Bosh,
You up and send them to the wash.
Too soon, too soon the socks return,
Too soon the horrid truth you learn;
Your woollen socks can not be worn
Unless a midget child is born,
And either sockless you must go,

Or buy a sock for every toe.
Woollen socks, woollen socks!
Infuriating paradox!
Hosiery wonderful and terrible,
Heaven to wear, and yet unwearable.
The man enmeshed in such a quandary
Can only hie him to the laundry,
And while his socks are hung to dry,
Wear them once as they're shrinking by.

THE THIRD JUNGLE BOOK

Why does the Pygmy
Indulge in polygmy?
His tribal dogma
Frowns on monogma.
Monogma's a stigma
For any Pygma.
If he sticks to monogmy
A Pygmy's a hogmy.

WHAT'S IN A NAME? SOME LETTER
I ALWAYS FORGET

Not only can I not remember anecdotes that are racy,
But I also can't remember whether the names of my Scottish friends
      begin with M-c or M-a-c,
And I can't speak for you, but for myself there is one dilemma with
      me in the middle of it,
Which is, is it Katharine with a K or Catherine with a C, and
      furthermore is it an A or is it an E in the middle of it?
I can remember the races between Man o' War and Sir Barton, and
      Épinard and Zev,
But I can't remember whether it's Johnson or Johnston any more
      than whether you address a minister as Mr. or Dr. or simply
      Rev.
I know a cygnet from a gosling and a coney from a leveret,
But how to distinguish an I-double-T from an E-double-T Everett?
I am familiar with the nature of an oath,
But I get confused between the Eliot with one L and one T, and the
      Elliot with two L's and one T, and the Eliott with one L and
      two T's, and the Elliott with two of both.
How many of my friendships have lapsed because of an extra T or a
      missing L;
Give me a simple name like Taliaferro or Wambsganss or Toporcer
      or Joralemon or Mankiewicz that any schoolboy can spell,
Because many former friends thought I was being impolite to them
When it was only because I couldn't remember whether they were
      Stuarts with a U or Stewarts with an E-W that I didn't write to
      them.

REFLECTION ON INGENUITY

Here's a good rule of thumb:
Too clever is dumb.

GENEALOGICAL REFLECTION

No McTavish
Was ever lavish.

SAMSON AGONISTES

I test my bath before I sit,
And I'm always moved to wonderment
That what chills the finger not a bit
Is so frigid upon the fundament.

ONE MAN'S MEED IS ANOTHER MAN'S
OVEREMPHASIS

I salute the section of our lordly Sunday journals which is entitled
      Scores of College Football Games Continued from Page One,
Because there a flock of not very notorious institutions of learning
      find their annual place in the sun.
Yes, the football season is a kindly time of year,
And during it we read of campuses of which at other times we do not
      often hear.
Would a playwright, for instance, ordinarily select Aurora as the
      Alma Mater for his hero?
Yet it is here recorded that Aurora one week held Wright Jr. to a
      six-to-six tie and the next week took the measure of
      Wartburg, nineteen to zero.
Yes, and the St. Cloud Teachers are an aggregation that no
      college-lover can conscientiously shelve,
Because they nosed out the Bemidji Teachers thirteen to twelve.
Oh ye of little faith who take Yale and Notre Dame for your Alpha
      and Omega,
What about Hiwassee, which outscored Biltmore, and Dillard, which
      engaged in a Homeric deadlock with Talladega?
When better endowments are offered,
Well, what's the matter with Augustana and Millsaps and Spearfish
      and Gustavus Adolphus and Wofford?
So if anybody makes derogatory remarks about the football season
      let us answer with scornful defiance,
And meanwhile let us not forget that Huron beat Yankton six to
      nothing on the very same day that Jamestown smothered
      Wahpeton Science.

FUNEBREAL REFLECTION

Among the anthropophagi
One's friends are one's sarcophagi.

REQUIEM

There was a young belle of old Natchez
Whose garments were always in patchez.
When comment arose
On the state of her clothes,
She drawled, When Ah Itchez, Ah scratchez!

LITERARY REFLECTION

Philo Vance
Needs a kick in the pance.

WHAT IS BIBBIDI-BOBBIDI-BOO IN SANSKRIT?

When people tell me French is difficult, I show my dimple.
French is simple.
My pen is cosmopolitan, not parochial.
I am at home in French either classical or collochial.
I can pronounce *filet mignon* even while chewing it,
And I can and will fluently translate popular songs such as
        "Everybody's Doing It."
Tout le monde est faisant le, faisant le, faisant le,
Tout le monde est faisant le,
Faisant quoi?
Dindon pas!
Vois ce ragtime couple débonnaire,
Vois-les jeter leurs épaules en air,
C'est un hibou,
Un hibou, un hibou,
Où?
I think that even Mr. Berlin would agree that this has life and
        movement,
And that the few changes are an improvement.
That ragtime couple, for example, instead of just being vaguely over
        there,
They are now obviously in some expensive club, they are debonair.
And the substitution of *c'est un hibou, un hibou, un hibou* (it's an
        owl, it's an owl, it's an owl) for *c'est un ours, c'est un ours, c'est*
        un ours (it's a bear, it's a bear, it's a bear)—
That is a veritable *coup de tonnerre,*
That is a truly superior brand of merchandise,
Because in French *ours* (bear) might be confused with *oursin* (sea
        urchin) and what would a debonair owl-loving ragtime couple
        want with a fishy batch of sea-urchindise?
I feel I have built myself a monument of more than bricks and
        mortar,
And, having gained the gratitude of Mr. Berlin, I am now leafing
        through the works of Mr. Oscar Hammerstein and Mr. Cole
        Porter.

THE WENDIGO*

The Wendigo,
The Wendigo!
Its eyes are ice and indigo!
Its blood is rank and yellowish!
Its voice is hoarse and bellowish!
Its tentacles are slithery,
And scummy,
Slimy,
Leathery!
Its lips are hungry blubbery,
And smacky,
Sucky,
Rubbery!
The Wendigo,
The Wendigo!
I saw it just a friend ago!
Last night it lurked in Canada;
Tonight, on your veranada!
As you are lolling hammockwise
It contemplates you stomachwise.
You loll,
It contemplates,
It lollops.
The rest is merely gulps and gollops.

* WENDIGO: In the mythology of the northern Algonquians, an evil spirit;
one of a fabulous tribe of cannibals.

WEBSTER'S UNABRIDGED DICTIONARY

DON'T LOOK FOR THE SILVER LINING,
JUST WAIT FOR IT

The rabbit loves his hoppity and the wallaby loves his hippity.

I love my serendipity.

Let none look askance;

Serendipity is merely the knack of making happy and unexpected
discoveries by chance.

Only yesterday I was bored by a bore—there is no topic that be
isn't inept on it—

And when I pointed out a piece of chewing gum on the sidewalk, he
was too busy talking to listen, so I soon made the happy and
unexpected discovery that he had stepped on it.

It was serendipity when a recent hostess of mine in Philadelphia
apologized for serving ham and eggs because she had
forgotten to order scrapple,

Just as it was when I found a bow tie I could wear that didn't rise
and fall with my Adam's apple.

Also when I found a hole in my pocket which I had tickets for a
harp recital in, or in which I had tickets for a harp recital, to
put it properer,

So instead of the harp recital we had to see the Marx Brothers in *A
Night at the Opera.*

If your coat catches on a branch just as you are about to slip over a
precipice precipitous,

That's serendipitous,

But when you happily and unexpectedly discover that you don't
have to go to the dentist or the chiropodist,

That's serendopitist.

THE MAN WITH TWO NEW SUITS

Who is that well-dressed handsome man?
Is everybody's eager cry,
I make response, for the fleeting nonce:
Excuse me, it is I!
The clangorous bells their homage pay,
The jubilant whistle toots,
And the murmur grows, Look, there he goes,
The man with two new suits!

The first is a tasteful quiet gray,
The second is a quiet brown;
One wouldn't suppose such reticent clothes
Would so excite the town.
The coats display no waspish waist,
The trousers boast no pleats,
But the collars fit like Glyn and It,
And Oh the lordly seats!
On the gleaming steps of the City Hall
The Mayor takes his stand,
With welcoming teeth, and a laurel wreath
And a gold key in his hand.
The City is yours, the Mayor cries,
And the guard of honor salutes,
And the gaping crowd cheers long and loud
For the man with two new suits.

The brown one has a single breast,
And the breast of the gray is double,
And they mold the form to the perfect norm
Where the scapulae cease to trouble.
The trousers nestle around the hips,
Then flow like a weeping willow—
Oh as gay am I as a butterfly,
Yet snug as the armadillo!

The old suit bagged across the knees,
And it also bagged behind;
The foraging moth had pierced its cloth,
And the nap was neatly shined,
I gave that suit to a shabby tramp,
I thought his poverty earned it,
And he said What's that? And then he spat,
And he took it out and burned it.

But now bring forth your noblest malt,
Your noblest barley and grape,
Triumphal parade and cavalcade
And torrent of ticker tape!
Now man and child shall work no more,
But seize their zithers and lutes,
And spend their days in endless praise
Of the man with two new suits!

THEATRICAL REFLECTION

In the Vanities
No one wears panities.

THE HAPPY ENDING OF MR. TRAIN

Once there was a man named Mr. Train who wasn't called
      Choo-choo, which in itself is odd.
Furthermore, he knew a Mr. Rhodes who wasn't called Dusty, and a
      Mr. Sloan who wasn't called Tod.
And they felt very unpopular not to be called Tod and Dusty and
      Choo-choo,
Because this was back in the days when if you were popular you
      were called Stinky or Baldy or the Tennessee Shad, and
      chicle had just replaced tobacco as the new chew.
Well, of their unpopularity they grew wearier and wearier,
Until they got together and decided that they were unpopular
      because they were superior,
And Mr. Sloan was asked by Mr. Rhodes, and Mr. Train, who kept
      going CHOO-choo, CHOO-choo, CHOO-choo, choo-CHOO,
Just how superior are YOU?
And Mr. Sloan replied that even as a child he had been familiar
      with Homer's *Iliad* and Xenophon's *Anabasis*,
And he knew that the classical word for a clump of trees was
      coppice, so that he always went over the river and into the
      clump of trees to play coppice and robberses,
And Mr. Rhodes and Mr. Train said You are still unpopular and
      alone,
You are not Tod, or even 's Liniment, you are still just Mr. Sloan.
And the aesthetic Mr. Rhodes boasted, I am superior because to my
      fiancée who to marry me was waiting until I got a steady job I
      said It's not too good, it's truly too bad you waited,
Because I did have a steady job teaching Art for seven years, but
      Art just graduated.
And Mr. Sloan retired at once to his coppices and bosky abodes,
Murmuring, No Dusty he, nor even the Colossus of, he was born,
      lived, and will die, as Mr. Rhodes.
But Mr. Train, he ain't say nuffin'
Just set on de sidin', a-tootin' and a-puffin'.

ALL, ALL ARE GONE,
THE OLD FAMILIAR QUOTATIONS

Who was born too soon? I will tell you who was born too soon:
    Francis Bacon, Baron Verulam.
Therefore he could not ask his friends, *Why is Charles Lamb like
    Baltimore,* and supply his own answer, *Because he is deep in
    the heart of Mary Lamb.*
Who was born too late? I will tell you without further parley:
It was I, because I cannot remember whether it was Charles Lamb or
    who, who on the death of his last nearest and dearest
    pathetically exclaimed, *Now there is no one left to call me
    Charlie.*
I am always getting entangled in such mnemonic snarls,
But from internal evidence it was obviously someone named
    Charles,
So it couldn't have been Scrooge or Marley.
Nor could it have been Charles II, because there was always
    somebody to call him Charlie.
It would have been duck soup or pie or jam
If he had said, *There is no one left to call me Elia,* then I would have
    known it was Lamb.
If I could but spot a conclusion, I should race to it,
But Charles is such a simple name that I can't put a face to it.
Still, I shouldn't complain, since it is its simplicity that gives it its
    pathos;
There would be no poignancy in saying, *There is no one left to call
    me Charlemagne or Lancelot or Athos.*
People prefer the simple to the grandiose,
And I do not believe that even in an antique land anybody would
    sympathize with anybody who went around saying, *There is
    no one left to call me Ozymandias.*

I'LL GET ONE TOMORROW

Barber, barber, come and get me;
Hairy torrents irk and fret me.
Hair and hair again appears,
And climbs like ivy round my ears;
Hair across my collar gambols;
Down my neck it wayward ambles;
Ever down it trips and trickles,
Yes, and where it trips, it tickles.
Barber dear, I wish I knew
Why I do not visit you,
Why I grudge the minutes ten
In your sanitary den,
Why I choose to choke on hair
Rather than to mount your chair.
Men no busier than I
Weekly to your office hie;
Men no braver than myself
Confront the armory on your shelf;
Men no wealthier than me
Gladly meet your modest fee,
And for a multiple of a dollar
Keep the jungle off their collar.
I alone am shy and flustered,
A solitary, cowardly custard,
Shaggy as a prize Angora,
Overrun with creeping flora.
Barber, barber, you're in luck;
The bell has rung, the hour has struck.
Sloth is strong, but hair is stronger;
I cannot stand it any longer.
Barber, barber, here I come;
Shake up the odorous bay rum;
Bring on your shears, your scythes, your snippers,
Bring on your crisp, electric clippers;

Employ a dozen extra sweepers;
Bring giant harvesters and reapers;
I warn you that a bumper crop
Waits to overwhelm your shop.
Barber, barber, be verbose,
Be anything, but clip me close;
Leave me razored, leave me scissored,
Leave me hairless as a lizard;
Barber, barber, singe and scald;
Barber, can't you make me bald?
I'd be the happiest of men,
And never think of you again.

CHACUN À SON BERLITZ

French is easy.
At speaking French I am the champ of the Champs Elysee,
And since I can speak Parisian without a flaw,
I will tell you why the crows, or les corbeaux, always win their battle
    against the scarecrows: it's on account of their esprit de caw.

THERE WERE GIANTS IN THOSE DAYS
or
MAYBE THERE WEREN'T

When people bandy about bright sayings they like to attribute them
     to celebrities celebrated for their witticism,
Hoping thereby both to gain prestige and forestall criticism.
Thus many people in London have had their dispositions soured
By being cornered by other people and told stories attributed to
     Mr. Shaw or Noel Coward,
While over here, if people tell an anecdote either hygienic or spotty,
Why, they attribute it to Dorothy Parker, only they usually cozily
     refer to her as Dottie.
I have never heard an anecdote attributed to William Henry
     Harrison, or Rutherford B. Hayes,
So let us respectfully attribute the following titbits to their
     posthumous praise.
When William Henry Harrison faced a knotty problem he didn't
     wonder what would Gerald K. Smith or Earl Browder do,
He simply recounted the story of the two jealous Indian ranees who
     met on elephant-back and one ranee stroked her coiffure and
     said, Here's a pretty hair-do, and the other ranee stroked her
     elephant and said, Here's a pretty howdah-do;
And once when Rutherford B. Hayes found himself losing at
     backgammon,
Why, he casually upset the board and asked, Did you hear about
     Lord Louis Mountbatten, he asked a soldier in Burma, Are
     you Indo-Chinese? And the soldier said, No suh, I'se out-do'
     Alabaman.
Kindly do not attribute these anecdotes to the undersigned,
Kindly attribute them to these two hitherto unsung statesmen, who
     are dead and probably won't mind.

CAPTAIN JOHN SMITH

Captain John Smith was a full-blooded Briton,
The same as Boadicea and Bulwer-Lytton,
But his problem and theirs were not quite the same,
Because they didn't have to go around assuring everybody that that
    was their real name,
And finally he said, This business of everybody raising their
    eyebrows when I register at an inn is getting very boring,
So I guess I'll go exploring,
So he went and explored the River James,
Where they weren't as particular then as they are now about names,
And he went for a walk in the forest,
And the Indians caught him and my goodness wasn't he
    emborrassed!
And he was too Early-American to write for advice from Emily Post,
So he prepared to give up the ghost,
And he prayed a prayer but I don't know whether it was a silent one
    or a vocal one,
Because the Indians were going to dash his brains out and they
    weren't going to give him an anaesthetic, not even a local
    one,
But along came Pocahontas and she called off her father's savage
    minions,
Because she was one of the most prominent Virginians,
And her eyes went flash flash,
And she said, Scat, you po' red trash,
And she begged Captain John Smith's pardon,
And she took him for a walk in the gyarden,
And she said, Ah reckon Ah sho' would have felt bad if anything
    had happened to you-all,
And she told him about her great-uncle Hiawatha and her cousin
    Sittin' Bull and her kissin' cousin King Philip, and I don't
    know who-all,
And he said you'd better not marry me, you'd better marry John
    Rolfe.

So he bade her farewell and went back to England, which adjoins
    Scotland, where they invented golf.

THE LITERARY SCENE

I

The Marquis de Sade
Wasn't always mad.
What addled his brain
Was Mickey Spillane.

II

Some words, like ugly courtiers,
Should lag behind the portieres.
Here's two such hippopotami:
Ambivalence, dichotomy.
I deprecate their prevalence,
Dichotomy, ambivalence.
Why do the learned quarterlies
Such couthless cant immortalize?

III

How many miles to Babylon?
Love-in-a-mist and Bovril.
Are there more Sitwells than one?
Oh yes, there are Sacheverell.

AWAY FROM IT ALL

I wish I were a Thibetan monk
Living in a monastery.
I would unpack my trunk
And store it in a tronastery;
I would collect all my junk
And send it to a jonastery;
I would try to reform a drunk,
And pay his expenses at a dronastery.
And if my income shrunk
I would send it to a shronastery.

COMMON SENSE

Why did the Lord give us agility
If not to evade responsibility?

14

FOOD FOR THOUGHT

*"Breakfast is an institution that I don't know who
commenced it,
But I am not for it, I am against it."*

CELERY

Celery, raw,
Develops the jaw,
But celery, stewed,
Is more quietly chewed.

THE CARAWAY SEED

The Abbé Voltaire, alias Arouet,
Never denounced the seed of the caraway;
Sufficient proof, if proof we need,
That he never bit into a caraway seed.

THE SHAD

I'm sure that Europe never had
A fish as tasty as the shad.
Some people greet the shad with groans,
Complaining of its countless bones;
I claim the bones teach table poise
And separate the men from boys.
The shad must be dissected subtle-y;
Besides, the roe is boneless, utterly.

THE EIGHT O'CLOCK PERIL

Breakfast is an institution that I don't know who commenced it,
But I am not for it, I am against it.
It is a thoroughly inedible repast,
And the dictionary says it is derived from the words *break*, meaning
      to break, and *fast*, meaning a *fast*, so to breakfast means to
      break your fast.
Well that just shows how far you can trust a dictionary,
Because I never saw a definition that was more utterly fictionary.
The veriest child could see it doesn't check,
Because if the first syllable of breakfast means *to break*, why is it
      pronounced *brek*?
Shame on you, you old lexicographers, I shall call you
      laxicographers because you have grown very lax,
Because it is perfectly obvious that the first syllable in breakfast is
      derived from the far-famed Yale football cheer, which is
      Brekekekex co-ax co-ax,
And did you even get the second syllable right? Why a thousand
      times No,
Because the *fast* in *breakfast* doesn't mean fast, *abstinence from
      food*, it means *fast*, not *slow*.
So with that in mind we can peek behind the scenes
And then we can see what *break-fast* really means,
It means that if you wake up in the morning feeling unappetized and
      sickly,
Why you are confronted by a meal and the entire Yale football team
      coaxes you with an axe to eat it quickly.

TRY IT SUNS. AND HOLS.; IT'S CLOSED THEN

I know a little restaurant
Behind a brownstone stoop
Where *potage du jour* is French
For a can of onion soup.

You order a Martini without an olive in it;
They bring you a Martini, it has an olive in it.
Throw the olive on the floor,
That's what the floor is for.

The tables teem with ladies
Tuned up by Mistress Arden,
And Muzak fills the air
With "In a Persian Garden."

You order legs of frog, and please omit the garlic;
They bring you legs of frog, all redolent of garlic.
Throw the frogs' legs on the floor,
That's what the floor is for.

The Daiquiris are flowing
Before the meal and after;
The smoke from fifty filter tips
Is shaken by the Schraffter.

You ask them for an ash tray, a receptable for ashes;
They do not bring an ash tray, instead they bring a menu.
Throw the ashes on the floor,
That's what the floor is for.

I know a little restaurant
Where client and agent grapple,
Where *ananas au kirsch*
Is French for canned pineapple.

You ask them for the check, for *l'addition*, for the bill;
They do not bring the check, they bring another menu.
Throw the menu on the floor,
Walk quickly through the door,
That's what the door is for.

QUICK, HAMMACHER, MY STOMACHER!

Man is a glutton,
He will eat too much even though there be nothing to eat too much
      of but parsnips or mutton.
He will deprecate his paunch,
And immediately afterwards reach for another jowl or haunch.
People don't have to be Cassandras or Catos
To know what will happen to their paunches if they combine hot
      biscuits and strawberry shortcake and French fried potatoes,
Yet no sooner has a man achieved a one-pound loss
Than he gains two through the application to an old familiar dish of
      a new irresistible sauce.
Thus cooks aggravate men's gluttony
With capers and hollandaise and chutney,
They can take seaweed or pemmican
And do things to them in a ramekin,
Give them a manatee that has perished of exposure
And they will whip you up a casserole of ambrosia,
Which is why a man who digs his grave with his teeth's idea of life
      beyond the grave is definite,
There's a divine chef in it.
Men are gluttons,
And everybody knows it except tailors, who don't leave room enough
      at the edge to move over the buttons.

THE SNARK WAS A BOOJUM WAS A PRAWN

A giant new prawn has been dredged up near Santiago, Chile . . . it is succulent and mysterious . . . . The new prawn has not been named, a fact that is causing no concern in Chile.—TIMES

Could some descending escalator
Deposit me below the equator,
I'd hunt me a quiet Chilean haunt,
Some Santiago restaurant;
The fact I speak no *Español*
Would handicap me not at all,
Since any language would be aimless
In ordering a tidbit nameless;
I'd simply tie my napkin on
And gesture like a giant prawn,
Then, served the dish for which I yearned,
Proceed to munch it, unconcerned.
Happy crustacean, anonymous prawn,
From distant Latin waters drawn,
Hadst thou in Yankee seas appeared,
Account executives would have cheered,
Vice-presidents in paroxysms
Accorded thee multiple baptisms;
Yea, shouldst thou hit our markets now,
Soon, prawn, wouldst thou be named—and how!
I see the bright ideas drawn:
Prawno, Prawnex, and Vitaprawn;
And, should upper-bracket dreamers wake,
Squab o'Neptune, and Plankton Steak.
Small wonder thou headest for Santiago,
Where gourmets ignore such frantic farrago;
That's exactly where I myself would have went if I'd
Been mysterious, succulent, unidentified.

I CAN'T HAVE A MARTINI, DEAR,
BUT YOU TAKE ONE
or
ARE YOU GOING TO SIT THERE
GUZZLING ALL NIGHT?

Come, spread foam rubber on the floor,
And sawdust and excelsior;
Soundproof the ceiling and the wall,
Unwind the clock within the hall,
Muffle in cotton wool the knell
Of doorbell and of decibel.
Ye milkman and ye garbage man,
Clink not the bottle, clash not the can;
Ye census taker, pass on by,
And Fuller Brush man, draw not nigh;
Street cleaner, do not splash or sprinkle;
Good Humor man, forbear to tinkle;
Ye Communists, overt or crypto-,
Slink past this shuttered house on tiptoe,
And cat, before you seek admittance,
Put sneakers on yourself and kittens;
Let even congressmen fall quiet,
For Chloë is on her latest diet,
And when Chloë is straightening out her curves
She's a sensitive bundle of quivering nerves.
Me you will find it useless to quiz
On what her latest diet is,
So rapidly our Chloë passes
From bananas to wheat germ and molasses.
First she will eat but chops and cheese,
Next, only things that grow on trees,
Now buttermilk, now milk that's malted,
And saccharin, and salt de-salted,
Salads with mineral oil and lemon in,
Repugnant even to palates feminine,
Lean fish, and fowl as gaunt as avarice,

And haggard haggis and curds cadaverous.
Today may bring gluten bread and carrots,
Tomorrow the eggs of penguins or parrots,
Because Chloë's dietetic needs
Shift with each article she reads.
But whatever her diet, from whence or whither,
When Chloë's on it, there's no living with her.

REFLECTION ON THE VERNACULAR

In cooking *petits pois*, or lesser peas,
Some use receipts, and some use recipes.
In spite of opposition warm,
I choose to use the former form.
In fact, though you may think me gossipy,
I plan to settle near Lake Ossipee,
And when my settlement is complete,
To change its name to Lake Osseipt.

THE BANQUET

Oh, here we are at the mammoth banquet
To honor the birth of the great Bosanquet!
Oh give a look at the snowy napery,
The costly flowers, the sumptuous drapery,
Row on row of silver utensils
Poised for action like salesmen's pencils,
Waiters gaudy as sugar plums,
Every waiter with seven thumbs,
Stream upon stream of gaudy bunting,
And lady commuters lion hunting,
The gleaming teeth at the speaker's table,
The clattering, chattering, battering babel.
Sit we here in the great unquiet
And brood awhile on the evening's diet.
As soggy and dull as good advice,
The butter floats in the melting ice.
In a neighboring morgue, beyond salvation,
The celery waits identification.
Huddled thick in an open vault,
Mummified peanuts moult their salt.
Out of the napkin peers a roll,
With the look of a lost and hardened soul.
The cocktail sauce, too weak to roister,
Fails to enliven the tepid oyster.
The consommé, wan as Elizabeth Barrett,
Washes over a drowning carrot.
Next, with its sauce of gummy tartar,
The sole, or flounder, or is it a garter?
And, be it Seattle or Cincinnati,
O'Sullivan's Rubber chicken party;
Parsley potatoes, as tempting as soap,
String beans, hemp beans, and beans of rope.
And the waiter would sooner give you his daughter

Than give you another glass of water.
Pineapple salad next, by George!
That ought to raise your sunken gorge!
And green ice cream, sweet frozen suet,
With nuts and raisins sprinkled through it.
At sight of vari-colored *gâteaux*
The innards reel, as on a *bateau*.
At last the little cups belated
Of coffee dated, or inundated.
Chairs creak as half a thousand rumps
Twist them around with backward bumps.
A thousand eyes seek out, as one,
The beaming chairman on his throne.
He rises luminous through the smoke
Of banquet tobacco, or poison oak.
He bows, he coughs, he smiles a bit,
He sparkles with imitable wit—
Rabbi Ben Ezra, fly with me;
The almost worse is yet to be.
Let us arise and leave this banquet—
And by the way, Rabbi, who *was* Bosanquet?

THE ABSENTEES

I'd ride a cock horse to Banbury Cross
For giblet gravy and cranberry sauce,
Two treats which are held in reserve by the waiter
Till you've finished your turkey and mashed potater.

PARSLEY FOR VICE-PRESIDENT!

I'd like to be able to say a good word for parsley, but I can't,
And after all what can you find to say for something that even the
        dictionary dismisses as a biennial umbelliferous plant?
Speaking of which, I don't know how the dictionary figures it as
        biennial, it is biennial my eye, it is like the poor and the
        iniquitous,
Because it is always with us, because it is permanent and
        ubiquitous.
I will not venture to deny that it is umbelliferous,
I will only add that it is of a nasty green color, and faintly
        odoriferous,
And I hold by my complaint, though every cook and hostess in the
        land indict me for treason for it,
That parsley is something that as a rhymer I can find no rhyme for it
        and as an eater I can find no reason for it.
Well, there is one sin for which a lot of cooks and hostesses are
        some day going to have to atone,
Which is that they can't bear to cook anything and leave it alone.
No, they see food as something to base a lot of beautiful dreams and
        romance on,
Which explains lamb chops with pink and blue pants on.
Everything has to be all decorated and garnished
So the guests will be amazed and astarnished,
And whatever you get to eat, it's sprinkled with a lot of good old
        umbelliferous parsley looking as limp and wistful as Lillian
        Gish,
And it is limpest, and wistfulest, and also thickest, on fish.
Indeed, I think maybe one reason for the disappearance of Enoch
        Arden
Was that his wife had an idea that mackerel tasted better if instead
        of looking like mackerel it looked like a garden.
Well, anyhow, there's the parsley cluttering up your food,
And the problem is to get it off without being rude,
And first of all you try to scrape it off with your fork,
And you might as well try to shave with a cork,

And then you surreptitiously try your fingers,
And you get covered with butter and gravy, but the parsley lingers,
And you turn red and smile at your hostess and compliment her on
  the recipe and ask her where she found it,
And then you return to the parsley and as a last resort you try to eat
  around it,
And the hostess says, Oh you are just picking at it, is there
  something wrong with it?
So all you can do is eat it all up, and the parsley along with it,
And now is the time for all good parsleyphobes to come to the aid of
  the menu and exhibit their gumption,
And proclaim that any dish that has either a taste or an appearance
  that can be improved by parsley is *ipso facto* a dish unfit for
  human consumption.

REFLECTIONS ON ICE-BREAKING

Candy
Is dandy
But liquor
Is quicker.

ISN'T THAT A DAINTY DISH? NO!

I am tired of gadgets with cocktails,
I am awfully tired of gadgets with cocktails,
My heart leaps down when I behold gadgets with cocktails
With me they have outlived their popularity.
Gadgets with cocktails are stultified
Gadgets with cocktails are stertorous
Gadgets with cocktails are stark and stagnant
And for them I have no patience or charity.

I don't want any toast covered with vulcanized caviar
Or any soggy popcorn covered with cheesy butter or buttery cheese,
I don't want any potato chips or Tiny Tootsie pretzels or pretzel
       sticks,
And I don't want any crackers coated with meat paste or bargain
       pâté de foie gras particularly please.

Do not hand me that plate filled with olives unripe and overripe,
Anchovies whether curled or uncurled I have concluded not to
       abide,
Kindly mail all those salted peanuts and almonds to the Collector of
       Internal Revenue,
As well as all the little heart-shaped sandwiches filled with squashy
       stuff that when you pick them up they squirt out at the side.

Maybe somewhere there is somebody who would like the stuffed
       eggs and diminutive frankfurters,
Or who could look the stuffed celery in the eye and voluntarily
       chew it,
Maybe there is a Chinaman in China who would care for that slab of
       fumigated salmon,
And that thing whatever it is rolled up with a toothpick sticking
       through it.

Hostesses never tire of gadgets with cocktails,
Hostesses sit around thinking up new gadgets with cocktails,

They prowl through the papers hunting tricky gadgets for cocktails,
And if they don't serve more than other hostesses they are swamped
      with humiliation and grief;
Gadgets with cocktails to you, my dear Mrs. Marshmallow,
Gadgets with cocktails to you, Mrs. Rodney St. Rodney,
Gadgets with cocktails to you and all other hostesses,
And I'll take some bread and butter and a slice of rare roast beef.

ONE TIMES ONE IS EIGHT

Either old magic or new math
Into our house has beat a path.
How else could Einstein or Diogenes
Explain an exploit of our progeny's?
While at the table with his ilk
A child upsets a glass of milk.
The glass held half a pint when filled,
And half a gallon when it spilled.

OUT IS OUT

Come in, dear guests, we've got a treat for you,
We've prepared a different place to eat for you!
Guess where we're going to have our dinner!
Everyone guess! Who'll be the winner?
The dining room? Heavens! It's hereby stated
That dining rooms are dreadfully dated.
What in the world could be more plebeian
Than to eat in a place in which you can see in!
The living room? No, you're off the path;
No, not the bedroom; no, not the bath;
And not the cellar, and not the attic;
The kitchen? No, that's too democratic.
Do you all give up? Well, listen and hark;
We're going to dine outdoors, in the dark!
No lights, because there aren't any plugs,
And anyhow, lights attract the bugs.
Oh, it's drizzling a little; I think perhaps
The girls had better keep on their wraps;
Just strike a match and enjoy the way
The raindrops splash in the consommé.
You probably won't get botts or pellagra
From whatever lit on your pâté de foie gras.
Now, you're not expected to eat with skill,
And everybody's supposed to spill;
If your half-broiled chicken leaps about,
That's half the excitement of eating out;
If you dust it with sugar instead of salt,
It's everyone's fun and nobody's fault;
And if anything flies in your mouth, perchance,
Why, that is mystery, that's romance!
Such a frolic and such a lark
It is to eat outdoors in the dark!
The dandiest fun since I don't know when;

Would you eat in a stuffy old room again?
Oh yes you would, you lukewarm liars,
And I'll see you tomorrow at the cleaner's and dyer's.

TASTE BUDS, EN GARDE!

Although I'll eat the strawberry when frozen
It's not the very berry I'd have chosen.
The naughty admen claim with gall divine
That it is better than the genu-ine,
New language they devise to sing its praise,
But only *le bon Dieu* can coin a *fraise*.

THE STRANGE CASE OF MR. PALLISER'S PALATE

Once there was a man named Mr. Palliser and he asked his wife,
    May I be a *gourmet*?
And she said, You sure may,
But she also said, If my kitchen is going to produce a Cordon Blue,
It won't be me, it will be you,
And he said, You mean *Cordon Bleu*?
And she said to never mind the pronunciation so long as it was him
    and not *heu*.
But he wasn't discouraged; he bought a white hat and *The Cordon
    Bleu Cook Book* and said, How about some *Huitres en Robe
    de Chambre*?
And she sniffed and said, Are you reading a cookbook or Forever
    Ambre?
And he said Well, if you prefer something more Anglo-Saxon,
Why suppose I whip up some tasty *Filets de Sole Jackson*,
And she pretended not to hear, so he raised his voice and said,
    Could I please you with some *Paupiettes de Veau à la Grecque*
    or *Cornets de Jambon Lucullus* or perhaps some nice *Moules
    à la Bordelaise*?
And she said, Kindly lower your voice or the neighbors will think
    we are drunk and *disordelaise*,
And she said, Furthermore the whole idea of your cooking anything
    fit to eat is a farce. So what did Mr. Palliser do then?
Well, he offered her *Œufs Farcis Maison* and *Homard Farci St.
    Jacques* and *Tomate Farcie à la Bayonne* and *Aubergines
    Farcies Provençales*, as well as *Aubergines Farcies Italiennes*,
And she said, Edward, kindly accompany me as usual to Hamburger
    Heaven and stop playing the fool,
And he looked in the book for one last suggestion and it suggested
    Croques Madame, so he did, and now he dines every evening
    on *Crème de Concombres Glacée*, *Côtelettes de Volaille
    Vicomtesse*, and *Artichauds à la Barigoule*.

EVERYBODY EATS TOO MUCH ANYHOW

You gulp your breakfast and glance at the clock,
Through eleventh hour packing you gallop amok
You bundle your bags in the back of the car,
You enter, she enters, and there you are.
It's au revoir to your modest abode,
You're gipsies, away on the open road;
The conversation is sweet as clover,
With breakfast practically hardly over.
"Darling, light me a cigarette?"
"At once and with all my heart, my pet;
"And by the way, we are off the track;
"We should have turned left a half-mile back."
You swing around with a cheery smile,
Thus far, a mile is only a mile.
The road is romance, so let it wind,
With breakfast an hour or so behind.
Under the tires the pebbles crunch,
And through the dust creep thoughts of lunch
The speedometer sits on a steady fifty
And more and more does lunch seem nifty.
Your eyes to the road ahead are glued,
She glances about in search of food.
She sees a place. She would like to try it.
She says so. Well, you're already by it.
Ignoring the road, you spot an eatery;
The look of it makes her interior teetery.
She sees a beauty. It's past and gone.
She's simmering now, like a tropical dawn.
She snubs the excuse as you begin it:
That there'll be another one any minute,
She says there won't. It must be a plot;
She's absolutely correct. There's not.
You finally find one. You stop and alight.
You're both too annoyed to eat a bite.
Oh, this is the gist of my gipsy song:

Next time carry your lunch along.

THE KIPPER

For half a century, man and nipper,
I've doted on a tasty kipper,
But since I am no Jack the Ripper
I wish the kipper had a zipper.

THE SWEETBREAD

That sweetbread gazing up at me
Is not what it purports to be.
Says Webster in one paragraph,
It is the pancreas of a calf.
Since it is neither sweet nor bread,
I think I'll take a bun instead.

COFFEE WITH THE MEAL

A gentlemanly gentleman, as mild as May,
Entered a restaurant famed and gay.
A waiter sat him in a draughty seat
And laughingly inquired what he'd like to eat.
"Oh I don't want venison, I don't want veal,
But I do insist on coffee with the meal.
Bring me clams in a chilly group,
And a large tureen of vegetable soup,
Steak as tender as a maiden's dream,
With lots of potatoes hashed in cream,
And a lettuce and tomato salad, please
And crackers and a bit of Roquefort cheese,
But waiter, the gist of my appeal,
Is coffee with coffee with, coffee *with* the meal."
The waiter groaned and he wrung his hands;
"Perhaps da headwaiter onderstands."
Said the sleek headwaiter, like a snobbish seal,
"What, monsieur? Coffee with the meal?"
His lip drew up in scornful laughter;
"Monsieur desires a demi-tasse after!"
Monsieur's eyes grew hard as steel,
He said, "I'm ordering coffee with the meal.
Hot black coffee in a great big cup,
Fuming, steaming, filled right up.
I don't want coffee iced in a glass,
And I don't want a miserable demi-tasse,
But what I'll have, come woe, come weal,
Is coffee with, coffee with, coffee *with* the meal."
The headwaiter bowed like a poppy in the breeze;
"Monsieur desires coffee with the salad or the cheese?"
Monsieur said, "Now you're getting warmer;
Coffee with the latter, coffee with the former;
Coffee with the steak, coffee with the soup,
Coffee with the clams in a chilly group;

Yes, and with a cocktail I could do,
So bring me coffee with the cocktail, too.
I'll fight to the death for my bright ideal,
Which is coffee with, coffee with, coffee *with* the meal."
The headwaiter swiveled on a graceful heel;
"Certainly, certainly, coffee with the meal!"
The waiter gave an obsequious squeal,
"Yes sir, yes sir, coffee with the meal!"
Oh what a glow did Monsieur feel
At the warming vision of coffee with the meal.
One hour later Monsieur, alas!
Got his coffee in a demi-tasse.

YORKSHIRE PUDDING

Let us call Yorkshire pudding
A fortunate blunder,
It's a sort of popover
That tripped and popped under.

THE PIZZA

Look at itsy bitsy Mitzi!
See her figure slim and ritzy!
She eatsa
Pizza!
Greedy Mitzi!
She no longer itsy bitsy!

ARE YOU A SNODGRASS?

It is possible that most individual and international social and
      economic collisions
Result from humanity's being divided into two main divisions.
Their lives are spent in mutual interference,
And yet you cannot tell them apart by their outward appearance.
Indeed the only way in which to tell one group from the other you
      are able
Is to observe them at the table,
Because the only visible way in which one group from the other
      varies
Is in its treatment of the cream and sugar on cereal and berries.
Group A, which we will call the Swozzlers because it is a very
      suitable name, I deem,
First applies the sugar and then swozzles it all over the place
      pouring on the cream,
And as fast as they put the sugar on they swozzle it away,
But such thriftlessness means nothing to ruthless egotists like they,
They just continue to scoop and swozzle and swozzle and scoop,
Until there is nothing left for the Snodgrasses, or second group.
A Snodgrass is a kind, handsome intelligent person who pours the
      cream on first,
And then deftly sprinkles the sugar over the cereal or berries after
      they have been properly immersed,
Thus assuring himself that the sugar will remain on the cereal and
      berries where it can do some good, which is his wish,
Instead of being swozzled away to the bottom of the dish.
The facts of the case for the Snodgrasses are so self-evident that it is
      ridiculous to debate them,
But this is unfortunate for the Snodgrasses as it only causes the
      sinister and vengeful Swozzlers all the more to hate them.
Swozzlers are irked by the superior Snodgrass intelligence and
      nobility
And they lose no opportunity of inflicting on them every kind of
      incivility.

If you read that somebody has been run over by an automobile
You may be sure that the victim was a Snodgrass, and a Swozzler
      was at the wheel.
Swozzlers start wars and Snodgrasses get killed in them,
Swozzlers sell waterfront lots and Snodgrasses get malaria when they
      try to build in them.
Swozzlers invent fashionable diets and drive Snodgrasses crazy with
      tables of vitamins and calories,
Swozzlers go to Congress and think up new taxes and Snodgrasses
      pay their salaries,
Swozzlers bring tigers back alive and Snodgrasses get eaten by
      anacondas,
Snodgrasses are depositors and Swozzlers are absconders,
Swozzlers hold straight flushes when Snodgrasses hold four of a
      kind,
Swozzlers step heavily on the toes of Snodgrasses' shoes as soon as
      they are shined.
Whatever achievements Snodgrasses achieve, Swozzlers always top
      them;
Snodgrasses say Stop me if you're heard this one, and Swozzlers stop
      them.
Swozzlers are teeming with useful tricks of the trade that are not
      included in standard university curricula;
The world in general is their oyster, and Snodgrasses in particular.
So I hope for your sake, dear reader, that you are a Swozzler, but I
      hope for everybody else's sake that you are not,
And I also wish that everybody else was a nice amiable Snodgrass
      too, because then life would be just one long sweet
      harmonious mazurka or gavotte.

MY DEAR, HOW EVER DID YOU THINK UP
THIS DELICIOUS SALAD?

This is a very sad ballad,
Because it's about the way too many people make a salad.
Generally they start with bananas,
And they might just as well use Gila monsters or iguanas.
Pineapples are another popular ingredient,
Although there is one school that holds preserved pears or peaches
    more expedient,
And you occasionally meet your fate
In the form of a prune or a date.
Rarely you may chance to discover a soggy piece of tomato looking
    very forlorn and Cinderella-ry,
But for the most part you are confronted by apples and celery,
And it's not a bit of use at this point to turn pale or break out in a
    cold perspiration,
Because all this is only the foundation,
Because if you think the foundation sounds unenticing,
Just wait until we get to the dressing, or rather, the icing.
There are various methods of covering up the body, and to some,
    marshmallows are the pall supreme,
And others prefer whipped cream,
And then they deck the grave with ground-up peanuts and
    maraschinos
And you get the effect of a funeral like Valentino's,
And about the only thing that in this kind of salad is never seen
Is any kind of green,
And oil and vinegar and salt and pepper are at a minimum,
But there is a maximum of sugar and syrup and ginger and nutmeg
    and cinnamum,
And my thoughts about this kind of salad are just as unutterable
As parsnips are unbutterable,
And indeed I am surprised that the perpetrators haven't got around
    to putting buttered parsnips in these salmagundis,
And the salad course nowadays seems to be a month of sundaes.

THE CLEAN PLATTER

Some singers sing of ladies' eyes
And some of ladies' lips,
Refined ones praise their ladylike ways,
And coarse ones hymn their hips.
The *Oxford Book of English Verse*
Is lush with lyrics tender;
A poet, I guess, is more or less
Preoccupied with gender.
Yet I, though custom call me crude,
Prefer to sing in praise of food.

Food,
Yes, food,
Just any old kind of food.
Pheasant is pleasant, of course,
And terrapin, too, is tasty,
Lobster I freely endorse,
In paté or patty or pasty.
But there's nothing the matter with butter,
And nothing the matter with jam,
And the warmest of greetings I utter
To the ham and the yam and the clam.
For they're food,
All food,
And I think very highly of food.
Though I'm broody at times
When bothered by rhymes,
I brood
On food.

Some painters paint the sapphire sea,
And some the gathering storm.
Others portray young lambs at play,
But most, the female form.
'Twas trite in that primeval dawn

When painting got its start,
That a lady with her garments on
Is Life, but is she Art?
By undraped nymphs
I am not wooed;
I'd rather painters painted food.

Food,
Just food,
Just any old kind of food.
Go purloin a sirloin, my pet,
If you'd win a devotion incredible;
And asparagus tips vinaigrette,
Or anything else that is edible.
Bring salad or sausage or scrapple,
A berry or even a beet.
Bring an oyster, an egg, or an apple,
As long as it's something to eat.
If it's food,
It's food;
Never mind what kind of food.
When I ponder my mind
I consistently find
It is glued
On food.

FURTHER REFLECTION ON PARSLEY

Parsley
Is gharsley.

WHAT, NO OYSTERS?

There is no R in the month of May,
There's none in the month of June,
And the days of the dog, July and Aug.,
Glide past on R-less shoon.
Then where are you going, my pretty maid,
And what will you find to eat
While the oyster broods in inedible moods
In his lonely bridal suite?

"I'm going a-feasting, sir," she said,
"I am on my way to dine.
Let the succulent bivalve cling to its bed,
Methinks I am doing fine.
For the chowder laves the fragrant clam
In the old New England style,
And if corn on the cob with my teeth plays hob,
I'll remember not to smile.

The baby lobster scarlet gleams
Next a mound of fresh asparagus;
While the blue point dreams connubial dreams,
I'll munch till my veins are varacus.
Lo, luscious now as an infant's lisp,
The strawberry, tart and juicy,
And soft-shell crabs as sweet and crisp
As a nocturne by Debussy.

Though there is no R in the month of May,
And none in the month of June,
Nor the days of the dog, July, and Aug.,
You can stuff till you're fit to swoon—
Who's that a-ringing the doorbell so,
Louder than doorbell ought to ring?
Why, it's half a dozen oysters, bowing low,
And their mouths are simply watering."

THE PARSNIP

The parsnip, children, I repeat,
Is simply an anemic beet.
Some people call the parsnip edible;
Myself, I find this claim incredible.

THE CANTALOUPE

One cantaloupe is ripe and lush,
Another's green, another's mush.
I'd buy a lot more cantaloupe
If I possessed a fluoroscope.

ASSORTED CHOCOLATES

If some confectioner were willing
To let the shape announce the filling,
We'd encounter fewer assorted chocs,
Bitten into and returned to the box.

15

WRITING, FOR BETTER OR VERSE

"A regular poet published a book,
And an excellent book it was,
But nobody gave it a second look,
As nobody often does."

THAT'S FUNNY, WASN'T IT? NO, IT WONT BE

Stranger, ignore yon loud bassoon
And harken, ere thou departest,
To the plaintive notes of a minor tune,
The wail of the comic artist.
The shadows lengthen across his career,
Each day is a new conundrum,
As the wingèd horses of yesteryear
Are progressively shot from under him.

His predecessors had ready themes,
Dependable sturdy stanchions,
And never foresaw in their direst dreams
The birth of a social conscience.
A permanent company they employed
Of dramatis personae;
There were Abie and Ike, and Pat and Mike,
And Rastus, Ole, and Tony.

But the humor that once raised mirthful whoops
Grew more and more precarious;
The facetious baiting of minor groups
Seemed less and less hilarious.
So the artist discarded the racial joke
And packed it away in camphor,
And assembled a group of risible folk
That nobody gives a damn for.

There's the couple marooned on the desert isle
With a caption faintly risqué,
And the portly sultan with lecherous smile
And entourage odalisqué,
The fakir complete with his bag of tricks,
The witch doctor, his cousin-german,
The felon reviewing his awkward fix,
And the khan on the flying Kirman.

So far, so good, but the world is filled
With sensitive True Believers,
There may come a complaint from the Sultans' Guild
Or the Magic Carpet Weavers.
How long can the ink-stained wretch rely
On his file of new sidesplitters
In the face of a logical outraged cry
From the Union of Counterfeiters?

Stranger, the wedding feast is done,
But linger, ere thou departest,
To murmur a prayer, just a little one,
For the soul of the comic artist.
May he sit secure on a laughing star
And cartoon on heavenly ceilings
The saints, who so superior are
That nothing can hurt their feelings.

LAMENTS FOR A DYING LANGUAGE—IV

Those authors I can never love
Who write, "It fit him like a glove,"
Though baseballs may be hit, not "hitted,"
The past of "fit" is always "fitted."
The sole exception worth a *haricot*
Is "Joshua fit de battle ob Jericho."

EVERYTHING'S HAGGIS IN HOBOKEN
or
SCOTS WHA HAE HAE

That hero my allegiance earns
Who boldly speaks of Robert Burns.
I have an inexpensive hobby—
Simply not to call him Bobbie.
It's really just as easy as not
Referring to Sir Wally Scott,
But many, otherwise resolute,
When mentioning Burns go coy and cute.
Scholars hip-deep in Homer and Horace
Suddenly turn all doch-an-dorris;
Fine ladies who should pose and purr
Roll out a half-rolled Highland burr;
Conventioneers in littered lobby
Hoist their glasses in praise of Bobbie;
All, all Burns-happy and Bobbie-loopy,
They dandle him like a Scotian kewpie.
I'll brush away like gnats and midges
Those who quote from Bobbies Southey and Bridges;
I will not snap my Hopalong gun
At admirers of Bobbie Stevenson
(To be Bobbied is no worse, I guess,
Than being enshrined as R.L.S.);
I'd even attempt to save from drowning
Maidens who dream of Bobbie Browning;
But of Robert Burns I'm a serious fan
He wrote like an angel and lived like a man,
And I yearn to shatter a set of crockery
On this condescending Bobbie-sockery.
Well, I'm off, before I break the law,
To read Tommy Hardy and Bernie Shaw.

EVERYBODY MAKES POETS

Poets aren't very useful,
Because they aren't very consumeful or very produceful.
Even poets of great promise
Don't contribute much to trade and commerce,
To which, indeed, even poets of great achievement
Are a positive bereavement,
Because they aren't very sensible,
Because they think buying and selling are cheap and lousy and
        reprehensible,
And this is a topic about which poets are people to whom you
        cannot tell anything,
Because they are people who cannot afford to buy anything and are
        seldom glib enough to sell anything.
Some poets are bitter,
But they are preferable to the poets who are all of a twitter,
But even the poets who are all of a twitter are as dependable as
        Rotary
Compared to what each of them has around him which is a rapturous
        coterie,
Because every poet is threatened constantly by one disaster,
Which is that a lot of otherwise thwarted male and female ladies will
        go around calling him Master,
And then there is nothing to do but surrender,
And then it is good-by old poetry, hello old theosophy and gender,
And yet on the other hand if a poet isn't fed by a lot of male and
        female ladies who are affected,
Why, until long after he is dead or gets the Pulitzer Prize, why he is
        neglected.
So my advice to mothers is if you are the mother of a poet don't
        gamble on the chance that future generations may crown him.
Follow your original impulse and drown him.

CALLING SPRING VII-MMMC

As an old traveler, I am indebted to paper-bound thrillers,
Because you travel faster from Cleveland to Terre Haute when you
    travel with a lapful of victims and killers.
I am by now an authority on thumbprints and fingerprints and even
    kneeprints,
But there is one mystery I have never been able to solve in certain
    of my invaluable reprints.
I am happily agog over their funerals, which are always satisfactorily
    followed by exhumerals,
But I can't understand why so many of them carry their copyright
    lines in Roman numerals.
I am just as learned as can be,
But if I want to find out when a book was first published, I have to
    move my lips and count on my fingers to translate Copyright
    MCMXXXIII into Copyright 1933.
I have a horrid suspicion
That something lies behind the publisher's display of erudition.
I may be oversensitive to clues,
But I detect a desire to obfuscate and confuse.
Do they think that because a customer cannot translate
    MCMXXXIII into 1933 because he is not a classical scholar,
He will therefore assume the book to have been first published
    yesterday and will therefore sooner lay down his XXV cents
    or I/IV of a dollar?
Or do they, straying equally far from the straight and narrow,
Think that the scholarly will snatch it because the Roman copyright
    line misleads him to believe it the work of Q. Horatius
    Flaccus or P. Virgilius Maro?
Because anybody can make a mistake when dealing with MCMs and
    XLVs and things, even Jupiter, ruler of gods and men;
All the time he was going around with IO he pronounced it Ten.

I AM FULL OF PREVIOUS EXPERIENCE

Newspapermen say that of all work, newspaper work is the
      infernalist,
But nevertheless I am studying up to be a journalist.
I do not aspire to be a Pearson or a Pegler or a Gunther,
I don't think I will ever be selected as a Book-of-the-Monther,
I don't hope to score any scoops or beat any deadlines,
But after a careful ten-year examination of the press I do think I
      have caught the knack of writing facetious little headlines.
Suppose a marmoset escapes in a saloon and mingles with the
      imbibers,
Why, "Monkey Business" is the heading expected by the
      subscribers,
And when a steer escapes on the way to the slaughterhouse and is
      recaptured by a cowboy from Madison Square Garden my cup
      is doubly full,
Because then I can write either "A Bum Steer" or "Throwing the
      Bull."
What can be apter than "Fowl Play" when the minister's Rhode
      Island Reds disappear at dawn,
Or be it Mrs. Somebody-or-other's of 13 South Water Street's
      amorous Pekinese that is missing, what could be more
      appropriate than "Dog-Gone"?
My, my, in the names of animals how many cryptic little giggles are
      hidden;
Which of you could guess what type of creature is referred to in
      items entitled "A Cat-astrophe" or "Poor Fish" or "Gets
      Farmer's Goat," or "No Kiddin'"?
No, I may never win any prizes from Mr. Pulitzer,
But when it comes to supplying the customers with little jokes for
      their breakfast table I will always be in there pitching
      honestly and trulitzer.

I MUST TELL YOU ABOUT MY NOVEL

My grandpa wasn't salty,
No hero he of fable,
His English wasn't faulty,
He wore a coat at table.
His character lacked the color
Of either saint or satyr,
His life was rather duller
Than that of Walter Pater.

Look at Grandpa, take a look!
How can I write a book!
His temper wasn't crusty,
He shone not forth majestic
For barroom exploits lusty,
Or tyranny domestic.
He swung not on the gallows
But went to his salvation
While toasting stale marshmallows,
His only dissipation.

Look at Grandpa, take a look!
How can I write a book!

My Uncle John was cautious,
He never slipped his anchor,
His probity was nauseous,
In fact he was a banker.
He hubbed no hubba hubbas,
He wore two MacIntoshes,
Also a pair of rubbers
Inside of his galoshes.

Look at my uncle, take a look!
How can I write a book!

My other uncle, Herbie,
Just once enlarged his orbit,
The day he crushed his derby
While cheering James J. Corbett.
No toper he, or wencher,
He backed nor horse nor houri,
His raciest adventure
A summons to the jury.

Look at my uncles, take a look!
How can I write a book!

Bound my ancestral menfolk
There hangs no spicy aura,
I have no racy kinfolk
From Rome to Glocca Morra.
Not nitwits, not Napoleons,
The mill they were the run of,
My family weren't Mongolians;
Then whom can I make fun of?

Look!
No book!

ROLL ON, THOU DEEP AND DARK BLUE
COPY WRITER—ROLL!

GREGORY PECK
   makes that
      HEMINGWAY
       kind of Love to
         JOAN BENNETT
           in "THE MACOMBER AFFAIR"
               —(ADVT.)

I beard a pouting siren
Cry o'er a classic sea,
Please to remove, Lord Byron,
Your hand from off my knee!

No silver-tongued Don Juan
Shall henceforth do me wrong;
Though you sing like Mrs. Luhan,
I do not hear your song.

Go chant it to the lemming,
Go coo it to the dove;
I'm waiting for that Heming-
That Hemingway kind of love.

To think that Mr. Steinbeck
Once roused my amorous fires!
Now debutantes in Rhinebeck,
They read him to their sires.

And now my lip is bitten,
And now my heart makes moan,
With envy I am smitten
For Gregory and Joan.

A cinematic cordon
Is drawn around my heart,
So we'll go no more, George Gordon,
A-roving ere we part.

Though the heavens are a cup for
The pearly moon above,
Go away; I'm saving up for
That Hemingway kind of love.

LECTURER IN BOOKSTORE

Behold best-selling Mr. Furneval,
Behind a pile of books to autograph,
Like a bearded lady at a carnival
Hoping to sell her fly-specked photograph.

A PARABLE FOR SPORTS WRITERS,
SOCIETY COLUMNISTS, BOND
SALESMEN AND POETS
or
GO GET A REPUTATION

I

Ezra Æsop, at eighty-eight,
He published a volume of verse.
The rhymes were ragged,
The meter wilted,
The prosody prosy,
The stanzas stilted.
But other poets at eighty-eight,
Patriarchal or celibate,
Might—conceivably—
Might—believably—
Might—finally, irretrievably—
Have seized the muse by the horns and tail,
And written a volume worse.
So the red fires burned,
And the banners flew,
And the fat nymphs danced
In the pagan dew,
And the mountains skipped like little lambs,
And editors squandered telegrams,
And over deserts,
And under oceans,
Through Rotary, Red Men, Elks and Yosians,
The word flew East and the word flew West,
Flew with the wings of a drummer's jest,
That the book of the era, beyond debate,
Was the book by the poet of eighty-eight.
O, Excellent Ezra! the people cried,
He might have doddered,
He might have died,

He might have entered a monastery,
He might have adopted his secretary.
But what did he do?
He studied at home,
Then up and published a slender tome.
So they borrowed early and purchased late
The book by the poet of eighty-eight,
And El Dorado had no bonanzas
Like Ezra Æsop's elderly stanzas.

II

Rosalie Ransome, going on six,
She published a volume, too,
And Heaven pity the heretics
Who neglected to read it through.
For the word was out,
In palace and cot,
Of the teensy, weensy, talented tot,
And gangsters gossiped of Rosalie Ransome,
Who lisped iambics,
And lisped 'em handsome.
The public panted,
The press grew giddy,
At the very thought
Of a lyrical kiddy,
And professors pawned their Shelley and Keats
To purchase Rosalie's youthful feats.

III

A regular poet published a book,
And an excellent book it was,
But nobody gave it a second look,
As nobody often does.
He was going on half-past thirty-five,
So it didn't keep him long alive.

THE STRANGE CASE OF THE RENEGADE
LYRIC WRITER

Once there was a lyric writer named Mr. Amazon,
And being a lyric writer he spent most of his days with his pajamas
 on.
Since he wrote words for the music in musical comedies,
Why, he noted a great similarity between singers and the man-eating
 horses of Diomedes,
Because although the singers couldn't eat the tunes—you could
 always recognize the tunes as Chopin's or Rodgers's or
 Schumann's—
Well, they ate his lyrics the way the man-eating horses of Diomedes
 ate humans.
He was always complaining that Gee whiz,
Some people had to swallow their own words but singers only
 swallowed his;
And he swore that if he ever met a female singer who would
 pronounce his words he would offer her his heart and hand
 and undying loyalty
And 12½ per cent of his royalty.
Then one day he heard a new female singer in rehearsal
And his feelings underwent a reversal.
Her enunciation was fabulous,
He heard every one of his rhymes, even the most polysyllabulous;
So to show his admiration and confidence he wrote a new song
 especially for her, beginning "The Leith police releaseth us,
 releaseth us the police of Leith,"
And on opening night he sent her a perfect rose, but it seems she
 was a Spaniard and she sang the song with the rose between
 her teeth.
Mr. Amazon couldn't even distinguish a vowel,
It was like hearing a candidate with a loose tooth talking to a barber
 through a hot towel.
Mr. Amazon no longer writes lyrics, he writes radio commercials:
 because there is one fact on which be finally pounced:

When a writer rhymes sour stomach with kidney tubes it may not be
    prosody but boy, is it pronounced!

IF HE SCHOLARS, LET HIM GO

I like to think about that great French critic and historian,
    Hippolyte Adolphe Taine.
I like to think about his great French critical and historical brain.
He died in 1893 at the age of sixty-five,
But previously he had been alive.
He wrote many books of outstanding worth,
But this was before his death, although following his birth.
He tried to interpret human culture in terms of outer environment,
And he knew exactly what the biographers of Rousseau and Shelley
    and Lord Byron meant.
His great philosophical work, *De l'intelligence*, in which be
    connected physiology with psychology, was written after
    meeting a girl named Lola,
And greatly influenced the pens of Flaubert, de Maupassant, and
    Zola.
He did much to establish positivism in France,
And his famous *History of English Literature* was written on purpose
    and not by chance.
Yes, Hippolyte Adolphe Taine may have been only five foot three,
    but he was a scholar of the most discerning;
Whereas his oafish brother Casimir, although he stood six foot seven
    in his bobby-socks, couldn't spell C-H-A-T, cat, and was
    pointed at as the long Taine that had no learning.

DON'T GUESS, LET ME TELL YOU

Personally I don't care whether a detective-story writer was
    educated in night school or day school
So long as they don't belong to the H.I.B.K. school.
The H.I.B.K. being a device to which too many detective-story
    writers are prone,
Namely the Had I But Known.
Sometimes it is the Had I But Known what grim secret lurked
    behind that smiling exterior I would never have set foot
    within the door,
Sometimes the Had I But Known then what I know now I could have
    saved at least three lives by revealing to the Inspector the
    conversation I heard through that fortuitous hole in the floor.
Had-I-But-Known narrators are the ones who hear a stealthy creak
    at midnight in the tower where the body lies, and, instead of
    locking their door or arousing the drowsy policeman posted
    outside their room, sneak off by themselves to the tower and
    suddenly they hear a breath exhaled behind them,
And they have no time to scream, they know nothing else till the
    men from the D.A.'s office come in next morning and find
    them.
Had I But Known-ers are quick to assume the prerogatives of the
    Deity,
For they will suppress evidence that doesn't suit their theories with
    appalling spontaneity,
And when the killer is finally trapped into a confession by some
    elaborate device of the Had I But Known-er some hundred
    pages later than if they hadn't held their knowledge aloof,
Why they say Why Inspector I knew all along it was he but I
    couldn't tell you, you would have laughed at me unless I had
    absolute proof.
Would you like a nice detective story for your library which I am
    sorry to say I didn't rent but owns?
I wouldn't have bought it had I but known it was impregnated with
    Had I But Knowns.

I BURN MONEY

The song about the happy-go-lucky fellow who hasn't time to be a
          millionaire strikes me as pretty funny,
Because I am pretty happy-go-lucky myself but it isn't lack of time
          that keeps me from being a millionaire, it's lack of money.
But if anybody has a million that they're through with it,
Well, I know what I'd like to do with it.
My first acquisition would not be a lot of Old Masters or first
          editions or palatial palaces,
No, it would be to supply each of my pairs of pants with its own set
          of galluses.
I can also think of another extravagance with which to startle all
          beholders
Which is an attendant with no other duties than to apply
          anti-sunburn lotion to that vulnerable spot you can't get at
          yourself either by reaching over or under your shoulders.
Likewise I have an idea which should earn the gratitude of every
          regular-dinner eater alive,
Which is to promote a regular-dinner that when you order oysters or
          clams on it you get six oysters or clams instead of five.
My next goal is one to reach which I should probably have to sink
          into debt,
But it would be worth it because it is the development of a short,
          hot, harsh, quick-burning, full-of-nicotine cigarette.
A million dollars could also be well spent in hiring somebody to
          invent some better rhymes for wife than rife and knife and
          strife,
But I think what I would really do if I had a million would be to buy
          a million dollars' worth of books written by me and then
          besides having a lot of good books I could sit back and live
          on the royalties for the rest of my life.

FROM A MANHATTAN TOMB

I know that a little verse is a versicle but I don't know if a little
      phrase is a phrasicle
But I do know that at the moment I feel too too alas and
      alackadaisicle.
What though around me is the hustle and bustle of a great city at its
      labors?
What though I am hemmed in by the most industrious and ingenious
      kind of neighbors?
What though young people are joining forever or parting forever with
      each tick of the clock?
What though Mr. Belloc admires Mr. Chesterton or Mr. Chesterton
      admires Mr. Belloc?
What though to produce the Sunday papers thousands of square
      miles of Canada are deforested?
What though in an attempt to amuse the public thousands of writers
      and actors and things are utterly exhorested?
What though young humans are getting born and old humans are
      getting deceased and middle-aged humans are getting used to
      it?
What though a Bronxville husband has discovered that he can put
      the baby to sleep by reading Proust to it?
All these things may be of great moment to those who are concerned
      with them in any way,
But how are they going to help me to get through the day?
For I have had to eat luncheon while I was still sorry I had eaten
      breakfast and I shall have to eat dinner while I am still sorry
      I ate luncheon
And my spirit has been put through the third degree and thrown into
      a very dark dank dismal dungeon.
Why do people insist on bringing me anecdotes and allegories and
      alcohol and food?
Why won't they just let me sit and brood?
Why does the population swirl around me with vivacious violence

When all I want to do is sit and suffer in siolence?
Everybody I see tries to cheer me up
And I wish they would stop.

SO THAT'S WHO I REMIND ME OF

When I consider men of golden talents,
I'm delighted, in my introverted way,
To discover, as I'm drawing up the balance,
How much we have in common, I and they.

Like Bums, I have a weakness for the bottle,
Like Shakespeare, little Latin and less Greek;
I bite my fingernails like Aristotle;
Like Thackeray, I have a snobbish streak.

I'm afflicted with the vanity of Byron,
I've inherited the spitefulness of Pope;
Like Petrarch, I'm a sucker for a siren,
Like Milton, I've a tendency to mope.

My spelling is suggestive of a Chaucer;
Like Johnson, well, I do not wish to die
(I also drink my coffee from the saucer);
And if Goldsmith was a parrot, so am I.

Like Villon, I have debits by the carload,
Like Swinburne, I'm afraid I need a nurse;
By my dicing is Christopher out-Marlowed,
And I dream as much as Coleridge, only worse.

In comparison with men of golden talents,
I am all a man of talent ought to be;
I resemble every genius in his vice, however henious—
Yet I only write like me.

I am fond of the late poet Sir John Suckling.

He may have been no Swan of Avon, but he was a pretty talented
       Twickenham Duckling.

Along with a gift for poesy, he was possessed of ingenuity and
       effrontery;

John Aubrey tells us that he *"invented the game of Cribbidge. He*
       sent his Cards to all the Gameing places in the countrey,

Which were marked with private markes of his; he gott twenty
       thousand pounds by this way."

Which was not then, nor is now, hay.

I suspect that sometimes the poet Suckling and the poet Herrick
       used to meet

To exchange ideas about ladies' feet.

Herrick took the first leap;

He said that Mistress Susanna Southwell's pretty feet crept out and
       drew in again like snails playing at bopeep.

As I have said, Suckling was no Shakespeare or Housman;

Neither was he a snail man: he was a mouse man.

So he looked up from his marked cards and loaded dice,

And said he knew a bride whose feet stole in and out beneath her
       petticoat like little mice.

As he plucked a fifth ace from under the seat,

He might have added that this bride was afraid of mice, and
       succumbed to the vapours trying to run away from her own
       feet.

Aubrey says of Suckling, *"He died a Batchelour,"*

Than which, considering his callous attitude toward brides, nothing
       could be natchelour.

VERY LIKE A WHALE

One thing that literature would be greatly the better for
Would be a more restricted employment by authors of simile and
    metaphor.
Authors of all races, be they Greeks, Romans, Teutons or Celts,
Can't seem just to say that anything is the thing it is but have to go
    out of their way to say that it is like something else.
What does it mean when we are told
That the Assyrian came down like a wolf on the fold?
In the first place, George Gordon Byron had had enough experience
To know that it probably wasn't just one Assyrian, it was a lot of
    Assyrians.
However, as too many arguments are apt to induce apoplexy and
    thus hinder longevity,
We'll let it pass as one Assyrian for the sake of brevity.
Now then, this particular Assyrian, the one whose cohorts were
    gleaming in purple and gold,
Just what does the poet mean when he says he came down like a
    wolf on the fold?
In heaven and earth more than is dreamed of in our philosophy
    there are a great many things,
But I don't imagine that among them there is a wolf with purple and
    gold cohorts or purple and gold anythings.
No, no, Lord Byron, before I'll believe that this Assyrian was
    actually like a wolf I must have some kind of proof;
Did he run on all fours and did he have a hairy tail and a big red
    mouth and big white teeth and did he say Woof woof?
Frankly I think it very unlikely, and all you were entitled to say, at
    the very most,
Was that the Assyrian cohorts came down like a lot of Assyrian

cohorts about to destroy the Hebrew host.
But that wasn't fancy enough for Lord Byron, oh dear me no, he had
      to invent a lot of figures of speech and then interpolate them,
With the result that whenever you mention Old Testament soldiers to
      people they say Oh yes, they're the ones that a lot of wolves
      dressed up in gold and purple ate them.
That's the kind of thing that's being done all the time by poets, from
      Homer to Tennyson;
They're always comparing ladies to lilies and veal to venison,
And they always say things like that the snow is a white blanket
      after a winter storm.
Oh it is, is it, all right then, you sleep under a six-inch blanket of
      snow and I'll sleep under a half-inch blanket of unpoetical
      blanket material and we'll see which one keeps warm,
And after that maybe you'll begin to comprehend dimly
What I mean by too much metaphor and simile.

LINES TO A WORLD-FAMOUS POET WHO FAILED TO COMPLETE A WORLD-FAMOUS POEM
or
COME CLEAN, MR. GUEST!

Oft when I'm sitting without anything to read waiting for a train in a
    depot,
I torment myself with the poet's dictum that to make a house a
    home, livin' is what it takes a heap o'.
Now, I myself should very much enjoy makin' my house a home, but
    my brain keeps on a-goin' clickety-click, clickety-click,
    clickety-click,
If Peter Piper picked a peck o' heap o' livin', what kind of a peck o'
    heap o' livin' would Peter Piper pick?
Certainly a person doesn't need the brains of a Lincoln
To know that there are many kinds o' livin', just as there are many
    kinds o' dancin' or huntin' or fishin' or eatin' or drinkin'.
A philosophical poet should be specific
As well as prolific,
And I trust I am not being offensive
If I suggest that he should also be comprehensive.
You may if you like verify my next statement by sending a stamped,
    self-addressed envelope to either Dean Inge or Dean Gauss,
But meanwhile I ask you to believe that it takes a heap of other
    things besides a heap o' livin' to make a home out of a house.
To begin with, it takes a heap o' payin',
And you don't pay just the oncet, but agayin and agayin and agayin.
Buyin' a stock is called speculatin' and buyin' a house is called
    investin',
But the value of the stock or of the house fluctuates up and down,

generally down, just as an irresponsible Destiny may destine.

Something else that your house takes a heap o', whether the builder
come from Sicily or Erin,

Is repairin',

In addition to which, gentle reader, I am sorry to say you are little
more than an imbecile or a cretin

If you think it doesn't take a heap o' heatin',

And unless you're spiritually allied to the little Dutch boy who went
around inspectin' dikes lookin' for leaks to put his thumb in,

It takes a heap o' plumbin',

And if it's a house that you're hopin' to spend not just today but
tomorrow in,

It takes a heap o' borrowin'.

In a word, Macushla,

There's a scad o' things that to make a house a home it takes not
only a heap, or a peck, but at least a bushela.

THE NONBIOGRAPHY OF A NOBODY

There is one major compensation for being a minor literary figure,
Said Mr. Curmudgel, a minor literary figure.
Particularly, said Mr. Curmudgel,
A minor literary figure who
Has led a life bespectacled and unspectacular,
The kind of life, said Mr. Curmudgel,
The kind of life that Solomon Grundy lived,
Leaving behind no meat, just a white skeleton of dates.
Born, married, sickened, died and that's the lot.
There's little there for ghouls to feed on.
At least I know, said Mr. Curmudgel,
That when the reticent New Hampshire soil
Reluctant yields me one small oblong of nonbreathing space
There will be none to grind my bones to make their bread,
To speculate both on my sex and what strange uses
I may have made of it,
To snivel over my death wish drowned in alcohol or blood sports,
My secret gnawing envy of my peers,
To cram the public maw with spiteful hearsay
Authenticate only by vociferous claim to intimacy,
To friendship, good fellowship, and unique piquant revelations
Garnered over the rum pot.
Let me say once for all, said Mr. Curmudgel,
I was never a Golden Boy by self destroyed,
And the hairs on my chest at last count numbered three.
No spate of As I Knew Hims
Will lie like empty beer cans around my modest stone,
No carrion crows regurgitate juiceless shreds of me,
No middle-aged actors searching for the comeback trail
Clamor to cast their versions of me on the screen.
Two inches or one in the *Times* and the printers are through with me,
    I'll rest in peace,
A Solomon Grundy of American letters.
Solomon Grundy, said Mr. Curmudgel thoughtfully,

Married on Wednesday, took sick on Thursday, died on Saturday.
By God, said Mr. Curmudgel,
Obviously an alcoholic with a death wish!
He slipped the cover from his dusty typewriter.

GOD BLESS THE GIDEONS
or
THERE'S ALWAYS THE KING JAMES VERSION

High near the mountain or low near the ocean,
Hard by the spa, it's the same old hotel,
Born of a Middle Victorian notion,
Reaching full stature, with ell tacked on ell.

Septuagenarians crowd its verandas,
Leathery lady and fragile old man,
Sunning like lizards or dozing like pandas,
Dreaming of dinner, American plan.

Far past the TV room, far past the cardroom,
Deep in a cranny encompassed by nooks,
Dim as a dungeon and grim as a guard room,
There is the library, these are the books—

Gone the gay jackets with blurbs parading,
Along the spine the titles are fading:
If Winter Comes, by A. S. M. Hutch.,
Castle Craneycrow, George Barr McCutch.,
The Amateur Gentleman, Jeffery Farnol,
Hilda Lessways, Bennett, Arnol',
Calvin Coolidge, C. Bascom Slemp,
Over the Top, Arthur Guy Emp.,
The Green Hat, Michael Arlen,
Blind Raftery, Donn Byrne's Irish darlin'.
Here lie Cosmo Hamilton, A. Hamilton Gibbs,
Joan Lowell, Trader Horn and their fabulous fibs,
The Art of Thinking, a tattered *Freckles*,
And an early, early Beverley Nichols.

Forty years on, when, afar and asunder,
Ashes are those who are reading today,
Strangers will gaze on our leavings with wonder,
Sum up an era and turn to croquet.

Behind glass doors not wholly hidden,
A literary kitchen midden,
The musty rubble of a race
Which fed on Kinsey and *Peyton Place*.
De Sade and *Valley of the Dolls* consort
With *Story of O* and *The Chapman Report*,
The *Tropics*, and other tins of sex;
Also, *The Agony and the Ecs.*,
Advise and Consent, by a Mr. Drury,
That life of Harlow, unhappy houri,
And yes, *How Probate to Avoid*,
And *Papa Hemingway*, not by Freud;
Memoirs of Getty, mystery Croesus,
And *Are You Running with Me, Jesus?*
In a corner, *This Is My Beloved*,
Penned by a twentieth-century Ovid,
And at one end, cleared by the courts,
A mildewed batch of Grove Press orts.

Golden pens and royalties must,
As chimney sweepers, come to dust.

A STRANGE CASEMENT OF
THE POETIC APOTHECARY

Poets are always in search of the right word, the adjective that is
      inevitable,
Because an ill-chosen adjective induces levity in the reader, and no
      poet wishes to be levitable.
A poem filled with the right words is more enjoyable, and therefore
      takes longer to read;
Hence the old Louisiana saying "The *mot juste*, the less speed."
When, for instance, Keats refers to "magic" casements he is no
      poetaster who a mass of trite, meaningless phrases spawns;
He did not slap down the first adjective that came to mind because
      he had left his thesaurus at Fanny Brawne's.
Whosoever thinks so, his ignorance of both Keats and casements is
      absurd;
If Keats speaks of a casement as "opening," then "magic" is the
      only possible word.
In the matter of casements Keats was no dreamy lotophagic;
He knew that if a casement was either openable or shuttable it was
      manifestly magic.
Keats could have written a lot more odes and died with money in the
      bank
But for the long hours he wasted trying to twist little widgets that
      were rusted stuck and yanking handles that wouldn't yank.
If his casements were like mine, when open they would not admit
      the breeze, and when shut they would not exclude the rain,
And when he looked through them he could not see Shelley or
      anything else plain.
So anybody who thinks there is a *juster mot* than "magic," I suggest
      they join the lowing herd and wind slowly o'er the lea,
And leave casements to Keats and me.

I yawn at the daily gossip columns,
A circling procession of tawdry names,
Publicity puffs and malicious hints,
And furtive games.

Where, then, shall I turn for honest gossip?
(I am one who on gossip thrives.)
Well, hand me over that sprightly volume,
John Aubrey's *Brief Lives*.

Here are noble foibles and durable crotchets,
Odd trifles passed over by Pepys and Evelyn,
Old bachelors' tales that outstretch old wives';
Here's gossip to revel in.

So lively they leap from Aubrey's notebooks,
Scholar and soldier, poet and peer,
That when they sneeze you cry "God bless you!"
After three hundred year.

Have ever you heard of James Bovey?
Neither had I, neither had I.
Yet he was unique among his fellows;
Aubrey tells why:
"Red-haired men never had any kindnesse for him. In all his Travills
    he was never robbed."

Have ever you heard of Sir Mathew Hale,
Fountain of legalistic lore?
He was Lord Chief Justice in Charles's England,
And furthermore,
"He was a great Cuckold."

Have you heard of the libel on Ben Jonson?
Neither had I, neither had I,
Till I read a remark parenthetically dropped
By my favorite spy:
"He killed Mr. Marlow, the Poet, on Bunhill, comeing from the
Greencurtain play-house."

When I doubt the genius of Edmund Waller,
Fellow-feeling banishes doubts;
I picture him with his laurels bedraggled,
A butt for louts:
"He haz but a tender weake body, but was alwayes very temperate.
They made him damnable drunke at Somersethouse, where, at
the water stayre's, he fell downe, and had a cruell fall. 'Twas
pitty to use such a sweet swan so inhumanely."

Thomas Hobbes had his day in court,
The philosopher had his dazzling day;
His friend recorded it, loyally risking
Lèse-majesté.
"The witts at Court were wont to bayte him . . . . The King would call
him the Beare: Here comes the Beare to be bayted: (this is too
low witt to be published)."

Credulous Aubrey with spaniel ears,
Friskily ranged a gamy century,
Dismissed himself and his guileless art
In a humble entry:
"How these curiosities would be quite forgott, did not such idle
fellowes as I am putt them downe!"

A POSY FOR EDMUND CLERIHEW BENTLEY

Walter Savage Landor
Stood before the fire of life with candor.
Coventry Patmore
Sat more.

Robert Browning
Avoided drowning,
Unparallelly
To P. B. Shelley.

Robert Herrick
Was an odd sort of cleric.
Another one
Was John Donne.

Charles Algernon Swinburne
Glowed less with sunburn than with ginburn.
Alfred Lord Tennyson
Settled for venison.

Did Dryden
Predecease Haydn?
Or did Haydn
Predecease Dryden?
When it comes to dates
I'm at sevens and eights.

A BRIEF GUIDE TO RHYMING,
or
HOW BE THE LITTLE BUSY DOTH?

English is a language than which none is sublimer,
But it presents certain difficulties for the rhymer.
There are no rhymes for orange or silver
Unless liberties you pilfer.
I was once slapped by a young lady named Miss Goringe,
And the only reason I was looking at her that way, she represented a
    rhyme for orange.
I suggest that some painter do a tormented mural
On the perversity of the English plural,
Because perhaps the rhymer's greatest distress
Is caused by the letter *s*.
Oh, what a tangled web the early grammarians spun!
The singular verb has an *s* and the singular noun has none.
The rhymer notes this fact and ponders without success on it,
And moves on to find that his plural verb has dropped the *s* and his
    plural noun has grown an *s* on it.
Many a budding poet has abandoned his career
Unable to overcome this problem: that while the ear hears, the ears
    hear.
Yet he might have had the most splendiferous of careers
If only the *s*'s came out even and he could tell us what his ears
    hears.
However, I am happy to say that out from the bottom of this
    Pandora's box there flew a butterfly, not a moth,
The darling, four-letter word d-o-t-h, which is pronounced duth,
    although here we pronounce it doth.
Pronounce? Let jubilant rhymers pronounce it loud and clear,
Because when they can't sing that their ear hear they can
    legitimately sing that their ear doth hear.

AN ENTHUSIAST IS A DEVOTEE IS A ROOTER
or
MR. HEMINGWAY, MEET MR. STENGEL

Into the Grand Canyon of the Colorado
Drop, my boon companion, the word "aficionado."

Brand me as provincial, hoot me for a jingo,
Hint that I'm an Oedipus to love my mother lingo,
On my reputation cast a nasty shadow,
Adamant you'll find me anent "aficionado."

Never may I languish prey to xenophobia.
Sydney Smith admire I, and Luca della Robbia,
And should Fate transport me into regions foreign
I could wear a chlamys, I could wear a sporran;
Yet, gazing at the Parthenon, strolling through the Prado,
Art lover I might be, but no aficionado.

Monosyllabic Master, whither are we heading,
Since you thrust upon us this verbal featherbedding?
You who freed the language of fetters euphemistic,
You who taught us terseness, muscular and fistic,
You whose prose is soldierly, Spartan and Mohican—
Why employ ten letters to do the job that three can?

This reproachful tribute to a first-class writing man
Comes from no aficionado,
Just
A loyal
Fan.